Belisarius

For Betsy Gash
A Dream Fulfilled

Belisarius
The Last Roman General

Ian Hughes

Pen & Sword
MILITARY

First published in Great Britain in 2009 by
Pen & Sword Military
an imprint of
Pen & Sword Books Ltd
47 Church Street
Barnsley
South Yorkshire
S70 2AS

ISBN 978-1-84415-833-1

A CIP catalogue record for this book is
available from the British Library

Typeset in 11/13 Ehrhardt by Concept, Huddersfield, West Yorkshire
Printed by the MPG Books Group in the UK

Pen & Sword Books Ltd incorporates the Imprints of Pen & Sword Aviation,
Pen & Sword Maritime, Pen & Sword Military, Wharncliffe Local History,
Pen & Sword Select, Pen & Sword Military Classics, Leo Cooper,
Remember When, Seaforth Publishing and Frontline Publishing.

For a complete list of Pen & Sword titles please contact
PEN & SWORD BOOKS LIMITED
47 Church Street, Barnsley, South Yorkshire, S70 2AS, England
E-mail: enquiries@pen-and-sword.co.uk
Website: www.pen-and-sword.co.uk

Contents

Acknowledgements

Many people have made this book possible and I would like to take this opportunity to thank a few for their exceptional support.

Firstly, I would like to thank Nik Gaukroger and Niall Taylor for their support with background material and Chris Lillington-Martin for access to his thesis on the location of the Battle of Dara.

For their help in allowing me to use their photographs I would like to thank: Adrian Wink of Armamentaria for pictures of reconstructions of Roman/ Byzantine equipment; Zach at beastcoins.com, and Joseph Sermarini and Richard of forumancientcoins.com for giving permission to use photographs of coins from their sites; Chris Constantine of spitfirehorsebows.com for both the pictures of bows and the illuminating discussions on the difference between the symmetrical and asymmetrical bow; Roberto Piperno of romeartlover.it for permission to use the pictures of the gates of Rome; Anik Messier of Bishop's Stortford, England, for the photos of Carthage; and Dorieo21 of Flickr for permission to use the photo of Belisarius asking for alms on the decorative plasterwork in the archway of the Palazzo Beneventano del Bosco, Sicily. Finally, I would like to express my deepest gratitude to Adrian Fletcher for permission to use his pictures of the mosaics of Justinian and Theodora at San Vitale.

I would like to thank Dr Kaveh Farrokh for permission to use his line drawings of Sasanid equipment, both those previously published and those unpublished prior to this book, and Peter Inker for his labours on the drawing board to produce the drawings of some of the troops who took part in the wars described.

However, without the patience and guidance of three people this book would not have been written: to Phil Sidnell for having faith in an unknown and for fielding endless questions about the processes of book-publishing; to Joanna for putting up with endless discussions on 'some bloke called Belisarius' and for reading endless drafts of the book with patience and clear insights; and finally to Adrian Goldsworthy for both his recommendation and his endless patience in answering queries and reading drafts of the finished product. Without them, you would not be reading this. However, despite our best efforts at achieving perfection, no doubt mistakes have been made and the responsibility for these rests solely on my shoulders.

List of Illustrations

List of Maps

Introduction

The main aim of this book is to tell the story of one man: Flavius Belisarius. According to no less an authority than the eminent historian John Julius Norwich, 'In Belisarius [Justinian] had found one of the most brilliant generals in all Byzantine history'. Despite this, his story is now relatively little known, especially when compared to the giants of the ancient world such as Julius Caesar, Alexander the Great and Hannibal.

This is a strange situation, for the story is one of excitement and adventure – the dramatic account of Emperor Justinian and his attempt to rewind the clock and restore the western empire to imperial rule, which gives us the paradox of a Roman emperor trying to capture Rome. Although the undertaking is usually seen as a failure, Africa, Italy and a large part of Spain were retaken.

Certainly one of the most celebrated, renowned and revered generals of late antiquity, Belisarius was chosen by the Emperor Justinian to spearhead this projected reconquest of the western empire. His subsequent accomplishments in the province of Africa (modern Tunisia) and Italy have elevated Belisarius to his standing as one of the greatest generals who ever lived, and certainly one of the greatest in Byzantine history.

The military activity is set against the context of a Christian empire, where divisions within the church often had a wide political impact. There were also widespread political divisions and one result of these was that Belisarius, early in his career, led his troops in the massacre of thousands of civilians during the Nika Riots of 532. In spite of his actions, he remained a major political and military figure who became loved by the people, and is depicted alongside the Emperor Justinian in a mosaic in the Church of San Vitale in Ravenna.

Compared to the earlier Roman Empire and the later 'Byzantine' Empire, the period of Justinian and Belisarius remains relatively unknown. Those historians who have covered the period have tended to do so only briefly, concentrating on the social, legal, political and economic aspects of Justinian's reign and merely outlining the military campaigns of Belisarius. As a consequence, the strategies, tactics, armies and enemies of Belisarius are now poorly known. Yet there is no real reason for this situation. The era is relatively well documented and Procopius, Belisarius' secretary, wrote *History of the Wars*, a detailed account of Belisarius' campaigns in Persia, Africa and Italy. They are comprehensive and are generally accepted as the relatively trustworthy account of an eye-witness. Procopius also wrote *The Secret History*, a 'tabloid' account of the reign of Justinian, which is famous for its intrigues, backstabbing and character assassination. When used alongside other, less well-known, authors it is possible to build quite a detailed picture of events.

Therefore, together with the stimulating story of Belisarius there is an analysis of warfare in the period. The new, changed Roman Army was at war with three different enemies: the exotic army of the Persians, which sometimes included elephants; the army of the Goths, which relied more on cavalry; and the totally mounted 'knight' army of the Vandals (a precursor of the later, medieval knights). Recent research has improved our knowledge of the organisation of these armies and this allows a new emphasis and analysis to be made of the military campaigns of Belisarius.

In order to keep the length of the book within reasonable limits two compromises have had to be made. The first is that I have attempted to limit descriptions of events to those which directly impinged on Belisarius' life, otherwise it would be difficult to keep the story to a single volume. The reign of Justinian is replete with wars, barbarian invasions, international diplomatic manoeuvrings, internal political squabbling and revolts, and a major outbreak of bubonic plague. To include them all would not only make tedious reading but would also expand the book into at least a trilogy. A slightly wider remit has been attempted in the chronology, but, again to keep this within acceptable limits, many events have not been included. Only where it is necessary to explain the background to the narrative does the account shift away from Belisarius – for example, to describe the revolt in Africa following Belisarius' conquest and so clarify the need for his recall.

The second compromise is that I have attempted to avoid an in-depth discussion of modern controversies that have arisen concerning any of the main players, or of the reliability of the sources that are used except where these are central to the story. At such a point a brief explanation of the debate will be included, but the story will be built upon the version of events I feel most likely to be true. However, readers should note that I do not claim to be infallible. Anyone wishing to delve deeper into the controversies and the events surrounding the life of Belisarius or into the reign of Justinian is referred to the bibliography. The books mentioned usually include their own bibliographies of even wider reading.

At the end of the book an attempt will be made to judge Belisarius as a general using the most basic of standards. However it is hoped that the book will give the reader enough information so that they can judge Belisarius' capabilities for themselves.

Spelling

As is increasingly the case when studying ancient history, especially when studying cultures which do not share a common alphabet, and even more so in an epoch of great change and disruption such as the sixth century, decisions have had to be made concerning the spelling of names and places.

When dealing with the peoples of the eastern Roman Empire and the 'barbarian' successor states in the west, I have retained the traditional, Latin versions of names and places (for example, Belisarius and not Belisarios, Procopius and not Prokopios, Justinian and not Iustinianos etc). In this way I have attempted to avoid confusion for the reader used to this form of spelling. It is also likely that, given their perception of themselves as *Romanoi* or Romans, the individuals would not be too upset at such a use.

However, when dealing with the Persian Empire there is a slightly greater difficulty. The forms of names traditionally used in the West have been based upon Roman/Latin approximations, suitable for use when addressing/ describing 'barbarians'. In an attempt to counter the possible negative image this can foster, a form of spelling based upon modern research has been used (for example, Khusrow and not Chosroes, Kavadh and not Kobad or Kobades etc.). This is not an attempt to be 'politically correct', but a desire to recognize that the Sasanid Persian Empire was a great civilised power worthy of being dealt with on their own terms, rather than through the sometimes-patronising eyes of the Greeks and Romans.

Nomenclature

In order to avoid confusion, the following names of empires and peoples will be used throughout the book:

- For the empire based upon Constantinople the terms 'Byzantine', 'Byzantines' and 'the Byzantine Empire' have been used throughout this book rather than 'Romans', 'Romans' and 'the east Roman Empire'. This is not due to any emphasis upon the differences between east and west, or a decision as to when these differences became so profound that the eastern empire needs to be renamed. It is simply to avoid potential confusion, since a large section of the book deals with Belisarius' campaigns in Italy and the naming helps to clarify when either the troops under Belisarius or the citizens of the city of Rome are being described.
- 'Goths' and 'Gothic' always refers to that branch of the Goths, now known as the Ostrogoths, who settled in Italy. The term Visigoth will always refer to that branch which was settled in Aquitaine before later expanding into Spain.

Sources

Procopius

Our main source for the wars of Belisarius is Procopius. Born around the year 500 in Caesarea, Palestine, he lived until approximately 565.* After obtaining a traditional education in the Greek classics, he attended law school – possibly at Berytus (modern day Beirut) – before becoming a *rhetor* (barrister) and travelling to Constantinople. In 527, the first year of Justinian's reign, Belisarius

---

* All dates given are AD unless otherwise stated.

Belisarius: The Last Roman General

was appointed a general in the war with Persia and Procopius became Belisarius' *assessor* (legal advisor) and private secretary.

Procopius served alongside Belisarius in the war and then accompanied Belisarius to the court at Constantinople when he was recalled from the east. He was thus an eyewitness not only to Belisarius' involvement in the Persian Wars, but also to the events surrounding the Nika riots of 532. Procopius then stayed with Belisarius for the invasion of Africa, but remained there after the general's recall to Constantinople and so missed the events in Sicily. He later rejoined Belisarius for the Gothic Wars in mainland Italy, ultimately witnessing the capture of the Gothic capital, Ravenna, in 540. However, by the time that Belisarius returned to Italy in 544 to fight against the Gothic rebellion, Procopius no longer appears to have been a member of his staff. As a result of serving on Belisarius' staff, Procopius is an eyewitness to most of the events in his books. Furthermore, during this time he would have become acquainted with many of the top military leaders, and they would later be able to provide him with an excellent source for those events that he did not personally witness.

Procopius wrote the *History of the Wars* in eight books. Books 1 and 2 describe the wars in Persia, Books 3 and 4 the Vandalic War, and Books 5, 6 and 7 the Gothic War. These were first published together and describe events down to early 551. He later added an eighth book to bring the entire history up to the final destruction of the Gothic kingdom by the general Narses in 554. Whilst primarily a history of the wars fought during the reign of Justinian, the *History of the Wars* also includes information on non-military affairs such as the Nika Riots and the plague of 540.

It should be noted that recent work by Averil Cameron (1996) has resulted in a greater understanding of Procopius. It would appear that as time and his work progressed he slowly lost faith in Belisarius, which is why his portrayal of his hero slowly declines from adulation to scepticism. However, despite some inaccuracies, his work does stand up to modern criticism and is, on the whole, reliable despite the bias.

Another book that Procopius wrote is *De Aedificiis*, a panegyric praising Justinian for his empire-wide building programme. This can be seen as a belated attempt to gain the emperor's favour. Justinian is unlikely to have been impressed at his portrayal in *the Wars*, where he is given a lower profile than Belisarius and is sometimes criticised in the book, for example due to a perceived lack of support for the great general.

Also attributed to Procopius is *Anekdota*, also known as *The Secret Histories*. Published after the deaths of Justinian and Belisarius, this is an undiluted attack upon the morals and behaviour of Justinian's inner court, and especially upon the Empress Theodora. Its revelation of intrigues, betrayal and scandal makes interesting reading and gives us an engrossing if sordid portrayal of court life in the sixth century. However, we should probably not take the book at face value, since it is likely to include events that have been blown out of proportion or inaccurately reported.

As a final note, the exact date of Procopius' death is unknown, yet in 562 Belisarius was accused of taking part in a conspiracy against Justinian in front of the urban prefect – Procopius. Although the possibility that this is the same Procopius must be deemed slight, it is an intriguing notion that Procopius may in his later years have had to sit in judgement of his one-time mentor.

Agathias

Agathias (or Agathias Scholasticus) was born around the year 536 at Myrina in Asia Minor, and died some time after 582. He travelled to Alexandria to study law before travelling to Constantinople to work in the courts. A poet and historian, he was persuaded by friends to write a continuation of Procopius following the death of Justinian in 565. Written in five (unfinished) books, *On the Reign of Justinian* is the main source for the period 552-559. Book 1 and the first half of Book 2 deal with Narses' campaigns in Italy. The remainder of Book 2 covers the war fought against Persia in Lazica up to the death of the Persian general Mermeroes (Mihr Mihroe), which was probably in 555. Book 3 continues the conflict in Lazica until the Byzantine victory at Phasis and the subsequent Persian withdrawal. Book 4 contains details of the peace treaty following the Battle of Phasis and Book 5 gives some details on the situation after the treaty. As a historian he is generally less well-regarded than Procopius, yet he remains practically the only secular source for the history of the end of Justinian's reign.

Other sources

Alongside the two main sources are several others, only these are of less significance. Some fail to cover the specific period, such as Jordanes' *Getica* ('On the Goths'), or they deal specifically with the history of the Church, such as Zacharias Rhetor's *Historia Ecclesiastica*. Other writers with information along these lines include Vigilius, John Malalas, John of Nikia and Marcellinus Comes, who wrote a continuation of the annals of Eusebius in the sixth century. Yet, although in many cases they cover areas outside our remit and tend to treat the military aspects in less detail, they can be used to supplement, check or correct our main sources. They can also be used to fill in the background detail concerning the religious, social and economic concerns of the time and so give us a context in which to work.

The detailed information we can gain from the sources should not prevent us from remembering that they were all written with a purpose. Even when this purpose is openly declared, the bias can easily be forgotten and then become accepted by later generations as fact: all writing of history is subject to the biases, desires and politics of the people who write it. The truth of this will become apparent as the story of Belisarius unfolds.

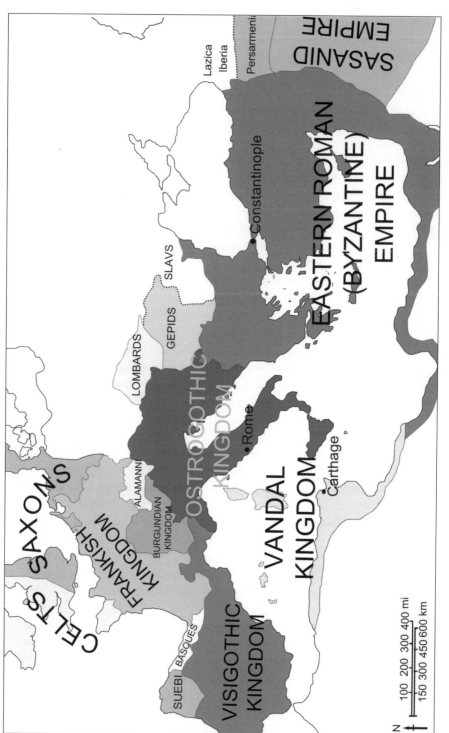

Map 1: *Europe on the accession of Justinian.*

Chapter 1

Historical Background

When Theodosius the Great died in 395 the Roman Empire was still recognisable in shape, if not in function, from the empire of Augustus. Over the intervening centuries some provinces had been gained, such as Mesopotamia, Dacia and Britain. Although some, like Dacia, had been lost again, these gains and losses made little difference to the overall map of the empire.

Internally, however, things were different. The old senatorial order had been replaced by a new system of rank, and the large legions upon which the empire had been founded had also changed. Gone was the *legio* of 5,000 or so men with supporting cavalry units (*alae*) and more flexible *auxilia* infantry formations. In their place was a complex new army with the increasingly elaborate hierarchy required to run it. The army was now split into two. On the frontiers were the *limitanei* (land frontier) and *riparienses* (river frontier) formations, comprising *legio* and *auxilia*, supported by *alae*. Stationed in the cities to the rear were new formations which have been interpreted by modern authors as 'mobile field armies'. These comprised 'new' units of *auxilia palatina*, *legiones palatina* (both infantry), *vexillationes* (cavalry) and the *comitatenses* or 'field army' regiments of which the majority were formed by dividing older formations. The infantry units appear to have been of around 1,200 men, the cavalry around 4–600 strong.

In theory, these rear 'mobile' armies were under the command of a high-ranking officer and would deal with any enemy that broke through the frontier defences. The belief is that they could also be transferred to a different part of the empire without visibly weakening the frontiers and so inviting barbarian attacks. The fact that the system rarely functioned effectively at this level and was seldom – if at all – used in this manner has tended to be overlooked by historians.

The empire was also in the process of dividing internally. The west now spoke derivatives of Latin and looked to the imperial past of Augustus and his heirs for their role models. The east was increasingly speaking Greek and focusing for their guidance upon Greek and Persian models of royalty and systems of government. This divide was, in effect, given official sanction upon the death of Theodosius when his sons split the empire, with Honorius taking the west and Arcadius taking the east. This resulted in an increasing tension between the rival empires. The eastern upper hierarchy now tended to see their western equivalent as being barbarians who were behind scientifically, aesthetically and culturally. In contrast, the western upper hierarchy saw the easterners as being effete Greeks with their increasing subservience to the emperor (based on Persian models) and their employment of 'un-Roman' eunuchs and other Persian influences.

In both halves of the empire there had been a growth in the number of barbarian generals rising to high posts and positions of power within the empire. Individuals of 'Germanic' origin such as Merobaudes, Bauto and Stilicho in the west, and Gainas and Tribigild in the east became politically powerful and had followings of barbarian troops to support their positions. The result was that barbarian kings and leaders on the fringes of the empire realised that they could increase their power and personal prestige whilst working within the framework of the imperial administration. With luck and skill they might even rise to the post of *magister utriusque militae* (Master of all the Troops), with the added title of *patricius* – hence this era sometimes being given the designation 'Patrician Rome'.

Although the post of *magister utriusque militae*, the most senior military post in the empire, was always desirable in itself, by the late fourth century the holder of the post in the west was actually in control of the empire. They dictated policy and often – especially later – made and unmade emperors. Obviously, the position was highly prized and the political fighting to obtain it was accordingly vicious, usually ending in the death of the loser.

The two empires also faced completely different problems with regards to foreign invasion and internal revolt, and as a result of these the financial burden was becoming more and more insupportable in the less-civilised and wealthy west. In both halves of the empire foreign invasion was a constant threat.

The Balkan question

Although many barbarian tribes were to invade the Balkan provinces that were nominally part of the eastern empire, pickings here were relatively lean and invaders were increasingly tempted to go west. Furthermore, where possible, barbarians who were defeated by the eastern empire were not allowed to remain at large as *foederati*, large groupings of barbarians keeping their own leaders and ostensibly serving the Romans. Instead, the defeated barbarians were dispersed as settlers and so merged with the local population. As an example, when the Hun Uldin invaded Thrace he was defeated and killed. Thereafter, his followers were widely separated and settled. In this way they could not reunite and cause further trouble to the empire.

Moreover, invaders could never take Constantinople by force and so could never reach the economically-vital regions of Asia Minor; although the Balkans was repeatedly ravaged, the heartland of the empire remained secure. Therefore, as a result of the geographical nature of the empires, and since invaders invariably turned west after first attacking the Balkans, for the purposes of this chapter the Balkans are included in the background history of the western empire.

The West – including the Balkans

In the west, Julian's victory over the Alamanni at the Battle of Strasbourg (Argentoratum) earlier in the century (357) was only a temporary respite in a series of wars that were to overwhelm the western empire. For it was at about this time that the Huns were making their first impact upon the west. They destroyed the Gothic empire of the almost mythical King Ermanarich, forcing some of the Goths to flee westwards in search of sanctuary. In 376 such a group of Visigoths were allowed to enter Roman territory by Valens. However, they were badly treated and revolted. Joining with a second group that had forced entry into the empire, they won the Battle of Adrianople in 378, a battle which destroyed a large part of the eastern army and killed the emperor Valens himself. However, the losses the Visigoths themselves had suffered, plus the rapid recruitment of fresh troops by Valens' replacement Theodosius I, resulted in a stalemate, and in 382 a treaty was signed by Theodosius that granted the Visigoths land between the Danube and the mountains of the Balkans.

At first glance this would not appear to be a problem for the west, since only the east had suffered from the ordeal. Yet, despite repeatedly ravaging the Balkans, the Visigoths – and all invaders after them – could not take Constantinople or force the eastern empire to surrender to their demands. The Balkans were simply not vital to the survival of the east, being relatively poor economically. In the end, the Visigoths set the precedent and headed west, where there were fewer obstacles to their movement, and where Rome itself lacked the massive fortifications and protection given to Constantinople.

It was at this time (c.395–400) that Alaric emerged as leader of the Visigoths. A strong warrior and politician, he invaded the west and made demands on the western government. During the course of the ensuing war the centre of government was moved from Milan (Rome had long been abandoned as too remote) to Ravenna, which behind its marshes was easier to defend. In 402, after much political and military intrigue, Alaric was defeated at Pollentia by Stilicho, *magister utriusque militae* of Emperor Honorius, and forced to withdraw.

Increased political manoeuvring followed, but in 406 Constantius III rebelled in Britain and was proclaimed emperor. Moreover, on the last day of 406 a force of Vandals (a coalition of the Asding Vandals and the Siling Vandals), Sueves and Alans invaded Gaul across the frozen Rhine. The resultant emergency led to an agreement in 407 whereby Alaric was made *magister militum* (Master of the Troops), Stilicho remaining in the superior post of *magister utriusque militae*. Alaric was also given land for his followers and was to be paid an annual tribute. The settlement was undone in 408, when Stilicho was arrested, refusing to allow his barbarian bodyguard to protect him. He was then executed and the regular soldiers of Italy, seizing their opportunity, rose and massacred the families of the barbarians that had been recruited by Stilicho. Constantius III crossed from Britain to the continent, but the Vandals, Sueves and Alans were left to roam Gaul at will.

The barbarian troops whose families had been killed, a force estimated as high as 30,000 men (though 10,000 is a more likely number), understandably joined Alaric, who promptly invaded Italy and besieged Rome. The Roman senate paid him off, but, being rebuffed by the Emperor Honorius in Ravenna, he returned to Rome and proclaimed Priscus Attalus as a puppet emperor. Finally, in late August 410, Rome was sacked for three days. The event shocked the inhabitants of the empire, even stimulating the eastern empire to send troops, but was of little political consequence, since Rome was no longer the seat of power and the emperor in Ravenna made no concessions.

The year before, in 409, the Vandals, Sueves and Alans that had invaded Gaul passed into Spain, where they set up kingdoms of their own. During the course of this the Vandal coalition of Asding and Siling separated, with the Asding Vandals and the Sueves taking the northwest province of Galicia, the Alans taking Lusitania, and the Siling Vandals taking Baetica. The provinces of Carthaginiensis and Tarraconensis appear to have been left to their own devices.

In Italy, after the sudden death of Alaric in 411, his successor Athaulf led the Visigoths into Gaul. Here they were blockaded into submission and were then sent to Spain to attack the Germanic settlers there. After wiping out the Siling Vandals and the majority of the Alans, the Visigoths were recalled and settled in Aquitaine in 418.

Following the attack, the Asding Vandals could never feel safe in Spain and King Gaiseric led them, along with the remnants of the Alans and the Asding Vandals, across the Straits of Gibraltar into Africa in 429. The Sueves stayed in northwest Spain. Advancing along the North African coast, by 435 the Vandals forced the Romans into a treaty whereby the Vandals gave military aid in return for land. Yet the treaty was probably due to the activities of east Roman troops in Tripolitania putting pressure on the Vandals, without which the Vandals may easily have taken Carthage. In fact, shortly afterwards, the military manoeuvres of the eastern empire in Tripolitania ceased, and in 439 the Vandals struck and secured the city for themselves.

As previously stated, the main cause of the turbulence in the west was the arrival of the Huns. Ferocious warriors, the Huns destroyed the Gothic power east of the Danube and by around 375 had built up an empire opposite Rome. The Huns were powerful enough to extract payment of annual tribute from the eastern empire, and when this was refused they would attack and ravage the

Balkans. The greatest and most (in)famous of their leaders was Attila (433–53). Attila was not satisfied with the petty raiding of his forbears. Instead, after agreeing a treaty with the eastern empire, he assembled an army and in 451 prepared to invade the west.

Attila did not head towards Italy, but instead invaded Gaul. He knew that the provinces of Gaul had been devastated by repeated despoilment by barbarian tribesmen and that they were disunited. He even sent an embassy to the Visigoths, now settled in Aquitaine, attempting to persuade them to ally with his cause against the Romans. Gaul would be a much softer target than Italy.

In Italy there had been a minor revival. After the execution of Stilicho, the post of *magister utriusque militae* was retained in the hands of Roman generals. Constantius and later Flavius Aetius both waged successful wars against barbarians and their use of diplomacy was enough to revive some of the strength of the Roman west. It was Aetius that faced the Huns under Attila. He persuaded the Visigoths to support him in the war, arguing that the Huns were the common enemy of all in the west. He also convinced several smaller tribes, such as individual tribes of the Franks and Alans, to support him in the war. Slowly the empire gathered its forces.

Attila advanced as far west as the city of Orleans, which was besieged. This was the farthest that any of the nomadic tribes were ever to penetrate; even the Mongol Empire was never to pierce this far into Europe. But upon the approach of the imperial alliance, the Huns fell back to the Catalaunian Plain near Troyes. The battle that followed determined the fate of Europe. Victory to the Huns would have left large areas of the west under the Hunnic yoke, with unknown ramifications for the present day. As it was, a close victory for the Romans forced the Huns to retire, although the Visigothic king, Theodoric, perished in the battle. The Huns withdrew to the Hungarian plain.

This was not quite the end of the story. Attila, realising that he could not take Gaul if the Visigoths remained hostile, decided to strike at Italy after all – possibly assuming (correctly) that the Visigoths would not leave their homes to fight for a foreign country. He invaded Italy in 452, sacking Aquileia and capturing Milan. However, a meeting with Pope Leo I followed and, surprisingly, Attila again returned home to Hungary. It is possible that his retirement was caused more by fear of disease, or possibly due to reports reaching him of eastern Roman troops attacking his homelands, than by anything said by the Pope. Whatever the reason, he never repeated his attacks. The following year he died after celebrating his marriage to a new wife.

The threat from the Huns rapidly receded. Their empire passed to Attila's sons, but they did not have the ability to maintain it. In 454 the Hunnic subjects, led by the Gepids, revolted and defeated their masters at the Battle of the Nedao. The Hun empire rapidly disintegrated and, rebuffed in their attempts to blackmail the eastern empire in the Balkans, the Huns finally retreated to the Russian steppe.

However the end of the west was in sight. In 454 the Emperor Valentinian III killed Aetius in person. The emperor was in turn killed by Petronius Maximus on 16 March 455, Petronius becoming emperor on 17 March. In the confusion surrounding these events, the Vandals moved swiftly and in late May of the same year they sailed from Africa and sacked Rome. Due to his cowardice during the attack, Petronius was killed by the Roman citizenry as he fled. With the west in confusion, the Vandals quickly proceeded to annex Tripolitania, Sardinia and the Balearics.

In the meantime, the Visigoths had slowly consolidated their rule. In 451 their king, Theoderic I, had been killed fighting alongside Aetius at the Battle of the Catalaunian Plains, yet when Euric came to the throne only fifteen years later he expanded his realm, incorporating most of southern Gaul and the greater part of Spain – except for the Sueves and the Basques – during his long reign (466–84). Despite some unsettled legal fictions, the western emperor now only controlled Italy and Sicily.

Paradoxically, with the death of Attila, the west could envisage a recovery, but this would probably take more than the resources of Italy and Sicily alone. However, action was needed and it was decided to attack the weakest and most easily-recoverable area under barbarian control. Furthermore, the barbarians in question had recently sacked Rome. In 461 the latest western emperor, Majorian, with his *magister utriusque militae*, Ricimer, attempted the reconquest of Vandal Africa. The army was sent via the land route through Spain and a fleet was mobilised to transport the army across the Straits of Gibraltar. Unfortunately, the fleet was destroyed by the Vandals, the attempt failed and Majorian himself was later killed, allegedly on the orders of Ricimer.

Shortly thereafter, Anthemius, an eastern general distantly related to the House of Constantine, was made emperor upon the recommendation of Leo I in Constantinople. A second attempt upon Africa was now launched with massive eastern aid. In June 468 a fleet of 1,100 ships and up to 30,000 troops anchored near Cape Bon, a short distance from Carthage. However, the Vandal fleet arrived and sent in fireships to disrupt the Romans. In the ensuing chaos, some ships were set on fire, some collided and others were attacked by the Vandals. It was the end of the second attempt to reconquer Africa, as the survivors scattered and the idea of a joint venture was never resurrected.

When Ricimer died in 472 another general, Gundobad, took his place as *magister utriusque militae*. But Gundobad seems to have recognised that things were never going to be the same again, and when his father died he left Italy to become a king of the Burgundians alongside his brothers.

At this late stage the collapse of the west was clearly visible and this fact was now acknowledged. In 474 the Vandals were recognised as independent by the new eastern emperor Zeno, and in 475 the Visigothic kingdom of Toulouse was so powerful that the western emperor, Julius Nepos, confirmed the Visigoths in the territories in their possession.

With Gundobad gone, Ecdicius briefly became *magister utriusque militae* before he was forced to yield by Nepos, who gave the post to Orestes. This proved to be a mistake, since Orestes gathered the troops in Italy and forced Nepos to retire to Dalmatia. Orestes then made his own son, Romulus Augustulus, emperor.

Unfortunately, army pay was now in arrears and the troops, mainly composed of Germanic recruits and mercenaries, petitioned Orestes concerning their upkeep. When this was ignored, they declared their leader Odovacar as the new *magister utriusque militae*. Orestes was killed and, in lieu of pay, land was distributed to the troops. Odovacar then sent a message to the Emperor Zeno, asking that he be made *patricius* and pointing out that the west no longer needed an emperor, since Zeno could easily fulfil that task. Zeno's response was so worded that it could cause no offence to Nepos in Dalmatia, still legally emperor, whilst granting Odovacar the powers he requested. Consequently, in 476 Odovacar deposed the last recognised western Roman emperor, Romulus Augustulus. However, in a strange scene of clemency, Romulus was not killed but granted an annual income of 6,000 *solidi* and he retired to live at Castellum Lucullanum, near Naples in Campania.

Odovacar now attempted to stabilise his position. He regained full control of Sicily by paying tribute to the Vandals, and on the death of Nepos in 480 he annexed Dalmatia. Despite these gains, he was forced to cede Provence to King Euric of the Visigoths, who was now far more powerful than the western emperor.

The final stages in the disintegration of the western empire had now almost been reached. Spain was in the hands of the Visigoths, the Sueves and the native Basques. In Gaul, the expansion of the Franks under Clovis caused the destruction of the Kingdom of Soissons (the creation of a revolted Roman general, not officially part of the empire) in 486, whilst in 507 Clovis drove the Visigoths out of Gaul and into Spain. Between the Franks in Gaul and the Goths in Italy lay the independent kingdom of the Burgundians. In Africa and the western Mediterranean, the Vandals ruled their maritime empire.

Meanwhile, large groups of Goths had been settled in the Balkans. As part of the peace treaty which followed their devastation of Illyricum, the child Theoderic the Amal had been sent to the court of Constantinople as a hostage at the age of eight. He was forced to pass ten years in the capital before he was released and returned to the Balkans, finally rising to take control of the Goths. At this time there were two rival groups of Goths in the Balkans, those led by Theoderic and another led by Theoderic Strabo (the Squinter). When Strabo died in 481, the two bands coalesced to form a formidable army, strong enough to threaten the eastern empire's control of the area. In 483 they came to terms with the Emperor Zeno, but later devastated Thrace and even threatened Constantinople. Finally, Theoderic reached an agreement with Zeno. It was decided that he would invade Italy and oust Odovacar from his rule.

Entering Italy, Theoderic beat Odovacar in battle on the River Adige. As a result, Odovacar fled to Ravenna and political and military manoeuvring then ensued, until on 11 August 490 Theoderic won a second victory on the River Addua, near Milan. Odovacar retreated to Ravenna once more, where he was besieged. A peace treaty was made between the two leaders, but on 15 March 491 they both attended a banquet where Theoderic killed Odovacar with his own hand.

Theoderic now set about establishing his power. With regards to the barbarian kingdoms around him, he adopted a policy of moderation and established a network of marriage alliances. He himself married Audufleda, sister of the Frankish king, Clovis, whilst one of his daughters, Theodegotha, married the Visigothic king, Alaric; the other daughter, Ostrogotho, married Sigismund, son of Gundobad of the Burgundians. In addition, in 491 he married his sister Amalafrida to King Thrasamund of the Vandals, ensuring a cessation of the Vandal occupation of, and attacks upon, Sicily. Theoderic was now a relative of all of the major barbarian powers settled on once-Roman soil.

By promoting toleration between his own Gothic Arian followers and the Catholics, he ensured the support of the Pope and the Catholic Church for his rule and, finally, in 497 the Senator and ex-Consul Festus completed his mission to the imperial court at Constantinople, and the Emperor Leo granted his support for Theoderic. With his patchwork of marriage alliances and diplomacy, Theoderic had established himself as the central power base in the west, a position he strove to retain until his death in 526, the year before the accession of the Emperor Justinian.

The East

In contrast to the confusion and chaos in the western half of the empire, the events of the eastern half (excluding the Balkans) up to the accession of Justinian are fairly easy to reconstruct and understand.

Dealing first with the employment of barbarian officers and generals, the situation reflected that of the west until the rise to power of the Goth Gainas. Gainas and his rival, Tribigild, were attempting to gain supreme power in Constantinople. Finally, Gainas secured imperial support from the Emperor Arcadius and subsequently forced Tribigild to submit. He then subjected the emperor and Constantinople to what amounted to a reign of terror. The horror lasted until 400, when the citizens of the city rose up and killed Gainas, going on to massacre 7,000 Gothic troops.

This did not end the power of 'barbarians' in the eastern army. By 457 Aspar, an Alan, had risen to military power and become virtual ruler of the east. The Emperor Leo I enrolled Isaurians from the mountainous regions of southeastern Anatolia as a counter to the Germans. He also promoted the Isaurian Zeno, with whom he replaced Aspar when he had him murdered in 471. The Germans in the army deserted and joined the Goths in the Balkans, so enhancing Gothic power. In 474 Leo died and Zeno inherited the empire. He it was that sent the enlarged Gothic army under Theoderic to invade Italy.

The final crisis in non-imperial attempts to control the throne came in the reign of Anastasius, Zeno's successor. The Isaurians, who had been enrolled as a counter to the Germans, themselves led an uprising. However, this was crushed by Anastasius, which freed the capital from foreign control and seems to have been decisive in maintaining the freedom of the east from the domination of barbarian generals.

In terms of defence, the vast majority of the eastern frontier needed little in the way of a strong military presence. Egypt and the Arabian provinces had the advantage that their frontiers rested upon deserts. Although later the Bedouin and Arabic tribes would unite under the banner of Islam and conquer all of the territories up to Asia Minor, in the time leading up to the age of Justinian the tribes were disunited and unable to mount anything other than minor border raids. As a consequence, both the Persians and the Byzantines adopted the same method with regard to the Arabic tribes: they attempted to persuade those tribes with whom they had influence to unite and attack the opposition. This resulted in each of the major powers having as their allies one major tribal grouping, the Byzantines' being the Ghassanids, the Persians boasting the Lakhmids. In reality, these alliances cancelled each other out, leaving the frontiers relatively quiet and unthreatened.

The main burden in the southern desert regions bordering Egypt and the trade routes around Arabia was diplomatic and financial rather than military. Justinian and his predecessors concentrated most of their efforts on Nubia, Ethiopia and Himyar. By shrewd political manoeuvring the Byzantine emperors managed to keep open the trade routes that crossed the Indian Ocean and traversed the Red Sea before arriving in Egypt. The continued revenue this maintained was a welcome boost to the imperial treasuries, especially as the overland silk routes were now in the hands of barbarians such as the Huns, who could use this fact to their own advantage. However, as a consequence of the physical safety of their eastern and southern frontiers, the armies in these provinces slowly lost most of their military attributes and became in effect simple military policemen.

To the northeast, bordering the Black Sea, the Byzantines did have some trouble with the peoples of the Caucasus Mountains. On the whole this consisted of minor raids by peoples such as the Tzani (who were subdued during the reign of Justinian), but this frontier needed to be relatively heavily defended since tribes and nations from beyond the Caucasus Mountains could cross the passes and sweep down into the plains. An example of this is when the Huns devastated large areas of Persian and Roman territory in the year 395.

However, the main enemy in the east was the Persians. In relations with the Sasanid dynasty the eastern Roman emperors were dealing with a political entity with many of the same internal tensions and problems as they had themselves inherited. Furthermore, the Persians had a far greater imperial history to look back on.

Unfortunately, the politics, policies and wars of the Persian frontier have tended to be either ignored or relegated to the footnotes by modern western historians, with the emphasis being on the Byzantine Empire in general, and Justinian in particular. Although this trend is now being redressed, there is still a long way to go.

Persia is usually portrayed as the enemy of Rome, a threat that remained constant and needed to be neutralised. It is interesting to note the claim of modern historians that Sasanid Persia was far more aggressive than its Parthian predecessor had been. The Sasanids are viewed as being intent on reconquering the lands ruled by the ancient Achaemenid Empire between the sixth and fourth centuries BC. This included most of Asia Minor and the Aegean, now part of the eastern Roman Empire. Yet despite their claims, they made no attempt to seize these areas on occasions when the Romans were weak.

For example, following the disastrous defeat and capture of Valerian in 260, the Persians were content with raiding Syria (where they sacked Antioch) and Cappadocia. The strength of the forces they employed may also have been overestimated, since they were surprised and defeated as they returned home by the army of Palmyra, hardly a state of international military power. A similar case occurred when in 363 the Emperor Julian was defeated and killed. His successor Jovian was forced to make humiliating terms to extricate himself and the remains of his army from the ruin, yet the Persians were content with the territory and bases in Mesopotamia that they received. There was no ensuing invasion to make maximum capital of explicit Roman weakness.

Still, given their earlier claims to the Achaemenid Empire, it would appear strange that they give the impression that they were content with their achievements and did not aspire to further accretions of territory. This is probably due to such claims being made for two reasons. Firstly, being a dynasty founded by Ardashir as recently as 226, the kings were likely to be eager to focus attention upon a common external enemy and away from internal affairs. There was no better way to achieve this than appeal to historical sentiment concerning the ancient Achaemenid dynasty. Secondly, an aggressive stance would help to strengthen their initial diplomatic activity with the Romans. An aggressive attitude might cause anxiety in the Roman capital and so make them hesitate before invading Persia whilst the Sasanids secured their new kingdom.

These condsiderations highlight the fact that modern perceptions concerning Romano-Persian relations tend to be extremely simplistic, and lack an in-depth historical basis. Political relations between the Romans and the Persians were not always hostile. An example of this concerns the Hunnic attack of 375 already mentioned. The Darial Pass in the Caucasus Mountains had been the main route followed by the Huns, and the pass was in Persian-controlled territory. Therefore, the two powers agreed that the pass needed fortification and a permanent garrison to prevent a recurrence of the raid. The Persians built and manned the fortifications, but the Romans agreed to cover a large part of the ensuing costs. Although a rare occurrence, the example does give notice that relations between Rome and Persia were often more complex than appears at first glance.

The same is also to a great extent true of the Romans. Although some of their greatest generals, such as Trajan and Septimius Severus, had managed to capture the Persian capital and were in a position to enforce their will, on the whole they do not seem to have seriously contemplated the conquest of either the entire Persian Empire or any significant proportion of it, being content with smaller gains of easily-digested territory.

Nor should it be forgotten that the Persians had long frontiers in the east that were constantly under threat. For example, in 440 the White Huns had destroyed the Kushans and proceeded to terrorise eastern Parthia, their attacks culminating in the death of King Peroz in 484. Furthermore, they too were prone to civil wars, even after Varham V neutralised much of the internal strife by conceding many of his royal prerogatives in 421. Around the year 484, shortly before the reign of Justinian, there was a civil war between Peroz's sons, Kavad and Zamasp.

With this in mind, it is easy to come to the conclusion that what Roman emperors desired from Persia was a relatively-strong buffer state that was easy to negotiate with, protecting Rome from barbarians further east. Most of the time Rome needed to focus upon the Rhine and Danube frontiers and would prefer it if Persia was similarly preoccupied with events on her other frontiers. Whenever Persia became too strong and posed a threat, the Romans gathered an army, invaded, and attempted to reduce the Persians to their acceptable role. What the Persian kings wanted was a Rome that would not be strong enough to dictate terms but which would always be there as an external threat to help unite their kingdom. There was also little chance that the Persians could conquer Rome, since Roman military might far outweighed their own.

It is not, therefore, unreasonable to conjecture that most of the large-scale Sasanid invasions of imperial territory, such as on the occasions that they reached Antioch, were either to deflect domestic criticisms and reduce internal pressure for political change, or a counterattack to restore the balance in Persia's favour after a damaging defeat. The need for equilibrium helps to explain the fact that conflict in the east was centred not upon large-scale battles and capturing territory, but upon sieges, small-scale victories and the establishing of spheres of interest and relatively minor territorial gains. When, in 395, this balance was seriously threatened, the two empires combined to neutralise the threat.

It is interesting to note that when the system broke down in 607, a full-scale invasion of Rome by Khusrow II quickly resulted in the capture of Mesopotamia and Syria, with Egypt falling in 616. A counter-invasion by Heraclius caused the deposition and murder of Khusrow by his own nobles, who then sued for peace in 628. The whole affair weakened both empires and the recently united Arabs, fired by Islam, wiped out the Persian Empire completely (637–49) and conquered all of the non-European Byzantine territories outside Asia Minor by 646.

Therefore, when Justinian came to the throne in 527 he inherited relatively stable frontiers in the east, where the only real threat was from the Persians, who appeared willing to play a game of small-scale warfare. However, this was liable to change at minimal notice, so there would always be a need to maintain a large military force in the East.

Chapter 2

The Byzantine Court and the Early Life of Belisarius

The Bureaucracy in Constantinople

A Roman emperor could not hope to run the empire alone. As a consequence, over time a large bureaucracy built up which increasingly gained a life of its own. From significantly earlier than Justinian's reign, the various military and bureaucratic posts were much prized. For the higher echelons of the bureaucracy this was with a view to becoming one of the emperor's closest advisors, or, for the most optimistic, perhaps even being raised to the throne in person – though it is unlikely that such lofty ambition was the norm.

In many instances the power behind the throne was likely to be a member of the imperial family, for example Justina the mother of Valentinian III or, on a lesser scale of influence, Euphemia wife of Justin – although Euphemia had to vie with Justinian for most influence with Justin. Even when such an influential individual existed, for most candidates the aim was to rise through the ranks and become a close advisor to the emperor – one of his intimate circle. In this way they would have a hand in controlling the destiny of the empire and, as a small dividend, become fabulously wealthy. For the heart of the imperial bureaucracy was, to all intents and purposes, corrupt.

There was a large number of important and influential imperial posts, with innumerable lesser posts below them. At the top of the pile were the prefects of the East (Thrace, Asia and Egypt), and the prefect of Illyricum (Dacia, Macedonia and Greece). There was also the prefect of Constantinople and the quaestor of the sacred palace (head of the Privy Council). Furthermore, the top jobs were merely the heads of sections. As a guide to the size of some of these departments, one major bureau of the government was under the *comes sacrarum largitionum* (Count of the Sacred Largesses). His department was divided into eighteen sub-groups, each of which was graded into seven classes in order of rank.

Over all of these was the *magister officiorum* (Master of Offices), who had authority over all of the civil service, especially secretarial departments in the palace, but also the *cursus publicus* (public post), the *agentes in rebus* (secret service) and the state arms factories. These state officers were served by huge numbers of clerks and assistants.

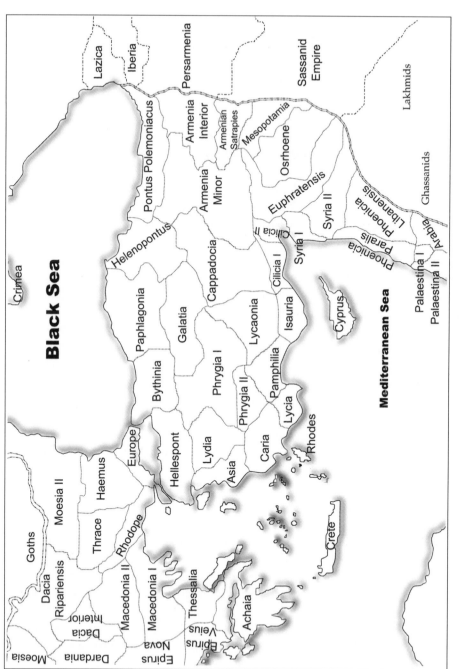

Map 2: Provinces of the Eastern Roman Empire.

Yet these were only the civilian posts. There were also the military ranks, such as the *magister utriusque militae* (Master of all the Troops) previously mentioned and the *magister militum per Orientem* (Master of Troops in the East), plus a long series of ranks down to the commanders of pairs of units within the army.

On the civilian side, all of the preferred posts brought with them a measure of power and access to the higher positions in the hierarchy. But most of all, the uppermost ranks gained access to the emperor and some, such as the *magister officiorum*, gained control of who had an audience with the emperor. This was a very privileged position and was often abused. The bribes needed to secure an audience with the emperor would remain a source of disgust to petitioners in Constantinople until the end of the empire. Of course, if you offended an upper dignitary, it was unlikely that you would see the emperor at all.

On the military side, there was the prestige and fame of winning major battles, which in itself would bring wealth and power. There might also be the added temptation of rebellion – if your army was large enough and there were enough troops in your command loyal enough to challenge the emperor himself. As a result, the top army posts were only awarded to men the emperor thought he could trust, and even then not without restrictions – as we shall see later.

Apart from the power of the top assignments, there was much to be gained from a civil appointment. In the Later Empire society was very highly stratified, and in the uppermost echelons rank was graded according to position in the hierarchy. It is easy to understand why rank was important to the workforce; it let them know where they stood in relation to each other.

All senators now ranked as *clarissimus* (illustrious), yet this was now on only the third tier of the pecking order. The higher rank of *spectabile* (notable) was now only granted, for example, to some of the higher provincial governorships plus some eunuch officers of the imperial bedchamber. The top level, *illustris* (famous), was reserved for consuls, patricians and occupiers of the uppermost ministries within government. As a further bonus, alongside the rank and titles came extra privileges, such as protection from prosecution in the courts and *sportulae* (fees on the side); it was usually possible to recover the money spent on gaining a post in this manner.

As a result, to avoid being left on the third tier as a *clarissimus*, senators now needed jobs in the government in order to progress. In this they came into contention with upwardly-mobile members of the equestrian 'middle classes'. This was especially the case in the army, where many of the latter coveted posts involving military rank so that they would be eligible for the *annona* (entitlement to provisions).

Accordingly, competition for jobs was fierce and usually revolved around a combination of family/personal influence, a patron's personal recommendation and, of course, bribery. Nor should it be thought that this was reserved for the comparatively lower echelons of the bureaucracy. The story goes that when the Emperor Anastasius died, his chief eunuch, Amantius, told the general of the palace guards, the *comes excubitorum*, of his plans to elevate one of his associates to be emperor. Consequently, he gave the general a large amount of gold with which to bribe the soldiers. Although the story may not be true, the fact that it could be told and be believed shows the level that such bribery could reach. Incidentally, the plan failed: the Excubitores guard unit proclaimed their general, Justin – who had been given the gold – as emperor on the following day. Not surprisingly, he kept the gold. He happened to be Justinian's uncle and immediate predecessor.

To modern readers the whole system might be seen as corrupt beyond repair, yet some modern bureaucracies in western Europe still appear to function on patronage and recommendation – depending upon which schools and university the applicant attended. Nor should historians of the Republic and Early Empire condemn it. It was the natural extension of the Republican 'patronage' system taken to its logical extreme. Indeed, by the fifth century payment for office had become the norm and in 444 Theodosius II had even regularised and regulated it by law. Furthermore, it is likely that the level of bribery was usually kept within acceptable limits, even ignoring existing legislation. Anyone upsetting the balance by spending too much money may have been labelled an 'upstart' and been the victim of a backlash from higher ranks anxious to preserve their positions. Looked at from the outside the system may well have been corrupt, but this should not blind us to one salient point: it worked. It not only worked, but it lasted until Constantinople fell in 1453.

Alongside the scheming and plotting to ensure that the top posts were filled with 'suitable appointees' (ie your own men), there was another side to imperial politics. This was the 'class' struggle that was pursued at all levels between the established, cultured and highly-educated elite against the poorly-educated men that nevertheless achieved high rank, especially during the course of a military career. Indeed, this may have been a source of the resentment of Procopius in the *Anekdota*, since he portrays Justin as an ill-educated buffoon who needed a stencil in order to write the word *legi* ('I have read this') on documents for them to become legally valid.

For aristocratic families raised in the classical tradition of Greek, Latin and rhetoric, to have an 'illiterate peasant' from an unknown village in Thrace as emperor was likely to be particularly galling. They would have been unable to show their classical education by alluding to events from Homer or Virgil in his presence, since he would clearly not have understood the reference, nor comprehended and acknowledged their skills.

Hardly less appalling would be the expected round of promotions from within the emperor's intimate circle. These would likely come from those closest to him, who would undoubtedly be of similar, rough, peasant stock. Furthermore, it is likely that they would oust men who had spent a fortune and lost years of their lives to reach their soon-to-be-lost lofty positions. The background intrigues and political schemes of those who had lost out would have likely taken on a sharper, more personal edge, even amounting to vendetta.

Yet it is clear that Justinian's uncle, Justin, recognised that to many he remained unacceptable. It is interesting to note that he ensured that Justinian obtained a classical education at Constantinople so that Justinian would not face, either openly or in secret, the derision or disdain that was likely to be aimed at Justin. Yet the tutoring Justinian received could not eradicate the lowly nature of his birth or stop the aristocracy disliking being subservient to him. After all, although he was the nephew of an emperor, he would probably still be seen as a lowborn peasant, and it is unlikely that he could eradicate all trace of his Thracian accent when speaking Greek or Latin.

Upon being made emperor, Justinian did not act in a manner to endear him to the nobility. As we have seen, their main source of prestige and power was employment in the civil service, and Justin had already made many changes. In order to decrease the amount of revenues being spent on administration, Justinian ordered a cut-back in the civil service. Many lost their jobs and their status, and in return acquired a sense of injustice and betrayal.

The very size of the civil service and the large part it played in the lives of the nobility and upwardly mobile did mean that change was always resisted. Such an attitude was probably one of the causes of Byzantine stagnation; in particular, the Byzantines believed that the emperor reflected the glory of God and his employees reflected the role of the angels. Therefore, Byzantine methods of operation were a reflection of Divine practice and were thus clearly perfect and needed no alterations. As a result, any change, whatever the motive, was not only unnecessary but verging on blasphemous. Furthermore, the trend for some time had been towards Greek replacing Latin as the language of the law. This was seen by many as a betrayal of their Roman heritage, and by some at least as a break with tradition bordering on the sacrilegious: in an age of superstition, such a rupture with their ancestral past was a bad omen.

It is when looking at the prejudice inherent in the noble classes that we need to take note of our sources. It is probable that most of the invective aimed at Justinian, his wife Theodora and Belisarius' wife Antonina in the *Anekdota* of Procopius was solely due to their being seen as of too common a stock for high positions at court. It should not be forgotten that Procopius had early acquired a traditional education in the Greek classics and law, implying that his family was relatively wealthy. Furthermore, the likelihood of his being of at least middle rank is reinforced by his appointment to such a high position as secretary to the new *magister militum per Orientem*, Belisarius, at a relatively young age. Procopius' family may have had wealth, a relatively distinguished ancestry and long-standing connections at court; Justinian, Theodora and Antonina did not. This was likely to be of some importance later in Belisarius' career.

It is also conceivable that Procopius was further dismayed by the rivalries, jealousies and intrigues that took place at the court. Normally, if an emperor was a member of one of the older, noble families, individuals would know roughly what to expect and where they stood in the pecking order. With Justin and Justinian being outsiders, it is likely that the uncertainty of the times resulted in a more frenzied court life than was the norm. An example of this took place in 541, when the Empress Theodora and Antonina conspired against John of Cappadocia, the praetorian prefect and a personal enemy of Theodora. It was an open secret that John desired to become emperor. Antonina arranged to meet him and induced him to reveal how he would achieve his objective. This was related to Theodora and John lost his job, his wealth and his personal property, but was exiled as a monk rather than being executed, possibly for fear of rousing residual aristocratic support against the emperor.

On the whole, Procopius appears to have been sickened by the political rivalries, jealousies and intrigues present in the court during the reign of Justinian, to the point where he wrote the *Anekdota* as a rebuke to all of the people involved. It is possible that he began his career with an idealistic view of the emperor and his court, and when this was at odds with reality he felt no option but to voice his disgust.

Finally, there was Justinian's relationship with Theodora. Justinian himself realised that neither he nor Theodora fit well into the imperial model. It is possible that, alongside his obvious attraction to the eminently-unsuitable courtesan Theodora, lay the tempting possibility of further irritating the arrogant nobles of the court. For Theodora had a chequered background. Her father was apparently a man who was a bear keeper at the Hippodrome and her mother was allegedly an acrobat. This was not a woman who could or would expect to be welcome in polite society.

Yet there was a major aspect of Theodora's past that would endear her to Justinian. They were both attached to the Blues. Blue and Green were originally the colours associated with the two principal teams of chariot racers at the Hippodrome. By the time of Justinian, the two factions had left simple racing behind and had assumed semi-political status. The Blues tended to be the party of landowners and the Graeco-Roman aristocracy; the Greens were affiliated with trade, industry and the civil service. Naturally, wishing to reform the civil service, Justinian tended to sympathise with the Blues.

The antagonism between the two parties could easily expand into full-scale riots, yet, far from attempting to diminish their influence, Justinian and Theodora seem to have allowed their favouritism for the Blues to enable the Blues to gain the upper hand. This was to have far-reaching consequences for Justinian's reign, especially during the Nika riots, as we shall.

The importance of the tensions and conflicts both at court and in the capital city will become clearer when we look at the life of Belisarius in detail. All that needs to be remembered at this stage is that politics and society in the imperial city were fraught with tensions and violence, factors that were to have an enormous impact upon the career of Belisarius himself.

Belisarius

It is unfortunate in the extreme that the rise to power of Justin and Justinian should be concurrent with the birth and early career of Belisarius. The existing sources for this period concentrate upon the ascent of Justin and the activities of Justinian as the power behind the throne and then as emperor himself. The fact that the sources are unclear concerning much of the early lives of the emperors Justin and Justinian gives an indication of their lack of coverage for the lesser personality of Belisarius.

Belisarius appears to have been born in the town of Germana – now Saparevska Banya in western Bulgaria – sometime around the start of the sixth century (probably between 500 and 505). Although nothing is known concerning his family or his upbringing, it is conspicuous that nowhere in the *Anekdota* does Procopius mention his ancestry. Although this may be due to a lingering regard for the general, given the nature of the *Anekdota* it would seem natural that, if he was as lowborn as Justinian, Theodora and Antonina, the fact would have been mentioned, if only as a comparison to the objects of Procopius' hatred.

The theory that Belisarius was of a relatively high status gains further credence when it is linked to the story of John the Cappadocian related above. John clearly expected Belisarius' wife to support John's attempt to gain the throne, yet there is no evidence to suggest that Belisarius conspired against Justinian. As a consequence, John's trust is only understood if he expected the support of a fellow noble against the Thracian upstart, especially considering the friendship of Antonina and Theodora.

The supposition that Belisarius was relatively noble may also be one of the causes for the relative lack of criticism he received in the *Anekdota* of Procopius. A possible reason for Procopius' tirade against Belisarius may be that Procopius expected Belisarius to move on from the conquest of Africa and Italy to the conquest of the empire. That he did not may have been a deep source of disappointment to Procopius, not simply because the lowborn Justinian remained in control, but also because of the benefits he himself could have expected from his former superior had he become the new emperor. Yet the denunciation does not have the same venom as that against Theodora and Justinian.

Therefore, it seems natural to deduce that Belisarius was not a penniless peasant but a member of the higher classes in his town of birth, possibly a *decurion* or *curiale* (town councillors) or higher. Such prominence would also help to explain his lofty position in the army at a very early age.

The whole edifice of Byzantine politics would undoubtedly have affected the young Belisarius. As we shall see, it was certainly to affect him after his marriage, when it is likely to have made him suspicious of the motives of others. This may have been especially the case in the military aspects of Byzantine diplomacy, since he appears to have been relatively unconcerned with civil politics.

On the other hand, we should not forget that the cities of the empire strove to reflect the conditions of Constantinople. The 'Mother of Cities' was a role model for all and it is likely that the manner of rank and promotion were the same in Belisarius' home town as the capital city, if on a much smaller scale. Therefore he is likely to have developed political skills growing up, especially if his family were of some importance in Germana, which would have stood him in good stead in his early career.

Furthermore, we should remember that both Justinian and Belisarius were from Thrace. The majority of the inhabitants of the east spoke Greek, but because of its western orientation the Thracians generally spoke Latin as their second language (Thracian being their first). Justinian and Belisarius therefore shared several common bonds: a language, a place of origin, but mainly their relative youth. It is quite likely that Belisarius was a far more pleasing companion for Justinian than any of the Greek–speaking, older military men that probably surrounded him.

There is one other factor to take into account. In about 522 Justinian met Theodora. As we have already seen, she was not an ideal match for such an important political figure, and it is possible that Belisarius was influential in maintaining their relationship, simply by giving advice to Justinian on how to manage the episode. It is likely that Belisarius would have a much greater knowledge of these matters and be able to help with sound political advice if he was originally of a higher social class than Justinian and knew the way that the aristocratic mind worked.

It is regrettable that so much about the future general must remain conjecture. Yet, given the nature of the surviving sources and the fact that in many instances the early lives of important figures were seen as irrelevant by contemporary writers, this is all we have until shortly before Justinian was declared emperor in 527. For Belisarius is first mentioned as an officer in Justinian's bodyguard before Justinian became emperor. He probably joined the army at about 18 years old, though an age as low as 16 is possible. We do not know at what level he joined the army, but if he joined as an ordinary soldier he was promoted exceedingly quickly. Given that the earliest he is likely to have been born is 500, this implies that he took only around ten years to rise through the ranks and become an officer in the guard of the *magister utriusque militiae*. By the time a Roman soldier was appointed general he would normally expect to be at least 35 years old.

The reason for this meteoric rise is unknown. He either utilised excellent family connections, possessed an outstanding personal physique and manner, or he was an outstanding military talent, or took advantage of a combination of the three. There is no claim in Procopius that Belisarius was outstanding physically – although he is given a certain military bearing – and he does not stand out as particularly powerful in the mosaic in the church of San Vitale (Plate 1). He may have been exceedingly well connected, with powerful patronage to promote his career, yet this is nowhere mentioned and a middle-class upbringing seems eminently more likely. Yet, as we will see later, he had one further advantage: his personality. Throughout his career he appears to have behaved in a sensible and trustworthy fashion. Although he may have been outstanding militarily from an early age, it is more likely that his loyalty and trustworthiness were what attracted the attention of his fellow country-man, the future Emperor Justinian.

The fact that upon Justinian becoming emperor Belisarius was appointed to a senior post and placed in command of troops in a war with Persia confirms that he was a close personal friend of the emperor, that his military talents were outstanding and that he had an exceptional personality.

Whatever the cause, Belisarius now steps from the shadows cast by Justin and Justinian and stands in the full spotlight of history, to be judged on his own merits.

Chapter 3

The New Roman Army

For any student of the earlier Roman Empire, the force that Belisarius took control of for the Persian Wars was a strange entity. The 'Roman' army was in the process of change. It was no longer the army of the early Empire, with its c.5,000 man legions forming the backbone of the fighting force. During the reigns of Diocletian, Constantine and their successors, a series of reforms had changed the face of the army. Although the number of legions had increased, they had been reduced in strength to around 1,000 men. There had also been an increase in the number of cavalry and *auxilia* units. Although the cavalry units had been reduced to a strength of approximately 300 men, the *auxilia* probably remained 500 men strong. The result was a much larger, well-balanced army combining foot and horse, close combat and missile weapons, whilst still retaining many of the traditional Roman elements. In contrast, by the reign of Justinian the army would scarcely have been recognisable as Roman by Julius Caesar or Pompey.

The Battle of Adrianople marked a major watershed for the Roman army. Although not the catastrophe often portrayed by historians, it was the beginning of the evolutionary period within the military that would result in the army of Belisarius.

The battle ended with the loss of a huge number of trained troops. Although conscription could rapidly renew the numbers lost, the recruits did not have time to receive the levels of training given to their predecessors. More difficult to replace was the vast amount of lost equipment. It is clear that the official *fabricae* (state factories) would struggle to replace the sheer volume of equipment lost, and it is probable that large numbers of smiths and ironworkers were hired to help to make good the losses of the East.

The new workers had no training in producing the complex Roman helmets that were spun from a single piece of iron. As a consequence, they produced basic styles, copied from steppe or Sasanid examples, as will be shown. The process of change had probably begun before the Battle of Adrianople: the eastern Roman army may have already been coming under steppe influences due to changes in fashion, but the after-effects of the defeat were to hasten the shift over the following decades.

Not long after Adrianople, the Romans finally came into direct contact with the Huns. Fearsome warriors mounted on sturdy ponies, the Hunnic cavalry were easily capable of riding rings around the Roman infantry, picking them off with their powerful bows whilst the infantry remained virtually powerless to respond. Needless to say, the Huns held Roman infantry – indeed any infantry – in contempt.

Following the collapse of the Hunnic empire after the Battle of the Nedao in 454, many Hunnic bands and individuals were recruited as mercenaries by the eastern empire. Naturally, they brought their strategy, their tactics and their contempt for the infantry with them. The army of the Empire began a rapid change. The spear and javelin-armed cavalry units that had been the backbone of the cavalry since the days of Augustus were retrained in the use of the bow. The new formations – now named *hippo-toxotai* (horse-archers) – retained the armour for the riders, yet achieved speed and manoeuvrability thanks to the strength of their Cappadocian horses. However, they did not adopt the use of barding or other horse armour; although some earlier units had used barding, both the Romans and the Persians appear to have stopped using it by the time of Belisarius. On the subject of horse armour, much has been made of the existence of the Leones Clibanarii unit in Egypt, which according to its name should have been equipped with armour for the front of the horse. Yet the name of the unit was likely to remain unaltered long after the use of such armour had been abandoned. Also, the unit was stationed in Egypt, a peaceful province, where the use of armour had probably fallen out of favour when the units involved had been given the option of purchasing their own. As a consequence, the continuation of the unit named Leones Clibanarii does not necessarily prove that Roman cavalry units continued to use barding for their horses.

Roman, or as they will now be referred to – Byzantine, cavalry do not seem to have employed the asymmetrical bow favoured by the Huns, using instead a more standard symmetrical bow that was much easier to produce in the large numbers necessary to re-equip the entire cavalry arm. However, like the Huns they relied on the power and accuracy of their shooting to cause casualties. This can be compared to the reliance upon the sheer massed volume of fire preferred by the Sasanids and their Parthian predecessors.

Organisation

The Byzantine cavalry units appear to have declined from their traditional strength. Although the actual strength of units is unclear, it is possible that the army had by now begun its transformation into the Byzantine army of the *Strategikon* of Maurikios. If this is the case, cavalry would now have been formed in *banda* of around 300 men. There would be ten men in a *decharchia*, five *decharchia* in an *allaghion*, two *allaghia* in a *hekatontarchia* and three *hekatontarchiai* in a *bandon*, totalling 300 men plus officers, musicians and other supernumeraries, all led by a *tribounos*.

To complete the tale, in later practice there were a variable number of *banda* in a *chiliarchy*, commanded by a *chiliarch* (from *chilias*, a thousand, although a *chiliarch* usually commanded between 2,000 and 3,000 men). Two or three *chiliarchs* were gathered in a *moira* (plural: *merē*) led by a *merarch*, who commanded perhaps 5,000–6,000 men and never more than 7,000; three *merē* formed a *dhoungos*. Since the emphasis at this time was upon the cavalry, it is probable that the cavalry, rather than the infantry, were the first to be reformed upon the new model.. Although actual strength is likely to have been less than 300 due to deaths, desertion and recruitment difficulties, thanks to their perceived importance and improved status it is likely that the cavalry attracted recruits far easier than the infantry and so were nearer to their paper figure in reality.

With the increasing importance of the cavalry in the eyes of the generals came an increase in training, with exercises in all-round shooting, speed of manoeuvre, and hand-to-hand combat. This was mirrored by a comparative decline in the training available for the infantry, which lost much of its élan and combat ability. By the time of Belisarius, the infantry were sometimes expected to turn and run when charged by cavalry – as was to happen to Belisarius at the Battle of Rome.

If the infantry had already begun their change in unit size, there would now in theory be sixteen men in a *lochagias*, four *lochagiai* in an *allaghion*, two *allaghia* in a *hekatontarchia*, and two *hekatontarchiai* in an *arithmos*, leading to a paper strength of 256 men, again led by a *tribounos*. This unit recalls the division used by Alexander the Great in his phalanxes, or pike blocks. It gives a square of infantry with sixteen men per side, enabling the unit to turn to face any direction necessary without a loss of frontage or force. It is eminently suitable to troops wielding a large pike of 4m or more in length, for whom greater depth can be an advantage. It is not necessarily suitable for troops wielding spears and swords.

As a consequence, the spear and sword-armed infantry (it is probably wise not to use the title *legiones* anymore, as this can cause confusion) under Belisarius probably retained their paper strength of approximately 1,000 men. Again, in reality it is unlikely that many of them managed to maintain these numbers in the field. The infantry, previously supported by the *auxilia*, were now supported by an increasing number of foot archers, drawn up either to the side or in the rear of the infantry to give supporting fire.

The size of the specialist archer units is open to question. In the *Notitia Dignitatum*, most *auxilia* units are assumed to be 500 strong. There does appear to have been at least one exception, where such a unit was 1,000 strong, equating to one of the *cohortes milliaria* (one-thousand strong cohorts) of the army of the earlier imperial period. However, the reorganisation may have been used to standardise the size of units, in which case the single large exception would have been amended. Consequently the archers were probably organised in units of 500 like the earlier *auxilia*, or much less likely 1,000 similar to the spearmen. They used the traditional Roman bows as used by the cavalry. On the other hand, due to their lower height coupled with the relatively poor visibility on dusty battlefields, it is likely that these archers relied on sheer numbers of arrows rather than on the accuracy and power of their mounted counterparts.

It is unknown if there was a pattern to the rearmament, for example with the old *legiones* retained as the close-combat arm and the *auxilia* equipped with bows. If there was, it is likely that the change was governed by seniority and influence rather than troop type, with the *Palatina* retaining their shock role and the units of lower rank becoming archers.

The troops described above appear to be the descendants of the 'field armies' described by the *Notitia Dignitatum*, supplemented by some of the frontier troops where necessary. Still stationed in towns and on the frontiers were the *numeri* ('bands'). Mustering around 200 men in each unit, they were often brigaded in pairs under the command of a *tribounos*. They seldom appear to have been used in the field, being too small to sustain casualties and too poorly trained to be effective in combat. They were thus left to garrison strategic points, forts and cities outside the remit of the regular army.

The formation which the Byzantine cavalry adopted in battle is unclear. Later Byzantine practice was to assume a close formation, which relied on arrow numbers prior to contact and the impact of heavily armed troops in the front ranks during combat to defeat the enemy. Hunnic practice was to adopt a loose formation and fire at the enemy at point blank range. This would force the enemy to either charge to relieve the pressure, or it would cause their formation to be disrupted. If charged, the Hunnic cavalry could evade, leaving the enemy disorganised on blown horses. When the enemy were either disrupted through charging or because of missile fire, any available Hunnic cavalry could close formation and deliver a charge in the hope of breaking the enemy. If the charge failed to rout the enemy, the cavalry would withdraw and repeat the process. If the charge succeeded, the horsemen could either pursue or turn to a fresh target.

Given the employment of large numbers of Huns, and the success that the Huns had had with their tactics, it is far more likely that the Byzantines adopted the latter method, using a loose formation. Only later would the Byzantines adopt closer formations, probably under the influence of their Sasanid adversaries.

When looking at the battles fought by Belisarius it is important to bear one more factor in mind: of the 1,000 men theoretically in an infantry unit, when the troops took the field some would be left behind in their garrison to receive and train new recruits, and act as a permanent base. Of the nominal total it is more than likely that the absolute maximum fielded by any infantry unit in battle would be 800.

Finally, we can look at the total strength of the army at the time of Justinian. The calculations are complex and have been covered in great detail by Treadgold (Treadgold, 1995, pp. 59–64). His figures are rough approximations based on the numbers given in various sources, primarily Agathias. Despite the difficulties surrounding them, they appear to fit the facts and are given in the following table.

Army	Commander	Strength
praesental army I	Emperor/*magister utriusque militiae*	20,000
praesental army II	Emperor/*magister utriusque militiae*	20,000
Army of the East	*magister militum per Orientem*	20,000
Army of Thrace	*magister militum per Thraciam*	20,000
Army of Illyricum	*magister militum per Illyricum*	15,000
Army of Armenia	*magister militum per Armeniam*	15,000

Although the figures given date to 559, it is unlikely that they had been altered to any great extent during the wars in the west and the ongoing wars with Persia. By this time, the eastern armies of the *Notitia Dignitatum* had declined in numbers. The new statistics reveal armies which are divisible by 5,000, which is also the average size of a *moira*, as described above.

Allies and Mercenaries

The loss of the traditional heavy cavalry armed with spear and javelins was to some extent offset by the recruitment of *foederati*, unassimilated barbarians armed in their native styles serving under Byzantine command. These included spear-armed troops from the northern frontiers, for example Goths and Heruls, who slowly adopted Byzantine drill, whilst retaining their own distinctive weapons. These troops later formed the nucleus of the Optimates guard unit.

The Byzantines continued to use non-Roman horse archers such as the Huns and other nomadic tribes from the east. These were known as *ethnikoi*, and they appear to have been used as specialist troops, especially where their scouting ability was concerned. Both *foederati* and *ethnikoi* troops became an increasing feature of the Byzantine military system.

The *bucellari* (personal guards) were named after the *bucellatum*, the dried biscuit or hard tack which was issued as rations in the field. They appear to have originally comprised the more heavily-armed barbarian, and especially steppe, nobles and their retainers serving directly under the general who had hired them. As a consequence, the majority were armed with their traditional equipment, namely a *kontos* (lance), a bow and possibly a small shield. (It should be noted however that the lance, whilst being the requisite length, was never used by the Romans in the couched manner that became prevalent in the later Middle Ages. Instead, it was used underarm and two-handed.) Forming the core of a general's *comitatus* ('fellow troops', 'personal army') in the Justinian period, by the time of Belisarius this equipment had become the norm, later spreading to other units of the cavalry.

The *bucellarii* were recruited by the generals under whom they served, not by the emperor, and so had loyalty only to the general that hired them, not to the empire or to the emperor in Constantinople. Although this was a situation fraught with danger for the emperor, there was little that could be done to change things. As mercenaries, they paid for their own equipment before hiring themselves to whoever was willing to pay them, or to generals in places where the chances of plunder were great. They had no desire to become soldiers who were only for show around the emperor.

The reduction in the power and status of the legions, the reliance upon horse archers and the employment of mercenary troops armed in their own fashion marked a distinct phase in the development of the Roman army. In effect, the old Roman army was gone.

Defensive Equipment

Alongside the change in the nature of the army, there was a corresponding change in dress and equipment. It has always been assumed by scholars that the Roman army retained many features throughout the Roman and Byzantine periods. In the earlier empire, the state-owned *fabricae* (factories) manufactured weapons, shields, armour and helmets. These were then distributed around the empire. Furthermore, helmets, body armour, shields and swords would be manufactured to specific patterns, depending upon whether the unit receiving them was a *legio* (legion), *ala* (cavalry) or *auxilia* (non-Roman infantry) unit. Many writers have assumed that the model remained true throughout the empire.

The theory does not take into account a major change in practice in the era approximate to the fall of the west. Earlier, money was deducted from troops' wages to pay for the equipment that they used. However, Anastasius changed the system in 498 or thereabouts. The soldiers were now paid 'in full', but they were expected to equip themselves out of their own purse. The large increase in pay meant that service in the army now became a viable career again; conscription was no longer needed and the army increased in size. The new levels of willing manpower available may have been a factor in Justinian's attempt to reconquer the west.

It is likely that the equipment that they bought depended upon several factors. Certainly, there was the obligation to fulfil their duties, and in this it is likely that they would purchase offensive weapons consistent with that of their unit, otherwise they would be a liability to their comrades. It is possible that these were still supplied specifically by the government in order to avoid confusion. It would also be necessary to buy equipment that would identify them as belonging to their unit; either they would have helmet plumes of the same colour or their shields would be painted with a colour or pattern to match that of their colleagues, or both.

Yet within specific limitations, there would be a great deal of flexibility according to their personal tastes. Specific weapons, such as swords, were doubtless bought for individual preference, since weight, length and 'feel' are highly individual aspects of weapons. In addition, the more expensive defensive items would not be to everyone's taste. Helmets and body armour could have been bought and tailored to fit, with the individual having to balance the greater cost of chain mail with its excellent defensive properties against the cheaper but more easily-damaged scale armour. Nor was this all. There was the possibility of using quilted linen armour, or even of relying upon a large shield and having no armour to cover the body at all. Furthermore, in provinces such as Egypt and Spain where there was little danger of military duties, with the troops acting more as a police force, there would have been little incentive for the troops to buy armour which they were never likely to use.

The same factors also apply to helmets. Although it is common to find helmets described as either 'infantry' or 'cavalry' helmets, it is likely that by the later period covered here there was a considerable overlap of helmet usage between the various services of the army. Since it was down to cost and personal taste, a relatively rich infantryman could probably afford the same helmets – or better – than the less well-off among the cavalry.

Therefore, the common image of units wearing exactly the same equipment should no longer be considered the norm. There was likely to be a variety of helmets, shields and armour within each unit, with only the colours of crests and/or shields defining the parent unit of the soldier. The main limiting factor would be availability. The equipment needed to re-equip the army, following both the defeat at Adrianople and the decision to change the armament of the cavalry, had to be manufactured in eastern *fabricae*: the *fabricae* of the west having by now been lost. This would have greatly reduced production and is likely to have caused shortages in some areas for at least some time.

In light of these considerations, it has been thought best to look at the equipment of the troops by equipment type, rather than by whether it is deemed to be worn by infantry or cavalry units by modern historians and archaeologists.

Helmets
There were a few types of helmet available for the soldier of Belisarius' army to purchase.

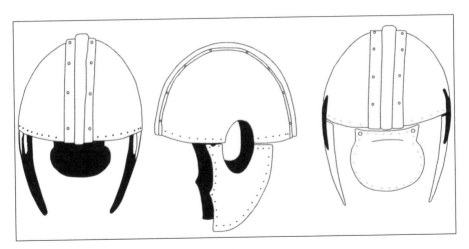

Illustration 1: Roman ridge helmet (after James).

The first types are known as 'ridge helmets'. Although they came into use as early as the late third century, these types continued in use for a very long time and were probably still in use during the wars of Belisarius: indeed, coins dating between the fourth and sixth centuries depict emperors wearing variants of the type, although this may be due to tradition in the imagery rather than contemporary fashion.

Ridge helmets came in two varieties. The archetype of these is known as 'Intercisa', named from the site where the first remains were found. These helmets were constructed from two halves, joined along the centre by a metal strip. There were three varieties of joining strip found on the site. Those of Intercisa 1 and Intercisa 2 were relatively broad and low, that of Intercisa 3 was narrow and high. These differences might simply be ascribed to production techniques and overall design effect of the finished helmet rather than profound differences in manufacture.

However, on Intercisa 4 the ridge projected far above the bowl of the helmet, forming a large metal crest. In art these metal-crested helmets are shown on various manuscripts, but it is likely that the soldiers portrayed are guardsmen. Therefore the difference between Intercisa 4 and the others may be that this helmet was worn by officers or guardsmen, worn to distinguish them from others in battle. This remains doubtful, however, since some of the

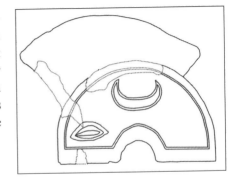

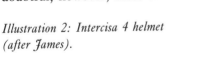

Illustration 2: Intercisa 4 helmet (after James).

Intercisa 1, 2 and 3 helmets appear to have had holes and fittings for the attachment of crests. If this is the case, the large metal crest of Intercisa 4 would have been less noticeable, especially in battlefield conditions.

Finds of similar helmets at Berkasovo were made from either two halves or four quarter pieces, but also include 'nasals' to guard the nose. Although such nasals are known from the Classical Greek period, this is unlikely to have represented a return to classical styles. Such patterns were popular amongst peoples from the steppes, such as the Huns, who appear to have been the source for many of the designs in the Byzantine army of this period. A similar example was found at Burgh-on-Sands in England (Plate 17).

The second type of helmet is known as a 'spangenhelm', from the German word *spangen*, which was applied to the inverted T-pieces with which such helmets were constructed. The spangenhelm was made from four or six shaped iron plates, attached to a brow band at the base and then connected together at the sides by the aforementioned *spangen*, made from gilded copper-alloy plates. The helmet was surmounted by a disc to hold the completed assembly together.

Unlike earlier helmets, where cheek pieces and neck guards were integral parts of the helmet, in all of these helmets they were made separately and attached to the lower rim of the helmet. This was likely to have been for ease and low cost of production.

Illustration 3: The Concesci helmet (after James).

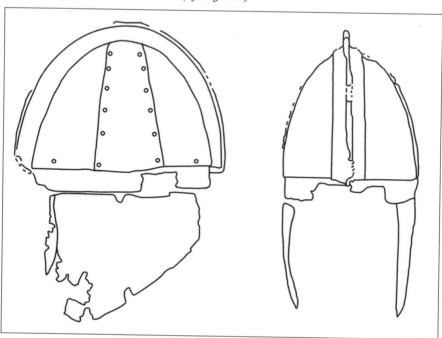

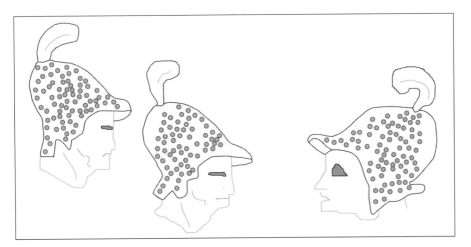

Illustration 4: Detail of the David and Goliath plate (Ian Hughes).

With all of these helmets it must be born in mind that the corroded iron remains that are usually all that is left of the helmet can disguise its form when originally worn. All of the helmets described could be, and possibly were, adorned with gold, silver or other metal sheeting, or might have been tinned to enhance their appearance. Some may also have added paste gems or semi-precious stones to make them even more imposing.

A further option for head protection appears to have been a coif of either chain or scale mail designed to be worn over the head in a similar fashion to a modern balaclava. Unfortunately, although possibly represented in art, no finds of such equipment have been found and the exact design remains in the realm of conjecture.

As a final note, an early seventh-century artefact known as 'the David and Goliath Plate' shows infantry wearing highly-decorated cloth covers over the top of their helmets. These would have acted as protection for the helmets themselves in inclement weather, and their decoration could have aided in individual and unit recognition. The date of their introduction is unknown. There is no evidence for their use in the sixth century, due to their inability to survive as archaeological artefacts and the lack of contemporary descriptions and artwork. However their use by the armies of Belisarius remains a possibility.

Armour

For body protection there were, again, a variety of armours that could be purchased. The most familiar of these to modern readers is likely to be chain mail. Small, individual rings of iron are interlinked and riveted together to form a strong and flexible – if very heavy – armour. However, the process of manufacturing the thousands of iron rings needed, plus the large amount of time necessary to rivet the links together, make this a very expensive piece of kit.

As a second choice there was scale mail. In this, a large number of scales are joined together to form a protective cuirass. The method of joining the scales produced two variations of the armour. In one, the scales are joined with either wire or string to their neighbours to left and right, as well as to a cloth or leather backing material to produce a relatively flexible armour. However, there would be a weakness in the armour between the horizontal rows of scales, which are not joined. In the alternative method, the scales are also joined to the adjacent scales above and below to form a rigid set of armour. The loss of flexibility would be offset against the elimination of the weakness between the rows.

A third form of armour is known as 'lamellar' armour. Narrow elongated plates of metal were vertically laced, not wired, to form a very rigid style of armour. Whilst there was little in the way of flexibility, the armour was strong and, due to the method of manufacture, relatively cheap. The form was increasing in popularity at this time under heavy steppe, particularly Avar, influences; this was a fashionable style of armour.

In all of the above examples the armour was designed to cover the torso of the wearer. In addition, fashion now dictated that sleeves were being worn long, usually down to the elbow, and that the skirt of the armour would reach down to the knee. Where necessary, it was designed with a split for ease of wearing by cavalry.

Unless the soldier was prepared to enter battle completely unarmoured, there was one further form of armour he could wear. This was the *thoracomachus* ('chest/thorax protector') or *subarmalis* ('below the armour'), which, as the name suggests, originated as a padded undergarment to be worn below heavy metal armour. There is no archaeological evidence for this armour, yet there are a few pictorial and literary sources available that show it was worn. Similar to the much later medieval akheton, layers of linen or other suitable material were stuffed with a soft filling of some form, for example goats' wool. This produced a tough, padded armour that could absorb some of a blow's force, whilst still being very flexible and extremely cheap. Indeed, it is feasible that many of these would have been hand made by the owner to save on armour costs.

To supplement the body armour there was a limited variety of leg, arm and hand armours available.

The *ocreae* (greaves) used to protect the lower leg had been in use since before the time of Scipio Africanus in the third century BC. They had evolved from the clip-on version of the early Greek city states into a style that was attached to the leg by leather straps. They were now made from either iron or wood, and were constructed from long pieces which ran vertically up the leg, a form similar to the lamellar armour mentioned above, but in this context known as 'splint' armour.

For the arms there were two sorts of defence available. *Manicae* ('sleeves') are segmented defences made of iron, copper alloy or leather. They are shown on the Adamklissi monument, where they were probably worn to defend the upper arm against the feared Dacian *falx*. They continued in use until at least the period under discussion, and they are included in the *Notitia Dignitatum* along with the items produced by the state-owned munitions factories. Although useful

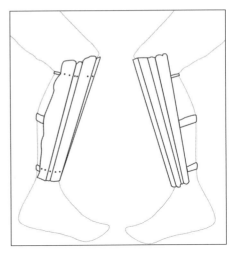

Illustration 5: Greaves (after Stephenson).

in protecting the vulnerable right arm (the left arm being behind a shield), their added expense may have resulted in only a few, if any, being worn by Belisarius' troops.

The other arm defences available were vambraces. These were made in the same way as the splint greaves mentioned earlier, their difference from *manicae* being that they only protected the lower arm. These may have been in greater demand than *manicae*, since the trend was to wear elbow-length armour and a vambrace would complete the arm protection at relatively little additional cost. However their use by horse archers was probably limited due to their restricting the movement of the right arm, for which flexibility was paramount when drawing and aiming a bow, and the possibility of interfering with a clean release.

Finally, there were gauntlets. These appear to have been made by stitching shaped metal plates onto a leather glove, either worn separately or as an extension of a *manica* or vambrace. Whatever method was used, they would be invaluable in giving the wearer some protection for the otherwise extremely vulnerable right hand. Unfortunately, although we know they were available, there is very little evidence for their manufacture and use. It is possible they they proved restrictive in the use of the bow, and so were deemed unsuitable for use by cavalry units.

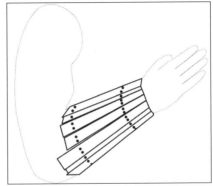

Illustration 6: Vambrace (after Stephenson).

Shields

Shields were now made using simple plank construction, with the face at least being covered in leather to help maintain shield integrity. The old plywood shields of the earlier empire were now a thing of the past.

Up until at least the start of this period the use of shields by horsemen had declined but shields began to come back into fashion at roughly the time of Belisarius' wars. The Byzantine cavalry was now primarily armed with a bow. This necessitated a change in the size and shape of the shields, which now became small and circular, as opposed to the large ovals that had dominated previously. These small cavalry shields were slung from the neck and attached to the upper left arm. This allowed the wearer both to use the bow at distance, and to utilise the limited protection that such a shield offered when in hand-to-hand combat.

Foot archers also appear to have had small shields, which they hung from their belts when not in use. However, these were a last-ditch defence, since the archers were very vulnerable to attack by all opposing troops except for similarly-equipped archers, and would be expected to use evasive tactics if charged.

The spearmen were still expected to use the long oval shield that became common during the preceding centuries, although the size and precise shape of these was likely to be up to the individual purchaser.

All the shields of a given unit would probably have been painted in a 'regimental' pattern, or at least the same colour. Yet it should be borne in mind that during the course of a campaign shields were absorbing blows aimed at the bearer, and so could become severely damaged. It is unlikely that field replacements would have been painted with a highly complex pattern; a simple facing colour would have been more likely. It should also be remembered that in a unit with a maximum strength of only 1,200 men, each man would have been known to his comrades, at least by sight.

Weapons

In the employment of weapons, it is likely that the choice would not necessarily have been left to the individual; it is probable that the main offensive/defensive weapon would have been provided by the state – although the cost would then have been deducted from the soldier's pay. In this way, uniformity of weapons within a unit would help to define the unit's main function and also eliminate the confusion that could arise from personal choice. Yet it must be remembered that the specific size or weight of, for example, a sword is a personal factor and may have resulted in such weapons continuing to be left up to the choice of the individual.

Spears and javelins

The main weapon for the infantry was the spear or javelin. Although usually seen as being used for different purposes, with the spear being retained in the hand and the javelin used as a missile weapon, there is actually little difference between the two apart from size. It is obvious that the heavier weight of the spear made it harder to throw, whilst the lightness of the javelin makes it less robust as a close combat weapon. Therefore, specialist units who were either designated as shock troops intended only for close combat, or skirmishers intended only for missile action, may have been given weapons of specific size and weight. However, for the majority of troops it is likely that the weapon supplied was of an intermediary size and so could be used for either purpose.

Spicula *and* angones

The classic *pilum* of the earlier empire had now fallen out of use. Its replacements were the *spiculum* (plural: *spicula*) and the *angon* (plural: *angones*). Both of these fulfilled the same function as the earlier *pilum*, but their design omitted the thin metal shaft that extended behind the iron head of the *pilum*, which may have been perceived as a weakness when facing cavalry. They were also easier, faster and cheaper to manufacture than the *pilum*.

It is likely that both the *spiculum* and *angon* were still expensive to make when compared to a normal spear, so it is unlikely that they would have been made for universal distribution. Therefore, only the wealthiest of the foot troops may have bought one of these, despite their superiority in most circumstances to other spears and javelins. It is more likely that a minority of specialist units would have been equipped with these weapons by the state.

Plumbatae

Also known as *mattiobarbuli*, *plumbatae* were a form of dart. In theory there were two types. The *plumbata mamillata* was the standard form, consisting of a shaft, a head and a large lead weight in the centre to aid penetration. The *plumbata et tribulata* had three spikes radiating from the lead weight. This meant that any darts which missed their targets and landed on the ground could instead act as caltrops, with the spikes hindering enemy movement – especially of cavalry. Unfortunately, although there are many examples of the *plumbata mamillata* in the archaeological record, there are as yet no finds of the *plumbata et tribulata*. Since the weapon is only attested in *De Rebus Bellicis*, written by an anonymous author in the third century, the possibility remains that it did not actually exist except in the imagination of the author.

Close-order infantrymen, and cavalry, could carry several of these weapons. They would be used immediately prior to contact, and modern reconstructions attest to their efficiency, especially at close range.

Lances

Used two-handed and underarm, the lance has often been seen as coming into its own only after the invention of the stirrup. Yet, as a note of caution to those who still maintain that the momentum of striking an enemy would dismount the rider unless stirrups are worn, Heliodorus and Plutarch describe the ability of such weapons to impale two opponents simultaneously. Unfortunately, the wooden shafts of these weapons have all rotted away, leaving only the metal heads behind. Without the shaft, the heads have probably been classified as either spear or javelin heads. It is likely that in order to work effectively, the shaft would need to be at least 8ft in length, otherwise it would be difficult to correctly balance the lance and have enough overlapping the head of the horse to make it a viable weapon frontally.

Swords

The style of sword used had also changed from earlier centuries. Three distinct new types are seen in the archaeological record. The first, the 'Straubing/Nydam' type was between 68 and 80cm long, and was less than 4.4cm in width. The second, the 'Lauriacum/Hromowka' type was only 55.5 to 65.5cm long, but had a width of up to 7.5cm. The final examples are of the double-edged 'Avar' type, and are much longer at 100 to 107cm. All had wood, bone and/or ivory hilts which have long since perished.

Much has been made of the difference in sword types, yet the diversity can easily be ascribed to fashion or simple regional variations. Furthermore, due to their wide difference in styles, the idea has arisen that they were produced to face different troop types. This is extremely unlikely.

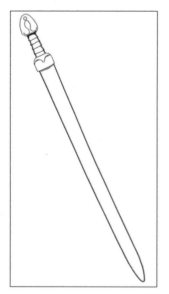

Firstly, there would have been large logistical difficulties in ensuring that troops who may be faced by heavily armoured warriors, for example, had the correct style of sword. Secondly, the troops had to buy their own weapons: they would clearly not be willing to pay for two swords and carry both during a campaign, only deciding on the day of battle which they should use. This is clearly unrealistic. The most that needs to be said is that troops with the option would probably buy the one that they preferred – possibly with horsemen buying the longer Avar type to give them extra reach – but again it would come down to cost and personal preference.

Illustration 7: Late Roman sword of Straubing/Nydam type from Köln (after Bishop and Coultson).

Bows

Apart from the javelin, the main missile weapon was the bow. The Romans appear to have changed the bow in use at some point from around the second century onwards. Prior to this they had used the older 'static-limb' bows, usually deriving their power from the compression of the wooden fibres that formed the body of the bow. Later, they adopted the more powerful horn-composite reflex bows that had been developed on the steppes of Central Asia.

The advantage of the new composite reflex bows is that they were more powerful than the older types whilst still being smooth and easy to fire. After the adoption of the new bow, the Romans (and then Byzantines) copied the Hunnic practice of concentrating on power and accuracy when firing, rather than using the Sasanid tactic of relying more on sheer volume of arrows delivered.

The Byzantines also adopted the 'up-to-date' steppe and Central Asian fashions of an hour-glass or box-shaped quiver, allowing the cylindrical quiver to fade away. Again, this is where personal taste came in to which item of equipment should be bought; the same bow as the rest of the troops is likely to have been enforced for military reasons, the style of quiver was personal taste.

At this point it is important to mention the extensive use of mercenary Hun units by the Byzantine army. Although in theory their use was simply an extension of the Byzantine conversion to horse archery, they had a formidable reputation as warriors and archers. This is mainly due to their adoption of the asymmetrical composite bow. Perceived as an adaptation for use by mounted bowmen, in the asymmetrical bow the lower limb is shorter than the upper limb. This results in a bow that is easier to fire from horseback, since the lower limb tends to make less contact and be less interfered with by the horse.

Yet this does not take all of the known factors into account. Extensive research by modern bowyers and archers has established that, although the asymmetrical bow requires much more skill and is much harder to master than the symmetrical bow, the end result is an archer that is far superior to one using the symmetrical bow. The asymmetrical bow excels in really high poundages (the amount of power needed to draw back the string) which gives greater range and power, is faster to fire, and performs far better with a thumb ring. In tests a fair degree of accuracy and power can be achieved even with flightless arrows by an archer trained in the use of the thumb-ring.

Consequently, it would appear that archers trained in the use of the asymmetrical bow would far surpass even the best-trained users of the symmetrical bow. It is not surprising that Hunnic warriors, trained from infancy in the use of a more effective bow, managed to achieve such a fearsome reputation when using it.

Sling

The existence of a unit with *funditores* (slingers) as part of their title has resulted in the acceptance of the continuing use of the sling as a missile weapon, and indeed its use since at least the fourth millennium BC implies the same. However, the continuation of the unit title does not necessarily mean that the unit definitely retained the sling. It is possible that the unit conformed to the contemporary practice and was converted to archers. A theory based upon the fact that the sling was retained as being more effective against armoured targets than the bow has its merits, but the simplification of supply and the ease of use of the bow must make the concept questionable. Unfortunately, the use of the sling must remain in the realm of conjecture.

Siege Equipment

The art of siege warfare dates back to the Assyrians of the seventh century BC, if not before. It had been absorbed through the ages by different cultures, until finally the Romans had learned it from the Greeks. The Romans had made it a weapon of terror, using it to intimidate any city unwise enough to resist them. The epitome of their siegework is probably that employed against the Jewish fortress of Masada, where even today the ramp built to allow the siege towers to reach the walls still remains after nearly 2,000 years.

In their sieges the Romans made use of a large array of machines and techniques, ranging from tunnels to undermine the walls, to *scorpio* bolt-shooters, *onager* rock-throwers, battering rams and movable siege towers. In defence they would use the countermine, *scorpio*, *onager*, incendiary projectiles, boiling water and boiling or flaming oil. These techniques were both complex and sophisticated, and the Romans were past masters in the art: a city besieged by the Romans was in serious trouble.

Overall, the Byzantine military machine, despite recent innovations and evolution, remained a very capable opponent. Capable of beating any adversary in the field, it was also capable of reducing even the strongest fortification. That is why many of the enemies of Rome waited until a period of chaos or confusion within the empire before striking, hoping to profit from Byzantine weakness whilst the Byzantines were unable to defend themselves or launch a counterattack of their own.

Despite the changes, the Byzantine army retained a strong tradition of success, and was capable of defeating any of its enemies. When Belisarius was appointed as a general in the Persian campaign, he took control of a formidable fighting machine.

Chapter 4

The Persian War

The Romano-Persian Wars to 527

In previous centuries, the Romans and Sasanids had fought each other to a virtual stalemate. The Romans and Byzantines found it difficult to face either the earlier Parthian or the later Sasanian cavalry when the armies deployed on the open plains prevalent in the west of Persia. More than once they had suffered heavy defeats at the hands of the Persian aristocratic heavy cavalry and accompanying horse archers. For example, Rome lost at the Battles of Carrhae in 53 BC and at Urumia in 36 BC. However, the Romans could also win, as at the Battles of the Taurus in 39 BC and Gindarus in 38 BC, and at the Battle of the Tigris in AD 115. The invasion of Julian in AD 363 resulted in three battles during which the Romans won tactically but strategically were forced to retreat after the death of Julian.

Taking the experience of these battles into account, Roman and Byzantine attacks tended to divert to the north, generally going through Christian Armenia before coming down through the more hilly terrain prevalent there, which they could use to their advantage. Roman armies that forgot this lesson were usually heavily beaten, while those that remembered usually captured the capital city of Ctesiphon and so gained a victory. Thanks to its strategic importance, the kingdom of Armenia had by the time of Justinian been divided between the two great powers. The name Armenia was retained for the area governed by Rome, while the Persian-controlled remainder of the country was now labelled Persarmenia.

Recognising each other's weaknesses, warfare in the region had gradually become one of limited gains, dominated by raids and sieges; open, large-scale warfare usually resulted in the weakening of both, leaving them open to attack by third parties. It is in this context that Belisarius was appointed to high command in the year 527.

The causes of the war lay in the earlier history of Romano–Persian relations. In the fifth century, there had been a tradition of peaceful cooperation. The Emperor Arcadius had even asked King Yazdigerd to adopt Theodosius, Arcadius' son, to help ensure support for his accession to the throne. Yazdigerd had agreed and his support had proved of inestimable value to the young Theodosius.

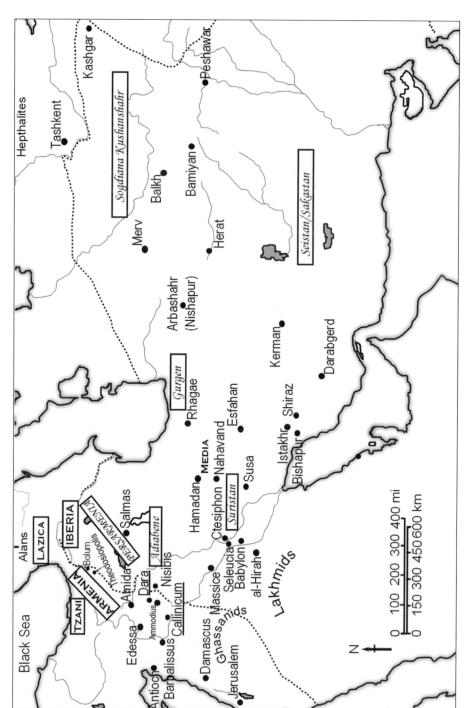

Map 3: Sasanid Persia.

Yet the overall impression gained is that relations were based upon the poor financial position of the Persian king and his ability to raid the Roman east to help his finances. Accordingly, whenever there was a drastic shortfall of money, the Persians would ask for a subsidy. If this was paid peace prevailed; if not, the Persians would attack, capturing as many cities, fortifications and prisoners as possible before the arrival of substantial Roman reinforcements made the Persians withdraw. The fact that the Romans and Byzantines often paid the subsidies shows the plain economic truth: it was usually cheaper to pay the Persians than it was to gather the troops, fight a war, and then pay for replacement equipment, train recruits and pay for the repairs to the eastern infrastructures that had been damaged by the conflict.

Yet not all emperors agreed to pay. In 502 the Persian King Kavadh requested subsidies from the Emperor Anastasius to pay the Hepthalites who had helped him to regain his kingdom during a civil war. When Anastasius refused to pay the tribute, Kavadh invaded Armenia, capturing Theodosiopolis, Martyropolis and Amida. The Byzantines were already at war with the Bulgar Huns, who were ravaging the Balkans, so Kavadh faced little opposition at the start of the war. However, the situation in the Balkans slowly stabilised, allowing reinforcements to be sent east. Then, in 505, the roles were reversed; the Hepthalites invaded eastern Persia. Faced with war on two fronts, in 506 Kavadh agreed to a truce lasting for seven years. In the end, it lasted for twenty.

Anastasius asked for advice from his generals, who recommended the building of a new, secure forward base for the army, who were otherwise at a disadvantage logistically. Whilst the Persians were still occupied on their eastern front, Anastasius quickly built a fortress and supply base at Dara (sometimes spelt Daras). By the time the Persians were in a position to interfere it was too late; although Anastasius paid compensation, Dara remained.

In 527, the now-ageing Kavadh asked the emperor, by this time Justin, to adopt his son Khusrow in a manner similar to that of Arcadius and Yazdigerd in the previous century. After taking legal advice, Justin offered only a limited form of adoption as befitted a 'barbarian'; the full form would have entitled Khusrow to inherit the empire. Kavadh understandably interpreted this as an insult, especially since Yazdigerd had proved faithful to the Byzantines in the earlier adoption. Kavadh declared war.

The early war and the appointment of Belisarius

The first Persian attack was upon Iberia, a Christian country allied to Rome, with whom the Persians were at odds over religion. They were promised substantial aid by Rome but received only a few troops to help them. Shortly afterwards the Persians invaded Lazica. The whole country was overrun and the Lazican king, Gurgenes, fled to Constantinople. The initial Persian attacks were a complete success.

The first Byzantine move was an invasion of Persarmenia. Following standard procedures, Sittas and Belisarius led a force into Persarmenia which plundered widely and returned with booty and captives (Procopius, *History of the Wars*, I.xii.20–23). The incident is of note in that it is the first appearance of Belisarius as an individual. Both Sittas and Belisarius are described as bodyguards of the Emperor Justin's nephew, Justinian (Proc., *Wars*, I.xii.21), although Sittas was soon to be appointed *magister utriusque militum praesentalis* after Justin's death. It is also clear that Justinian had control of the campaign in the east, although his uncle Justin remained the emperor throughout this period.

Since the expedition had been a success, the invasion was repeated. However, by this time the Persians had been able to make preparations for the defence. In an unnamed battle, Sittas and Belisarius were beaten by the Persians under Narses and Aratius, who we will meet again later. Unfortunately, no details of the encounter survive.

At the same time, a Byzantine force under the command of Libelarius of Thrace, the *magister utriusque militum*, had crossed the border near Nisibis and entered enemy territory. The army, however, retired immediately upon hearing of the defeat in Persarmenia, and Libelarius was reduced in rank for the absolute failure of the attack.

It was around this time that the *dux Mesopotamiae* (commander of the troops in Mesopotamia), Timostratus, died. It is likely that Sittas had been the senior commander during the defeat in Persarmenia, yet, while he retained his post, it is possible that Belisarius' conduct in the lost battle had been more deserving of note. The lack of a detailed narrative of the battle means we have no way of knowing the truth. Whatever had happened, Belisarius was promoted *dux Mesopotamiae* in place of Timostratus, most likely on the orders of Justinian, consequently assuming command at the headquarters of the *dux* at Dara.

Events were not looking favourable for the Byzantines when Justin died in August and Justinian ascended the throne. Justinian began a major reform of the eastern armies. Apart from revising some of the provincial commands, Justinian also created the post of *magister militum per Armeniam* to help in the war against Persia. As part of the reforms, he brought in a large number of fresh, young officers to command the newly-created positions.

A major part of the strategy against the Persians was the building and maintaining of fortified posts along the frontier, of which the most important was Dara. As a continuation of this policy, an attempt was now made to fortify a site in the desert at Tanurin, south of Nisibis. Realising what was happening, the Persians brought an army to the site and so the work was halted.

To counter this, a Byzantine force was brought together, with a large number of troops under the command of their many individual leaders, including Belisarius; Cutzes, one of two *duces Phoenices Libanensis* (commanders of the

Map 4: Justinian's reorganisation and the Persian War.

troops in Phoenices Libanensis) based at Damascus; and Buzes, the other *dux Phoenices Libanensis*, who was based at Palmyra.

Here there is a major fault in our sources. This is the battle described by Procopius as taking place at Mindouos (Proc., *Wars*, I.xiii.2–8). Unfortunately, Procopius appears to have conflated two distinct battles – one at Tanurin and one at Mindouos – into one. Since Tanurin is to the south and Mindouos to the north of Nisibis, it is probably preferable to follow Zacharias Rhetor (Zacharias of Mitylene) and John Malalas and accept that there were two distinct battles. We now, therefore, need to consult Zacharias and Malalas for a clarification of events.

Zacharias (*Historia Ecclesiastica*, ix.2) records the battle as follows:

> Accordingly, a Roman army was mustered for the purpose of march- ing into the desert of Thannuris [Tanurin] against the Persians under the leadership of Belisarius, Cutzes, the brother of Buzes, Basil, Vincent, and other commanders, and Atafar, the chief of the Saracens. And, when the Persians heard of it, they devised a stratagem, and dug several ditches among their trenches, and concealed them all round outside by triangular stakes of wood, and left several openings. And, when the Roman army came up, they did not perceive the Persians' deceitful stratagem in time, but the generals entered the Persian entrenchment at full speed, and, falling into the pits, were taken prisoners, and Cutzes was killed. And of the Roman army those who were mounted turned back and returned in flight to Dara with Belisarius; but the infantry, who did not escape, were killed and taken captive. And Atafar, the Saracen king, during his flight was struck from a short distance off, and perished; and he was a warlike and an able man, and he had had much experience in the use of Roman arms, and in various places had won distinction and renown in war.

The description shows a common feature of the warfare of this period – the digging and concealment of trenches and pits. On this occasion, the Byzantines failed to detect the pits in time, and so the infantry were defeated, the cavalry escaping to Dara with Belisarius. It is noteworthy that both Buzes and Cutzes are described by Procopius as being 'inclined to be rash in engaging with the enemy' (Proc., *Wars*, I.xiii.5). It is possible that they were blamed for the defeat, encouraging their soldiers in a rash attack and so falling into the Persian trap. Despite the loss, Belisarius was yet again not blamed for the defeat.

The same passage in Zacharias (*HE*, ix.2) is also noteworthy in that it gives us our first glimpse of the personality of Belisarius: 'Belisarius . . . was not greedy after bribes, and was kind to the peasants, and did not allow the army to injure them. For he was accompanied by Solomon, a eunuch from the fortress of Edribath'. This description of Belisarius' character is informative. His refusal to take bribes, which implies incorruptibility, his willingness to take advice – in this case from Solomon – and his control of the army are all noteworthy. These are attributes that would stand him in great stead later in his career.

After this battle Justinian ordered Belisarius to construct a fort at Mindouos, north of Nisibis. The story is again told by Zacharias (*HE*, ix.5):

> The Romans, when Belisarius was duke ... wished to make a city at Melebasa [Mindouos]; wherefore Gadar the Kadisene was sent with an army by Kavadh; and he prevented the Romans from effecting their purpose, and put them to flight in a battle which he fought with them on the hill of Melebasa.

Again Belisarius had been defeated. Yet in 529, possibly as a reward for escaping the defeat at Tanurin and the manner of his conduct at Mindouos, Belisarius was recalled and promoted *magister militum per Orientem* in succession to Hypatius, with instructions to make preparations to invade Persia.

A large army was now assembled and Belisarius advanced towards his former base at Dara. He was joined by the *magister officiorum*, Hermogenes, who was to assist in organising the troops, and Rufinus as an ambassador – for already both sides were contemplating peace (Proc., *Wars*, I.9–11). There was now a lull in military activities as negotiations began. Although it is not stated specifically in our sources, the time Belisarius now had was probably spent in improving the quality of his army. The army had been dealt a series of defeats at the hands of the Persians. Morale would have been at a very low ebb, and training and discipline in the army appears to have been poor; this is clear from the speech Procopius (*Wars*, I.xiv.14) has Perozes make to his men before the third day of the battle of Dara:

> But seeing you considering why in the world it is that, although the Romans have not been accustomed heretofore to go into battle without confusion and disorder, they recently awaited the advancing Persians with a kind of order which is by no means characteristic of them, for this reason I have decided to speak some words of exhortation to you

Although doubtless a literary device to enhance the drama and promote Belisarius' abilities, there is no doubt a grain of truth in these words. The Persians had won a string of victories over the Byzantines and this would tend to demoralise the Byzantines, making them unwilling to fight and so making their dispositions clumsy and slow.

It is to Belisarius' credit that he took steps to train the army and improve morale, for the peace negotiations broke down. Before the conclusion of any treaty, the Persians first wanted to take Dara, which had been a source of resentment since its construction by Anastasius. Accordingly, a Persian army of 30,000 men advanced towards Dara led by Perozes, and set up camp near the town of Ammodius.

The Sasanid Persian Army

Although the Sasanid army, like that of the Romans/Byzantines, had also been subject to change over the centuries, this was to a far smaller degree, mainly focusing upon equipment modifications. Following the final overthrow of the Parthians at Firuzabad in 224, many powerful Parthian families had joined the Sasanids. As a consequence, the Sasanid army inherited many of the traditions of the Parthian army, although several details were subject to change.

Sasanid society was divided into four main groupings, namely: priests, warriors, scribes and commoners. The warrior caste, which included royalty, nobles and the aristocracy, was further divided into three classes based upon rank. The first rank was that of the top seven families in the empire. These were the Sasans themselves, the Aspahbad-Pahlov (from Gurgen, north Persia), the Korin-Pahlov (from Shiraz), the Suren-Pahlov (from Seistan/Sakastan), the Spandiyadh-Pahlov (from Nihawand, near modern Teheran), and the Giuw.

The second rank were the *azadan*, or upper nobility. These families could trace their Aryan ancestry back as far as the Achaemenid Empire.

The first and second classes combined to form the *savaran*, the elite armoured cavalry. Included in the *savaran* were some of the elite units of the Sasanid army. For example, there was the Pushtighban (Royal Guards) unit, comprising approximately 1,000 men stationed in Ctesiphon; the Gyan-avspar (Those Who Sacrifice Their Lives), also known as the Peshmerga, formed from men who had distinguished themselves in battle; and the Zhayedan (Immortals) unit, comprising 10,000 men, emulating the Immortals of Darius the Great.

The third rank of the warrior class were the *dekhans*, or lower nobility. Unable to enter the *savaran*, these warriors formed the core of the Sasanids' light horse archers.

The image of Sasanid infantry is dominated by the *paighan*, or conscript infantry. Equipped with a spear and large shield, their low morale and poor quality is seen to typify the plight of Sasanid foot troops. Their task was to serve as pages to the *savaran*, assault fortifications, excavate siege mines, and look after the baggage train. It is true that they were available in huge numbers; the *Chronicon Anonymum* (66.203.20–205.7) depicts an army led by Khusrow I consisting of 183,000 troops. Of these, 120,000 are *paighan*. Yet 40,000 of the total are other Sasanid infantry, with the balance being cavalry.

A major source of foot warriors were the native Medes. Mede infantry could be armed with spear, shield, chain mail and ridge helmets; these were highly regarded and could even be deployed in the centre of the battle line behind the *savaran*. A further source of recruits was the Dailamites. These may have been armed with a mixture of weapons, including battleaxes, bows, slings, and daggers, but Agathias (3.7–9) describes them as carrying 'both long and short spears [*sarissai* and *xysta*] ... and a sword slung across one shoulder'. Apparently capable of both skirmishing and close combat, they were an infantry force respected even by the Byzantines.

A large proportion of the infantry force which may have been classed as part of the *paighan*, but which were highly regarded by the Sasanids, were the foot archers. They were armed with the traditional composite bow and, when possible, with a large shield. In attack they were used to disrupt enemy formations prior to the *savaran*'s assault; in defence they were to disrupt, or even halt, enemy attacks.

Allies and Mercenaries

Alongside the native troops were the allies and mercenaries who were used to supplement the army. The Armenians supplied both cavalry and infantry to the Sasanid army and were highly regarded by them. The elite Armenian cavalry were trained and equipped as the *savaran* and were considered their equal. The remainder of the cavalry joined the light horse archers. The Armenian infantry, armed with spear and sling, were also well respected by the Sasanids and boosted the overall quality of the infantry forces available.

Finally, there were the troops supplied by, for example, the Lakhmids, Alans, Kushans, Saka and Hepthalites. Mainly composed of light horse armed with bows and/or javelins, when combined with the Sasanid light horse archers they made formidable opponents.

Although most allies provided light horse troops, the exception was the Lakhmids. An Arab tribe, the Lakhmids were very highly rated, and, like the Armenians, their cavalry was trained and equipped to fight alongside the *savaran*. They were a major ally, assisting the Sasanids in their wars with the Byzantines and helping to neutralise the threat of the Ghassanids, an Arab tribe allied to the Byzantines.

Elephants

One major difference between the Byzantines and the Sasanids was the latter's use of the war elephant. Imported from India, the elephant was guided by a trained mahout, who sat astride its neck, and a turret-like howdah carrying two or three warriors armed with bows or javelins strapped to its back. The elephant had three functions. One was to provide a missile platform, allowing the archers in the howdah to rain arrows on the enemy from a higher vantage point affording greater vision to the archers and partly negating the enemy's use of shields for protection. The second was to cause fear and consternation to the enemy. Much has been made of the fear the elephant inspires in horses unused to their presence, yet the sight of such a large creature bearing down would also have been terrifying for enemy foot soldiers. Third, the elephant was capable of smashing into enemy troops and causing widespread death and chaos, which could then be exploited by supporting troops. In order to help the process, it was common to give the elephants alcohol prior to battle. This would aid in making the elephant aggressive, helping to override the serene instincts of an otherwise relatively peaceful creature. In theory, and many times in practice, the elephant could be a battle-winning weapon.

Unfortunately, the theory did not always work in the field. Elephants, like most animals, do not like the noise, confusion and pain found on battle-fields, and were therefore liable to become uncontrollable – on more than one occasion turning away from the enemy and running back through their own troops, killing and disordering them as they went.

The double-edged nature of the elephant resulted in it always being a risky weapon to use, and it is noticeable that the Byzantines – ever willing to adopt successful enemy weapons – did not maintain any war elephants for their own use, except in the games. They were rarely used in the wars against the Byzantines.

Organization

In the main, it would appear that the Sasanids organised their own troops – at least their cavalry, if not necessarily their infantry or the allied troops – using a decimal system, although it must be admitted that the evidence is sparse. The smallest unit mentioned was the *vasht*. Although no figure is given for the size of this formation, earlier practice would suggest a strength of approximately 100 men. A larger unit was the *drafsh*, which appears to have numbered around 1,000 men. Finally, the largest division was the *gund*, probably of about 10,000 men.

Although based mainly upon deduction and previous practice, support is given to the theory by the fact that armies were usually stated to have had around 10,000 men, led by a *gund-salar* (general). If we allow for a personal bodyguard of up to 2,000 men, the general might have a total of around 12,000 troops. However, in the field the numbers would have varied due to disease/illness, injury or any of the other factors that could reduce unit rosters. Also, it should be borne in mind that historians such as Procopius tended to give round figures, meaning that anywhere between around 8,000 to around 12,000 may have been rounded to 10,000, therefore this hypothesis should be treated with caution.

Leadership

A full muster of the standing army, or *spah*, could be led by the king or, more rarely, by his deputy, the *vuzurg-framandar* (great commander). In the main, however, the command of the army usually fell to the *eran-spahbad*, who was usually a member of one of the seven top families. If he was unavailable to lead an army, or the army was simply a small defensive force, command could devolve upon the *spahbad* or the *marzban*. These both combined the roles of general and local governor, though only the *spahbad* appears to have been given the power to conduct formal negotiations.

The total strength of the Sasanid army in the late sixth century has been estimated at approximately 70,000 troops. If this is accurate, then there may have been four *gund*, each of around 12,000 men, with a seperate field army of approximately 22,000 men – including the 10,000 *Zhayedan*, the 1,000 *pushtighban*, the *gyan-avspar* and other guard units – being called to muster in Ctesiphon, under the command of the king, should the need arise.

Defensive Equipment

Helmets

Helmets were similar in form to those worn by the Byzantines, both having derived from the same Iranian and steppe originals. They included ridge helmets and spangenhelms, with the addition of chain mail hanging from the rims of the helmets as further protection to the head, neck and face. The main stylistic difference was that in the *bashlyk* type of spangenhelm, the bowl formed a higher peak than in the Byzantine variants, possibly to aid in the deflection of vertical blows to the head.

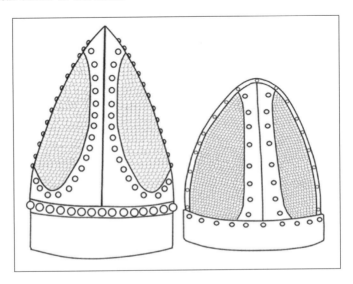

Illustration 8: Two distinct types of Sasanid helmet (after Farrokh).

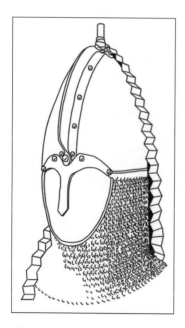

Illustration 9: Sasanid helmet found at Dura-Europos (after James).

Like Byzantine helmets, all of these could be overlaid with gold and/or silver or be tinned, and have semi-precious stones attached to improve appearance.

Armour

Again, the armour worn was similar – if not identical – in style to the types worn by the Byzantines. This included lamellar, scale and chain mail armour. However, unlike the Byzantines, it appears that the Sasanids commonly combined the various types into one piece of armour, designed to utilise the best properties of each type to cover the most appropriate area of the body. As a consequence, a *savaran* horseman may have worn chain mail overlaid with lamellar armour to give extra protection to the torso, coupled with laminated defences for the arms and legs. He may also have worn a *bazpan* (armoured glove) to protect one or both hands.

However, probably due to the cost and complexity of manufacturing such complex armour, plain mail seems to have been slowly becoming the norm for the Sasanid army.

Shields

The spearmen of the *paighan* infantry, and on occasion the foot archers, carried a large oblong, curved shield made from wicker and rawhide. The Dailami infantry are described by Agathias (3.7–9) as carrying shields and bucklers. This suggests a mix of types according to personal preference, but possibly tending towards a smaller, round type that could be used for skirmishing. However, it should be noted that Agathias describes these troops as being capable of both skirmishing and fighting at close quarters, so the evidence is not conclusive.

On the whole, the Sasanid horse archers did not carry any shields, relying upon the speed of their mounts to evade the enemy; but some of the allied cavalry contingents, such as the Alans, did carry a form of small buckler to enable them to compete in hand-to-hand combat. It may have been this that motivated the *savaran* to begin wearing a small buckler attached to the left forearm to help protect them when in battle. Yet this may also tie in to a change in outlook for the Sasanid heavy cavalry.

Horse Armour

The heavy defences of the earlier period of the Sasanid Empire were now in decline, possibly as a result of their experience fighting enemies such as the Huns and Hepthalites, who relied on mobility and firepower. The complete covering for horses found, for example, at Dura Europos, were being replaced by a *chamfron* (head) and *crinet* (neck) covering that protected only the head, neck and frontal chest areas of the horse. This marks part of the transformation of the *savaran* back into a force relying on archery followed by momentum and mobility to break the enemy, rather than simply their close-formation charge. Yet even these may have been in decline.

Weapons

Lances and Spears

The lances used by the *savaran*, and the spears used by some allied cavalry and the infantry, are likely to have resembled those used by the Byzantine cavalry of the same period. Unfortunately, none have survived to enable us to have a clear picture of their appearance, although depictions in art such as the bas-reliefs at Firzubad and Naghsh-e-Rustam give us some idea of their length and thickness, and the manner of their use.

As noted above, the Dailami troops are described by Agathias (3.7–9) as armed with 'both long and short spears'.

Swords

The swords used by the Sasanids appear to have been long and relatively heavy, being 1–1.11m in length and between 5 and 8.5cm in width. Unfortunately, excavated examples have been too corroded to allow a full reconstruction, so it is impossible to decide if they were designed mainly for either cutting or thrusting. However, there is a possible clue in the distinctive angled grip. This is very similar to the

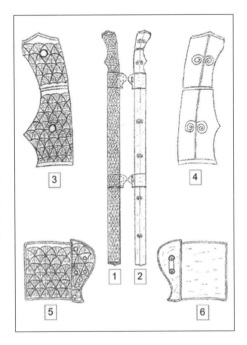

Illustration 10: Late Sasanian Sword:
Entire sword from front (1) and back (2).
Sword Handle at front (3) and back (4).
Sword Mount at front (5) and back (6).
(Drawings by Kaveh Farrokh, 2004.)

'semi-pistol' grip of the British 1908 pattern cavalry sword, which is generally considered the best sword ever issued to the British cavalry. This is partly because the 1908 sword was optimized purely for thrusting. The angle of the grip ensured that when the arm was extended, the blade naturally aligned with it, so there was a straight line from sword point to shoulder. As a consequence, when charging the sword was positioned to allow the rider to use the point at speed, effectively like a lance thrust, transmitting the full momentum of the horse into the blow; although this is not to say that it was not possible to cut with it too. It is worthy of comment that the Sasanids had the curved grip fifteen centuries before British sword makers, after a long drawn-out process and scientific study, arrived back at essentially the same solution.

Other close combat weapons

Maces, axes and whips could also be used by the cavalry, as well as the infantry, in a Sasanid army. Whilst the use of maces, axes and spears needs no explanation, it is likely that the whip was used in a similar manner to the Hunnic lasso. Whilst it could inflict wounds that were not lethal, its main function may have been to entangle the opponent and unbalance him, so enabling the warrior to dispatch him with relative ease.

Bows

Archery was returning to favour, as has been noted above, mainly due to the impact of groups such as the Huns and the Hepthalites. The Sasanid bow was of standard Central Asian composite design, and was employed by the majority of the cavalry as well as a proportion of the foot soldiers.

Sasanid archery relied on four factors for success: penetrative power, speed of delivery, volume of arrows and accuracy. The emphasis upon speed and concentrated volume in a small area is highlighted by a Persian device, the *panjagon* ('five device'). This machine allowed five arrows to be fired with one draw, which, although not particularly accurate, did allow for a very large number of arrows to land simultaneously in a relatively small space. Unfortunately, none of these weapons has survived, so it has been impossible to replicate one and conduct experiments to establish how accurate the device was or measure the force and penetrating power of its arrows.

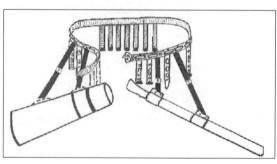

Illustration 11: Late Sasanian belt: Turco-Avar lappet style suspension for swords and quivers found in Nehavand. (Drawing by Kaveh Farrokh, 2004.)

Siege Equipment:

Unlike the Parthians, the Sasanids learnt the art of siege warfare, probably from the Romans/Byzantines. To this end, they used the same type of siege equipment as the Byzantines. Although it is unlikely that they could greatly improve upon the Byzantine designs or methods, they soon came to match them in their skills in both the assault of fortifications and their defence.

Such, then, was the army with which Peroz now threatened Dara.

The Battle of Dara

The clash at Dara highlights one of Belisarius' favourite tactics when fighting a battle. He was primarily a defensive commander, a theme that we will return to throughout the course of the book.

Roman/Byzantine battles against the Persians were historically fraught with danger. The high mobility of the Persian cavalry, and their resultant ability to control the battlefield, had only been partly offset by the previously-mentioned changes taking place within the Byzantine army – especially the greater reliance

Diagram 1: Dara the initial deployment for the battle.

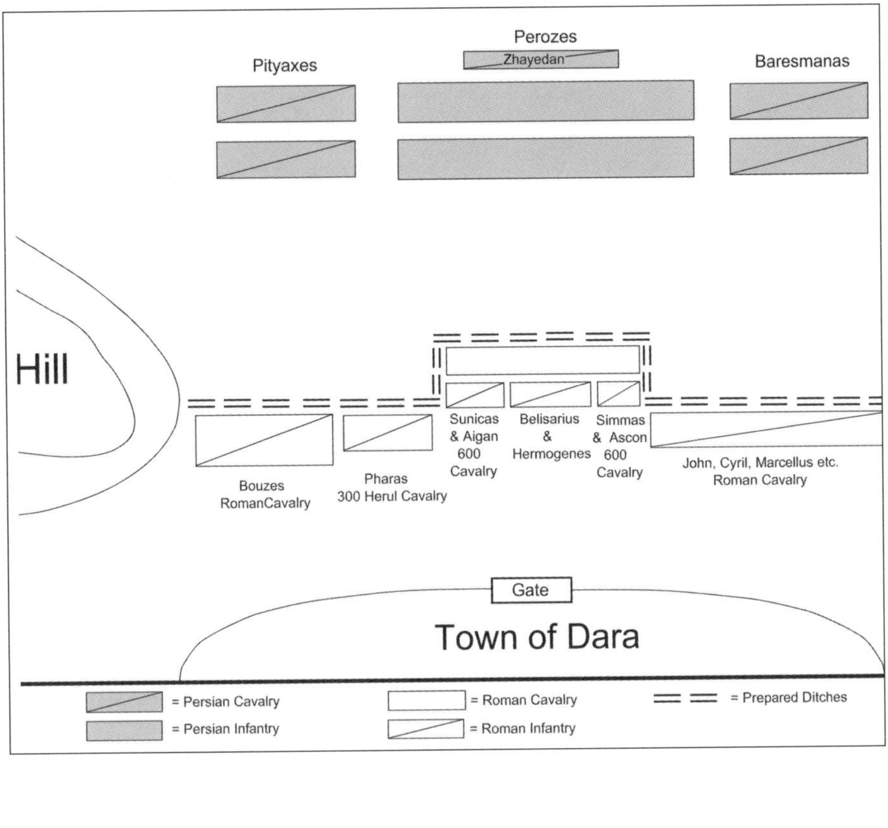

Pityaxes — Perozes / Zhayedan — Baresmanas

Hill

Sunicas & Aigan 600 Cavalry — Belisarius & Hermogenes — Simmas & Ascon 600 Cavalry

Bouzes Roman Cavalry — Pharas 300 Herul Cavalry — John, Cyril, Marcellus etc. Roman Cavalry

Gate

Town of Dara

= Persian Cavalry   = Roman Cavalry   === = Prepared Ditches
= Persian Infantry   = Roman Infantry

upon cavalry. The result of their tactical dominance had been their battlefield superiority in the preceding century. Belisarius was aware of this difficulty and he employed the time-honoured tactic of digging ditches to help compensate for his disadvantage, as shown in the diagram.

Yet the arrangement of the ditches suggests more; it is difficult to impose your will upon the enemy when they have the greater mobility, but Belisarius wanted to guide the battle towards a specific series of events. Therefore, the ditches were dug to a particular layout in the expectation of these events unfolding. In effect, the centre was advanced and the wings refused. Belisarius engineered events so that the main strike would occur on the flanks.

Stationed behind the front trench were the infantry, with a reserve of cavalry, under Belisarius and Hermogenes. Echeloned back and to the left of the infantry and positioned behind the ditches were Buzes with some Byzantine cavalry and Pharas the Herulian with 300 Herulian cavalry. To the right of these, stationed behind the infantry and so out of sight of the Persians, were Sunicas and Aigan with 600 cavalry. The right wing mirrored the left: a large force of Byzantine cavalry was stationed on the right behind the ditches, and behind the infantry to their left were Simmas and Ascan with 600 cavalry.

Diagram 2: Dara the revised deployment for day three.

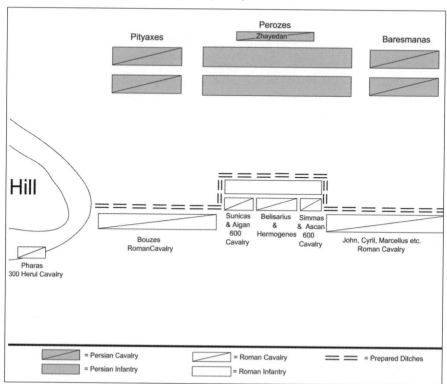

The plan appears to have been simple: the Persian wings would advance and slowly force back the relatively-weak Byzantine cavalry, with the ditches helping to keep the Persian advance at a slow pace. Once they had advanced past the reserve cavalry units stationed behind the infantry, these would be able to attack the Persian cavalry in the flank and rear, hopefully causing them to panic and rout. The task of the infantry was to maintain their position and pin the enemy centre.

As the Persians approached, their leader, Perozes (described by Procopius as *mirranes*, possibly equating to the *marzban* of the Persian army) sent a message to Belisarius to prepare a bath for his arrival. Belisarius ignored the message, but ensured that all was prepared for battle the following day.

On the morning of the next day, both sides drew up in their battle formations, the Byzantines as described above and the Persians in deep formations, then stopped. Both armies waited. The Persians believed that if they waited until after noon, the Byzantine troops, who usually ate before noon, would be hungry and weaker, so would in all likelihood give way. The Persians, who traditionally ate later in the day, would then prove to be the stronger. Therefore it was not until the afternoon that a force of Persian cavalry

Diagram 3: Dara the Persian left attacks and the Roman ambush strikes.

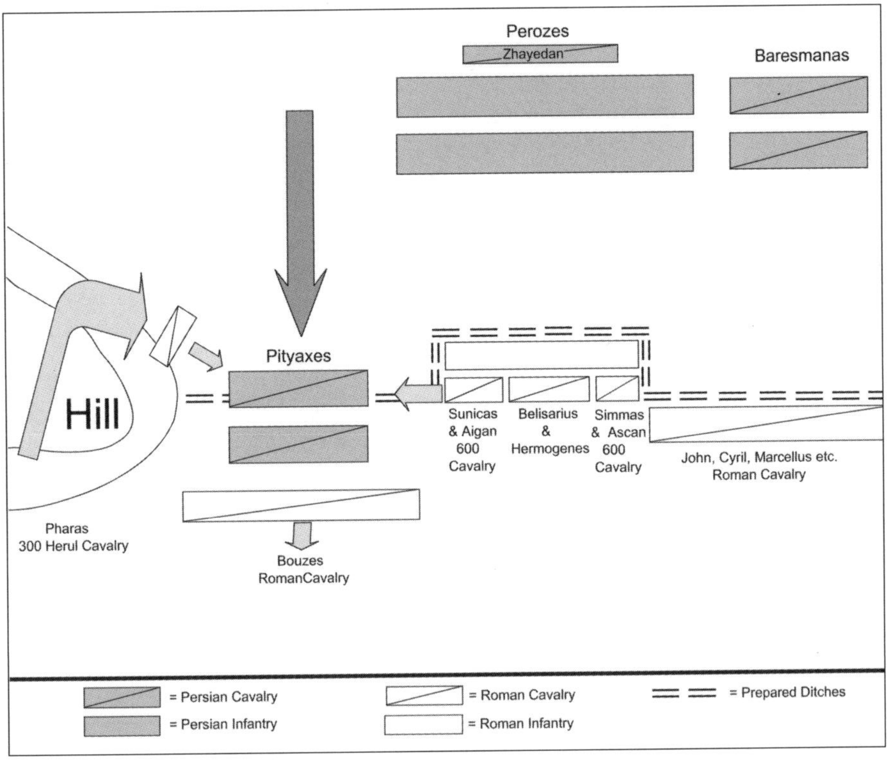

on their right wing attacked the troops with Buzes and Pharas. The Byzantines retired a short distance to their rear, but the Persians – possibly sensing a trap – refused to pursue. Consequently the Byzantines advanced again and forced the Persians to retire in their turn.

Shortly after, there was a challenge to single combat by a Persian youth, who was killed by Andreas, a trainer in a wrestling school. A further challenger was also killed by Andreas, before the armies retired to camp for the night.

On the second day, the respective generals realised that any attempt at battle was hazardous given the equality of forces and so they exchanged letters in an attempt to entice either the enemy to withdraw or to accept battle at a disadvantage. The attempt failed.

By the third day Perozes had been reinforced by 10,000 men and, with his numerical superiority assured, the Persian army prepared for battle. Perozes divided his army in two, forming two parallel lines, each formed of an infantry centre flanked by cavalry. The 10,000 men of the Zhayedan (Immortals), he stationed in reserve behind both lines. The idea was to rotate the front and back lines, enabling tired troops to have a rest whilst still keeping the Byzantines

Diagram 4: Dara the Persian attack is driven back. Seeing the Persians reinforcing their left, Belisarius reinforces his right wing.

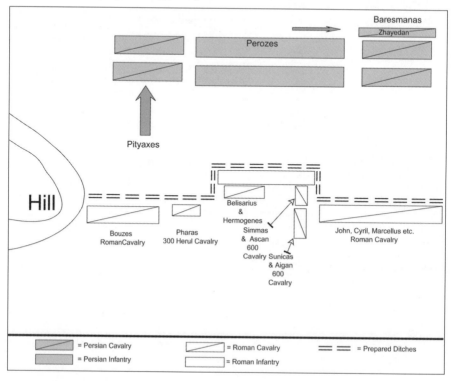

under intense pressure. Perozes himself controlled the centre, with Pityaxes on the right with the Cadiseni, and Baresmanas on the left.

However it was also on the third day that Pharas, the leader of the Heruls, suggested a small alteration in the Byzantine plan. He proposed that he lead his Heruls behind the hill on the left flank, then, when the enemy were fully engaged, he would lead them over the hill and strike the Persians in the rear. Belisarius and Hermogenes approved the plan, and the cavalry under Buzes expanded their frontage to cover the gap this created, thus ensuring the Persians did not detect that part of the cavalry force was now missing from its place in the line.

After again waiting until the afternoon, the Persians finally closed the distance between the armies and an exchange of missiles began. The advantage that the Persians had with more men and their rotation system – which went unnoticed by the Byzantines – was offset by them firing against the wind. Once the supply of missiles was exhausted, the cavalry of the Persian right wing advanced to contact.

Diagram 5: Dara the Persians attack, the Romans fall back and their reinforcements take the Persian attackers in the flank and rear.

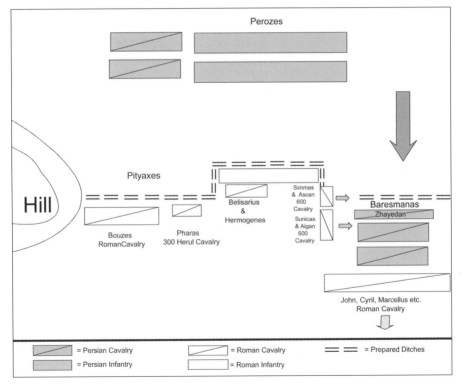

After fierce fighting, the Byzantine left was driven back and was beginning to give way when the Heruls under Pharas appeared over the crest of the hill and charged into the flank and rear of the advancing Persians. As Pityaxes' men wavered, Sunicas and Aigan with their 600 men attacked them in the other flank. The Persians broke and fled back to the shelter of their infantry, leaving 3,000 dead behind them.

Meanwhile, Perozes reinforced his left flank with some troops drawn from the second line and the Zhayedan in preparation for an assault on the Byzantine right wing. Fortunately, this was seen by Belisarius and Hermogenes and they accordingly ordered some of their own reserves, plus the troops under Sunicas and Aigan, to join Simmas and Ascan, sheltering behind the infantry on the right flank.

When this second Persian onslaught struck, the Byzantine right wing recoiled. This exposed the flank of the attackers, which the newly-combined troops attacked, driving through the Persians and splitting the Persian army in two. As the Persian wing turned to meet the attack, the recoiling Byzantines

Diagram 6: Dara with their right defeated and their left encircled, the rest of the Persian army flees.

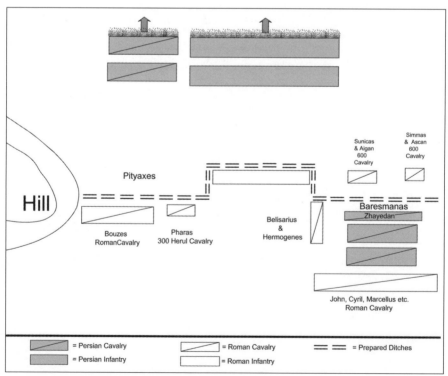

rallied and charged. Sunicas killed Baresmanas and the Persian left wing, attacked from two directions, was surrounded, 5,000 men being killed.

At this point, the Persian centre threw down its arms and fled, closely followed by the remnants of the right flank. Many were killed in the ensuing pursuit, but Belisarius and Hermogenes did not allow the chase to continue for long. The Persians were renowned for their ability to recover from a rout and turn upon their pursuers: Belisarius did not want to lose a battle that had already been won.

This was not the end of the fighting. After the battle, the Persians sent an army into Armenia. Surprised by the forces of Dorotheus, the newly-created *magister militum per Armeniam*, and Sittas, *magister utriusque militum praesentalis*, the army was defeated and returned to Persarmenia. Reinforced, the Persians returned and at the Battle of Satala they were again defeated by Dorotheus and Sittas. Finally, Byzantine forces completed the conquest of the Tzani, and the brothers Narses and Aratius, who had earlier defeated Belisarius in battle, deserted to the Byzantines, followed by a third brother, Isaac, who also delivered the fortress of Bolum into Byzantine hands.

At about this time a brief glimpse is given into international politics. The Samaritans, unhappy at Byzantine rule, had previously been defeated in their revolt against the empire. In late 530, five Samaritans were captured in the vicinity of Ammodius, and when questioned under torture they revealed to Belisarius that there had been a plan to betray Palestine to Kavadh. Although unsuccessful, this illustrates the sometimes complex character of politics in the Middle East in the sixth century.

The Battle of Callinicum

In the Spring of 531 the Persians again invaded Byzantine territory. Yet this time there were to be major differences from previous campaigns. Following the advice of the Lakhmid commander Al-Mundhir (Proc, *Wars*, I.xvii.29–40), the Persians under the *spahbad*, Azarethes, invaded Commagene/Euphratensis (see Map 4). Procopius states that this was the first time that there had ever been an attack from this direction by the Persians (Proc, *Wars*, I.xvii.2–3 and I.xviii.3). Furthermore, Al-Mundhir himself accompanied the invasion, along with 5,000 of his troops. When deployed alongside the 10,000 Persian cavalry, the result was that Azarethes fielded an all-mounted army of 15,000 troops.

Caught by surprise, Belisarius at first hesitated in case this was a diversion, and he was unsure what to do about the defence of the traditional line of Persian attack. Eventually, he left garrisons in the cities of Mesopotamia and crossed the Euphrates to challenge the Persians, employing forced marches to catch the enemy. He had also been politically active and had obtained the services of 5,000 Ghassanid troops under Arethas. This gave him a total of

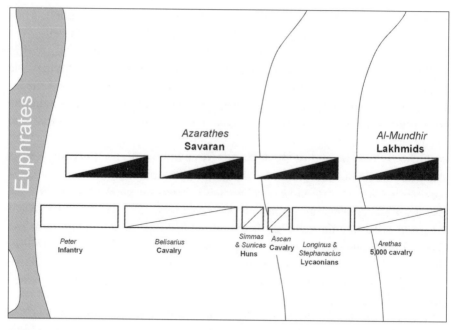

Diagram 7: Callinicum the deployment.

25,000 troops, both infantry and cavalry. Having made contact with the Persians, who had been busy pillaging the countryside, he set up camp at Chalcis, whilst the Persians were in the vicinity of Gabbula.

Faced with a superior force, Azarethes began to retire towards the Persian frontier. Belisarius followed a day's march behind, often using the deserted Persian camps of the day before to billet his troops. He finally caught up with the Persians in the vicinity of Callinicum on the day before Easter Day, 531.

According to Procopius, there was now a disagreement between Belisarius and his men. Belisarius did not want to give battle as to fight on Easter Day was disrespectful to God. Furthermore, his men would be required by their religion to fast on the day of the battle, leaving them weak and easily exhausted. However, the troops did want to fight and Belisarius eventually yielded to their wishes. The battle would be fought on Easter Day, 19 April 531.

The dispositions of the troops conformed to the terrain. As the Byzantines approached the battlefield, the River Euphrates ran along their left side, protecting that flank from attack. On the right the ground rose sharply. Therefore, Belisarius deployed his infantry, under the command of Peter, a soldier in the bodyguard of Justinian, with their left flank on the river. He personally took command of the centre of the line with the cavalry, whilst to his right were the Huns under Simmas and Sunicas. To their right was a further force of Byzantine cavalry under Ascan, followed by a body of Lycaonian

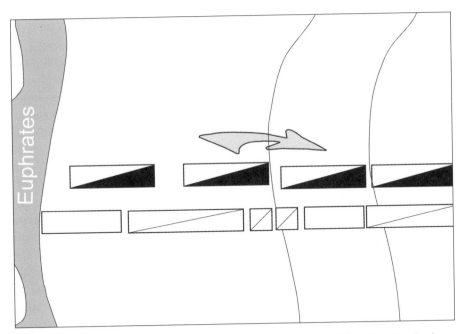

Diagram 8: Callinicum: the two sides close and the Persians reinforce their left flank deployment.

Diagram 9: Callinicum: the Roman right crumbles.

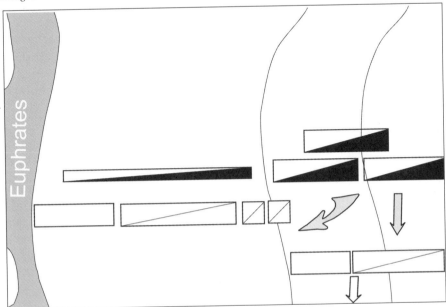

infantry under the command of Longinus and Stephanacius. On the right flank, where the ground rose, he stationed the Ghassanids under Arethas.

On the Persian side, Azarethes stationed his cavalry opposite the Byzantines, with the Lakhmids on his left facing the Ghassanids.

There was now an extensive missile exchange. Although the Persians fired a greater number of arrows, the majority of these were stopped by the Byzantine armour (Procopius, *Wars*, I.xviii.33). In contrast, the smaller number of Byzantine arrows had greater penetrative power, so the outcome was evenly balanced.

Towards the end of the exchange, Azarethes moved a large number of his cavalry to his left wing, stationing them alongside the Lakhmids. This was to prove critical; a similar move at Dara had been observed by the Byzantines and they had taken measures to counter the attack. This time, the move went unobserved and the attack proved decisive as, not being reinforced, the Byzantine right wing crumbled. The Ghassanids were put to rout, followed by the Lycaonians – Longinus and Stephanacius both being killed. The Byzantine cavalry on the right appear to have resisted, but it was to no avail, with Ascan also being killed in the fighting. Pressure now mounted upon the remainder of the Byzantine line until the rest of the cavalry fled, leaving only the Byzantine infantry to face the Persians. The infantry adopted the *fulcum* formation, the later equivalent of the famous *testudo* (tortoise), used to defend against heavy

Diagram 10: Callinicum the Roman cavalry routs, covered by the infantry who stand until the Persians retire.

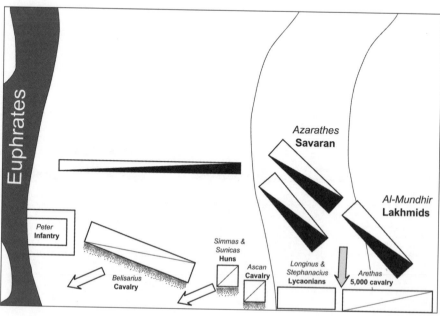

missile attacks. They formed up in a 'U'-shape, using the river to close the top of the 'U'. With foot archers in the centre of the 'U' giving overhead supporting fire, the infantry withstood the Persian attack until nightfall, when they escaped over the Euphrates to safety in Callinicum.

It is at the point, where the battle comes to the infantry, that there is confusion in the sources. Procopius has Belisarius retiring to the infantry, giving up his horse and fighting alongside them until nightfall (Proc, *Wars*, I.xviii.43). According to Malalas, Belisarius did not remain, but fled earlier in the battle, escaping by boat across the river. In this version, Sunicas and Simmas were the ones who dismounted with their troops to fight alongside the infantry (Malalas, 464). For reasons that will become clearer shortly, the version given by Malalas is to be preferred.

The Battle of Callinicum had ended in a clear defeat for Rome and Belisarius, wiping out the benefits of the earlier victory at Dara and giving the initiative once again to the Persians. The differences between the two battles now need to be explored.

The circumstances surrounding the two battles were entirely different. At Dara, Belisarius fought a defensive battle within strict geographical limits. Therefore, Belisarius had the opportunity to dig ditches designed for a specific plan, knowing that the enemy would come to fight him at that place as the Persians wanted control of Dara. Furthermore, his position at the centre, possibly on slightly raised ground, gave him a view of the whole battlefield, making it possible for him to see where the enemy were sending their reserves and enabling him to react accordingly. In addition, the Persian reliance on fluid cavalry tactics resulted in a tendency for them to strike at perceived weak points in the enemy line. Belisarius' use of ditches and his subsequent deployment at Dara allowed him to manufacture apparent weak points, tempting the Persians to attack and enabling him to pre-plan his counterattacks and rout the Persian assault troops.

Callinicum was a completely different sort of battle. Not being constrained by the objective of capturing a town, and not having any slow-moving infantry present, the Persians retained a complete fluidity of movement, enabling them to retain the strategic and tactical initiative. Furthermore, Belisarius did not have the time to examine the battlefield, plan a strategy and dig the trenches that he had at Dara. A further difficulty was that Belisarius personally took position on the lower ground, not on the hill, and he was therefore unable to see the enemy's tactical movement, which would have indicated a concentration of forces on his right flank.

In a similar manner to the battle at Dara, the Persians attempted to locate the Byzantine weak point, but in this case they succeeded in doing so, and then manoeuvred superior numbers of quality troops into a position from where they could attack with superior numbers. Once the Byzantine right wing had collapsed, the Persians simply rolled up the enemy from right to left, making sure to maintain their local superiority in numbers. As a further point, it must be noted that Belisarius again fought a tactically defensive battle. On this occasion, his personal deployment and tactics were poor. He placed himself in a position from where he could not observe the battlefield, and failed to keep a force in reserve to counter any Sasanid threat. As a result he was heavily defeated.

At the Battle of Callinicum we have two versions of Belisarius' actions as the tide of the battle turned against him. In Procopius, he dismounted and joined the infantry, fighting until the Persians withdrew and the infantry could cross the Euphrates and escape. Malalas has him fleeing from the field and leaving the infantry to their fate. We need to establish which one is true.

It is believed that Procopius did not give the true version of events, possibly in order to defend Belisarius from criticism. The main reason for this belief is that Procopius remains silent about the enquiry that was held under Constantiolus following the battle. We know from other sources, including Malalas (Malalas, 466) and Zacharias (Zach, *HE*, ix.6.17), that the enquiry took place, and that Belisarius was blamed for the reverses at Tanurin and Callinicum. Belisarius attributed the defeat at Callinicum to the impetuous request of his troops to fight, a claim supported by Hermogenes, who reported this version to the emperor (Malalas, 465). Belisarius was subsequently cleared of blame by the enquiry and joined the emperor in Constantinople. Nevertheless, he had lost his post as *magister utriusque militum per Orientem* and had been recalled by the emperor to Constantinople. He would not take part in the Persian war for a long time.

Chapter 5

The Nika Riots and Marriage

The Nika Riots

Whilst the Persian War was being fought in the east, Justinian was busy in Constantinople. Once he felt secure on the throne, Justinian began a major overhaul of the system acquired from his predecessors.

One of the most dramatic reforms undertaken was that of the law courts. Justinian ordered Tribunianus to head a commission to codify the vast accumulation of laws that had amassed over the preceding centuries. Their efforts were published in three books: the *Code* was published in 529, and the *Digest* or *Pandects* in 533. Following the *Digest*, there was a need to revise the *Code*, and the revision was published in 534. Also published in 533 was *Institutes*, a handbook for students in the law schools of Constantinople, Beirut and elsewhere. The whole purpose was to make the vast edifice of the laws accessible to every magistrate in a simplified version in manageable divisions. A last publication was the *Novels*, published after the rest and concerned solely with new legislation under Justinian dealing with areas where the *Code* was found wanting. Most of these publications would not be of importance in the life of Belisarius except for one major difficulty; imperial bureaucrats did not like change.

Unfortunately, despite his education and skill, Tribunianus began to acquire a reputation for greed, ensuring that lawsuits were decided in favour of either friends or the highest bidders. The general population gained an increasingly antagonistic view of him.

When he came to the throne, Justinian found that he had not inherited a healthy monetary situation. In order to remedy this, he placed John the Cappadocian in the post of praetorian prefect with orders to fill the treasury and reduce the cost of the civil service. John began to implement taxation in a new, ruthless manner which quickly earned him a reputation for greed and deviousness. His tax reforms also put a stop to many of the forms of bribery common in the civil service. This caused more unrest, since it was noted that John himself was becoming increasingly rich. Slowly, the general population began to feel the effects of John's policies.

As discussed previously, John's reforms of the civil service alienated many of the nobles, who lost both their income and their status when they lost their positions. They quickly swelled the ranks of the Greens – the faction associated with the civil service – while others who were disillusioned joined the Blues. The disaffected quickly found their voice in the growing circus factions, who over a limited amount of time became more and more of a problem.

In response, and because after five years on the throne he felt secure and able to rule without outside approval, Justinian now took measures to curb the influence and behaviour of the circus factions, both the Blues and Greens. The Blues understandably felt betrayed, whilst the Greens – swollen by the ranks of unemployed bureaucrats – perceived it as a further sign of imperial oppression.

The two factions became increasingly restive until on 10 June 532 they came to blows in the Hippodrome. Justinian sent in the troops and seven ringleaders were arrested and condemned to death. However, when they were taken down from the scaffold two were found to be still alive. They were rescued by a group of monks and taken to the monastery of St Lawrence. Unwilling to enter the monastery using violence, the city prefect, Eudaimon, posted armed guards outside the monastery in order to starve them out.

Unfortunately for Justinian, the two men were a Green and a Blue. Finding themselves with a common cause, the two factions united. When Justinian

Map 5: Constantinople.

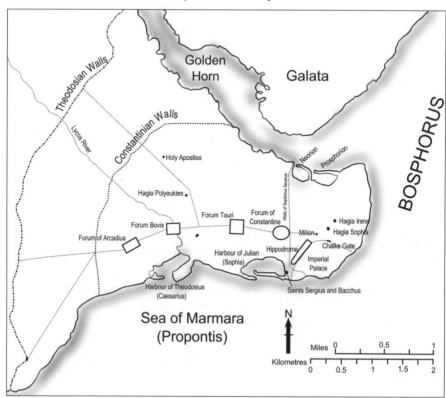

appeared in the Hippodrome three days later there was uproar. The two factions chanted 'Nika! Nika!' ('Victory! Victory!') and Justinian quickly realised that the chants were directed at him. The races began, but there was no reduction in the tension. Finally the races were abandoned and the crowd poured out of the Hippodrome, and headed to the palace of the city prefect. They killed the guards, freed all of the prisoners kept inside and then set fire to the building. They then continued to the praetorian prefecture, the senate house and the baths of Zeuxippus and those of Alexander, finishing at the churches of St Irene and St Sophia. All of these building and more were soon engulfed in flames.

On the second day the mob returned to the Hippodrome, calling for the removal of John of Cappadocia, Tribunianus and Eudaimon. Justinian granted their wish, but this did not placate the rioters; on the third day they demanded a new emperor – Probus, Anastasius' nephew – and when they found that he had left the city they set fire to his house and the revolt continued.

Tension remained high and on 18 January Justinian faced the mob in the Hippodrome, assuming full responsibility and promising an amnesty if the rioters now returned to peaceful ways. Unlike Anastasius twenty years before, Justinian was not held in reverence and his appeal failed.

The rioters now decided upon a new emperor. Anastasius had two more nephews available, both of whom were resident in the palace. However Justinian, possibly fearful of an assassination attempt, refused to allow them to remain. Despite their protests that should they be found by the mob they would be unwillingly forced to assume the crown, they were made to leave. Found by the rioters, the elderly Hypatius, who had had a distinguished military career, was taken to the Hippodrome. Having no imperial regalia, a necklet was appropriated from one of the crowd in place of a diadem and Hypatius was declared emperor.

In contrast to these events, according to the *Pascal Chronicle* (p. 339) sanity had begun to return to many of the Blues. They now began to become dismayed at the deeds taking place in their name, and realised that events had gone too far. Slowly, singly or in small groups, they began to leave the Hippodrome and return to their homes. Furthermore, the aged eunuch Narses – who had also remained loyal to Justinian – began to distribute gifts to members of the Blues. These either decided to return home or began to argue with the mob concerning the crowning of Hypatius.

According to Procopius, Justinian, unaware of this slow turn of the tide, now lost his nerve and prepared to leave; not only were the mob against him, the soldiers stationed in the palace had decided to remain neutral in the affair, neither helping nor hindering Justinian but simply waiting upon the turn of events. It was at this point that Theodora stood forth and made an impassioned speech for Justinian to stay and fight (Proc, *Wars*, I.xxiv.32–7).

Present in the palace were two of the emperor's loyal generals: Mundus, a Gepid with a sizeable force of Herul mercenaries, and Belisarius, with his *comitatus*, newly returned from the east. Accordingly, Mundus exited the palace by the Snail Gate whilst Belisarius headed towards the emperor's box in the Hippodrome along the short private route the emperors were accustomed to use. At the entrance to the Hippodrome there were soldiers stationed according to custom, but, when Belisarius called to them to open the door so that he could arrest Hypatius, they pretended not to hear him and stuck by their choice of neutrality. Baffled by their refusal to obey, Belisarius returned to Justinian and informed him that the troops were rebelling.

Justinian now ordered Belisarius to exit via the Bronze Gate and complete his mission. Clambering over the still-smoking ruins of the buildings in the area, Belisarius finally reached the Blue Colonnade and determined to take the narrow route via a small door to ascend to the royal seat and arrest Hypatius. However, the door was closed and held by men loyal to Hypatius. Belisarius did not want to attack, since he was worried that the defenders would hold him and that he would then be attacked from the rear by the rioters. He therefore determined to attack the rioters instead, as they were mainly unarmed civilians.

As a consequence, he bypassed the door and, followed by his *comitatus* of veterans from the east, he charged the mob. Unsurprisingly, they retreated amidst loud cries and screams. Attracted by the screams and seeing Belisarius and his men assaulting the rioters, Mundus gave the order for his own men to charge the crowd from where they were standing on the other side through the Gate of Death.

At this point Narses stationed his men at the exits in order to trap the rioters in the Hippodrome. A slaughter now ensued. Over 30,000 people died, and Hypatius and his brother Pompeius were arrested and executed, their lands and property being confiscated by Justinian. Later, possibly realising that they had had little control over events, Justinian returned the majority of the lands and property to their sons (Proc, *Wars*, I.xxiv.40–58).

So ended the Nika riots. Within a few weeks John of Cappadocia and Tribunianus had been reinstated, although their excesses were severely curtailed. However, whilst Tribunianus was to live for many years until he died from disease, and kept within the restraints laid down, John retained his brutal habits until brought down ten years later by the machinations of the Empress Theodora (Proc, *Wars*, I.xxv.1–36).

With the war against Persia over and the population of Constantinople cowed, Justinian felt free to undertake other adventures.

Marriage to Antonina

No details survive concerning the meeting, courtship or marriage of Belisarius and Antonina. Procopius nowhere mentions Antonina during the narrative of the Persian War, and she is not referred to in the passages concerning the Nika Riots. Given the fact that she travelled with Belisarius throughout the Vandalic War it is therefore assumed that the marriage took place after the riots but before Belisarius set sail for Africa. Although this is accepted – especially as she would most likely have been referred to in the sources – the argument is based on negative evidence; that she is not mentioned does not necessarily mean that she was not present during the episode of the Nika riots. Unfortunately, without further documentation, the matter must remain unclear.

What is clear is Procopius' dislike for Antonina, and this should be remembered when reading his account of her; throughout *Anekdota* she is ridiculed, especially concerning her nature, her reckless personal life, and her origins. For her grandfather and father were charioteers at the Hippodrome. Although as such they could be famous, and possibly relatively well-off, they would not be acceptable in polite society. Her mother, Thessalonica, was equally low-born, and was probably brought up as an actress – although Procopius refers to her as 'a prostitute in the theatre' (Proc, *Anekdota*, I.11).

Born around the year 484, and therefore up to twenty years older than Belisarius, she appears in her early life to have come into contact with the unsavoury type of individual common around the races at the Hippodrome, and so acquired a rather sordid reputation which was eagerly recounted by Procopius.

Procopius claims that she had many children before she married Belisarius. We know of only two for certain: Photius, a son by a previous marriage, and an unnamed daughter who married Ildiger, a high-ranking military commander who served under Belisarius in Africa and Italy.

Belisarius and Antonina had only one child, a daughter named Joannina who in 548 married Theodora's grandson Anastasius at Theodora's insistence, although she was under age. Following Theodora's death eight months after the marriage, Antonina separated the couple, much against their wishes, as they appear to have actually been in love.

Despite Procopius' dislike, Antonina would play a major part in Belisarius' career, especially since she was closely linked to the Empress Theodora. Yet, according to Procopius, there was a level of distrust and for this reason Antonina would accompany Belisarius on his greatest campaign (Proc, *Wars*, III.xii.2).

Chapter 6

The Invasion of Africa

Vandal History

When Gaiseric seized Carthage in 439 he originated a kingdom unlike any other contemporary Germanic state. The Vandal approach to occupying Roman territory was different to that of all of the other Germanic nations that arose on imperial soil: they eschewed all ideas of fitting into the existing Roman political, social and religious infrastructures in Africa. Leading tenants were sent into exile and their lands appropriated for Vandal warriors. Whilst other Germanic kingdoms of this time produced coins with the head of the ruling Roman emperor, the Vandals rejected this idea. Yet it is in the area of religion that the Vandals became the major exception. The Germanic tribes who had been converted to Christianity had not become Catholics like the majority of the empire, but had taken to Arianism. The teachings of Arius differed from the traditional Catholic faith concerning the nature of God. In Catholicism we find the Trinity of the Father, the Son, and the Holy Ghost, all parts of one God. In Arianism, the Father created the Son, who in turn created the world and later appeared on earth. In this theory the Son is not 'eternal', as he came after the Father, but is rather an instrument of Creation – a secondary god. Obviously, Arians were classed as heretics by the Catholic faith and the two religions could not be reconciled.

Other Germanic tribes lived with the fact that they were a religious minority and allowed the native population to continue to worship unmolested as Catholics. But Gaiseric's son and successor, Huneric (ruled 477–484), began a major persecution of the Catholics in Africa. This continued through the reign of Gundamund (ruled 484–496), only ending with the accession of Thrasamund in 496. Thrasamund ended the persecution, desiring instead to have Catholics converted willingly to Arianism by debate rather than by force. Hilderic (ruled 523–530) continued the policy, but by this time it was too late; the Catholics in Africa had too many martyrs to remember to enable them to forgive and forget.

Politically, things began well for the Vandals. Under Gaiseric they dominated the waters of the western Mediterranean, even sacking Rome in 455, so earning fear and respect from their neighbours. When the Ostrogoth Theoderic came to power in Italy, he accepted that the Vandals were a major political force and married his sister Amalafrida to the Vandal king, Thrasamund. She was accompanied by 1,000 Goths as a bodyguard. When Hilderic came to the throne, Amalafrida fled and gained sanctuary with the Berbers. She was later captured and imprisoned and her bodyguard were destroyed, charged with revolutionary designs against the throne (Proc, *Wars*, III.ix.3–4.). She died in captivity, probably in 525 or 526. This ended the alliance with Theoderic, but Theoderic decided to make no move since the Vandals were powerful and Hilderic had a personal friendship with Justinian. Justinian at that time was serving his uncle, Emperor Justin. The Goths did not have the power to face both the Vandals and the Empire.

Yet the Vandals were no longer the military force that had served Gaiseric in the initial invasions of Africa. In a war against the native Moors, Thrasamund's army had suffered a disastrous defeat, losing many troops. A renewal of the conflict under Hilderic also ended in a disastrous military defeat for the Vandals. Consequent to the military reverses and the loss of the Gothic alliance, Vandal political and military influence was in a steep decline. Hilderic responded by drawing closer to Justinian and appointing his cousin Gelimer, who had a high military reputation, as commander of the army. This was to prove a mistake.

Gelimer

Gelimer was a great-grandson of Gaiseric, and, as the second-eldest male descendant of Gaiseric, he was nominally next in line to the throne after Hilderic: Geiseric had arranged matters so that his eldest male descendant would ascend the throne in order to avoid the troubles that plagued direct succession, such as minorities and guardianships.

Following his appointment by Hilderic as commander of the army, Gelimer defeated the Moors in battle and then opened negotiations for an alliance. However, Gelimer was worried by the political course that Hilderic was following. He believed that Hilderic's apparent subservience to the emperor might result in his losing his standing as next in line to the throne. After his victory had enhanced his military reputation and increased his power base, he increasingly opposed the policies followed by Hilderic. Eventually, he began to claim that Hilderic was too weak and unwarlike to rule the nation and, almost inevitably, in May 530 Gelimer revolted with the general support of the Vandal nobles. Hilderic and his principal followers were imprisoned and Gelimer assumed power.

Upon coming to power, Gelimer attempted to establish positive political relations with his neighbours. He sent gifts to Justinian, who refused to accept them or to recognise Gelimer. Gelimer may also have attempted to open negotiations with the Goths in Italy, but this was anticipated by Justinian, who sent word to Ravenna advising that they not recognise Gelimer. At this time, not long after King Theoderic's death, King Athalaric was a minor and his mother, Amalasuintha, was acting as regent. Niece of the murdered

Amalafrida, she was also keen to secure Justinian's support for herself and her son. Any embassies from Gelimer were rebuffed.

Justinian now sent two embassies to Gelimer. In the first, he criticised Gelimer for rebelling, in the second he threatened war if Gelimer did not release Hilderic and other captives and allow them to travel to Constantinople. However, the chances of Gelimer releasing Hilderic were practically non-existent; it would destabilise his position if the 'true' king was in exile and available to return to cast out the usurper. Hilderic was retained in prison. At no point would Gelimer have seriously contemplated that the Empire would launch an attack upon Africa.

With his political overtures rejected, internal affairs now began to go awry for Gelimer. Although he had the reputation of an outstanding military leader, he was seen by many of his contemporaries as clever and unscrupulous. If Gelimer had remained above reproach in his personal dealings, he may have survived. Unfortunately, he quickly gained a reputation for greed, employing Bonifatius, a native from Byzacium, as a secretary. Perhaps with a background in Roman law, Bonifatius was used by Gelimer to seize the property of his enemies. Furthermore, Gelimer was now alleged to have executed many of the nobility. Support for Gelimer began to weaken, and it is in this context that the rebellions in Tripolitania and Sardinia took place.

The rebellions that occurred within the Vandal kingdom immediately prior to the Byzantine attack are generally perceived as a series of unconnected events that coincidentally conspired in Justinian's favour. In Tripoli, a citizen named Pudentius began an insurrection against Vandal rule and requested imperial assistance. Furthermore, Gelimer had given control of Sardinia to a man named Godas, said by Procopius to be a personal slave. Godas was ambitious enough to assume the role of an independent commander, but astute enough to realise that he needed outside support to maintain his independence. He quickly began negotiations with Justinian for aid.

Some aspects of the story need examination. That two important areas under Vandal control should rebel within a short space of time of each other is reasonable; after all, they had a king that had taken control by force, who was unlikely to be welcomed by everyone and who quickly obtained a reputation for unscrupulous behaviour. Yet these events occurred long after Gelimer assumed power and almost simultaneously with Justinian's planned invasion. The timing needs explanation.

It is reasonable to assume that both parties had been in touch with Justinian prior to their rebellion in an attempt to secure Byzantine support. It is likely that they both waited until Justinian was prepared to send aid before acting, since on their own they would be overwhelmed by Gelimer's response. Justinian would not be in a position to send assistance until 533. First he had to arrange peace on the eastern front in order to release the troops needed for the assault on Vandal Africa, and then he had to suppress the Nika revolt in Constantinople.

With such a long lapse of time, the evidence points to the timing of the rebellions being orchestrated from Constantinople: in short, Justinian was exercising his diplomatic talents and pulling the strings behind the scenes. This was due to the fact that once Gelimer had refused his demands to release Hilderic, Justinian had been busy politically. Recognising the Vandals' political isolation, Justinian realised that there was a chance to attack the Vandals before Gelimer could consolidate his position. Furthermore, it is likely that by this time he had received messengers from Godas in Sardinia and Pudentius in Tripolitania asking for his support in their prospective rebellions.

Justinian began to make the necessary diplomatic moves. He needed the support of the Goths, since they ruled the territories between Constantinople and Africa. Without them, Sicily would not be available as a base and the expedition would find it difficult to assault Africa with the necessary logistical support. However, it would be relatively easy to gain their assistance. As was noted earlier, the regent Amalasuintha had a personal enmity with the Vandals and was keen to cultivate the friendship of Justinian. She now gave her consent to the expedition landing in Sicily, further agreeing to establish a market in Syracuse where the Byzantines could buy provisions and horses.

With the western routes to Africa secure, the other major concern was the Persian frontier. It would be almost impossible to fight a war on two fronts. At war since 527, Justinian looked to his generals to act decisively. When Belisarius won the Battle of Dara in 530, Justinian must have hoped that peace could be achieved. Unfortunately, the loss at Callinicum in 531 postponed hopes of a secure frontier, but the death of Kavadh and the accession of Khusrow altered the balance of power. After extensive negotiations and threats, Kavadh signed the 'Endless Peace' in 532, Justinian agreeing to withdraw the head-quarters of the *dux Mesopotamiae* from Dara to Constantina, and pay 11,000 pounds of gold, amongst other conditions. Seen by some as an expensive peace, it nevertheless freed troops and reduced pressure on the eastern front. Justinian was now free to act against the Vandal usurper.

Throughout the existence of the Vandal kingdom there had been pleas for help from the native Catholics. Justinian could now use their pleas for help as a further justification for action, alongside his determination to punish the Vandal king that had defied him. With his clear grounds for attack, coupled with the Vandals' untrustworthy behaviour, Justinian had gained the support or neutrality of the kingdoms surrounding the Vandals. With the 'Endless Peace' in place he now had troops free with which to mount the attack. With his support there would be rebellion within the Vandal kingdom. The time had arrived for action.

It is notable that few indications are given by Procopius of any of these diplomatic manoeuvres. This is not a surprise. To safeguard the individuals plotting rebellion, details of the negotiations would be restricted to the few individuals who were involved in the plots. To ensure that the Vandals were unaware of the proposed landings in Africa, the diplomatic talks would need to remain as secretive as possible. It is not surprising that Procopius does not mention any of the diplomatic activity; he would certainly not have been privileged with such information. As a further point, with his intense dislike and contempt for Justinian – as revealed in *Anekdota* – it is improbable that he would have believed the emperor capable of such subtle political manoeuvring.

When Justinian revealed his purpose in council, the expedition was not greeted with enthusiasm by the emperor's advisors. Mindful of the disasters which had befallen the two previous attempts by the Empire to regain Africa, and frightened by the military prestige still attached to the Vandals, none of the military commanders wanted to be the one ordered across the ocean to Africa, the leader of the expedition not yet having been announced. Furthermore, John the Cappadocian and other financial advisors advised Justinian that the war would be too costly for the empire's now-limited resources. According to Procopius, at this point the emperor himself began to waver in his resolve, but a bishop reported a dream in which God had promised to help Justinian in the capture of Africa. Upon hearing this, Justinian regained his enthusiasm and announced the leader of the expedition (Proc, *Wars*, III.x.1–22).

Belisarius appointed commander

With everything ready for the invasion, all that was needed was a commander for the operation. Mundus, the *magister militum per Orientem* was reappointed *magister militum per Illyricum* in January 532. It is possible that at this time Belisarius was once again made *magister militum per Orientem*, although the actual dating of his appointment is obscure; he was definitely filling the post by February 533.

The choice of Belisarius has always been seen as obvious: he had proven himself in the Persian Wars by his superb generalship, he was a personal friend of the emperor, and he had recently proven his loyalty in the Nika Riots. Assured of victory due to his military gifts, he would not then rebel and set himself up as a rival to Justinian in Africa.

None of this makes sense. In Chapter 4 it was shown that Belisarius had lost the early, unnamed battle in Armenia, had been present for the defeat at the Battle of Tanurin, and had commanded at the battles of Mindouos and Callinicum, two further defeats. The only battle he had won was at Dara. Although this had been a superb victory won by outstanding generalship, the winning of one battle and the loss of four – although admittedly he may not have been in charge at two of them – does not indicate superior military ability.

Yet despite his defeats at the hands of the Persians, Belisarius had recently been cleared of incompetence by the inquiry led by Constantiolus. His conduct at Dara had shown that he did have considerable talent, although this was not always in evidence, so the potential for victory was there.

His friendship and loyalty to Justinian are beyond question, but again on their own they do not justify Justinian's decision to send Belisarius to the west. There must have been more to Justinian's choice of commander.

The reasons can be found in evidence regarding Belisarius that has already been seen. One of the major reasons for the choice of Belisarius was linguistic. Most of the generals of the eastern empire now spoke Greek rather than Latin: the population of Africa spoke Latin. Although it would be possible to provide a translator for a Greek-speaking general, and although it is probable that most senior generals had been taught Latin, a 'native' speaker such as Belisarius would have been the preferred choice, since he was less likely to antagonise the native Africans either by his attitude or by misinterpreting their language. Furthermore, Justinian was aware that western Latin speakers believed that Greek-speaking easterners were effete, untrustworthy Greeks. This made the Latin-speaking 'westerner' Belisarius – born in Germana , in or near Illyricum, a 'western' province – an obvious choice.

As a final confirmation of his suitability, there is the passage from Zacharias previously quoted, showing that Belisarius 'was not greedy after bribes, and was kind to the peasants, and did not allow the army to injure them.' The last thing Justinian would want would be to conquer the Vandals only to have the native Africans rise in revolt due to the troops being arrogant and treating them poorly; the idea was to conquer, not to have to repeatedly send troops to crush unrest.

Taking everything into account, there is unlikely to have been any other general in the service of Justinian who was as suitable as Belisarius to wage war in the west: the reinstated *magister militum per Orientem* would lead the expedition to Africa.

Preparation and Departure

In 533 Belisarius was officially given supreme command of the expedition. There was to be no dual command, as had been used in the east; Belisarius was in sole control, with the emperor confirming his position in writing. In order to reduce the burden of command, Justinian appointed Archelaus, a man with great experience who had previously been praetorian prefect of Byzantium and Illyricum, as prefect of the army and so in charge of the logistics

Justinian placed at Belisarius' disposal a mixed force of infantry and cavalry. According to Procopius (Proc, *Wars*, III.xi.1–21), the main force was composed of 5,000 Byzantine cavalry under the command of Rufinus, Aigan, Barbatus and Pappus, and 10,000 infantry, under the overall command of John, a native of Epidamnus/Dyrrachium, supported by Theodorus Cteanus, Terentius Zaidus, Marcian and Sarapis. A further element was a contingent of *foederati* led by Dorotheus (*magister militum per Armeniam*) and Solomon, Belisarius' *domesticus*.

Included amongst the generals were Cyprian, Valerian, Martinus, Althias, John and Marcellus. At about this time Justinian received a reply from the Vandal rebel, Godas, in Sardinia, stating that the troops would be welcome but that there was no need to send a commander. As a consequence, Cyril, one of the leaders of the *foederati*, was appointed to lead the expedition to Sardinia along with 400 men and was ordered to sail with Belisarius. Unfortunately, we are given no clear indication by Procopius as to whether the 400 men sent to aid Godas were included in Procopius' overall total for Belisarius' army or were an additional number of men.

Finally, there were two groups of mercenaries: 400 Heruls under Pharas and 600 Huns under Sinnion and Balas – the latter two being praised as men 'endowed with bravery and endurance' (Proc, *Wars*, III.xi.13.)

Serving alongside Belisarius were his personal *comitatus*, including spearmen, guardsmen and his *bucellarii*. Procopius does not appear to have included either the *comitatus* or the mercenaries as part of the total of 15,000 men, so it is possible that Belisarius' force amounted to at least 17,000 troops.

To carry the expedition 500 ships were gathered, varying in size between approximately 30 and 500 tons, being crewed by an additional 30,000 sailors (averaging sixty men per ship), mainly natives of Egypt, Ionia and Cilicia, with Calonymus of Alexandria as commander. To defend the transports, ninety-two *dromones* (literally 'runners': single-banked warships with decks covering the rowers) were prepared, with 2,000 marines to man them alongside their normal crew.

When taken together, the traditional view that Belisarius set sail with only 15,000 troops to conquer Africa does not appear to be correct. Certainly, the main body was the 15,000 men detailed by Procopius as being allocated to Belisarius, but the expedition also included 400 Heruls, 600 Huns, Belisarius' personal *comitatus*, and 2,000 sailors 'from Constantinople' manning the warships, who had been trained to fight as well as row (Proc, *Wars*, III.xi.16). There is also confusion over whether the *foederati* and Cyril's force of 400 men were included in the original total. Finally, there were 30,000 sailors. Even if we accept that the sailors on the transport vessels would not be very good as warriors and therefore do not add them to the total, this still leaves a force probably in the region of twenty thousand men. The equivalent of two old Roman legions plus *auxilia*, even in the earlier empire this would have been a force to be reckoned with. In 9AD Varus had lost three legions in the Teutoburgerwald, rated as one of the worst disasters in Roman military history. The invasion was not undermanned, nor was it a scratch force scraped together

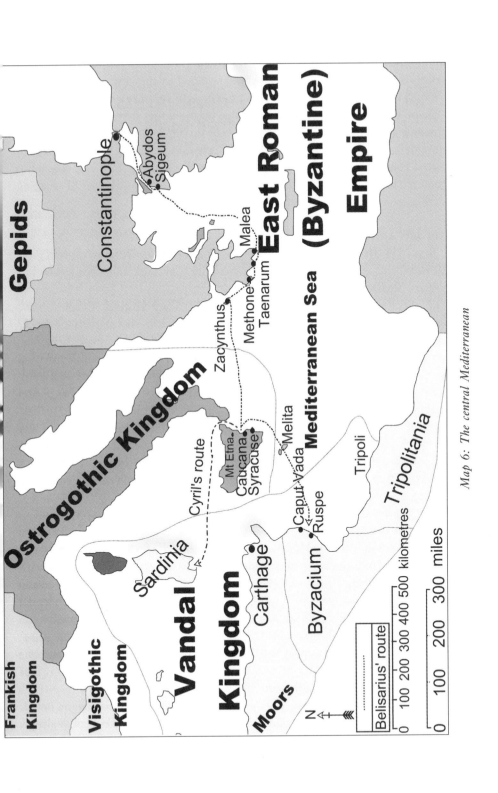

Map 6: The central Mediterranean

for a desperate adventure. It was a large, well-balanced force capable of over-coming the Vandals and may have contained a higher proportion of high quality, reliable troops than the armies stationed in the east.

Whilst the force was equipped along the lines of Byzantine forces as outlined in Chapter 3, there was a major difference between this army and that used by Belisarius at Dara and Callinicum: there was no opportunity to train the troops before departure. As we shall see, Belisarius would be forced by the weather to stop en route to Africa and this would allow him to organise the command structure, but at no point was he able to give the troops practice of working together as a unit. This was to have repercussions later.

The Invasion of Africa

In June 533 Belisarius and the army embarked at Constantinople and set sail, Belisarius being accompanied by his wife Antonina and his *assessor* and secretary Procopius.

The fleet sailed from Constantinople to Heraclea Perinthus (Eregli, on the Sea of Marmara), where they waited five days for the arrival of a large number of horses from the Thracian herds. They then moved to Abydos, where they were becalmed for four days. During their enforced stay, Belisarius reinforced his authority when two drunken Huns killed a colleague. The two were executed and a message sent to the army that Belisarius was in charge and discipline would be enforced (Proc, *Wars*, III.xii.7–22).

Whilst in Abydos measures were taken to ensure that the fleet would not become dispersed in bad weather. The three ships in which Belisarius and his staff sailed were marked out so that they were easy to locate. They had a portion of their sails painted red and lanterns erected to make them visible both day and night (Proc, *Wars*, III.xiii.1–4).

Once the wind strengthened, the fleet proceeded to first Sigeum, then across the Aegean to Malea.

From there they went to Taenarum (Caenopolis: Cape Matapan) and finally to Methone. Here the army was joined by Valerian and Martinus along with a further contingent of troops – how many we are not told – and, due to the lack of wind, Belisarius decided to disembark the troops. This done, he formed up the army and organised his forces, detailing which troops were under the command of which officers. This would have been a very necessary require-ment; with so many officers it would be easy for there to be confusion over command of the various troops and Belisarius averted the possible chaos that may have ensued upon landing in Africa.

It was at Methone that over 500 men died due to their eating infected bread, supplied, according to Procopius, by John the Cappadocian. Procopius alleges that instead of baking the bread properly, John had used the furnaces in the Baths of Achilles to save money, leaving the bread undercooked so that it quickly turned mouldy in the summer heat. Belisarius immediately took steps, ordering that local bread be provided to the troops, and sending a report to Justinian. Apparently, John went unpunished for the deed (Proc, *Wars*, III.xiii.12–20).

Once the troops who were able to had recovered, the fleet continued on to Zacynthus, where they took on fresh water to last them in crossing the Adriatic. Unfortunately, the winds were gentle and the water spoiled before the crossing was made. Only Belisarius and his table companions had fresh water; Antonina had had a small room constructed on board ship which she then part filled with sand. Pouring water into glass jars, she buried this in the sand and the water remained relatively pure (Proc, *Wars*, III.xiii.23–4). At last the ships arrived in Sicily, where they disembarked in a deserted area near Mount Etna.

We noted earlier that the movements of the general Cyril were unclear. Originally bound for Sardinia to help Godas, Procopius states that he joined Belisarius for the journey to Africa after Godas had declared that he did not need a Byzantine general, just some troops. It is clear that he sailed with Belisarius, but Procopius later has him rejoining Belisarius in Carthage following the Battle of Ad Decimum, after having discovered that Godas had been defeated and killed by Tzazon. The only logical place from which he could easily leave the expedition and travel to Sardinia was Sicily. As a consequence, it is likely that Cyril now set sail with his 400 men, planning to aid Godas in his rebellion.

Due to the length of the passage to Sicily, Belisarius had no up-to-date intelligence concerning the Vandals. According to Procopius,

> [Belisarius] did not know what sort of men the Vandals were . . . how strong they were in war . . . in what manner the Romans would have to wage the war, or what place might be their base of operations . . . [Furthermore], he was disturbed by . . . [his own] soldiers, who were in mortal dread of sea-fighting. (Proc, *Wars*, III.xiv.1–2)

Accordingly, he sent Procopius to the city of Syracuse, ostensibly to purchase supplies. This had been provided for in the agreement reached between the emperor and Amalasuintha before the fleet set sail. In addition to buying goods, Procopius was given secret orders to reconnoitre and find recent information about the Vandals and their preparations for the upcoming war. They were to meet again at Caucana (Porto Lombardo), to where Belisarius was moving the fleet.

Upon reaching Syracuse, Procopius met an old friend who was in business there. The man reported that his servant, who had returned from Carthage three days previously, claimed that the Vandals were totally unaware of the expedition. Furthermore, they had recently sent 5,000 of the best men of their army under Gelimer's brother, Tzazon, to Sardinia to crush the rebel Godas.

Gelimer was staying at Hermione in Byzacium, four days' journey from the coast. It would be possible to sail to and land in Africa before the Vandals were aware of their presence. Taking the servant with him, Procopius travelled to Caucana, where Belisarius could question the servant in person.

When they arrived, they found the army in mourning. Dorotheus, *magister militum per Orientem*, had died of illness and the troops suffered a great sense of loss. So did Belisarius, as Dorotheus was one of his best commanders. Despite this, upon hearing Procopius' news, Belisarius had the trumpets sounded and the army embarked. They passed the islands of Gaulus (Gozo) and Melita (Malta) before finally making landfall at Caput Vada (Ras Kabudia) near Ruspe, on the coast of Byzacena.

Prior to landing, a conference was held aboard Belisarius' ship, where the attendees agreed to his suggestion that they should land and establish a strong, fortified base. They therefore landed and on the same day completed a ditch and rampart behind which the army camped for the night. Whilst constructing the base, their digging unearthed a spring. Procopius claimed that this was an omen that God was with them (Proc, *Wars*, III.xv.32–36).

At this point Belisarius showed that he had learned from the mistakes of the past; he posted watchmen around the ramparts and on the ships, and ordered a protective screen of light fast vessels to sail around the fleet. This expedition would not be surprised by fireships, as had happened to Anthemius in 468. After around three months of travelling, the Byzantines had finally landed.

The Vandal Response

Gelimer does not appear to have taken the threat of Byzantine military action against Africa itself too seriously. However, recognising that the rebellion in Sardinia may attract imperial attention, he dispatched his brother Tzazon with 5,000 troops and a large proportion of the fleet to retake Sardinia before support could arrive from the east. The rebellion in Tripolitania was less serious, although the lack of manpower meant that this could only be suppressed once the troops had returned from Sardinia. Even so, it only appeared a matter of time before the situation returned to normal. In Autumn, 533, whilst Belisarius was in Sicily with the invasion fleet, Gelimer was in Hermione, four days' travel from the coast, having recently sent an envoy to Theudis, king of the Visigoths in Spain, to propose an alliance (Proc, *Wars*, III.xxiv.7).

Upon learning that Belisarius had landed in Africa, Gelimer reacted with commendable speed. He sent word to his brother Ammatas in Carthage to execute Hilderic and the other captives, and ordered him to gather troops in order to trap the Byzantines at Ad Decimum (Proc, *Wars*, III.xxvii.11). He then ordered Bonifatius to place his treasure on board a ship, with instructions to sail for Spain if the Vandals were overcome. Having given his orders, Gelimer travelled to join his troops for the battle against the Byzantines.

Chapter 7

The Vandalic War

The Vandal Army

The composition and recruitment of the Vandal army was completely different to that of the Byzantines. Whilst the Byzantines had a huge manpower pool, and by the era of Belisarius could rely on volunteers to fill the ranks, the Vandals had no such luxury. Their army was the 'nation in arms', with every able-bodied warrior joining the army when necessary.

We have no clear figure for the total Vandal population, and it should be remembered that the numbers given here, as well as elsewhere, are based upon logic and conjecture. Although reasonable, there is no guarantee that they are accurate.

Procopius (*Wars*, III.v.18) states that the Vandals had eighty *chiliarchs* (Germanic *thusundifath* – leader of 1,000). A plausible case has been made for the *thusundifath* being in control of 1,000 people, rather than 1,000 armed men, so giving us a total of 80,000 for the nation (Boss, 1993) although it must be remembered that they ruled a considerably larger number of 'native' Africans who did not contribute militarily to the state. This does not tell the whole story.

The post of *thusundifath* probably predates the Vandal invasion of Africa. Since the Vandals' increased in numbers whilst in Africa, as there were fewer major wars and the people could live at peace in a prosperous country with plenty of food, it is possible that the population may have climbed as high as 100,000 people. Rather than creating new *thusundifaths*, the swelling population would be allocated to the existing *thusundifaths*, whose allocation would have rapidly increased to more than 1,000 people. If each *thusundifath* only gained 250 people over the century in Africa, this would give us our total of 100,000.

This would allow for a plausible military base of approximately 25,000 men. However, unlike the Roman case, this was the total manpower available. Any military reverses would eat into this base, and only time would allow the numbers to recover as children aged and reached maturity, so enabling them to serve in the army. Furthermore, the number would have constantly varied due to the age, health and ability of the Vandal soldiers.

As has been seen, the Vandals were to suffer two heavy defeats at the hands of the Moors. The loss of manpower is unknown, since no accounts of the battles survive, yet if the Vandals only lost 5,000 men in the two defeats (such a casualty rate among the defeated being unexceptional in battles of the period) this would leave their army at around only 20,000 men. In this context, the 20,000 men allocated to conquer the province under Belisarius appears to be a realistic force for the invasion. Unfortunately, most historians have tended to follow Procopius' assessment of Vandal strength and consequently see the number allocated by Justinian as too small for the task.

Organisation

If the *thusundifath* were in charge of 1,000 (possibly more) people, this would give a reasonable strength of around 300 fighting men per *thusundifath* if all of the adult males are included, although it must be remembered that these may have been of variable quality. The Germanic nations may have adopted a decimal system for their organisations, either mirroring or influencing the Roman and Byzantine changes, so it is possible that there were 10 men led by a decurion, 100 men led by a centurion, and 300 men led by a *thusundifath*. Such figures are mere conjecture, since no record of Vandal organisation survives, but it is interesting to note that if there were eighty *thusundifath*, each leading 300 men, this would give 24,000 troops. With the inclusion of the king, the nobles, and their personal retinues, the figure rises to around 25,000.

When deploying for battle, it would be natural for the king and his nobles to take control of a varying number of *thusundifath*, depending upon the strategy and tactics being employed. As we will see, this flexibility suited the nature of Gelimer and his desire for elaborate battleplans.

Defensive Equipment

The Vandals had reached Africa via Gaul and Spain. Their travels in the west had done little to alter the style of their military equipment. Their isolation in Africa and their focus upon the western Mediterranean resulted in their being insulated from the Steppe influences that had transformed the Roman army.

Helmets

The Vandals appear to have relied upon simple spangenhelm designs for their helmets. These were cheap and easy to manufacture and had been used by Germanic tribes since before the Vandals began their perigrinations through the empire.

Body armour

Armour appears to have comprised of the traditional chain and scale mail, with the emphasis probably being upon the former. Given the nature of their attacks upon the western empire after having settled in Africa, it is possible that the vast majority of the troops would have armour that they had inherited or looted whilst raiding. Again, their tendency to refrain from attacks upon the eastern empire would have limited their contact with new trends and designs.

We have no information on additional equipment such as greaves and vambraces. Whilst it is possible that they were in use by the Vandals, there are no literary references to such equipment and none appear to have been found archaeologically.

Shields.
The Vandals appear to have retained the traditional large circular shields of their ancestors – there was simply no need for them to change. These would have been manufactured in much the same way as the Roman shields described in Chapter 3.

Offensive Weapons
In a similar manner to defensive equipment, Vandal swords would have been of traditional style. The *spatha* design was already ancient among the Germanic nations and had since been adopted by the western Roman army, wherein it had now been common for at least two centuries. Again, their raids on the west would have resulted in there being an abundance of such weapons available for the army.

It is in their use of the spear that the Vandals differed most from the Romans and Byzantines. They do not appear to have used the spear as a missile weapon, instead always retaining it in the hand for combat. The description of Germanic warriors in the *Strategikon* of Maurikios has them using their spears overarm (*Strategikon*, 3.5), a style also reflected in art.

Cavalry
The limited evidence available for the Vandals in Africa indicates that they may, uniquely amongst the Germanic nations, have converted their army into one based entirely upon cavalry. Probably in response to the mobility of their main enemies on land, the Moors and the Saharan Bedouin, their conversion to cavalry can be seen as an attempt to meet these on a more equal footing. In this situation their limited reserves of manpower would have been of great help; having the whole of the province of Africa in which to rear horses for only 25,000 men would have made the enterprise relatively straightforward, enabling the whole force to become cavalrymen.

Illustration 12: Tenth-century illustration of a traditional Germanic warrior.

The description of Vandal raiding parties attacking Europe and the Mediterranean islands fighting on foot do not prove the existence of infantry in Africa. The difficulty of transporting horses would have resulted in raiders being forced to leave their horses behind and necessitated their fighting on foot. Furthermore, at any time, members of the cavalry would have been able to dismount, depending upon the situation, although their response to the camels used by the Moors (described below) implies that such a situation was extremely rare.

Therefore, Belisarius and his army would be faced by an opponent composed of heavily-armed cavalry who expected to charge the enemy and engage them at close quarters with their spears. The flexibility of the Vandal army and the mobility of its mounted forces would make it a formidable opponent.

Yet it had one major drawback. Their defeats at the hands of the Moors showed that they were at a disadvantage when faced with opponents who relied upon skirmishing and the use of large quantities of missiles. In a surprising twist, the Moors had taken advantage of this weakness by surrounding their troops with a line of camels. When the Vandals attacked, their horses refused to approach the camels and the Moors were able to devastate the Vandals with missile fire from behind the camel screen. Having no missile troops of their own with which to counter this tactic, the Vandals eventually broke under the hail of missiles.

Training

The Vandals do not appear to have introduced regimented training regimes, such as those found in the Roman army. Each individual would practice with their friends and relatives, becoming adept at fighting with spear, sword and shield as well as riding a horse. However there appears to have been only limited training, if any, in unit manoeuvres and battlefield dispositions, an omission which the Vandals would regret when fighting the Byzantines under Belisarius.

Leadership

Leadership devolved upon the royal family and leading nobles. In the years preceding the Byzantine invasion the Vandals had suffered two large-scale reverses at the hands of the Moors. Appointed to the command of the war, Gelimer had defeated the Moors in battle, and begun negotiations. As a consequence, the morale of the Vandals was lifted, yet the limited experience of many of their leaders, and their reliance on the skills of Gelimer, may have left them with a serious disadvantage when compared to the seasoned and skilled leaders attending Belisarius, many of whom had served in the Persian War.

Belisarius' political strategy

For Belisarius and the Byzantine expedition the first night ashore passed quietly. Early the following morning an episode occurred that was to surprise the troops. Some of the men left the camp and picked some fruit, without either asking permission or paying for the goods. They were immediately subjected to corporal punishment, although Procopius does not give us any details of the form this took. Belisarius used the opportunity to gather the army together and outline that he expected them to behave in a civilized manner and that they were to treat the natives well. He also gave them the reasons for his demands: although the Vandals had been in control of the native 'Libyans' for almost a century, the Libyans were still Roman at heart; he was relying upon their active cooperation as spies, scouts, guides and a source of provisions. Actions such as theft would alienate the natives and encourage them to wholeheartedly join the Vandals. In that eventuality, the Byzantines would be in grave danger (Proc, *Wars*, III.xvi.1–6). The affair not only let the troops know what Belisarius expected from them, it also gave them viable reasons for his expectations. From this point forwards, the behaviour of the Byzantine troops towards the natives was to be exemplary.

Almost as if to prove the point that good conduct would encourage native support, Belisarius now sent a contingent of *bucellarii*, under an officer called Boriades, to the town of Syllectus. Approximately one day's march from the camp on the road to Carthage, the town would be a test of the natives' willingness to join the Byzantines. With strict instructions not to harm the inhabitants, Boriades and his men spent the day travelling to Syllectus and then passed the night camped outside the town. On the morning of the third day, they gained entrance by the simple ruse of joining a group of wagons going into the town. When the citizens became aware of what had happened, they willingly submitted to Belisarius – although the presence in their town of Byzantine troops left them with few alternatives.

The Vandals had maintained the Roman practice of sending urgent messages using fast couriers. These men changed horses kept at staging posts, positioned at regular intervals along major roads. The overseer of the public post, who maintained at least one of these staging posts, deserted to the Byzantines. At this point one of the actual messengers was captured. He was allowed to go free and paid to distribute a message from Justinian to the Vandal people. This stated that Justinian was not intending to make war on the Vandal people, only on the man who had imprisoned their rightful king. This attempt to divide the Vandals was to fail; the messenger only showed the message to a few people that he could trust, since he was afraid of the consequences should he be captured distributing propaganda and handed over to Gelimer (Proc, *Wars*, III.xvi.12–15).

Gelimer's Response

At the same time as Belisarius was making tentative moves to befriend the natives, Gelimer was moving to counter the Byzantine threat. Gelimer instantly concluded that the Byzantine army would travel along the coastal road, so passing through the valley at Ad Decimum. According to the instructions that he had already sent to his brother Ammatus, the troops in Carthage began to mobilise ready to march towards Ad Decimum from the north. Gathering a force from the area of Hermione, Gelimer marched north to rendezvous with his brother at Ad Decimum.

The Deployment of Belisarius and his march towards Carthage

Waiting for news from Syllectus, Belisarius organised the army for the march on Carthage. Three hundred *bucellarii* were placed under the command of John the Armenian, Belisarius' *optio* ('choice': in charge of Belisarius' finance), with instructions to scout the way forward and report any enemy activity. He was to remain at least twenty *stades*, approximately 2⅓ miles, ahead of the main force.* The 600 Huns under Sinnion and Balas were ordered to guard the left flank in a similar manner to John, also remaining at least twenty *stades* away from the main force.

Belisarius stationed himself in the rear, along with his *bucellarii* and *comitatus*, his best troops. Aware that Gelimer was last reported as being in the south of the country, this position would enable Belisarius to immediately take close control of the troops who would be under threat if Gelimer was to arrive and attack the Byzantines from the rear. Furthermore, with his mounted *bucellarii* in attendance, he would be able to advance instantly if there was a need to support any troops further forward who came under attack.

The rest of the army marched in the centre. The fleet was ordered to keep pace with the infantry as they moved along the coast road. No flank guard was placed upon the right flank as this was resting for the most part within sight of the sea and so was protected by the fleet.

The main army now advanced to Syllectus, where the men acted in such an excellent manner that the citizens decided to give their full support to Belisarius' venture. Furthermore, word of the restrained behaviour of the troops now paved the way for a peaceful advance towards Carthage, with the full cooperation of the towns and cities along the route.

Marching at a rate of eighty *stades* (approximately 9 miles) per day, the army advanced towards Carthage, staying at the towns of Leptis and Hadrumetum along the way. Finally, they came to Grasse, 350 *stades* (around 40 miles) from

---

* *Stades* is derived from the Greek unit of measurement, the *stadium*. This was a measurement of approximately 600 feet (180 metres). Twenty *stades* is therefore approximately 2⅓ miles.

Carthage, where the Vandal king had a palace. Although Belisarius realised that the Vandals would be close, their strength and position was as yet unknown. This was now to change. As the army prepared to settle for the night at Grasse, a detachment of the Byzantine rearguard clashed with some troops sent ahead by Gelimer. After a brief skirmish, both parties retired to their camps, but Belisarius was at last certain that at least some of the Vandals were in the vicinity and closing in behind him

Belisarius was now faced with the most dangerous part of the journey to Carthage. The road ran inland while the coast curved away to the north, forming the headland of Cape Bon. This meant that the fleet would have to sail out of sight around the Cape. Unable to keep close control of the fleet, he instructed Archelaus, the prefect, and Calonymus, the admiral, to take the fleet around the headland, but to remain at least 200 *stades* (c.22 miles) from Carthage. Maintaining the army's deployment as before, he set out on the morning of the fourth day on his way towards Ad Decimum. With the absence of the fleet, he had a maximum force of around 18,000 men.

The Strategies

There is no reference to the numbers of troops available to either Gelimer or his brother Ammatus at the approaching battle. With the whole army mustering, at the most, 20,000 men, due to losses in the wars with the Moors, and with 5,000 of the best men in Sardinia under Tzazon repressing the rebellion, this leaves a maximum of 15,000 men for Gelimer. Whether he was able to muster the total force is questionable. It is more likely that he had approximately two thirds of this number available, possibly 10,000 – 12,000 men. Yet even if he could have mobilised the whole available force, his tactics are likely to have remained the same; he would never have significantly outnumbered Belisarius.

Furthermore, Gelimer would still have had a major obstacle to overcome. He would find it difficult to unite his armed forces. The Byzantines were marching towards Carthage and so forming an obstacle between the south and the north. Gelimer needed a victory at Ad Decimum in order to unite his troops.

It seems likely that the majority of the troops were led by Gelimer, since otherwise he would not have had the confidence to detach Gibamundus with 2,000 troops, as will be seen later. The number of troops available to Ammatus is also unknown, but it is possible to estimate their strength. Procopius states that they were marching in groups of no more than thirty. If we allow one group per 50 yards, this computes to around 1,000 men per mile. Allowing that Ad Decimum was 8 miles from Carthage, this gives a maximum of around 8,000 men on the road. The actual figure would be significantly lower than this: the troops had to be at Ad Decimum and deployed for battle by the early

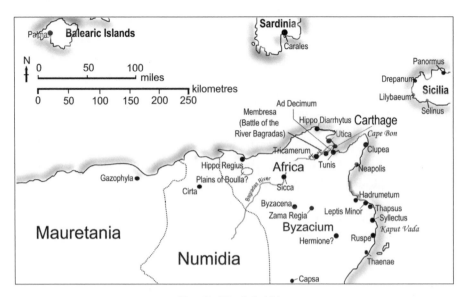

Map 7: Vandal Africa.

afternoon, and so would have left Carthage long before noon. Consequently, they would not occupy all of the 8 miles.

The number of troops available helps to explain Gelimer's plan for an ambush at Ad Decimum. With only 5–6,000 men himself, and with Ammatus having only around 6–7,000, he did not have the forces to face Belisarius in a pitched battle. He did, however, have enough men to mount an ambush that could potentially destroy the Byzantine army, or at least reduce their numerical superiority and weaken their morale. Furthermore, his experience of warfare against the nomadic Moors may have predisposed him to use an ambush as a natural form of warfare.

Ad Decimum was 70 stades (around 8 miles) from Carthage. According to Procopius, the road passed through a 'narrow passage' (Proc, *Wars*, III.xvii.11) and this is where Gelimer planned to ambush the Byzantines. The plan was simple: Ammatus was to move his troops from Carthage and block the northern exit from the valley. Once the Byzantines arrived, he was to attack the head of their column and drive it back into the valley, hopefully causing confusion and disorder, possibly even forcing Belisarius to commit his reserves. Whilst this attack was going in, Gelimer was to advance from the south and attack the Byzantines from the rear. With the extra confusion and dismay at having to fight in two directions, the Byzantines would then be annihilated and the war won.

The plan was elegant and simple, but there was one drawback: a lot would depend upon the timing of the attacks and they would not be easy to synchronize. According to Procopius, there were three roads in the vicinity heading towards Carthage, none of them visible from each other due to the hilly terrain. Coordination would be extremely difficult.

The first road was the coastal route being used by the Byzantines, which passed through Ad Decimum before heading towards Carthage. Gelimer had predicted that the Byzantines would use this road, since they needed to remain in contact with their fleet. His assumption had been proved correct when his scouts had made contact on the road the previous night. Ammatus would also use this road, but approaching from the opposite direction

The centre road was the one that came up from the south, and so was the one that Gelimer was using for his advance from Hermione. This road intersected the coastal route shortly before the pass at Ad Decimum. This piece of local knowledge had determined Gelimer in his desire to fight at Ad Decimum: the Byzantines would not know that the road from Hermione intersected the coast road here and so would be taken by surprise at his unexpected appearance at the junction.

It was the third road that was to cause Gelimer anxiety. This was further inland and bypassed the valley at Ad Decimum, following a separate route towards Carthage. If Ammatus was to follow Gelimer's instructions, Carthage would be left defenceless. With Sardinia and Tripolitania in open rebellion, Gelimer would have distrusted the natives. Even a weak Byzantine force advancing down this road would be unopposed and the Carthaginians were likely to open the gates to them. Winning a battle at Ad Decimum would be negated if Carthage itself was in enemy hands, since this could easily provoke more areas to rebel. Accordingly, Gelimer changed his plans and sent his nephew Gibamundus on to the road to ensure that Carthage remained secure. The diversion of 2,000 men away from the battle was a small price to pay to ensure that the city remained in Vandal hands. The move would also allow Gelimer to change his plans if it revealed that either the main body or at least a large detachment of Byzantine troops had already reached this road and were advancing upon Carthage, having bypassed his intended ambush at Ad Decimum.

Procopius gives a different reason for the detachment of Gibamundus. He claims that Gibamundus was to make a wide swing to the left before moving back in and attacking the Byzantines from their flank (Procopius, III.xviii.1). On close inspection this scenario would appear unlikely, since the eastern road was too far from Ad Decimum – according to Procopius, Gibamundus was travelling northwards forty *stades* (approximately 4½ miles) away from the battlefield. Any troops sent on this route would have little chance of taking part in the battle, since the intervening terrain was hilly and would slow down their movement accordingly. If the troops under Gibamundus were to attack the Byzantines in the manner described by Procopius, they would have stayed with the main force until nearer to Ad Decimum before moving a short way into the hills. With only a short distance to travel, they would then have been in an ideal position to fall upon the undefended Byzantine flank.

Gelimer's plan was relatively simple and only depended upon timing. In contrast, at no point did Belisarius want to fight a battle on that day. He still had no clear idea concerning the Vandal's strength or army composition. What he wanted was information which he could use in order to plan a battle for the following day at the earliest.

The Battle of Ad Decimum

Although usually described as a single battle, the action was actually fought in four distinct and separate phases, all either out of line of sight of each other or at different times.

Opening Moves

Following Gelimer's instructions, on the early morning of the fourth day after the invasion Ammatus (Gelimer's brother) ordered his men to follow him to the pass whilst he himself went ahead to scout the area and decide upon deployment.

As the Vandals marshalled their forces and marched towards Ad Decimum, Belisarius was nearing the valley. Around four miles from Ad Decimum, the Byzantines came upon a natural position which was an ideal place to act as a camp. Setting the infantry to fortify the place, and leaving the baggage and Antonina in relative safety, Belisarius led the remainder of his cavalry out to meet the Vandals. With John and his 300 men still scouting ahead and with the Huns still guarding his left flank, Belisarius set forth on the afternoon of the fourth day since their arrival in Africa. His plan was to locate the enemy and assess the strength and the composition of their army, before retiring to the safety of the newly-built camp and deciding upon a strategy for the ensuing battle. Accordingly, he sent the *foederati* under Solomon (Dorotheus having died in Sicily) ahead to contact John and try to locate the Vandal forces. He was unaware that John had already made contact and that the Battle of Ad Decimum had begun.

Phase I: The Defeat of Gibamundus

According to Procopius, two engagements occurred at approximately the same time. At around noon, Gelimer's nephew Gibamundus and his 2,000 men encountered the Huns as they travelled along the third road, close to Pedion Halon, forty *stades* (around 4½ miles) from Ad Decimum. Although out-numbering the Huns by odds of over three to one, the Vandals stopped when faced by a single Hun who rode ahead of his own forces and faced them alone. It is unknown why they stopped: possibly due to fear of a trap, possibly in amazement at the courage of the lone Hun, or possibly due to their surprise at finding enemy troops so far from Ad Decimum. Procopius chooses to

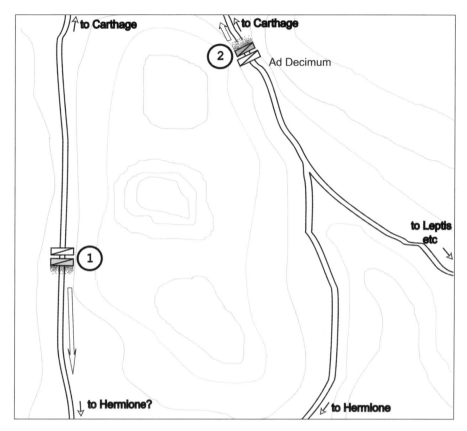

Diagram 11: The Battle of Ad Decimum 1
(1): phase 1 Gibamundus is defeated and killed by the Huns
(2): phase 2 Ammatus is defeated and killed by John and the comitatus.

claim that they were afraid due to the Huns' reputation as fierce warriors. Whatever the actual reason, their failure to act put heart into the Huns and they attacked the Vandals at full speed. Without attempting to resist, Gibamundus was killed and his men routed and completely destroyed (Procopius, *Wars*, III.xviii.18–20).

Phase II: The Defeat of Ammatus
Meanwhile, Ammatus had made a mistake that would prove extremely costly. Instead of gathering a large force and advancing towards Ad Decimum *en masse*, he had gone ahead with only a few troops to assess the proposed battlefield. The rest of his forces followed in small groups of no more than thirty men, stretching back in a long line towards Carthage.

Ammatus reached Ad Decimum around noon, at roughly the same time as Gibamundus was being defeated and killed. Unfortunately for him, he encountered John and his 300 *bucellarii*. Despite killing twelve of the *bucellarii*, Ammatus was himself killed and the remnants of his small force fled back down the road towards Carthage, with John and the *bucellarii* in hot pursuit.

Unable to concentrate their forces and mount a viable defence, the small groups of Vandals that the pursuing Byzantines encountered marching towards Ad Decimum abruptly turned and fled. The whole action quickly assumed a sort of domino effect. The trickle became a flood, with all of Ammatus' forces retreating towards Carthage. John advanced as far as the gates of the city before his men halted their pursuit. The road back to Ad Decimum was now littered with the bodies of dead and dying Vandals; Procopius stated that the carnage resembled a battle fought by 20,000 assailants rather than 300 (Proc, *Wars*, xviii, 11). The victors slowly began to drift back along the road, looting the bodies of the Vandal dead as they went.

Phase III: The Arrival of Gelimer

Meanwhile, the Byzantine *foederati* under Solomon – moving in advance of Belisarius – had reached the site of the initial fighting between John and Ammatus and had found the bodies of the troops who had died, including that of Ammatus himself. After questioning local inhabitants – presumably friendly thanks to the troops' excellent behaviour – they were at a loss as to what course to take, so climbed the nearby hills to gain a vantage point over the country thereabouts. Once on higher ground, they noticed a cloud of dust approaching from the south, following the line of the second road; it was Gelimer and the main Vandal force. The leaders of the *foederati* immediately sent messengers to Belisarius, urging him to march as quickly as possible to their assistance. They now argued over whether to retire or to attack the Vandals. However the decision was to be academic. In between the armies was a large hill, the highest in the area. Ideal as a place to establish a camp, with views over all of the surrounding area, individuals in both armies recognised its importance and began to fight to gain possession of the hill.

The Vandals reached the summit first and then, due to the advantage of being uphill as well as having superior numbers, their attack routed the *foederati*. Fleeing in panic, the *foederati* attempted to reach Belisarius and his reinforcements. They retreated until they reached a position held by Uliaris, the commander of Belisarius' personal guard, along with 800 of his men. The *foederati* expected the guardsmen to join with them and face any further attacks, but they now received a shock: upon hearing the news of the defeat, the Guard broke and fled down the road towards Belisarius and safety.

When the fleeing troops reached Belisarius, they halted. He ordered them to reform their ranks ready for battle and then reprimanded them for their flight. Afterwards, he listened to their reports. Realising that Gelimer had halted and that a large number of Vandals had already been defeated, he

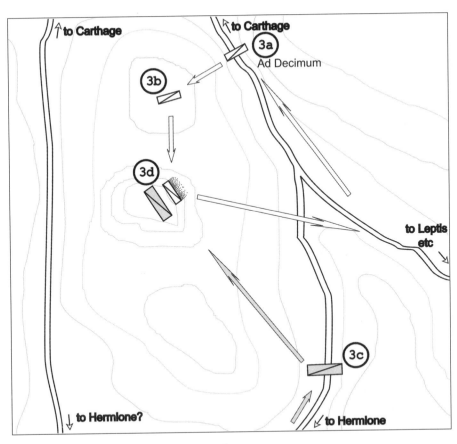

Diagram 12: The Battle of Ad Decimum 2
(3a): Solomon and the foederati *arrive and find Ammatus' body*
(3b): they climb a nearby hill to survey the terrain and see a cloud of dust, which is
(3c): Gelimer arriving on the battlefield
(3d): the foederati *and the Vandals fight over possession of a large hill: the* foederati *rout towards Belisarius.*

believed that he outnumbered the remaining Vandal forces at Ad Decimum. With the knowledge that he had an opportunity to strike a heavy blow at the Vandals; he ordered the troops to march at full speed towards Ad Decimum.

In the meantime, Gelimer himself had a choice to make. According to Procopius, he could have either immediately pursued the *foederati* or moved on to Carthage. Either choice would have been a disaster for the Byzantines. Pursuit would have caught Belisarius unawares and Procopius believes that the Byzantines would have been overrun and completely defeated (Proc, *Wars*, III.xix.25–27). A move towards Carthage would have encountered John and his 300 men, now busily engaged in looting the bodies of dead Vandals. The Vandals would easily have been able to kill them all. In addition, Gelimer would have been able to capture or defeat the Byzantine fleet, which had ignored its orders and advanced to within reach of the Vandal fleet in Carthage (Proc, *Wars*, III.xix.27–28). Instead, Gelimer descended from the hills at walking pace and so came upon the body of his brother Ammatus. Procopius asserts that Gelimer now began mourning for his brother and arranging for his burial, while his troops aimlessly milled around in the confined space.

The assessment is at fault. Obviously, Gelimer would want to take care of his brother's body. Yet, unlike Belisarius and Procopius, Gelimer was ignorant of the course of events. The nearby inhabitants had chosen their sides and so did not inform Gelimer of the nature of his brother's death. Expecting to meet his brother, instead he had found the body of Ammatus alongside those of only a few Vandals and a handful of Byzantines. He would have been at a loss to understand what had happened. Gelimer could not have foreseen that the armed forces from Carthage would be defeated by only 300 men. It would be natural to assume that the Byzantines had advanced faster than expected and either the Vandal forces had immediately fled when confronted with superior numbers, or Ammatus had ordered a retreat, himself dying as part of the rearguard. Gelimer therefore believed that the main body of the Byzantines had already passed and the troops that he had defeated had been the Byzantine rearguard. The main Byzantine force would by now be approaching Carthage.

With these conclusions, one option open to him was to advance immediately and try to attack the Byzantines from the rear in the open space around Carthage. On the clear ground he would quickly be seen and so lose the advantage of surprise. Furthermore, if he did not know already, he would guess that the enemy outnumbered his available forces. Such an attack was not a realistic option. The alternative was to wait until nightfall and send messengers into the town to gain a clearer understanding of what had happened. Then he could decide what to do; either retreat until Tzazon returned from Sardinia or mount an attack in conjunction with the forces remaining in the city. This is a more likely explanation for his delay at this vital moment in the battle. As he was arranging matters, asking for advice and deciding upon his options, disaster struck.

Phase IV: The Arrival of Belisarius and Defeat of Gelimer

At this point Belisarius arrived with his organised troops and swiftly attacked the disordered Vandals from an unexpected direction. Unable to withstand the assault, the Vandals fled, but not in the direction of Carthage. They were still unsure of events and it was probable that there was a substantial Byzantine force on the road to Carthage that could trap them. Instead, they fled off-road towards the relative safety of the Plains of Boulla and the road leading to Numidia. Gelimer had recently made alliances with some of the Moorish tribes in the area, so his decision was valid. This was to be a costly, though

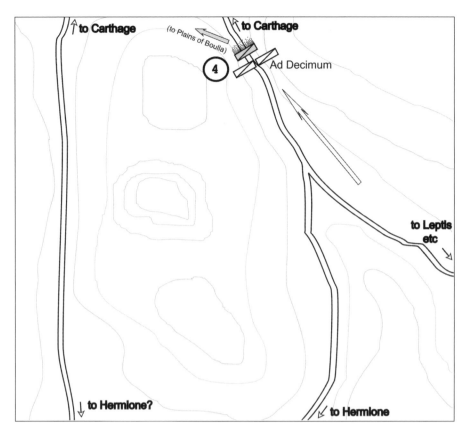

Diagram 13: The Battle of Ad Decimum 3
(4): Belisarius and the rallied troops advance and attack Gelimer whilst he is contemplating his next move: the Vandals rout towards the Plains of Boulla.

understandable, mistake. Although there was no way he could have known, his forces would easily have brushed aside John's 300 men, who were scattered and intent on gathering plunder, and so have reinforced the garrison at Carthage.

As Gelimer headed away from the city, there were now not enough troops in Carthage either to withstand a Byzantine assault or to stop the city's population from opening the gates to the victor. Furthermore, the walls had not been repaired and so would not withstand an attack without a large number of defenders. The Battle of Ad Decimum was over and Carthage lay open to the victor. Belisarius had won.

The Generalship of Belisarius and Gelimer

The standard interpretation of the battle has been that Gelimer's strategy was too complex, with his forces arriving at badly-timed intervals, allowing the Byzantines to crush each small group individually. Conversely, Belisarius is the genius that takes advantage of Gelimer's indecision and inability to control his troops to win the day. Based largely upon Procopius' account, which was written to acclaim Belisarius' talents as a general, the interpretations are too polarised and based upon the misleading factors already highlighted in the account of the battle.

Turning first to Gelimer, he immediately reaped the negative rewards of Vandal policy towards Catholics: the natives were willing to support Belisarius and withdrew their loyalty from Gelimer and, more importantly, failed to volunteer information at a critical point in the battle. His plan at Ad Decimum was excellent and made with commendable speed. It made good use of his background knowledge of the terrain and the movement rates of both his own and the Byzantine troops: he knew where and when he wanted to fight, and it was only because of Ammatus' mistake that this did not occur.

If Ammatus had left at the correct time with all of his forces, it is likely that he would have forced John to retire back along the valley. Belisarius would probably have moved forward and attempted battle with Ammatus, who would have been heavily outnumbered. Whilst Belisarius was deploying and preparing for battle, Gelimer would have arrived and Belisarius would have been in grave danger. Furthermore, Gelimer could not have foreseen that a small force of 600 Huns would have destroyed the 2,000 men under his nephew Gibamundus. Although this was to have no effect on the battle at Ad Decimum itself, it still highlights the unexpected course that all of the events took that day.

The arrival of Gelimer and the ease with which his men beat the *foederati* shows that the Vandals were capable troops who were willing to fight. More than anything, the battle emphasises the importance of luck upon the battle-field. The Byzantines were lucky to beat Ammatus; they were lucky to beat Gibamundus; and they were extremely lucky in that Gelimer halted in confusion at the unexpected find of his brother's body. At Ad Decimum, luck was definitely against Gelimer.

If Gelimer was unlucky, then it would be tempting to assume that Belisarius was simply lucky, for all of the reasons just listed. Yet there is more to his victory than blind chance. His decision to restrain the troops in their dealings with the natives was crucial. This enabled him to advance without having to lay siege to towns and secure in the knowledge that no armed forces would emerge from them to attack his rear. This allowed him to concentrate solely upon the Vandals. Furthermore, on the day of the battle the Libyans were willing to give his troops information, which they then withheld from Gelimer.

Belisarius' order of march also shows good judgement. The advance guard and the flank guard were crucial to avoid him being taken by surprise. Moreover, his positioning himself at the rear displays recognition that the main Vandal thrust was likely to come from the south.

His decision to establish a camp and leave the majority of the infantry to guard it is also commendable. He needed to gather information and the infantry could easily become a liability if a large number of enemy cavalry were present. Yet it is when he halted and began to build the camp that he made a major mistake that could have proved costly. He did not immediately send messengers to inform either John or the Huns that he had stopped. This allowed them to continue their advance, leaving them dangerously isolated and vulnerable. Furthermore, when he finally left the camp, he sent the *foederati* ahead to contact John, who by this time was already engaged in battle. There is no evidence that he also sent word to the Huns to inform them of the change in circumstances. With only a slight change in the course of events, both John and the Huns could have been heavily defeated. Gelimer's strategy could easily have become a reality.

Having censured Belisarius for these mistakes, we should note that when he was joined by the routing *foederati* and guard he had the presence of mind to stay calm, stop them, rebuke them and then ask for information. He also had the ability to see that the situation could be turned to his advantage. Realising that he had the opportunity to strike Gelimer whilst he was uninformed and off guard, he swiftly changed his plans and attacked. There is no point in being lucky if you do not have the wit to take advantage of your good fortune.

With the above factors in mind, it is possible to conclude that Gelimer was extremely unlucky and could not have foreseen the events that happened that day. Conversely, although Belisarius was extremely lucky, he should be commended for his sound judgement and quick thinking in the heat of battle. He was about to reap the rewards of the victory.

Carthage

John with the Byzantine cavalry and the 600 Huns under Sinnion and Balas returned and rejoined Belisarius at Ad Decimum with the onset of dusk. It was only now that Belisarius was to gain a full insight into all of the events of the day and comprehend the scale of his victory. The reunited cavalry passed the night at Ad Decimum.

On the following day the infantry left their camp and joined Belisarius, bringing Antonina with them. The whole army regrouped and advanced to Carthage, arriving as night was falling. Belisarius had them camp in the open even though the gates were open and the citizens lit many lights to illuminate the scene. He was still worried in case the Vandals had set an ambush in the city streets, and was also aware that his own troops might use the cover of night to sack the city unobserved should they be allowed in.

Having sailed around Cape Bon, the fleet was at first unaware of events, so sent men to the city of Mercurium for information. Upon learning of the victory, they approached Carthage, but decided to anchor at Stagnum, forty *stades* (approximately 4½ miles) from the city. Once anchored, Calonymus the admiral appears to have gathered a small group of sailors and ignored Belisarius' instructions. They proceeded to plunder the property of merchants at nearby Mandriacum.

On the morning of day six, Belisarius drew the army up in battle formations – he was still concerned about the possibility of a Vandal ambush – and reminded the troops to leave the citizens unharmed. The Byzantines finally entered the city, Belisarius occupying the palace of Gelimer and receiving delegations from the citizens. Almost immediately, there was an outcry and the merchants whose property had been taken demanded restitution. According to Procopius, Calonymus swore to return the goods but never fulfilled his oath. However, the merchants were appeased and calm restored.

Belisarius and his staff ate the meal that had been prepared in expectation of Gelimer's return whilst the troops were billeted around the city. Such billeting was the norm in a peacefully-occupied city, and the exceptional behaviour of the troops helped to cement the loyalty of the majority of the Carthaginians. In the afternoon Belisarius displayed the policy he would maintain towards the defeated Vandals. There were many of them around the city, staying in sacred buildings for sanctuary due to fear of retribution. Belisarius made pledges guaranteeing their safety and they were rounded up, disarmed and led to places of safety.

Belisarius also ordered the refortification of Carthage. The city walls had become ruinous in many places and so were useless as a means of defence; therefore Belisarius paid the native Carthaginians to build a ditch with stakes around the wall. Once this was complete, he felt secure enough to order work begun on repairing the decayed portions of the walls.

For the next few weeks Belisarius remained in Carthage to oversee the work, sending Solomon to Constantinople with an account of the events thus far. And his luck stayed with him. Whilst the events described above had been transpiring in Africa, Gelimer's brother, Tzazon, had completed the reconquest of Sardinia, killing Godas in the process. Unaware of the loss of Carthage, he dispatched messengers with details of his victory. These men sailed into Carthage and were captured. At around this point, the Byzantine general Cyril also sailed into the harbour, having journeyed to Sardinia and separately discovered that Tzazon was victorious and Godas dead. The extra men he brought to Carthage would have been a welcome reinforcement to Belisarius.

Additionally, the envoys previously sent to Spain to ask King Theudis of the Visigoths for an alliance had reached the Visigothic king. They had travelled very slowly and Theudis was informed of the loss of Carthage before they reached him. Naturally, he refused to make an alliance. Rebuffed, the envoys also returned to Carthage and were captured by Belisarius. In this way Belisarius was kept in touch with the larger events in the Mediterranean. Gelimer, on the other hand, was still awaiting information concerning either his envoys or his brother Tzazon.

Although by his retreat to Boulla Gelimer may have been counting on his new Moorish allies, the majority of the Moors did not want an alliance with him. Many sent envoys to Belisarius, some even including hostages, asking for the traditional symbols of office given to them by a Byzantine emperor, and promising to fight as Belisarius' allies. Justinian had evidently been aware of such an eventuality, and so had furnished Belisarius with the insignia before the fleet sailed. Belisarius sent the items plus large sums of money, but the Moors took no active part in the war and were to remain neutral until the outcome was inevitable.

In the period of calm which followed the battle at Ad Decimum, Gelimer did not remain idle. He distributed money amongst the farmers around the plain of Boulla, enticing many to maintain their allegiance to the Vandals. He further announced a fixed sum of cash for the head of every Byzantine brought to him. Many heads were produced, and he appears to have believed that the Byzantine army itself was gradually being eroded. However, they were the heads of Byzantine slaves and servants out of the city on business of their own. The Byzantine troops kept their heads and remained within the city walls.

Gelimer was soon joined by his Moorish allies, although they do not seem to have provided a sizeable force. As seen above, the majority of the Moors were biding their time before openly declaring their allegiance. Gelimer sent messages to his brother in Sardinia, informing him of events and recalling him to Africa. Tzazon sailed to Africa and then travelled across land to meet Gelimer at Boulla.

With the return of Tzazon and his forces, and with his own forces slowly increasing as fugitives from the battle made their way to join him, Gelimer decided to advance on Carthage. The decision was an easy one. The Vandals had been deprived of the majority of their bases as the natives had opted to support Belisarius. They could not afford to fight a protracted campaign as they did not have the manpower available for a war of attrition. A single, decisive confrontation was the only – probably highly desirable – option. A Vandal victory would cause many cities to change allegiance, and if the victory was overwhelming the invasion could be ended in one day.

Accordingly, he led his army towards Carthage, intent on drawing the Byzantines out of the city. Once there, they damaged the city's aqueduct and camped near the city. Although this allowed them to control many of the city's rural districts, they did not attempt to begin a siege or starve the Byzantines out. Gelimer did not want to waste men, since they were fast becoming a rare resource. He wanted a battle. Once in place, he waited, expecting either the native Carthaginians to change their allegiance, or for those troops in the Byzantine army who were fellow Arians, such as the Heruls, to change sides. He was soon in negotiation with the Huns. Unhappy, because they had been hired and, without their consent, transferred to Constantinople and then Africa, they secretly agreed to join the Vandals. They believed that if the Byzantines were victorious they would leave the Huns in Africa.

Belisarius did not share Gelimer's views on the desirability of a battle. Instead, he waited in the town until the walls had been completely restored, thus ensuring that he would always have a secure base. Realising that treachery was always going to be a possibility, he remained alert. Having caught a Carthaginian who had agreed to join the Vandals, he had him tried and then impaled. The sight of the gruesome execution appears to have had the desired effect. All moves by other Carthaginians to league with the Vandals halted.

Belisarius was likewise aware of the restless nature of the Huns. To avoid their betraying him, he gave them attention and banquets, finally tempting them to admit to their fears and to confess their agreement with Gelimer. He swore solemn oaths that once the victory was won they would be transported home with a suitable amount of booty. The Huns agreed to return to their original loyalty, whilst deciding – like the Moors – to wait and join the victor when the time came.

Once he felt secure with the loyalty of the people and the troops, Belisarius decided to oppose Gelimer in the field. It was now about three months after the landing in Africa. First, he sent out all of the cavalry and all of the *bucellarii* except for 500 men, together with the army standard, under the command of John the Armenian. John had orders to skirmish with the enemy if the opportunity arose, since Belisarius had recognised that the Vandals were unable to cope with skirmishing troops. He was on no account to accept a challenge to a full-scale battle.

The next morning, Belisarius followed with the remaining cavalry and the infantry. The army marched towards Tricamerum, approximately 150 *stades* (about 17 miles) from Carthage, where the Vandals were encamped. The Byzantine cavalry set up their own camp, leaving a large distance between themselves and the enemy.

The Battle of Tricamerum

On the following day Gelimer waited until just before midday before leading his troops out of their camp and ordering them to assume their battle formations with a small stream directly to their front. It could be that the habit of the Byzantines to take their meals at noon was well known: the Persians had similarly attempted to force the Byzantines into forming battle lines before they could eat their meal. Gelimer may have been using the same tactic of making the enemy fight on empty stomachs.

Yet there is a further reason behind his decision to attack. When assessing the numbers available, the Byzantine forces at this point look extraordinarily light. Belisarius had begun with 5,000 cavalry, not including his personal *comitatus* or the reinforcements led by Valerianus and Martinus which had joined the expedition at Methone. Although the Vandals had been defeated at Ad Decimum, they had nevertheless fought hard at times, inflicting casualties and so reducing the number of men available to Belisarius. It is unlikely that the army facing Gelimer was much more than 8,000 strong. The 10,000 or more infantry were yet to arrive at the battlefield.

Facing them, the Vandal army was likely to be slightly larger than the available Byzantine forces. Many men had been lost at Ad Decimum, either killed, taken prisoner, or seeking sanctuary after the battle. Their absence was more than compensated for by the arrival of Tzazon and his men from Sardinia. Taking into account the overall manpower available (see above, Chapter 5), and deducting the losses incurred, it would appear reasonable to suggest that Gelimer may have had a maximum of around 15,000 men. It is not surprising that he wished to attack before the Byzantine infantry arrived to balance the numbers.

Whatever the motive, the Byzantines were caught unawares. With extreme haste, the army prepared for battle and deployed across from the Vandals on the opposite bank of the stream.

It is sometimes difficult when reading Procopius to understand the narrative since he usually makes Belisarius the centre of events. However, a close reading of the text reveals that Belisarius only joined the main force just before the battle. Therefore, the deployment of the Byzantine troops was made by John the Armenian. John had deployed the troops and so had greater knowledge of what was happening. It made sense for him to remain in charge throughout the battle, so Belisarius only gave him 'advice'. Accordingly, John took his position in the centre of the battlefield with the *comitatus* and the standard.

On the left wing, Martinus and Valerian, John, Cyprian, Althius and Marcellus commanded a section of the Byzantine missile-armed cavalry, being reinforced by the *foederati* who were armed solely for close combat. The left wing is likely to have numbered around 3,500–4,000 men.

On the right wing were Pappas, Barbatus, Aigan and others with the balance of the regular cavalry. Again, this would suggest a maximum number of 4,000 men. The Huns were deployed apart from the Byzantine army. This would allow them to choose which side to join when they saw which was winning.

The Vandals deployed with Tzazon leading his veterans from the Sardinian campaign in the centre. To the left and the right the Vandal *chiliarchs* led the remainder of the army. Since the Byzantines were to concentrate upon the Vandal centre, and not upon a weaker wing, it is possible that the two wings were roughly equal in numbers. Behind the Vandal centre was a force of Moorish allies, the strength of which is completely unknown. Like the Huns, they waited until the battle had been decided before taking any action; they did not want to alienate their possible future masters by an untimely attack.

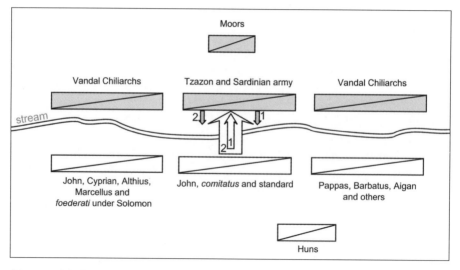

Diagram 14: The Battle of Tricamerum 1
1 Limited skirmish and Vandal controlled charge to relieve pressure
2 Larger skirmish and Vandal controlled charge to relieve pressure.

Gelimer himself travelled around the entire force, exhorting the men to fight bravely. He also ordered that they fight only with the sword, disdaining to use their spears or other weapons. This may have been a tactic to encourage close combat and so reduce the effects of large-scale Byzantine missile fire. Yet there is no record of him taking part in the actual fighting.

The battle opened with John following Belisarius' advice and sending a few troops to skirmish with the Vandal centre. The plan appears to have been to either shoot at the Vandals who would lose men and be unable to respond, or to provoke a counterattack that would lose momentum and cohesion as it crossed the stream. The enemy would then be easy for the outnumbered Byzantines to destroy. Tzazon was too wily to take the bait: a charge by the Vandals forced the Byzantine skirmishers to retire, but the Vandals did not attempt to cross the stream.

Seeing that the tactic had nearly worked and that the Vandals had no response to mounted archers other than to charge them, John now personally led out the *bucellarii*, and again was forced to withdraw without the Vandals crossing the stream. John or Belisarius now recognised that the Vandals were not going to take the bait, and that their losses from arrow fire alone were not going to be sufficient to cause them to withdraw. However, they also noticed that the two wings of the Vandal army had not moved to support Tzazon. As a result, John now led out almost all of the *comitatus*, including the standard, and attacked the Vandal centre. An extremely fierce hand-to-hand battle ensued, in the course of which Tzazon was killed.

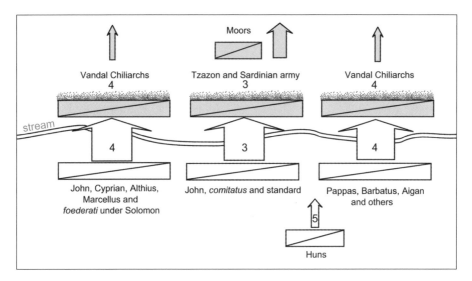

Diagram 15: The Battle of Tricamerum 2
3 John leads assault in the centre; Tzazon killed and Vandal centre routs
4 Byzantine general advance leads to the collapse of the Vandal army
5 The Huns join in the pursuit of the Vandals.

Procopius does not give us the detail we need to assess what happened next. It is possible that Belisarius (not John, who was now involved in the fighting), recognising that the Vandal centre was giving way and that the Vandal flanks were unlikely to intervene, ordered an all-out attack. The timing was crucial. The Vandal centre quickly collapsed in rout, the panic then spreading outwards to the wings. In a short space of time, the Vandal army was fleeing in terror. At this point, the Huns joined in the pursuit, declaring their allegiance to Belisarius.

However the pursuit was to be a short one; the Vandals returned to their camp, and, without the infantry, Belisarius did not have the necessary troops to assault the position. Instead, the Byzantine troops turned and began to strip the Vandal bodies of their belongings. According to Procopius, the Byzantines left fifty men dead on the battlefield, the Vandals 800. Although not in itself a large number, this was a significant proportion of the Vandal army. More than five per cent of the Vandal forces were dead, and there were many injured in the camp. Things were looking bleak for Gelimer.

In the afternoon the Byzantine infantry arrived. Belisarius now formed the entire army ready to attack the Vandal camp. It was not to be necessary. Gelimer, along with a few relatives and servants fled unnoticed. When the Vandals realised that their leader had gone, they too escaped from the camp as best they could. The Byzantines stormed the empty camp and took possession of all of the treasures which had been left by the Vandals. Procopius says that this was a vast sum, not only including many valuables made by and for the Vandals while they had been in Africa, but also including many treasures taken during their extensive sea-borne raids of the previous century.

In their frenzy for loot, Belisarius lost control of the troops: they spent the night pursuing the fugitives, killing the men and enslaving the women and children. Belisarius was deeply worried in case the Vandals should reform and attack the disorganised Byzantines, who would quickly fall under such an assault.

At daybreak Belisarius took up a position on a hill and harangued the troops concerning their behaviour. Slowly discipline was restored and Belisarius gave his orders. John and 200 men were to pursue Gelimer, not halting until his capture or death. Belisarius then gave pledges to those Vandal fugitives who had sought sanctuary in local churches. They were disarmed and sent under guard to Carthage. After finally gathering his army together again, Belisarius began his own pursuit of Gelimer.

The Generalship of Belisarius and Gelimer

The most notable aspect of Gelimer's generalship at Tricamerum is the lack of any mention of him by Procopius after the deployment of the troops. Unlike Tzazon, he does not appear to have fought in combat during the day, but to have joined his troops in retiring to the camp after their defeat. It would appear that Gelimer had deployed behind the stream hoping that the Byzantines would either deploy with an obvious weak point that he could quickly attack, or that the Byzantines themselves, being overconfident following their victory at Ad Decimum, would attack before they were reinforced by their infantry. In such a situation they would disorder their own troops as they crossed the stream, leaving them vulnerable to attack. When neither of these situations materialised, he appears to have done nothing, instead giving the advantage of the initiative to the Byzantines, an advantage they would exploit to the full.

The situation was the result of one major factor in Gelimer's experience in leading troops: he did not know how to deal with the Byzantine horse archers. Their range gave them the tactical advantage against troops who waited, so if he waited, they would slowly wear his army down. Furthermore, this would give time for the Byzantine infantry to arrive. Fast action was needed.

Yet if he attacked, the formation of his troops would be disrupted by the stream, so giving the advantage to the Byzantines. It appeared that either decision would result in a defeat.

Therefore, at the crucial point in the battle, Gelimer hesitated and was lost. His failure to adopt any meaningful strategy left him open to the afore-mentioned horse archers. They first weakened his centre with archery, before the *bucellarii* charged home and caused the centre to rout. The troops on the wings watched helplessly as the centre was put to flight and Tzazon killed.

Gelimer's inability to formulate a plan of attack or to make important judgments when needed had lost him the battle.

Gelimer's decision to flee from the Vandal camp also needs analysis. It is usually compared to his indecision at the Battle of Ad Decimum. There, Procopius has Gelimer grieving for his brother Ammatus, and so losing the battle when Belisarius attacks. In this instance, it is the loss of his brother Tzazon that causes Gelimer to lose heart. This is very simplistic and further factors need to be taken into account.

Gelimer had deposed Hilderic partly because of his inability to lead his men to victory in battle as a Germanic king should. Having lost two battles, Gelimer's leadership would now be under question, and it is likely that upon their return to the camp many of the Vandal nobles were regretting their decision to support his seizure of the throne. At least some of the nobles and warriors would have remained loyal in theory to Hilderic and his policies towards Justinian. Although powerless to prevent Gelimer taking the throne by force, they were likely to surrender to Belisarius when the tides of war turned against them, or even decide to attack Gelimer themselves. Finally, it is probable that many of Gelimer's most powerful and loyal supporters, such as his brothers, had been killed in the two battles. His position was now extremely weak. Those nobles and warriors left in the camp who had the least loyalty to Gelimer knew that their rule in Africa was at an end. They had neither the troops nor the will to continue the fight. However, they would have a good chance of escaping with their lives if they offered to surrender Gelimer to Belisarius in return for their safety. Gelimer would have been aware of this. Even before the Byzantine attack, the recriminations would have begun.

Recognising that he could no longer trust the nobles or the army to remain loyal and fight for him, Gelimer decided to escape before he was either killed or handed over to the Byzantines. Although not the act of a Germanic hero, the decision to flee probably saved his life. By now Bonifatius and the Vandal treasures should have been safely on their way to Theudis in Spain. Gelimer decided to join them.

Turning to the Byzantines, it is unclear what role Belisarius played in the battle. Although Procopius has him 'advising' John, it would seem clear that John was in control. By deploying the guard in the centre, opposite the Vandals' veterans from Sardinia, John's strategy appears to have been to weaken the Vandal centre by luring them into crossing the stream and being attacked at a disadvantage. He could then break through the centre, before rolling up the enemy's line to right and left. The morale of the rest of the Vandal forces would be suspect after their capitulation at Ad Decimum and the lack of a defence at Carthage. They might easily fly if put under enough pressure. Whether the plan was John's or Belisarius', it worked.

What is usually overlooked at this point is Belisarius' order of march, and the fact that he again sent the cavalry ahead. This resulted in over half of his army being unavailable when the time came for battle. Although it can be argued that the victories are all the more noteworthy in that they were actually won by less than ten thousand men, such a situation is not the mark of a great commander. At both the Battle of Ad Decimum and the later Battle of Tricamerum, Belisarius failed to keep his forces united and so risked all with only a small portion of the available forces. It is fortunate for him that the Vandals had fewer men than is often claimed, and that at the vital moment the Vandal leaders gave the initiative to the Byzantines.

The End of Vandal Africa

In the meantime, John the Armenian had been giving chase to the Vandal king. Finally, after five days and nights, the Byzantines had finally closed the gap and were close enough to engage. It was not to be: in a bizarre accident, Uliaris, one of Belisarius' aides, shot John with an arrow whilst aiming at a bird. John was struck in the neck and died shortly after.

As he came up with the advance party, Belisarius found them mourning their leader. He joined the mourning, providing funds for the regular maintenance of John's grave. After an investigation, it was concluded that the incident was purely an accident and Uliaris was given a full pardon for his part in John's death.

Gelimer continued his flight to Hippo Regius (Bona), from where he travelled to an ancient Moorish city called Medeus. Situated on the slopes of Mount Papua, the natives were allied to Gelimer and prepared to face a long siege. Having established Gelimer's position, Belisarius set Pharas the Herul along with his 400 men to blockade the city. Pharas and his Heruls were praised by Procopius as exceptional – for Heruls – in the manner of their conduct both on and off the battlefield (Proc, *Wars*, IV.iv.29–31). Obviously Belisarius shared his high regard for Pharas. Belisarius himself now returned to the nearby city of Hippo Regius, maintaining his policy of pledging safety to all of the Vandals currently in sanctuary. They were returned to Carthage under guard.

It may be recalled that Gelimer had given orders to his secretary Bonifatius to place the royal treasury on board ship in Hippo Regius and, if he saw that the Vandals were losing, to set sail for Spain and the court of King Theudis. Gelimer expected to join Bonifatius later, and calculated that Theudis would give him sanctuary.

When Bonifatius became aware that all was lost, he set sail as instructed for Spain. Unfortunately, adverse winds drove him straight back to Hippo Regius, and he was trapped in the harbour by a storm. Realising that he could not escape, he sent men to a sanctuary in the city with instructions to tell Belisarius that Bonifatius had the treasure, but not to reveal the whereabouts until they had been given pledges for Bonifatius' safety. Belisarius quickly agreed and so captured the last of the Vandals' treasure. Bonifatius was allowed to go free, retaining his own wealth and, according to Procopius, stealing a large sum from the Vandal treasury as well (Proc, *Wars*, IV.iv.41).

It is possible that it was only at this late stage that word reached Gelimer that his overtures to Theudis had been rejected. With few men and no money, his brothers lost and now no hope of a powerful alliance to help him, the end was near for Gelimer.

After many weeks of besieging Gelimer, Pharas grew weary of his task and led his men in an assault upon the city. Due to the steep approach and the alertness of the defenders, he was beaten back, losing 110 of his men. The episode proved that Pharas could not take the city, but also finally established that Gelimer could not escape. Following an exchange of letters and with starvation looming, Gelimer agreed to surrender providing that Belisarius gave pledges for his safety. Elated, Belisarius sent Cyprian to give the guarantees to Gelimer. The last king of the Vandals accepted them and was escorted to Carthage. The Byzantines had landed in September 533; by March 534 the Vandalic War was at an end.

Unwilling to wait for Gelimer to make a decision, Belisarius had not been idle. With the Vandal kingdom all but conquered, he had begun to take control of and reorganise the provinces that they had ruled. He sent the general Cyril with a large force to take control of Sardinia. As the natives were terrified of the Vandals and would be suspicious of claims that the Vandals had been defeated, Cyril was given Tzazon's head to take as a token of proof that the Vandals were no longer a threat to the island. Once in control of the island, Cyril sent a portion of his army to Corsica and that, too, now returned to the control of the empire.

Belisarius also sent other leaders to claim distant outposts of the Vandal kingdom. John, one of his officers, was sent to Caesarea (Cherchel) in Mauretania with a detachment of the *comitatus*.

Another John, one of Belisarius' guardsmen, was sent to Gadira and the fort of Septem, close to the Pillars of Hercules (Straits of Gibraltar). Apollinarius was sent to reclaim the Balearic Islands for the empire. He was an Italian who had lived in Libya and served Hilderic. When Hilderic was overthrown by Gelimer, Apollinarius was one of the ambassadors who travelled to Constantinople to plead for help. He had joined the Byzantine expedition and proved himself to be a brave and loyal fighter, especially at Tricamerum. Furthermore, Belisarius now sent troops to aid Pudentius and Tattimuth. Following the rebellion, they had been attacked by the neighbouring Moors. With Byzantine help, the Moors were repulsed and order restored.

All of the Vandals that had been captured or who had surrendered following Belisarius' pledges for their safety were gathered together in Carthage. Belisarius now awaited the spring, when he could take them to Constantinople and the emperor.

Belisarius also sent envoys to the Goths concerning the status of Lilybaeum in Sicily. He claimed that although Sicily was under Gothic rule, as Lilybaeum had been owned by the Vandals it, too, was now a part of the empire. The Goths refused to allow this. Embassies now passed between Belisarius and Amalasuintha, before the Gothic regent suggested that the matter should be put before Justinian for arbitration. Before Justinian could decide the case, circumstances in Italy were to change drastically.

Antonina

Antonina had accompanied Belisarius on the campaign. There are many possible reasons for this. Amongst them are the often-aired theories that Belisarius did not trust Antonina and forced her to accompany him so that he could keep an eye on her, or that Antonina wanted to maintain her influence over Belisarius (see, for example, Norwich, 1988, p. 206 for the former; *PLRE* IIIA, 1992, *Antonina*, 1, p. 92 for the latter).

There is something amiss here; Antonina was a close friend and agent of the Empress Theodora. If she did not want to go to Africa, an appeal to the empress couched in the correct way would have enabled her to stay in Constantinople. There is little reason to suppose that Belisarius could force her to go against her will. On the other hand, if she wanted to maintain her influence, surely it would have been better to remain with the empress than attempt to maintain her hold over a general, no matter how powerful he was.

Fortunately, another reason presents itself. Since Procopius does not mention the marriage of Belisarius and Antonina, nor tell us the length of the courtship, we are left to assume that both took place in the brief period between Belisarius' return from the east and his departure for Africa. The speed of the marriage and Antonina's inability to maintain her fidelity suggests that romance may not have been high on the agenda. Yet there was a major political reason for the union. Although Justinian and Belisarius knew each other well, and Justinian felt that Belisarius was trustworthy, Theodora had no such relationship with or trust in Belisarius. Yet Theodora was the power behind the throne as shown in the Nika Revolt. Before sending Belisarius on such a risky venture, she devised a scheme to ensure that Belisarius remained loyal. The marriage was a political union which enabled Theodora to keep a close watch upon Belisarius: Antonina could easily have reported any threat of rebellion or other misdemeanour to the empress. This is the reason why the two married in such haste, and also explains why Antonina accompanied Belisarius on his campaigns. Furthermore, it also explains her inability to remain loyal to the general – since she had few, if any, personal feelings for him.

The above would certainly help to explain one event narrated by Procopius in the *Anekdota*. Shortly before leaving for Africa, Belisarius had adopted a son by the name of Theodosius. During the voyage to Africa and the campaigns of conquest, Antonina and Theodosius had begun an affair, once even being caught by Belisarius himself (*Anekdota*, 1.18). Despite Belisarius' fury, Antonina had, according to Procopius, been able to give a plausible excuse and so defuse the situation. However, the affair would continue throughout the campaign in Italy that would shortly follow.

Belisarius may have had genuine feelings for Antonina, and this would explain his fury at her being unfaithful. Furthermore, his anger would also be justified in that her actions would make one of Constantinople's great generals a laughing stock. But in failing to act he reinforced the idea that he was dominated by Antonina.

Yet Belisarius' failure to act may have had other causes, apart from a possible emotional attachment. Antonina served the empress and any aggressive behaviour, however justifiable, was likely to be punished by the empress, or at least lead to his recall and demotion. In this situation, Belisarius could not win, and the number of possible influences and the complexity of the scandal leaves us in confusion over the actual state of affairs.

Belisarius triumphant

Before leaving Africa, Belisarius continued his reorganization of the provinces that had been retaken. He also had to determine how the troops could be deployed as garrisons to ensure the safety of the newly-won provinces.

At around this time a plot was hatched amongst some of the officers to topple Belisarius from power and so improve their own chances of promotion. Accordingly, they dispatched two messengers to the emperor (in case one was waylaid), claiming that Belisarius was planning to rebel and set himself up as king of the Vandals in Africa.

Belisarius was lucky enough to capture one of the messengers and so discover the details of the plot. When the second messenger reached Constantinople, the emperor decided to test Belisarius' loyalty. He informed Belisarius that he had a choice: he could either send the captured Vandals to Constantinople and remain behind in Africa, or he could accompany the Vandals and report in person to the emperor. If Belisarius was planning a revolt, he would definitely choose to remain in Africa. In the *Anekdota*, Procopius has Justinian accusing Belisarius of attempted betrayal and recalling him to Constantinople to answer the charge (Proc, *Anekdota*, 18.9). This is an extremely harsh interpretation of events by Procopius, intended to discredit the emperor in the eyes of the reader. At no point was Belisarius actually accused of treachery by Justinian.

When the messengers from Justinian arrived, alongside his aforementioned message they delivered a piece of legislation sent by the emperor. Dated 13 April

534, it decreed the manner in which the newly-reclaimed provinces would be garrisoned by the empire. Whilst making preparations for his return journey to Constantinople, Belisarius simultaneously began to put the edict into effect.

These arrangements proved premature. Until now the Moors had remained quiescent, mainly due to their fear of Belisarius. Upon learning that he was returning to Constantinople, they rebelled. Belisarius knew that he could not stay in Africa to deal with the rebellion in person; any hesitation could be interpreted as an attempt at revolt, as suggested by the conspirators. Therefore, he placed most of his *bucellarii* under the command of Solomon and ordered him to quash the rebellion. Belisarius now set sail for Constantinople, taking with him Gelimer, a large number of captive Vandals and a huge amount of treasure.

Possibly arriving in the same ship as the messengers, Tryphon and Eustratius were sent by Justinian as tax assessors to Africa. During the Vandal occupation the registers used for tax had been lost and the two men were instructed to hold a census upon which new taxes could be based. In the best traditions of imperial policy these men claimed the best estates in the name of the emperor and judged that Arians should be excluded from their sacraments. In a very short time the population of Africa began to regret the reconquest. There was one further mistake. Justinian or his ministers did not dispatch the pay for the army. Payment of wages was now overdue.

Belisarius arrived in Constantinople and was given a hero's welcome. Justinian granted him a triumph for his exploits in recapturing Africa for the empire. However, the triumph did not follow the traditional practice, as was the norm in earlier centuries. Belisarius walked from his home in the city to the Hippodrome, followed by Gelimer and the other Vandal captives from the war, plus the vast amount of treasure he had secured. Once in the Hippodrome, Belisarius and Gelimer both made obeisance to the emperor as he sat in the imperial box.

As a further honour, Belisarius was made *consul ordinarius* for the year 535, allowing him to celebrate a second, consular, triumph, in which he was carried around the city by the Vandal warriors in a consul's *curule* chair, distributing spoils from the war amongst the population as he went. Belisarius had definitely made his name as a general. His reconquest of lost imperial provinces and the sheer speed with which he had accomplished this would have left the population of Constantinople in shock; it was less than a year since he had left on an expedition which many had thought would end in disaster. He had now returned victorious.

However, the Emperor had not finished with Belisarius. The situation in Italy had changed in the period between Belisarius' landing in Sicily en route to Africa and his triumphant return to Constantinople. The relations between the court at Ravenna and Constantinople had fast deteriorated.

Chapter 8

The Invasion of Sicily and Southern Italy

Events Prior to the War

In 526, the year before Justinian became emperor, Theoderic the Great had died. He had ruled Italy since 493 and established a network of alliances and contacts to secure himself in his position as 'Ruler of Italy'. However, even before his death relations had soured between Theoderic and Justin, Justinian's predecessor.

Theoderic had been succeeded by his grandson Athalaric, but as Athalaric was a minor, being only eight years old, the actual power lay in the hands of his mother Amalasuintha. Well educated and desirous of good relations with Constantinople, she immediately attempted to reverse the downward trend in relations. Furthermore, she attempted to have her son reared in the classical Roman manner.

Not all of the Goths were happy with this state of affairs, seeing no need to form a close relationship with the emperor in Constantinople and being extremely unhappy that their so-called king was being raised as a Roman. Very quickly an opposition formed, centred upon Athalaric himself. His tutors were dismissed and he quickly fell under the control of men who turned him to drink and an unhealthy lifestyle. Contrary to the laws and customs of Theoderic, many Goths now began to secure property from Romans by force. Theoderic had been a strong king who could enforce his will; Amalasuintha did not have the strength or standing to enforce her will and follow his example.

One man who did well out of the seizure of Roman property was Theodahad. He was the son of Theoderic's sister Amalafrida, born during her first marriage. After the death of Theodahad's father, Theoderic had married Amalafrida to the Vandal king, Thrasamund, to cement one of his many alliances. As a cousin of the current king, and being of a legal age to rule, Theodahad may have had a strong claim to the throne when Theoderic died. If any such claims were made, there are no surviving records of them. He had a reputation for greed and for taking property whenever the opportunity presented itself; he was not a popular figure.

Amalasuintha attempted to halt the appropriations of property and have them returned to their Roman owners, which alienated Theodahad. He now devised a scheme whereby he would hand all of his lands to the emperor in Constantinople in return for a large sum of money, the rank of senator, and permission to pass the remainder of his life in Constantinople. Unfortunately for him, before this could happen he was denounced for his behaviour within Tuscany, called before Amalasuintha and forced to make restitution. Theodahad would never forgive her.

As a result of the growth of opposition to her rule, and with a possible hostile, though unpopular, candidate for the throne in existence, Amalasuintha's position began to weaken. Furthermore, the Goths were under increasing pressure from the Franks, who at this time were busy conquering Thuringia and dismembering the Burgundian kingdom. The Goths failed to make any territorial gains whilst the Franks were accumulating power

Amalasuintha was not idle. She decided to eliminate three of the leaders of those plotting against her and sent assassins against them. She also made plans in case the assassins should fail. Accordingly, she asked Justinian if he would be willing to grant asylum to her. Upon his assent, she dispatched all of her treasures and belongings to Epidamnus, and waited for the ship to return. If the assassins succeeded, she would remain; if they failed, she would flee into exile. The assassins succeeded and Amalasuintha determined to stay and attempt to remain in power.

Although during the course of these internal upheavals Amalasuintha had agreed to allow the empire's forces to stop in Sicily on their way to Africa, she may have believed that the attempt would fail and that both the Vandals and the empire would be weakened by the struggle. It was not to be; the speedy collapse of the Vandal kingdom resulted in her being surrounded by powerful neighbours. The Franks were now at the borders to the north, and the empire controlled all other areas surrounding Italy. Gothic power was beginning to look a shadow of its former self and many Goths blamed Amalasuintha for the situation.

Then, in 534, Athalaric died of a wasting disease brought on by his epic bouts of drinking; he was sixteen years old. Amalasuintha could no longer maintain her position by acting as the regent of her son. Consequently, her hold upon power weakened even further. Furthermore, at this sensitive point she received an envoy from Justinian, demanding that Lilybaeum be handed to the empire. In desperation, she sent a letter asking Justinian to think again. She doubtless hoped that the emperor would be lenient and allow the Goths to keep the city, since its loss would further weaken her position at home. However, Justinian realised that he had an opportunity to assume control of more than simply a part of Italy. Accordingly, he sent one of his most trusted envoys to Ravenna.

Peter the Illyrian was a citizen of Thessalonica. Trained as an orator, he had a gentle manner, was extremely discreet, and was outstanding in the arts of persuasion. Justinian believed that Peter was the perfect envoy, and so he was sent to open negotiations with Theodahad regarding his holdings in Tuscany. At the same time, he was commanded to open secret discussions with Amalasuintha,

Close up of the mosaic in the basilica of San Vitale at Ravenna showing the Emperor Justinian and, to his right, Belisarius. This is the only representation we have of Belisarius. (*Photo © Adrian Fletcher, www.paradoxplace.com*)

The mosaic in the basilica of San Vitale at Ravenna showing the Empress Theodora. Given the proximity of Belisarius to Justinian in the corresponding mosaic, it is possible that one of the two figures which are closest to Theodora is Antonina. (*Photo © Adrian Fletcher, www.paradoxplace.com*)

3. A plate showing a hunting sc[ene] depicting Khusrow I. The king i[s] using a hunting bow and the ho[rse] is not wearing any armour. Although not a battle scene, the plate shows the harness and method of firing the bow used b[y] the Sasanids. (*Cabinet des Medailles e[t] Antiques, Paris*)

4. Coin of Khusrow I wearing winged crown with three crescents and Pahlavi script. (*Courtesy of Beastcoins.com*)

5. Relief from Taq-i-Bostan, probably of Khusrow II (590–628). Although slightly later than Belisarius, the lower scene illustrates the trend for lighter equipment, as the horse is wearing only frontal armour. The carving also demonstrates the Sasanid method of using the lance over-arm.

6 & 7. Two views of the ruins at Carthage. They display the splendour and architectural development of the buildings constructed during the Roman period before the city was captured by the Vandals in 439. It is likely that these buildings were still functional when Belisarius recaptured the city in 533. (*Courtesy of Anik Messier, Bishop's Stortford, England*)

8. Coin of the Vandal king, Gelimer. Unlike the coins of other Germanic settlers within the Empire, this coin does not carry any reference to the emperor at Constantinople, highlighting the Vandals' freedom from imperial dominance. (*Courtesy of Forum Classical Coins*)

9. Roman infantryman. For protection he is wearing a simple ridge helmet of Intercisa 1 type and a coat of ring mail. He also carries an oval shield, the pattern being that of the Reges, described by Procopius as guarding the Flaminian Gate during the siege of Rome and identified as the Regii listed in the Notitia Dignitatum. It should be noted that there is little difference between this man and the German Infantryman in Plate 13, especially as many Romans and Goths would have worn helmets of a similar or identical pattern. (© *Peter Inker*)

A standard Roman cavalryman. Equipped with a plain quiver and a reflex bow, he is wearing a ¦angenhelm with a nasal, showing steppe influence. Although here shown shieldless, many Roman ¦rse archers may have carried shields during the Belisarian Wars, although this is uncertain. For ¦otection he is wearing ring mail and he has splinted greaves on his legs. (© *Peter Inker*)

11. Sasanid infantryman. Based on descriptions of the Median infantry, these troops were highly respected and could be used to form the centre of the Persian battle line behind the *savaran*. Armed with a spear and a sword, he is protected by a Sasanid-style spangenhelm, a coat of ring mail and shield and is capable of facing Roman infantry in a prolonged battle. (© *Peter Inker*)

Sasanid *savaran* cavalry. This man is protected by body armour consisting of lamellar strips for the shoulders, abdomen and upper thighs over a full coat of ring mail covering the body, upper arms and thighs. However it should be noted that the use of this complex and expensive armour is declining, with simple ring mail coats becoming increasingly common. On his head he wears a variant of the traditional Sasanid spangenhelm and strapped to his left arm is a small circular shield, which aids in his protection whilst not hindering the firing of a bow. Offensively, he is armed with a bow, a sword and a lance. (© *Peter Inker*)

13. German infantryman. This man represents the Gothic combat infantry present in Italy during t
wars, as well as any remnants of foot troops still extant in Vandal Africa. He wears a spangenhelm
coat of ring mail and carries a large shield for protection. The protruding boss was a relic from the
period of the German invasions of the western empire and may have been slowly being replaced k
simpler, more rounded variants. However the chronology of these changes is insecure and the
Vandals may have clung to more traditional styles in order to maintain their identity in Africa. Th
Goths, having taken control of the Roman *fabricae* in Italy, may have changed to a more standard,
Roman-style boss (as seen in Plate 9) by the time of Belisarius' wars. (© *Peter Inker*)

Gothic and Vandal cavalry. This man is wearing a coat of ring mail, a plumed spangenhelm and
rying a large shield for protection. Offensively he carries a spear and a sword for use in close
mbat: missile weapons were relatively rare in the cavalry of both the Goths and the Vandals, and
y seemed to have relied on their prowess in close combat to win battles. (© *Peter Inker*)

15. Modern reconstruction of an Intercisa 1 helmet of the late empire. The central strip joining the two halves of the bowl is conspicuous, as is the eye-shaped motif above the brow. (*Courtesy of armamentaria.com*)

16. Modern reconstruction of a Roman ridge helmet. Again, the central strip joining the two halves of the bowl is evident, however, on th reconstruction more decoration is shown on t bowl. (*Courtesy of armamentaria.com*)

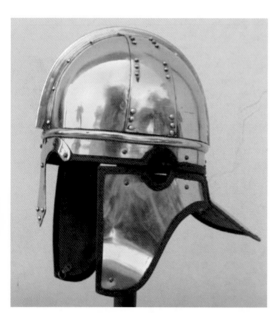

17. Modern reconstruction of the type of late Roman spangenhelm found at Burgh-on-Sands, England. Of a more complex design than the ridge helmets, the bowl is made in four parts, joined by a central strip and two iron *spangen* (from which the helmet gets its name). The nasal guard is evidence of the increasing influence of fashions from the nomadic races of the steppes. (*Courtesy of armamentaria.com*)

18. The remains of the helmet found at Interc and designated Intercisa 4. The high ridge pl is reminiscent of the plumes worn by troops earlier in the history of Europe and may be indicative of officer or guard status, although this remains theoretical. The pale sections indicate where reconstruction has taken place

19. This highly-decorated reconstruction of a spangenhelm is a reminder that, although only the iron core of these helmets remain in the archaeological record, the process of decoration (in this case gilding) may have resulted in a more spectacular appearance and suggests that the perceived uniformity of Roman troops is a modern misconception. (*Rheinischen Landesmuseums, Bonn*)

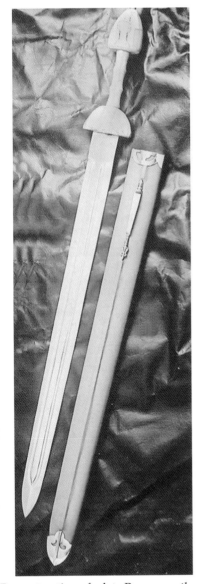

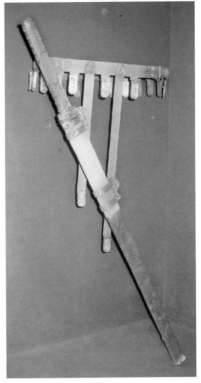

Reconstruction of a late Roman *spatha*. By time of Belisarius this style of weapon was nmon throughout Europe and was only wly being replaced by the styles in use on the pes in the east. (*Courtesy of armamentaria.com*)

21. A Sasanid sword and scabbard, probably dating to the seventh century. It is highly decorated, with the handle and other metal fittings being of gold. The distance from the scabbard to the belt is indicative that this was probably worn by a cavalryman, since the scabbard would otherwise have caught on the ground or low objects. (*Smithsonian Institute*)

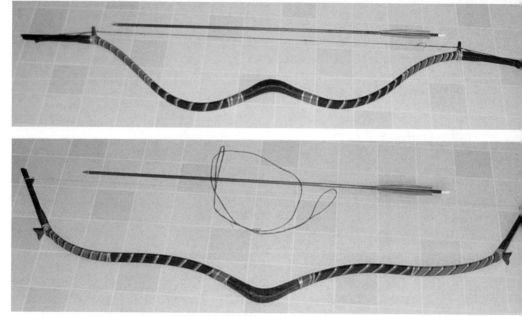

22 & 23. Modern reconstruction of an asymmetrical bow, strung and unstrung. Although seeming unwieldy to modern eyes, practice has shown that the asymmetrical bow may have other benefits than the ability to be fired more easily from a horse than a symmetrical bow, as when fired correc it demonstrates greater accuracy and power. (*Courtesy of spitfirehorsebows.com*)

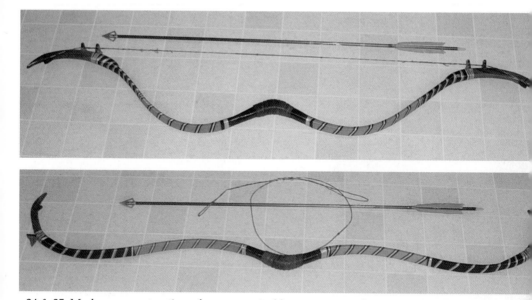

24 & 25. Modern reconstruction of a symmetrical bow, strung and unstrung. Whilst powerful, the were slightly more unwieldy when used on horseback and didn't have the 'sweet-spot' of the asymmetrical bow. (*Courtesy of spitfirehorsebows.com*)

The Milvian Bridge. When the Goths captured the bridge during the siege of Rome, they were ‿ to cross the Tiber and put the western walls of Rome under pressure. Without control of the ‿ge the walls to the west of the river would have been completely unthreatened. (*Courtesy of ‿.romeartlover.it*)

The Mausoleum of Hadrian. An integral part of the defences of Rome during the Gothic siege, statues that once lined the parapet were broken up by the defenders and used as missiles during Gothic assault. (*Courtesy of www.romeartlover.it*)

28. The Porta Pinciana (Pincian Gate). Under the personal control of Belisarius during the siege of Rome, it was used in a successful sortie against the Goths, and was also the scene of the penultimate attempt by Witigis to force entry into the city. (*Courtesy of www.romeartlover.it*)

29. The Porta Chiusa (Vivarium Gate) as drawn by Guiseppe Vasi in the eighteenth century. An attack on this section of the wall was defeated by Belisarius, Bessas and Peranius. The Goths were routed, suffering heavy casualties, and the siege engines in the vicinity burnt. (*Courtesy of www.romeartlover.it*)

The Porta Ostiensis (St Paul's Gate). The main gate leading towards the port of Ostia and the [sou]th, Procopius left via this gate when he was sent to Naples by Belisarius to gather supplies and [rei]nforcements for the beleaguered city. According to tradition it was rebuilt and refortified by [Bel]isarius during the later siege of Rome. (*Courtesy of www.romeartlover.it*)

The Porta Salaria (Salarian Gate) as drawn by Guiseppe Vasi. Under the personal control of [Bel]isarius during the siege of Rome, the gate was used for the first hit-and-run sortie against the [Go]ths. As the tactic was a success, it was later repeated many times during the siege. The gate was [dem]olished after being severely damaged by artillery fire in 1870. (*Courtesy of www.romeartlover.it*)

32. The Porta Flaminia (Flaminian Gate) as drawn by Guiseppe Vasi. As the Romans entered Rome by the Asinarian Gate, the Gothic garrison left by the Flaminian Gate. Initially the Flaminian Gate was under the control of Constantinus, then later of Ursicinus with the Reges. During the siege it was opposite the main Gothic camps and so under grave threat of attack, and as a result Belisarius ordered a wall built across the inside of the gate to ensure its safety. Later the wall was taken down prior to a sortie by the defending forces under Belisarius' personal command. (*Courtesy of www.romeartlover.it*)

33. Theoderic's palace as depicted in a mosaic in his palace chapel of San Apollinare Nuovo. Far from being the uneducated barbarians portrayed in popular culture, this building shows that the Goths acquired a more refined taste and were, by the time of Theoderic, the equals of the Romans in their appreciation of art, architecture and culture. (*Courtesy of the Yorck Project*)

the intention being to negotiate a deal wherein Amalasuintha would, like Theodahad, receive a welcome and estates in the east. In return, given her weakening position in Italy, she would hopefully agree to deliver the whole of Italy to the emperor. The envoys contacted Theodahad concerning his plans to give his lands in Tuscany to the emperor. They found him to be inclined to fulfil the agreement. Therefore they now returned to Constantinople, ready to complete the exchange with the emperor.

Unfortunately, circumstances were to change the situation in Italy beyond all recognition. Amalasuintha, in a bid to maintain her position, chose to associate herself with Theodahad, who after the death of Athalaric was the only heir to the throne. She tried to persuade him to accept the throne, but be bound by solemn oaths to allow her to remain the political power in Ravenna. It was to be a massive mistake. After taking the necessary oaths, Theodahad immediately had Amalasuintha imprisoned and assumed personal control of Italy.

When Peter reached Theodahad he learned of Amalasuintha's deposition and imprisonment. With such a drastic change of circumstances, Peter halted and waited for instructions from Justinian. The emperor decided to give his full support to Amalasuintha, in the knowledge that this would create immense internal political problems for the Goths, hopefully leading to divisions and strife throughout Italy. The message would be futile. Whilst the envoys waited and the message was composed, Amalasuintha was killed upon the advice of a handful of leading Goths; Theodahad does not appear to have resisted their demands to any great extent. When Amalasuintha was killed, Peter in effect declared war: 'because this base deed had been committed by them, there would be war without truce between the emperor and themselves' (Proc, *Wars*, V.iv.30).

Africa and Italy

The similarities between the events in Africa prior to the invasion and those in Italy are striking. In Africa a relative of the ruler had usurped the throne and given Justinian an excellent pretext for invasion: Theodahad had now done the same. The seizure of the throne had caused political divisions and so weakened the Vandals' will to fight: the same could now be true in Italy.

There was one major difference: when Justinian had decided to invade Africa, he had freed troops by the use of diplomatic manoeuvrings to gain peace with Persia. The peace had also released a general who could be trusted to lead the expedition. For the invasion of Italy, the general in question was already free, having perfectly timed matters by recently defeating the Vandals, and there were no other wars to distract Justinian from his intentions. Belisarius would lead the expedition to Italy.

It is unlikely that Justinian in Constantinople had a hand in the events occurring in Italy. In Africa, he had been in contact with rebels in order to time their revolt with his invasion. It is possible that his agents now made moves to contact district leaders in Italy, but there was little likelihood of a well-timed rebellion in this instance. The invasion of Italy, if it occurred, would be a very different event to the invasion of Africa.

Justinian was not prepared to fight the war alone if he could obtain help from other quarters. Accordingly, he sent a message to the Franks. In this, he explained his reasons for declaring war. The recent behaviour of the Gothic nobles towards their leader Amalasuintha was a major theme in the letter, but the fact that Italy – and especially Rome – was the ancient core of the Roman Empire was also given as a reason for invasion. The 'Romans' were only reclaiming what was rightfully theirs. The fact that the Franks were in competition with the Goths in northern Italy further enabled Justinian to invite the Franks to take part in the invasion, suggesting that they attack in the north and so split the Gothic armies. To that end, Justinian sent a large sum of money as encouragement, promising more when the Franks actually became active in the field. He could now only wait to see if the Franks took the bait.

The war did not, however, begin with either Belisarius landing with his troops in Italy or a Frankish invasion from the north. The first conflict occurred in Dalmatia (see Map 9). In 536 Gripas and Asinarius led a Gothic army into Dalmatia with the task of capturing Salona. Near the city they defeated and killed the Byzantine general Mauricius. Although they were in turn defeated by Mauricius' father, Mundus, and forced to withdraw, Mundus also died in the battle. Mundus' reputation as a general had kept the barbarians north of the Danube in check, and helped to restrict their raids. With his death, the Balkans were again open to invasion and this was to prove a thorn in Justinian's side in the coming years.

Sicily

For the proposed campaign, Belisarius was given fewer troops than for the African campaign. First among the troops listed by Procopius (*Wars*, V.v. 2–5) are 'four thousand soldiers from the regular troops and the *foederati*'. Unfortunately, the wording does not make it clear whether the *foederati* were included in the 4,000 or were additional to it. The cavalry were led by Valentinus, Magnus and Innocentius; the infantry by Herodian, Paulus, Demetrius and Ursicinus. Above these and serving directly under Belisarius were Constantinus, Bessas and Peranias. Belisarius was further allocated 3,000 Isaurians under Ennes, along with 300 Moors and 200 Huns. Finally, he was accompanied by the traditional *comitatus* of *bucellarii*, Procopius later stating that he had 7,000 *bucellarii* (Proc, *Wars*, VII.i.20). Belisarius was again given sole command of the expedition, retained his rank as *magister militum per Orientem*, and was accompanied by his step-son Photius, the son of Antonina by a previous marriage.

Although Procopius does not give us a breakdown of the troops, it is possible to estimate the proportions using the information given in Chapter 3. If we assume that the commanders listed as being in charge of the infantry and cavalry commanded separate units, the divisions may have been as follows: the cavalry consisted of two units, each of some 300 men, alongside approximately 600 *foederati*, led by Valentinus, Magnus and Innocentius; the infantry consisted of four units of around 700 men each, led by Herodian, Paulus, Demetrius and Ursicinus. Although these numbers are clearly estimates, and may not be correct, they do give us a basis from which to understand Belisarius' strategy and tactics.

With fewer troops than those given for the invasion of Africa, Belisarius was ordered to land in Sicily. However, Justinian was not prepared to fight a long war for the island. His instructions were to land in Sicily whilst declaring that he was heading for Carthage. Once on the island, he was to test the mood of the islanders. If they were loyal to the Goths, he was to sail on; if they were prone to accept imperial rule, he was to attempt to take the island. The reasons behind the strategy are simple: there were not enough troops available at such short notice to enable a full-scale campaign against the Goths of the sort that had been mounted against the Vandals.

It is probable that during his stopover in Sicily on the way to Africa, Belisarius had noticed that there were extremely few Gothic troops stationed on the island. Therefore, Belisarius was given what was available and ordered to test the islanders' loyalty whilst they were unguarded and before the Goths could send large-scale reinforcements. The strategy was a risk, but only a small one. At the first sign of resistance, Belisarius could sail on to Africa without appearing to have suffered a defeat.

Although not mentioned by Procopius, it is likely that Belisarius, prior to the landing, had given orders to the troops regarding their behaviour towards the natives in Sicily. At all times the Sicilians were to be treated with respect, ensuring their support for the invasion, as had happened in Africa. Belisarius landed in Sicily close to the town of Catana. The town immediately surrendered to him, a capitulation that was mirrored by all of the other towns and cities on the island except for Panormus. This is the only town mentioned by Procopius as having a Gothic garrison prior to their surrender. If the towns were undefended, their surrender is understandable.

At Panormus, the Gothic garrison refused to surrender, since the walls appear to have been maintained and they believed that Belisarius did not have the forces to take the city by storm, a belief which Belisarius shared (Proc, *Wars*, V.v.12–13). However, Belisarius had observed that the city walls did not surround the harbour. He therefore ordered his ships to sail into the harbour, where there was only a comparatively low wall. Once inside the harbour, it was realised that the masts of the ships were taller than the walls. Belisarius ordered small boats to be hoisted up to the height of the masts. When the boats were loaded with archers, they overlooked the city and the archers were able to fire down upon the defenders on the walls. Filled with fear at this development, the Goths quickly surrendered.

Within a very short space of time and with few, if any, losses, Belisarius had reconquered Sicily for the empire, his abilities as a general quickly overcoming the defences of the only town that had not immediately surrendered.

By coincidence, his arrival at Syracuse coincided with the end of his year serving as *consul ordinarius*. He entered the city amidst the applause of the army and citizens whilst distributing gold coins at random to the people and the troops. He remained at Syracuse for the winter, billeting the troops upon the population as was customary. As in Africa, there is no mention of troops behaving in an improper manner towards the natives of the island. Sicilian support for the invasion was assured.

Developments in Italy

When news of the reconquest of Sicily reached Theodahad and Justinian's envoy, Peter the Illyrian, Peter immediately began to increase the pressure on Theodahad. In the ensuing negotiations Theodahad was urged to accept the loss of Sicily, send a large gold crown to the emperor (with obvious implications) and agree to send 3,000 Gothic troops to aid the emperor whenever he demanded them. In effect, Peter was attempting to persuade Theodahad to acknowledge the supremacy of the emperor in Constantinople. Theodahad did not have the strength of character necessary to resist these pressures and shortly afterwards, and in fear of open war, he agreed to abdicate in favour of Justinian.

When the news reached Justinian he took immediate action. Peter and a fellow envoy by the name of Athanasius were instructed to reach a formal agreement, giving Theodahad the royal estates known as the *patrimonium* in return for a signature granting Italy to Justinian. Once they had the agreement in writing, the envoys were to send a message to Belisarius in Sicily requesting his presence in Italy. Accordingly, Justinian sent a message to Belisarius ordering him to prepare his troops and be ready to march to Ravenna at top speed upon receiving word from the envoys.

Developments in Africa

As was seen earlier, when Belisarius chose to return to Constantinople, the Moors had rebelled against imperial rule. Belisarius had left Solomon to put down the revolt and given him the greatest part of his *comitatus* to help deal with the situation. Upon hearing of the news of the rebellion, Justinian dispatched reinforcements under the command of Theodorus the Cappadocian

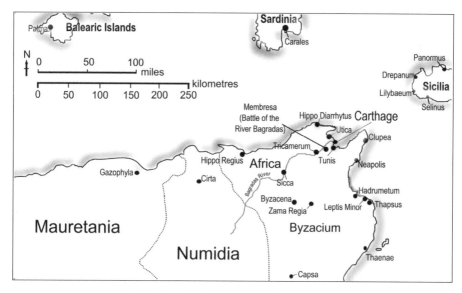

Map 8: The African mutiny (known sites).

and Ildiger, the son-in-law of Antonina, wife of Belisarius. These troops were desperately needed elsewhere, not least with Belisarius in Sicily, but Justinian could not afford the damage to his prestige of the loss of a province that had only recently been retaken.

The Moors were ravaging areas of Numidia and Byzacium, killing isolated troops as they went. Aigan, the leader of the Huns, and Rufinus the Thracian, the army's standard bearer, together with their detachments of cavalry, ambushed and destroyed some marauding Moors, but were in turn ambushed and killed. Morale in the Byzantine ranks fell.

Solomon now led the army against the largest group of Moors, marched to Mammes on the borders of Mauretania and very near to some mountains, built a stockaded camp opposite the Moors and prepared for battle. In preparation for the battle, the Moors adopted a tactic that had worked well against the Vandals. They formed a circle of camels around themselves that was twelve ranks deep. The women and children were placed in the centre, and most of the men were deployed on foot amongst the camels. They were armed with shields, swords, and javelins. The remainder of the men remained on horseback but deployed in hiding in the nearby foothills.

Solomon, realising that the Moors would have troops hidden towards the mountains, concentrated his forces upon the side of the circle facing away from the mountains, in order to avoid being attacked from his rear. Both he and his men were wary following the defeat of Aigan and Rufinus the Thracian. When the battle began the Moorish tactics seemed to be working: the Byzantine horses were frightened by the camels and panicked, resulting in the archers being unable to aim their bows. Sallying from their positions within the line of camels, the Moors began to cause casualties amongst the Byzantine cavalry.

Comprehending the danger, Solomon dismounted and ordered the troops to do likewise. With the majority of the troops protecting themselves with their shields, Solomon led 500 men around the circle of camels and attacked from the side nearest the mountains. Although this risked being attacked from the rear, he counted upon the defence here being weaker and his attack being able to make rapid headway. His assessment was correct. The few Moors stationed there quickly fled at his approach and the Byzantines killed around 200 camels. The rest of the army now moved around and entered through the gap that had been created. The Moors abandoned the defence and ran. The women and children caught in the middle of the camels were enslaved, the men were cut down as they ran. Procopius gives the figure of 10,000 Moors killed (Proc, *Wars*, IV.xi.55–6). Along with the slaves, camels and booty, the Byzantines now returned to Carthage.

Solomon now turned his attention to the Moors plundering Byzacium. As he advanced, the Moors retreated, taking refuge upon Mount Bourgaon, which had a gentle slope to the west and a very steep face on the east. It was a perfect place for defence.

After inspecting the site, Solomon ordered Theodorus, the *comes excubitorum*, to take 1,000 men and secretly scale the mountain from the east. At dawn, Solomon advanced the army to the foot of the mountain and waited. The Moors awoke to a Byzantine army below them and a large Byzantine force above them. Theodorus attacked from the top, Solomon from the bottom of the mountain. The Moors instantly broke and fled, allegedly losing 50,000 men in the pursuit whilst the Byzantines did not lose even a single man wounded. Victorious, Solomon again returned to Carthage.

With the year getting late, and the Moors plundering Numidia in small bands, Solomon established garrisons to help restrict Moorish attacks and waited for the passing of winter. Furthermore, at the same time news reached him of a rebellion in Sardinia. He also began to prepare the fleet for a campaign to the island in spring.

The campaigns did not materialise; when spring arrived, the Byzantine troops in Africa mutinied.

The African Mutiny

The reasons behind the mutiny are easy to understand. After the collapse of Vandal Africa, the Byzantine troops had captured most of the Vandal women and children. Shortly afterwards, many of the men had married the wives and daughters of the Vandals that had either been killed or transported to Constantinople. They now expected to inherit the land previously owned by the husbands or fathers of their new wives.

The marriages and expectations of the troops give us one clear insight into the policies of Justinian regarding the nature of the army sent to Africa. They clearly expected to remain in Africa as the garrison, and were quickly establishing themselves within the existing framework. With the arrival of Tryphon and Eustratius as tax assessors the situation changed. Along with their task of carrying out a census for taxation purposes, they also suggested that these lands should revert to the control of the emperor. Solomon agreed to this and when approached by the troops with their claim he refused to support them.

Furthermore, again following the arrival of Tryphon and Eustratius, Arian worship had been stopped and only Catholicism was now allowed. This was at odds with the needs of a large section of the Byzantine army, such as the Heruls, who were themselves Arians. As an additional blow, Justinian also forbade the baptism of any Arians. Understandably, the Arian troops were now extremely unhappy and were prepared to listen to Vandal bishops, who began to urge them to mutiny. To make matters worse, the entire army was very unhappy as they still had not been paid for their services in Africa. Although blame for this is hard to apportion, this bureaucratic mistake alienated a much larger proportion of the army.

Finally, the Vandal men who had been taken to Constantinople had been organised into five cavalry units and shipped to the eastern front. The majority ended up fighting against the Persians, but about 400 managed to overpower the sailors and had forced them to sail the ships back to Africa, where the Vandals now landed.

All of the above factors helped to provoke the troops to the mutiny that began at Easter. When the Arians in the army were barred from taking part in the religious rites surrounding the festival, they decided to act. The mutineers determined to kill Solomon on the first day of the feast, but when faced with the actual deed could not bring themselves to do it. On the second day the conspirators also failed to act. Realising that they could not kill him, possibly due to their respect for him as a general, they understood that every day that they failed to act increased their danger of discovery. Therefore, the majority of the mutineers left the city and began to plunder the countryside. The remainder stayed in the city and hid their thoughts.

Solomon attempted to keep the troops in the city loyal, but when the men saw that the mutineers outside the city were going unpunished and unrestrained, they gathered in the hippodrome and the revolt grew. Solomon sent Theodorus the Cappadocian to restrain them, but he was hostile towards Solomon and the mutineers now elected him as their leader. Taking full control, the mutineers ran amok in the city.

Realising that they were in danger, Solomon, Martinus and Procopius – who had not returned to Constantinople with Belisarius – took sanctuary in the palace. Entering the house of Theodorus after dark, they were captured and forced to dine with him. Theodorus appears to have convinced them that he was a pawn in the hand of the mutineers. After the meal, they were placed on board a ship and left the city. Solomon now sent a letter to Theodorus, commanding him to take control of the situation in Carthage at the soonest opportunity, so validating his actions. He then sent Martinus to Numidia with orders to join Valerian, the commander in the area, and attempt to regain the troops' loyalty with promises and bribes. Solomon himself now set sail for Syracuse, along with Procopius, to seek help from Belisarius.

Belisarius' return to Africa

Accepting that Theodorus was still going to follow Solomon's orders, and anyway had only been elected by the troops in the city, the mutineers outside the city had gathered on the plain of Boulla and elected Stotzas, one of Martinus' guards, as leader. Their purpose was to drive the remainder of the loyal troops out of Africa and take the country for themselves.

Stotzas armed all of the available men, a force of roughly 8,000 soldiers, ready to march on Carthage. He assumed that Carthage would easily fall to his attack. He further sent messages to the Vandals who had escaped in the Byzantine ships and returned to Africa, and also summoned those Vandals who had avoided capture after Belisarius' victories and had not yet been caught. When these were all gathered, they mustered an extra 1,000 men to fight for Stotzas. Finally, he was joined by a large number of slaves, which would have significantly added to the number of men he commanded.

Arriving at Carthage, he sent messengers to the city, ordering them to surrender. Both the people and Theodorus refused the demand, and announced that they were guarding the city for the emperor. They also sent Joseph, one of the household of Belisarius, to demand that Stotzas halt his attacks. Joseph was killed and the city besieged.

It was at dusk, the besiegers were in their camp and expecting the city to fall on the following day, when Belisarius arrived in the city with 100 men from his *comitatus*. On the following morning when they learned of his arrival, Stotzas and his troops packed their camps and quickly retired into the interior.

Belisarius gathered 2,000 of the loyal troops in the city, gave them promises and money, then set off in pursuit. He overtook the mutineers at the city of Membresa, 350 *stades* (around 40 miles) from Carthage. Both armies made camp outside the city, since it had no walls and was indefensible. On the following day there was fought the Battle of the River Bagradas.

Before the battle started, a high wind arose, blowing from Belisarius' lines into the faces of the mutineers. Since the wind would hinder their own missiles, whilst greatly helping those of Belisarius and his men, the mutineers decided to march to the flank, so turning the battlefield by ninety degrees and allowing the wind to blow lengthways between the armies. Belisarius, seeing that the enemy were moving across his front in disorder, immediately seized his opportunity; he gave the order to attack. Faced with being charged whilst unformed and from the flank, the rebels fled. Procopius claims that their flight was so precipitous that few of them were actually killed, and of those that were slain, most were Vandals (Proc, *Wars*, IV, xv. 40–46). As he had only 2,000 men, Belisarius did not pursue the enemy, instead allowing the troops to plunder the enemy camp. There the troops found a lot of money and the very women who were in part responsible for the mutiny in the first place.

The defeat was a catastrophe for the rebels, brought about by their having no clear leader with a clear objective. A competent general would either have compensated for the wind direction or kept a force in reserve to cover the main body of troops as they attempted to change their position. The lack of an effective general cost the mutineers the battle.

On the other hand, the battle shows the value of Belisarius as a general. He was lucky in that the enemy decided that they could not remain with the wind in their faces and so decided to attempt to change the axis of the battle. Yet there is more to his victory than good fortune. It needed good observation, quick reactions, and decisiveness when, seeing the enemy unformed and weakened by their manoeuvres, he ordered the assault. Any delay might have allowed the mutineers to reform and overpower his men by sheer weight of numbers. It was a stroke of genius by Belisarius.

Belisarius now returned to Carthage. Once back in the city, a messenger arrived, claiming that mutiny had broken out in Sicily and that his return was urgently required. Leaving Carthage in the hands of Ildiger and Theodorus, Belisarius returned to Sicily.

Stotzas retired to Gazophyla (Ksantina) in Numidia. Learning of his presence, and attempting to gain a victory before all of the mutineers could assemble, Marcellus, the newly-appointed dux, led his army against the mutineers. In his forces were the *foederati*, led by Cyril (the same who had overseen the conquest of Sardinia and Corsica), cavalry under Barbatus, and infantry under Terentius and Sarapis.

Once the two armies had camped near to each other, Stotzas entered the Byzantine camp alone and repeated the claims of the mutineers, asking that the army should join him rather than fight him. When it was clear that the troops were going to join Stotzas, the commanders took refuge in a sanctuary in Gazophyla. Finding them, Stotzas made pledges for their safety, but when they emerged he had them all killed.

When Justinian learned of this, he sent his nephew, Germanus, to take control of the province and bring the mutineers to justice. Using a combination of promises and bribes, as well as bringing the troops' pay, Germanus slowly restored the situation, regaining the loyalty of the majority of the troops. Stotzas marched on Carthage, hoping that his presence would tempt the troops to rebel again. When this failed, he retired, his army being caught at Scalae Veteres and defeated. Stotzas sought sanctuary in Mauretania, marrying a daughter of one of the chiefs and settling down. Germanus was recalled to Constantinople and Africa was left under the control of Solomon.

With Germanus in charge in Africa and the mutiny slowly being suppressed, Belisarius was now free to deal with events in Italy. He waited for word from the envoys surrounding Theodahad, knowing that the conflicts in Africa and Dalmatia meant there would be little in the way of reinforcements available to him.

The Start of the Gothic War

Theodahad was waiting for news from the emperor when he learned of the Gothic defeat in Dalmatia, coupled with the death of the Byzantine generals Mauricius and Mundus. Immediately regaining his courage and reversing his policy, he refused to sign the agreement handing Italy to the emperor and instead placed the envoys under guard.

When news came to Justinian of the victory in Dalmatia, the death of Mauricius and the imprisonment of the envoys, he sent Constantinianus into Illyricum to defend Salona. At the same time, Belisarius was ordered to invade mainland Italy.

As Constantinianus gathered his army, Gripas again led a Gothic force intent on capturing Salona. This time, he succeeded. However, when his spies reported the approach of the army led by Constantinianus, emphasising its great size, he abandoned the city – as the walls were in a poor state of repair – and withdrew to the nearby plains. Constantinianus learned of the retreat of the Goths and immediately advanced to take the city. Once inside, he began to make repairs to the walls. Recognising the futility of his position, Gripas returned to Ravenna, Constantinianus proceeding to gain control of Dalmatia and Liburnia, and the allegiance of the remaining Gothic inhabitants.

The Invasion of Italy

Upon receiving the orders to invade Italy, Belisarius acted. Leaving garrisons in Panormus and Syracuse, he sailed across the narrow strait to Rhegium. Facing him was Ebrimuth, who was married to Theodahad's daughter, Theodenanthe. Ebrimuth had been sent by Theodahad to guard the Straits of Messina when Belisarius had captured Sicily. In a surprise move, Ebrimuth and all his followers now surrendered to Belisarius. He was immediately sent to Constantinople, where he was given gifts and rewarded with the title of *patricius*. It is interesting to note that Gelimer had also been offered the rank of *patricius*, but this was only open to Catholics and Gelimer had refused to renounce his Arian faith. Ebrimuth obviously had no such religious conviction.

Map 9: Italy and Illyricum

Belisarius advanced further into southern Italy. Due to the defection of Ebrimuth, the area was now without Gothic defenders. The towns in the south of Italy, unused to war, also had no walls and therefore could not resist his advance. They soon surrendered. Belisarius quickly moved through Bruttium, Lucania and Campania until he reached the city of Naples.

Naples was excellently sited for defence and possessed walls that were in good repair. Moreover, it also had a Gothic garrison. Belisarius ordered his ships to enter the harbour, but to remain out of range of artillery sited on the walls. A fort in the suburbs of the city surrendered to him and he then requested the presence of envoys from the city.

Three of the envoys are named by Procopius. Stephanus appears to have been in favour of surrender to the Byzantines, especially when Belisarius promised him a large reward if he could convince the Neapolitans to surrender without a fight. Pastor and Asclepiodotus were friendly with the Goths and argued that the city should remain loyal to Theodahad.

Following the advice of Pastor and Asclepiodotus, the citizens sent a large list of demands to Belisarius. Only after he had agreed to them would the city surrender. No doubt the Gothic sympathisers believed that he would never agree to them When Belisarius agreed to all of the points, the citizens were about to accede to his requests when Pastor and Asclepiodotus reminded them of what would be in store for the city if they surrendered to the Byzantines but the Goths were ultimately victorious. The citizens refused to surrender and the siege began.

During the course of the siege Belisarius lost many men in fruitless and costly assaults, and, although he cut the aqueduct leading into the city, the inhabitants were able to survive on water from wells in the city. They also succeeded in sending a message to Theodahad asking for aid.

Part of Belisarius' strategy had been to take Rome before winter set in, and as the siege extended he began to make plans to lift the siege and advance on the ancient imperial capital. At this point he had a stroke of luck; an Isaurian had wanted to look at the workmanship of the ancients, and so had wandered in to the now-dry aqueduct. He quickly realised that, with a little work, a section of the aqueduct that was almost blocked by natural rock could be widened and so permit entry to the city. Belisarius sent workmen to complete the task, and, when the preparations had been made, he gave the Neapolitans one last chance to surrender before their city was put to the sack. Stephanus carried his message but the citizens refused to believe him.

Accordingly, Belisarius sent 400 men through the aqueduct, led by Ennes the Isaurian leader and Magnus, accompanied by 2 trumpeters and a large quantity of torches. In the dark, 200 of these men lost their nerve and returned with Magnus to Belisarius. Belisarius chose 200 replacements, and, gathering their courage, the 200 who had fled also returned to the aqueduct. The 600 men now made their way in to Naples.

In order to distract the guards from any noise the troops in the aqueduct might make, Belisarius had Bessas converse with those nearest the aqueduct in Gothic, urging them to yield and gain large rewards. Amidst the jeers of the guards, the 600 men advanced unnoticed into the city. After three quarters of the night had passed, the invasion party finally emerged from the aqueduct. They seized two towers in the northern wall, opposite Belisarius, blowing their trumpets and lighting the torches. Belisarius ordered an immediate assault, with attacks on all sides of the walls in order to pin down the defenders and to stop them sending reinforcements to the north wall. Finally, the gates were opened and the city was sacked, the women and children being taken as slaves and the soldiers acquiring vast amounts of booty.

After the initial frenzy, Belisarius was able to gradually restore order. He commanded that the women and children be returned to their families in order to cultivate the good will of the citizens. However, the booty was declared the prize of war and the soldiers were allowed to keep it as a punishment to the citizens for failing to surrender. Due to the stress of the siege, the Neapolitan envoy Pastor died of natural causes, but Asclepiodotus was killed by the citizens for giving advice that allowed the city to be sacked.

The Death of Theodahad

Hearing of the circumstances surrounding the loss of Naples, the Goths turned against Theodahad, since he had done nothing to send aid to the city. Meeting near Tarracina, they elected Witigis as leader of the Goths. Theodahad fled towards Ravenna, but a Goth named Optaris was sent by Witigis to bring him back dead or alive. Optaris decided upon the former. He caught up with Theodahad before he could reach Ravenna and killed him. The Goths now had a new, energetic leader. They prepared for war.

Chapter 9

The Siege of Rome

The Gothic Army

Numbers

The number of troops available to the Gothic kings is debatable. Procopius claims that during the siege of Rome Witigis led 150,000 men to assault the city (Proc, *Wars*, V.xvi.11). This is an extremely large number of men for the Goths in Italy to have available. The suspicion that it is an exaggeration is inadvertently supported by Procopius himself when he states that even with 150,000 men the Goths did not have enough troops to completely besiege the city; out of fourteen large gates, they only had enough troops to put pressure on five gates (Proc, *Wars*, V.xix.2–3). With 150,000 men, they should have been able to enclose the whole city wall, which is less than 15 miles long, with an average of 10,000 men per mile.

Since Procopius' figures have been found to be unreliable, we must turn to conjecture. Roy Boss, in *Justinian's Wars* (1993), states that the highest figure likely for the Gothic army would be 40,000 men, but that this would shrink due to the poorer members of the Goths losing their 'Gothic' status and becoming assimilated with the native Italians. He also notes that the number of troops available for field actions would be further diminished by the need to maintain garrisons at strategic points around Italy.

It is probable that Boss's estimates are near to the reality. First, his figures make sense when we are told that Witigis left a garrison of 4,000 men under Leuderis in Rome (Proc, *Wars*, V.xi.) 26). This would be a reasonable number of troops to defend Rome given the size of the city and its significance both morally and strategically. It is also a significant proportion (approximately 10%) of the overall available forces that he was forced to leave behind. Any less and the city would be indefensible, any more and his own forces would have been seriously weakened. Furthermore, despite Belisarius having invaded with only around 15,000 men, he had no difficulty in establishing control of Sicily and Southern Italy. After Belisarius had left garrisons in the south, Witigis was to realise that Belisarius had only a small force in Rome and hurried to attack him whilst he was heavily outnumbered.

It is possible to suggest, therefore, that following the desertions in the South and in Samnium, Witigis had at the most 20 – 25,000 men available for the siege. This would explain why he could not surround the whole city but only force Belisarius to defend the northern section. It would also allow for Witigis to send detachments to other areas, as will be shown, whilst still maintaining a heavy numerical superiority. However, if we increase the number of men available to a higher level, neither the strategy nor the tactics of either Belisarius or Witigis make sense – mainly due to Belisarius being heavily outnumbered and so taking unconscionable risks. Given his cautious nature, it is unlikely that Belisarius would take such risks regularly in the way that would have been required.

Organisation

The organisation of the Gothic army is unknown, but, given the evidence from the other Germanic nations in the west, it is also likely to have been based upon the decimal system. Therefore, the Goths may also have had their equivalent of a Vandalic *thusundifath* in charge of roughly 300 fighting men, with 100 men led by a 'centurion', and 10 men led by a 'decurion'. As is usual, the figures are conjectural but do align themselves with the practice of both the other Germanic nations and those of the reorganising Byzantines.

Equipment

Unfortunately, there is little evidence for the manner in which the Goths armed themselves, and what there is remains open to interpretation. Accordingly, three different views as to the arming of the Gothic cavalry still exist.

One of these is that held by E A Thompson. In his book, *Early Germanic Warfare* (1982), he claims that the Goths remained armed much as they had in the years before their entry into the Roman Empire. Therefore, they continued to be lightly-armoured horsemen, armed with spear and javelin. He proposes that there had been little change over the previous 2–300 years, but he allows that their entry into the Roman sphere may have allowed them to equip more men as cavalry and to rearm many of their infantry as foot archers.

Unfortunately, much of his argument revolves around the fact that there are few mentions of Goths wearing armour in the sources, it being restricted to named individuals in specific deeds. However, as Boss has noted (*Justinian's Wars*, 1993), the same methodology results in the Romans and Persians being, on the whole, unarmoured, since many of the references to these armies also only state that individuals 'wear armour'. Yet it cannot be deduced from this that the Roman and Persian rank and file went into battle without body armour.

There is a further factor to take into account. When they came into possession of Italy, the Goths inherited some of the *fabricae* listed in the *Notitia Dignitatum*, namely: the *fabrica* at Concordia for making arrows; the one at Verona for making shields and weapons; the one at Mantua for making armour;

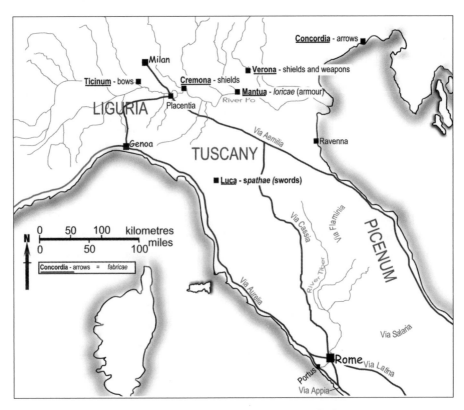

Map 10: Imperial fabricae *under the Goths.*

the one at Cremona for making shields; the one at Ticinum for making bows; and the one at Luca for making swords. It is almost certain that the Goths maintained these *fabricae* and arsenals for their own use, with a consequent upgrade in the number of troops having access to the types of armour pre-viously restricted to the nobility and their immediate followers.

The second theory is outlined by Herwig Wolfram in his book *History of the Goths* (1990). Here, he claims that the Goths' proximity to the Sarmatians earlier in their history led to their adoption of Sarmatian tactics and equipment.

Illustration 13: A traditional Germanic warrior from the Hornhausen Stone.

This 'sarmaticising' influence resulted in the Goths using a *kontos* (a heavy lance) two-handed to charge at the enemy rather than using javelins for skirmishing activities.

Supporting evidence can be found in Procopius, where he states that the Goths in Roman service against the Sasanids terrified the Persians 'with long spears in close array' (Procopius, *Wars*, II.xviii.24). Although possibly suggesting that the Goths were armed with a lance, the episode concerns the Goths arriving to support a group of fleeing troops. Further, the wording follows classical historical patterns,

Illustration 14: Horseman from the sixth-century Isola Rizza dish in the Castelvecchio Museum, Verona.

and may simply be a way of emphasising the cohesion and formation of the Goths as opposed to the disorganisation and lack of formation of the pursuing Persians. It should not, therefore, be used as evidence unsupported.

There is a further distinct problem with the theory. The Sarmatian cavalry had also tended to be equipped with weak bows alongside their *kontos*. It is difficult to accept that the Goths would have adopted the lance used by the Sarmatians without similarly adopting the bow, since the two weapons were an integral part of Sarmatian tactics. Furthermore, there is no mention of Gothic cavalry using bows in Procopius: during the battle of Rome the Goths remained stationary under the storm of Byzantine arrows – hardly likely if they had had the ability to strike back at the enemy, however poorly in comparison to Byzantine practice. Moreover, it would have been difficult to convince the Goths to remain stationary unless they had the additional protection afforded by a large shield, which was not a normal part of the Sarmatian panoply. There

is also the categorical statement in Procopius (*Wars*, V.xxvii.15) that the Goths and the Romans were armed completely differently, which would not have been the case had the Gothic cavalry likewise been armed with a bow. Consequently, the interpretation is open to doubt.

Illustration 15: Traditional Sarmatian warrior from a Bosporan grave stele (after Suliminski).

As further evidence that the Goths had not changed their methods, Boss (1993, p. 30) uses as confirmation the fact that a fourth-century historian, Ammianus Marcellinus, describes the Quadi as 'Sarmaticised' (Ammianus Marcellinus, xvii.12.1) but nowhere claims that the Goths had been similarly influenced. This argument, relying on negative evidence, is by its very nature unreliable and so must be used with extreme caution.

The third theory is that given by Phil Barker in *The Armies and Enemies of Imperial Rome* (1981), in which he claims that the Goths were armed with spear/javelin in continuation of earlier practice, but used the Italian *fabricae* to extend the use of armour to all of the cavalry. There is also the single line in Procopius where Belisarius notes that the Goths had no practice in mounted archery, were only accustomed to fighting with spear and sword, and had no means of defending themselves against mounted archers (Procopius, *Wars*, V.xxvii.27–8). Furthermore, also according to Procopius, Gothic cavalry threw their javelins at Ricilas, one of Belisarius' guards, as he was scouting, killing him in the process (*Wars*, VII.xi.24). Although, as Boss notes (1993, p.31), the javelin may have been retained either as a secondary weapon or merely have been used by the rear ranks of the cavalry, this is the only attested use of a specific weapon and should, therefore, take precedence over modern theories.

One factor that is not mentioned in the arguments outlined above is that of personal choice. In Chapter 3 it was seen that, even in the 'regimented' Roman army, personal choice of equipment had a large part to play. In the Gothic army, choice of weapon would have been an even more unregulated exercise. Therefore, it is likely that some Goths, especially any who had served in the east, may have chosen to change to the *kontus* under the influence of the Persians and of some of the *bucellarii* in the *comitatus* of the Roman generals (see Illustrations 14 and 15). As a consequence, it is reasonable to assume that there was a mixture of weapons and equipment throughout the Gothic army, although, given the literary and pictorial evidence, the use of the shorter spear is likely to have remained the dominant weapon of choice. It should be noted, however, that troops armed with the *kontos* are likely to have been grouped together in 'specialist' units, since the *kontos* is a more specialised weapon and its use may not have been suited to such troops fighting alongside spear armed cavalry. It should also be remembered, however, that the sparse nature of the evidence cannot lead us to a definite conclusion concerning the general arming of the Gothic cavalry.

It is also reasonable to claim that the Gothic cavalry wore chainmail armour and either the more traditional patterns of western helmets or possibly new forms of the spangenhelm type produced by the Italian *fabricae*. As a supplement to their traditional spear/javelin and large round shield, they are likely to have carried a Roman-pattern *spatha*, again produced by the Italian *fabricae*.

The idea that the Goths maintained production from the Roman *fabricae* is reinforced by the statements in Procopius that the Gothic army was equipped from arsenals controlled by the king (*Wars*, V.xi.28 and V.xvi.11). In the first of these references, both arms and horses were distributed amongst the troops; in the second, Witigis led horsemen and infantry, 'the most of them as well as their horses were clad in armour'. Although it is uncertain that the majority of the cavalry had armour on the front of their horses, the fact that this is mentioned by Procopius does suggest that at least some of them were so equipped.

The latter quote also gives us evidence for the nature of the infantry. Barker (1981) suggests that the infantry was composed largely of unarmoured archers, there to give supporting fire to the cavalry. However, Procopius' wording suggests the majority of the army was armoured, so implying that at least a large proportion of the infantry were heavy spearmen. The latter is reinforced to a degree by Belisarius' statement to his friends during the siege of Rome that the Goths had no answer to the Byzantine horse archers (Proc V. xxvii. 27). If the Goths had been able to deploy very large numbers of foot archers, Belisarius would not have been able to employ the hit-and-run tactics used during the siege of Rome, as the small numbers of Byzantine cavalry would have been very exposed in the face of the ensuing large volumes of infantry missiles.

In conclusion, it is possible to describe the Gothic army as based largely upon heavily-armoured cavalry using their traditional spears and javelins, with perhaps a few troops armed instead with the longer *kontos*. The infantry appears to have been dominated by heavily armoured spearmen, with an auxiliary force of archers to give supporting fire when needed. This army was very different to the totally-mounted Vandal armed forces, yet, as Belisarius was to quickly ascertain, they shared a major flaw when pitted against the Byzantines.

Belisarius recaptures Rome

Learning of the Byzantine invasion, the new king, Witigis' took steps to counter the offensive, proceeding to Rome with a large force of Goths and ordering the arrest of Theodegisclus, son of Theodahad. However, he was faced with a dilemma. Belisarius was expected to move north from Naples, but Constantinianus was in a strong position in Illyricum and could easily march into the north of Italy. Furthermore, the Franks were in a threatening position to the northwest of Italy.

Witigis decided to play for time. Leaving a garrison of 4,000 men under Leuderis in Rome, taking many senators as hostage and urging Pope Silverius and the Roman citizens to remain loyal, he moved to Ravenna. The city was strategically placed at the focus of the three possible avenues of attack. From here, he could move to repulse either the Franks or Constantinianus, or he could advance upon Rome should it be threatened by Belisarius.

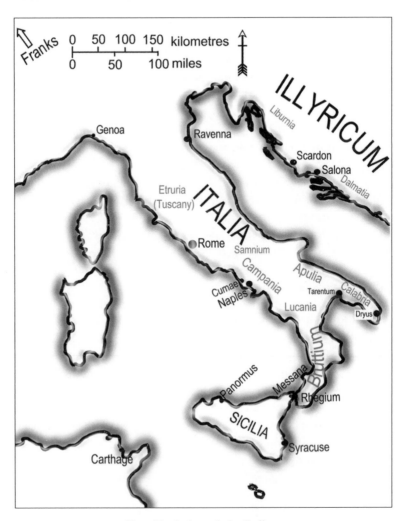

Map 11: Italy and the Balkans.

Once in Ravenna he made the political move of marrying Matasuintha, daughter of Amalasuintha, in an attempt to link himself to the house of Theoderic and so legitimise his rule. He also ordered a muster of all of the Goths, excepting garrisons, and he then armed the troops with weapons and horses (Procopius, *Wars*, V.xi.28).

At about this time, if not earlier, he sent envoys to the Franks. In order to ensure peace on one possible front, he ceded to the Franks those parts of Gaul still under Gothic rule. In return, the Franks not only agreed to remain nominally neutral, they also agreed to supply non-Frankish subject troops to aid the Goths in their war with the Byzantines. As they were supposed to be allied to the Byzantines at this time, they refused to allow actual Franks to join the Goths due to the potential political implications should they be recognised or captured. In accordance with the new agreement, Witigis ordered the troops acting as garrisons in Gaul to return to Italy, along with their leader, Marcian.

Whilst Witigis was making agreements with the Franks, both Calabria and Apulia had surrendered to Belisarius, as the towns had no walls, no Gothic garrisons, and no means of defence. With his rear and flank relatively secure, Belisarius prepared to advance upon Rome. He left 300 infantry to garrison Naples and another force to garrison Cumae; these were the only two fortified towns in Campania, so with their garrisons in place he believed that his rear was now secure.

As Belisarius began his advance, the situation turned unexpectedly in his favour. Pope Silverius and the Romans, scared by the sack of Naples, decided that they should surrender the city to Belisarius without a fight. Therefore, they sent the *quaestor* Fidelius of Milan as an envoy to inform Belisarius of their decision. It was only as the Byzantines approached that the Gothic garrison learned of the citizens' decision: as the Byzantines entered by the Asinarian Gate, the Gothic garrison left by the Flaminian Gate. The date was 9 December 536.

Leuderis, the Gothic commander, chose to stay in the city. Procopius assumes that this was due to shame (*Wars*, V.xiv.13), but he may also have been fearful of his reception by Witigis, having lost Rome without a fight. Leuderis, along with the keys of the city, was sent by a triumphant Belisarius to Justinian in Constantinople.

As he established himself in Rome, Belisarius received further proof that the Goths were no longer a united force aiming at the expulsion of the invader. Pitzas, the Goth in control of western Samnium, surrendered with all of his forces to Belisarius. Belisarius gave Pitzas a small number of his own troops and ordered him to retain the territory in the name of the emperor.

In a short space of time Belisarius had conquered the area of Italy south of Rome and Samnium. On the eastern side of the Adriatic, Constantinianus was in control of the areas of Illyricum and Dalmatia as far north as Liburnia. The war was going well.

The Gothic Reaction

Once in Rome, Belisarius ordered the digging of a moat around the city walls, following this with instructions for the repairs of those areas of the walls that had deteriorated due to neglect. Using Rome as a base, he also dispatched troops to the surrounding areas in order to bring more of the peninsula under his control.

Constantinus was sent with a large force of *bucellarii*, many spearmen, Huns, and other troops to secure the whole of Tuscany. Constantinus quickly captured Spoletium and Perusia, establishing a garrison at the former whilst he

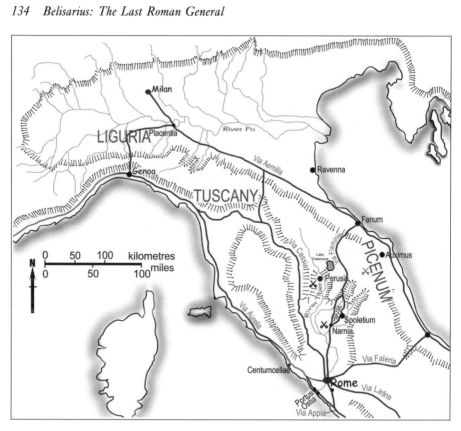

Map 12: Events prior to the siege of Rome.

held the latter with the rest of his forces. Whilst at Spoletium, he seized two daggers from a Roman citizen, an act that was to have grave repercussions, as will be described later. Bessas was dispatched with a smaller force and, upon his approach, Narnia surrendered to him without a fight. By the capture of these towns Belisarius had achieved control of the Via Flaminia, as well as other associated roads, which crossed the Apennine passes to the east and northeast of Rome.

Belisarius himself remained at Rome. He obviously foresaw a response from the Goths and expected it to be directed at Rome. Alongside the repairs to the walls, he stockpiled provisions for a siege, even though the Romans informed him that attempts to defend the walls were futile, and waited upon developments.

As the Byzantines settled into the towns they had taken, Witigis waited in Ravenna for the arrival of Marcian and his men from Gaul. When news reached him that Tuscany had been taken, but that Belisarius had remained in Rome, he realised that he had a chance to strike at the Byzantines whilst they were divided. He sent an army under the command of Unilas and Pissas to

Perusia. The army was larger than that commanded by Constantinus, but in the first battle of the campaign, the Byzantines were victorious, routing the Goths and killing most of them in the course of the pursuit. Unilas and Pissas were captured and sent to Belisarius in Rome.

When tidings of the defeat reached Witigis he decided to take matters into his own hands. He ordered Asinarius and Uligisalus to collect troops from the Suevi, according to his agreement with the Franks, before marching into Dalmatia and besieging Salona. To help with the attack, he assigned a fleet to help with the siege of the city. He personally took command of the majority of the Goths and marched on Rome.

Dalmatia

The Gothic forces assigned to this theatre were led by Asinarius and Uligisalus. When Asinarius left the force to collect the Suevian troops, Uligisalus continued the advance with the main body until he reached Liburnia. Shortly, he was faced by the Byzantines under Constantinianus and defeated at the Battle of Scardon (Proc, *Wars*, V.xvi.13; see Map 11). The Goths retired to the city of Burnus and awaited the arrival of Asinarius with the Suevic reinforcements. For his part, Constantinianus heard of Asinarius' mission and realised that he did not have enough troops to face the combined army. Therefore he withdrew to Salona, dug a moat around the walls and prepared for a siege.

Asinarius finally joined Uligisalus and the combined forces moved on Salona, accompanied by the fleet. Upon their arrival, they dug a ditch and stockade around the city whilst the ships completed the encirclement by closing off the harbour. After a short wait, a sortie by Byzantine ships in the harbour sank, captured or scattered the Gothic fleet. The Byzantines were able to sail in and out unmolested, though the Gothic troops maintained the siege by land.

Meanwhile, Witigis had been marching towards Rome. As he travelled south, he was informed of the small size of the Byzantine forces by fugitives fleeing from Rome. Perceiving that he greatly outnumbered Belisarius, he decided that victory would be easy if he could only trap the Byzantine general in Rome. Accordingly, he travelled as fast as possible, in the hope that Belisarius would not have time to make his escape.

Rome

In Rome, Belisarius had not been idle. By taking control of Spoletium, Perusia and Narnia, Belisarius had established strong points along the Via Flaminia and other, parallel routes across the central Apennines. In this way, he may have been hoping to delay and weaken the Goths before their arrival at Rome; a succession of sieges would have cost the lives of many of the Gothic warriors. In order to further delay their advance, he built a tower at the Milvian Bridge, posting Innocentius and a unit of cavalry as the garrison.

Hearing of Witigis' advance, and aware of how small his own forces were, Belisarius ordered Constantinus and Bessas to leave garrisons in those towns they deemed defensible, and commanded them to return to Rome with the remainder of their forces at top speed.

Constantinus did as he was ordered, leaving garrisons in Spoletium and Perusia, before returning to Rome. Bessas delayed and acted too slowly. Before he could organise his troops, the advance guard of the Gothic army arrived upon the plains outside Narnia. After a fierce encounter, the Goths were driven back, but, whilst pursuing them, Bessas became aware of the size of the forces arrayed against him. Consequently, he returned to Narnia with all haste, organised a garrison for the town, then travelled to Rome with the news that Witigis was approaching.

Witigis had displayed a strategic foresight that would have alarmed Belisarius. Rather than halting and besieging each of the cities in turn, Witigis understood that they were unimportant. The main target was Belisarius, the leader of the invasion, along with the city of Rome. As a result, he bypassed Narnia to the south, moved through the territory of the Sabines, and approached the Milvian Bridge unexpectedly.

Anticipating Witigis' imminent arrival, Belisarius set out from Rome and headed towards the Milvian Bridge with 1,000 cavalry in order to further impede the Goths' progress. As he neared the bridge, he was surprised to meet the vanguard of the Gothic army. As the Goths had approached the crossing, twenty two men of the garrison who were of Germanic descent had deserted to Witigis. The rest of the garrison had decided that they could not hope to hold their position and had fled south towards Campania. The Goths had crossed the river unopposed and met the forces under Belisarius by chance.

Unable to make tactical deployments due to the unexpected nature of the meeting, the Byzantine cavalry immediately joined combat with the Goths, Belisarius himself being in the front line of the fighting. On seeing this, the deserters pointed him out, instructing the Goths to attack the rider on the 'white-faced horse' (Proc, *Wars*, V.xviii.8). As the Goths focused their attention upon Belisarius, his bodyguards closed around him to protect him.

Finally, the Goths were routed. According to Procopius the Goths had lost 1,000 men. (*Wars*, V.xviii.14), but in the circumstances this appears to be a case of Procopius exaggerating the exploits of his hero. Belisarius now led the pursuit until the Goths reached their own main body, consisting of formed lines of infantry. The Byzantines were repulsed and the Gothic cavalry, reinforced by fresh men, forced the Byzantines to retire in their turn.

The Byzantines made a stand upon a nearby hill, causing the Goths to retire momentarily, before withdrawing towards Rome. They did not stop until they reached the Salarian Gate, only to find the Romans refused them entry. They had heard from fugitives that Belisarius had been killed and thought this was a Gothic ruse to enter the city unopposed.

Belisarius ordered his men to reform. When the Gothic pursuers came close he ordered a charge that scattered them, before again returning to the gate. Convinced, the Romans now allowed him to enter. The siege of Rome began.

The Siege of Rome

At the beginning of March, Witigis approached the city and detailed his men to build seven fortified camps from which they could maintain a partial siege, as he did not have enough troops to totally blockade the city. Instead, Witigis was relying on the low level of manpower available to the Byzantines and was expecting to win the war of attrition that sieges often became. Six of these camps were located so as to put pressure on the walls between the Flaminian and Praenestine gates.

The seventh camp was on the other side of the River Tiber on the Plains of Nero, and was manned by Marcian and his men, recently returned from Gaul. Not only would the camp put pressure upon the Cornelian and Aurelian gates, it would also secure the Milvian Bridge. Without this camp, the entire section

Map 13: The walls of Rome.

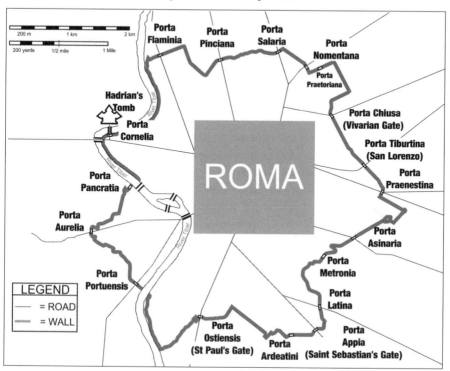

of walls on the west side of the Tiber would be free from threat, since apart from the Milvian Bridge the Goths had no means of accessing the western side of the river. As it was, the Goths only posed a direct threat to about half of the city walls. Witigis then broke the fourteen aqueducts that fed water to the city, began the construction of assault engines, catapults and mines, and began the siege in earnest. We are not sure of the exact date at which the siege began, only that it was sometime in late February 537.

Upon his return, Belisarius had immediately assigned his troops to their duties. He had placed one of his commanders at every gate with a detachment of troops. Bessas was at the Praenestine Gate, and Constantinus was at the Flaminian Gate, where Belisarius ordered a stone wall built inside to ensure that it was secure from attack. Belisarius had taken personal control of the Pincian and the Salarian gates, as these were most suitable as exits from which to launch sallies against the Goths. These four gates faced the Gothic approach and so were most in danger of attack. Belisarius had placed his most reliable officers in charge here. The remaining gates were assigned to his infantry commanders, since they were deemed to be less threatened by the Goths. He further ordered the siting of catapults and stone-throwers on the walls, ready for the expected assault of the Goths.

Shortly after the siege began, Bessas reported a rumour that a number of Goths had broken into the city. Belisarius sent men to investigate and, when they reported that no such thing had happened, he sent an order to all of his commanders ordering them to ignore all such rumours in the future and remain at their posts; Belisarius would deal with any real breakthroughs in person.

Once the Goths had broken the aqueducts, Belisarius took measures to ensure that they were blocked where they entered the city, so that the Goths could not repeat the strategy he had used to gain entry to Naples. However, the aqueducts had provided the power for the mills that ground the city's flour. Belisarius countered this by suspending water-wheels between two boats, mooring the boats in the Tiber, and using the force of the river to turn the wheels and grind the corn. Although the Goths released logs and other debris upstream in an attempt to destroy the floating mills, Belisarius ordered a chain to be hung across the river and the danger was averted.

As the siege progressed, the citizens began to feel the pressures of a city under siege. They began to share their dissatisfaction with each other and deserters brought the news to Witigis. As a result he attempted to open negotiations with Belisarius, but was rebuffed and the siege continued.

Having completed his preparations, at dawn on the eighteenth day of the siege Witigis launched his assault. Siege towers pulled by oxen, battering rams, and Goths with large numbers of scaling ladders approached the walls. Belisarius ordered his men to hold their fire until he gave the signal. As the Goths came within range, Belisarius fired three arrows at the enemy, each one finding a target. The other defenders now fired their bows at the attackers, but those around Belisarius were ordered to kill the oxen pulling the towers. When this was accomplished, the siege towers lay immobile and useless. The attack stalled. When a Goth was pinned to a tree by an artillery bolt the majority of the Goths withdrew out of range, and a sally by the defenders routed the remaining attackers. The Byzantines set fire to the engines and returned inside the walls. Procopius again inflates the figures and claims that in this assault 30,000 Goths were killed (Proc, *Wars*, V.xxiii.26).

At the same time at the Cornelian gate, which was defended by Constantinus, the topography and the plant cover enable the Goths to reach the walls without being seen. The Byzantine catapults could not fire down at them and the defenders were exposed to danger if they leaned far enough over the walls to aim their bows at the attackers. In desperation, the men on the top of Hadrian's tomb broke up the statues and hurled them down upon the attackers. The attack was repulsed and, as the Goths withdrew, they came under fire from the artillery on the walls. Similarly, an attack on the Pancratian Gate, held by Paulus, also made no headway.

Strangely, the Flaminian Gate, held by the Reges infantry unit (the descendants of the Regii of the *Notitia Dignitatum*) under the command of Ursicinus, was not attacked at all.

Events at the Porta Chiusa (Vivarium Gate) were different to the others. Here, the original wall had crumbled – possibly due to subsidence – and a section of wall had been added outside this to protect the damaged part. The space between the two walls was known as the Vivarium, as animals were often kept there. A Gothic mine had been dug in order to collapse the outer wall at this point. Bessas and Peranius, who were in control of this area, were hard pressed by the Goths and so sent to Belisarius for help. The arrival of the general restored morale and, taking note of events, Belisarius allowed the Gothic mine to complete its work. When the Goths entered the breach they found themselves faced with another wall. At this point Belisarius ordered Cyprian and his men to attack the Goths in the Vivarium. The Goths panicked and began to flee back through the breach. As the Goths were milling around in confusion at this unexpected setback, Belisarius launched a sortie that routed them and they fled in panic back to their camps. The victorious Byzantines again burned the Gothic siege engines and retired behind the walls.

The first Gothic attempt upon Rome had failed. Belisarius had shown his men that they could defeat the Goths, and had shown the Goths that the capture of Rome would not be as easy as Witigis had led them to believe. Belisarius' deployment of his troops, his rapid assessment of the situation, and his expert timing of sallies that caught the Goths unawares and resulted in them receiving heavy casualties, must all be applauded; this was a masterpiece of defensive warfare.

In spite of his successes, Belisarius knew that he did not have the forces to raise the siege or win the war. Consequently, he despatched messengers to Justinian requesting reinforcements, informing the emperor that in leaving garrisons in selected strongholds he had been force to reduce the number of available men to only 5,000. Procopius states that, as the Goths had 150,000 men, Belisarius requested reinforcements to bring him up to a parity with Gothic numbers (Proc, *Wars*, V.xxiv.1–9). This is clearly unrealistic, since the emperor did not have that number of troops in the entire imperial army, and is a further example of Procopius' willingness to exaggerate the numbers of the Goths in order to glorify the achievement of Belisarius. In fact, Justinian had already sent reinforcements. The *foederati* that had served alongside Belisarius in Africa, under Valerian and Martinus, had already been recalled to Constantinople before being dispatched for Italy. Unfortunately, the weather had trapped them in Greece. Belisarius was informed of their impending arrival and waited in Rome for their coming.

Recognising that he did not have enough troops, and that most of the men in the city could not work due to the siege, Belisarius enrolled the citizens to fight alongside the regular troops, paying them wages for their services. Since the men had no other means of income, the measure was a success as it increased Belisarius' manpower whilst at the same time increasing the loyalty of the citizens to their new commander. It was a brilliant stroke of propaganda.

Witigis

Baulked in his assault upon the city, Witigis decided that his next move would be to seize the Roman harbour at Portus. This is where incoming ships transferred their cargo to smaller boats and barges which then transported the goods upriver to Rome. Three days after the assault, he led his men south and captured Portus on or around 13 March 537, leaving 1,000 men as a garrison. The move increased the difficulties for the defenders. Although the Goths did not surround the city, Rome still had a large population to feed. These had been supplied by river, but with Portus taken supplies had to be landed at the port of Antium, which was near to Portus, taken overland to Ostia – a day's journey – and then taken overland from Ostia to Rome. Supplies in the city began to decline.

Angered by the treachery of the Roman citizens, Witigis sent orders to Ravenna that the senators earlier taken as hostage should be executed. Rumour of the order arrived early and a few of the senators managed to escape. The rest were killed.

Belisarius

Once he realised that the Goths, although repulsed, were going to maintain the siege, Belisarius sent the women and children to Naples in order to reduce the burden on the food supplies. The rations in the city would now last longer. He would also not need to worry about their safety should the Goths force entry to the city.

Worried about the possibility of treachery, he ordered the guards at the city gates to be rotated frequently in order to minimise their opportunity for betrayal. At night he sent men to camp near to the moat, safe in the knowledge that the Goths had not yet recovered from their defeat and would not attempt an attack on any such forces. These men helped to reduce the possibility of treachery by not allowing the Goths close access to the walls under cover of darkness.

A letter was now discovered, allegedly linking Pope Silverius to a plot to restore the city to the Goths. Forged by Julianus, the *praetorianus*, and Marcus, a *scholasticus*, the letter was given to Belisarius who ordered that Silverius be sent to Lycia. On 29th March Vigilius was ordained as the new Pope, allegedly by the order of Theodora. Justinian later ordered that Silverius be returned to Italy, pending an investigation. Belisarius surrendered him to the custody of Vigilius, whose men starved him to death. Vigilius is said to have promised to give Belisarius 200 pounds of gold for his support; it was not the only hint of scandal linked to Belisarius during the siege.

In a similar manner, Belisarius also ordered that many senators be sent out of the city to forestall any attempts at betrayal. Although the commoners had been recruited into the army and paid, so ensuring their loyalty, the Pope and the senators, being of a higher class, probably declined to take an active part in the defence. Feeling no obligations towards Belisarius, their loyalty was suspect, especially since they had already betrayed the city once before, when they had allowed Belisarius to gain entry.

Belisarius takes the Initiative

Twenty days after the Gothic capture of Portus, and twenty three since the failed assault, so probably around 5 April, Martinus and Valerian finally arrived with their 1,600 *foederati*. These cavalrymen were mainly Huns, Slavonians and Slavic Antae – cavalry archers of proven ability. More confident due to the reinforcements, Belisarius decided to adopt a more aggressive stance.

On the following day he instructed one of his bodyguards, by the name of Trajan, to take 200 *bucellarii* out of the city via the Salarian Gate to a nearby hill. Once there, the cavalry were to engage the enemy using only their bows, but, when the supply of arrows was exhausted, to retire to the safety of the city. At the same time, Belisarius ordered the catapults on that section of the walls to be made ready to cover the retreat.

Trajan carried out the order, riding to the hill and starting to shoot at the Goths. Disturbed by this new development, the Goths seized the equipment that they had to hand and rushed out of their camps. When all of their arrows were expended the Byzantines began their withdrawal, with the enemy in close pursuit. As they came within range of the walls the catapults began to fire, killing many of the Goths and prompting the rest to immediately abandon the pursuit and retire out of range. In this engagement Procopius claims that the Goths lost 1,000 men killed (*Wars*, V.xxvii. 11), but again the figure has been exaggerated for the benefit of Belisarius. It is unlikely that many Byzantines were casualties, since the Goths had little response to their use of archery.

Four days later, Belisarius repeated the tactic. On this occasion 300 *bucellarii* led by Mundilas, another of Belisarius' bodyguards, caused a greater number of casualties than the original sortie. Finally, after another lapse of a few days, Belisarius repeated the tactic, sending another guardsman, Oilas, again with 300 *bucellarii*. In the course of three engagements, Procopius claims that the Byzantines killed around 4,000 men, although doubtless he has distorted the number of Gothic losses.

Witigis

Procopius now describes Witigis' response to Belisarius' tactics (*Wars*, V.xxvii. 15–23). Without fully understanding the reasoning behind Belisarius' ruse, Witigis now attempted a similar stratagem. He sent 500 men to demonstrate near to the city without advancing near enough for them to suffer casualties from the catapults on the walls. Immediately grasping the situation, Belisarius sent 1,000 men under Bessas to engage the Goths. Forced to retire under a hail of Byzantine arrows, the Goths were surrounded and almost annihilated.

Failing to understand the reasons for the defeat, Witigis insulted the survivors and accused them of cowardice. Three days later, with 500 men gathered from all of the camps, Witigis again employed the identical ruse. The result was the same. This time, 1,500 of the *foederati* under Martinus and Valerian destroyed the Goths he had sent.

However, Procopius may not be telling the whole truth, either in order to magnify the abilities of Belisarius when compared to the (apparently inept) Witigis, or due to his inability to grasp the finer details of generalship. It is possible that Witigis was attempting to duplicate the ruse used by Belisarius, yet a close analysis of the text reveals the difficulties both he and Belisarius faced. It is too easily forgotten that the areas around the walls of the city would not have been open grassland. Instead, there would have been fields, vineyards, fences and all of the other obstacles presented by Roman farming techniques. In such restricted terrain, the bow would not have greatly outranged the javelin and, as a consequence, the attempt to replicate the ruse was not actually too far-fetched.

Yet there was one factor in which Belisarius was superior to Witigis: his supply of excellent junior officers and the superior quality of the troops he used. Trajan, Mundilas and Oilas were all members of his personal bodyguard and men who could be trusted to translate his orders into action. Furthermore, on these operations Belisarius did not send out the regular cavalry of the army, using instead small numbers of his personal *comitatus*; *bucellarii* of proven ability and daring. These superior troops with excellent leaders fulfilled the task perfectly.

Witigis did not have such a luxury. His leaders and troops were not as highly trained and efficient as the bodyguards and *bucellarii* and so failed to follow the plan, allowing themselves to be surrounded and practically annihilated. Three days later, Witigis repeated the attempt, but again his troops were defeated with heavy loss.

Yet it may be that Witigis was not actually attempting to repeat the Byzantines' tactic. It is possible that he was, at least in part, attempting to seize the initiative and deprive Belisarius of the terrain near to the walls from which to effect his hit-and-run tactics. By occupying the high ground outside the city walls from which the Byzantines had been launching their attacks, he may have been pre-empting their assaults and attempting to tighten the siege, whilst at the same time ensuring that army morale remained high. Whichever theory is correct, the strategy failed: The Goths were defeated and Belisarius retained the initiative, which was to be the undoing of the Goths.

Recognising their danger, the Goths now reverted to maintaining the siege: when Belisarius repeated his tactics, the Goths simply drove the Byzantine cavalry away by a controlled charge that did not leave them vulnerable to a counter-attack or from missiles from the city walls.

The episode illustrates Belisarius' ability as a general; it was a superb use of the strengths of his horse archers – mobility and firepower – against the weakness of cavalry that relied on hand-to-hand combat to defeat the enemy. On the other hand, Witigis' attempt to use the stratagem demonstrates that, although he understood what was happening, he did not have the highly-trained manpower necessary to repeat Belisarius' tactics for himself.

It was at about this time that Belisarius confided to his friends that he had always been confident of victory over the Goths. Like the Vandals, the Gothic cavalry had no answer to the Byzantine horse archers, being unable to close with the enemy and fight whilst still suffering casualties from a distance. Only if vastly outnumbered and threatened with encirclement would the Byzantines be in any danger of defeat by the Vandal horsemen. Although in theory the Gothic foot archers could be used to counter the threat, these were – understandably – too timid to face the Byzantine cavalry on their own, and so needed a covering force of heavy infantry to act as a screen. Unfortunately for the Goths, the heavily-armed men manoeuvred too slowly, allowing the Byzantine horsemen to move away from the threat of the archers.

The Battle of Rome

It was their very success in these skirmishes that was to be the undoing of
the Byzantines. The troops began to put pressure on Belisarius as they now
believed that they could beat the Goths in an open battle. At last he agreed, yet
he wanted the battle to be fought on his terms. Therefore he continued with
the stratagem of sallies as detailed above, hoping for an opportunity to lead the
remainder of his men out and so take the Goths by surprise. The hope did not
materialise; the Goths remained vigilant and were always ready for such a move.

Finally, Belisarius abandoned his hopes and gave orders for the troops
to deploy for a more traditional, set-piece battle. He sent Valentinus and his
men out of the Aurelian Gate on to the Plains of Nero. Their instructions were
to harass and pin Marcian and his men in their camp, and not allow any
reinforcements to cross the bridge to the east bank of the river. On no account
were they to become engaged in a pitched battle.

Belisarius was also faced with the problem of what to do with the Romans.
Many of them had volunteered and wanted to fight the Goths. As they were
untrained and of dubious quality, they could easily be routed by an enemy
attack. Belisarius therefore deployed them through the Pancratian Gate and
had them form a dense formation close to the left bank of the river. In this way,
these untried troops would help to pin down the Goths whilst not actually
being in any danger. Only if Belisarius gave the signal were they to advance and
attack the enemy. It was an ingenious way of solving a knotty problem, since
any refusal to use them could lead to a drop in their morale with a subsequent
refusal to fight in their own defence any longer.

On the east bank, Belisarius had a similar problem. Most of his infantrymen had by now acquired horses captured during the many sorties against
the Goths. During the quiet periods of the siege they had been training as
cavalrymen and Belisarius now decided that the main effort against the Goth
should be fought entirely as a cavalry action. The remnants of the infantry that
were without horses, composed of unmounted Isaurians, were to be drawn up
near the moat to act as a rallying point behind which the cavalry could reform if
they encountered any difficulties.However the morale of the army was high and
the infantry were unhappy about being left with such a minor role. Two of
Belisarius' guardsmen, Principius and Tarmatus, argued that the poor showing
of the infantry was due to the poor quality of their officers, who ran away as
soon as danger threatened. It was not surprising that their men would follow
suit. These officers were now mounted and were part of the cavalry arm.
Principius and Tarmatus argued that if Belisarius allowed them to lead the
infantry, the infantry would fight and not run away. Eventually Belisarius
agreed. Leaving a small number of men to guard the gates, the rest of the
infantry were deployed to the rear of the cavalry, where they could still act as a
rallying point. Yet it was clear that Belisarius did not trust the infantry, since

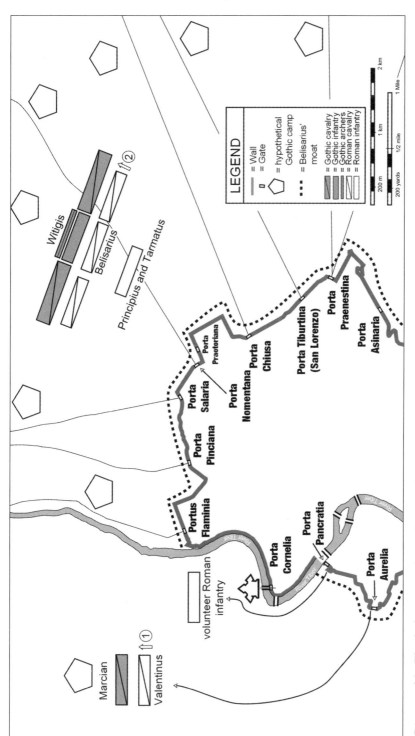

Diagram 16: The deployment and initial phase of the Battle of Rome. (1): Valentinus advances and engages Marcian. (2): The Byzantine cavalry advances and engages the Goths.

they were deployed in such a way that if they routed, they would not disrupt the ranks of the cavalry as they fled.

The Gothic army deployed in a very traditional manner. In the centre were the 'heavy-armed men', protecting the archers from attack by the Byzantine cavalry. The Gothic cavalry were split fairly evenly between the two flanks. Witigis did, however, order his troops to deploy as far away from the city as possible, lining his men up immediately before the camps. He believed that the sheer size of his army would lead to victory and he wanted the Byzantines to be as far away from the city as possible when they broke. In this way, his men would have more distance in which to pursue the Byzantines before they reached the cover of the walls, and this would enable them to cause the maximum number of casualties. Although Witigis was not of the same calibre as Belisarius, as was seen above in his attempt to emulate Byzantine tactics, it is clear that he did have a grasp of at least some of the basic elements of warfare.

The battle on the east side of the river began in the expected manner. With Belisarius and Witigis at the back urging their troops to perform great deeds, the Byzantines advanced to within missile range and began firing at the Goths. The Goths, however, did not act to remove the threat; they simply stood their ground, absorbing the casualties.

Obviously, the Byzantines were happy with this state of affairs, but slowly began to close the distance between the lines. Gradually, as the gap between the armies closed, the Byzantines began to grow tired and their supplies of ammunition began to dwindle. They were now close enough to charge the Goths, as is shown by Athenodorus of Belisarius' guards, and Theodoriscus and George of Martinus' guards, repeatedly charging at the Goths and killing many with their spears (Proc, *Wars*, V.xxviii.20–21). Yet as the fighting gradually became face-to-face, the Gothic archers also began to cause casualties in the Byzantine ranks, many of the horses being killed or wounded. The wounded and those unhorsed sought sanctuary in the city, reducing the troops at Belisarius' immediate disposal.

The slow attrition of the Byzantine ranks did not go unnoticed. At last, the Goths reacted. Either spontaneously, as suggested by Procopius (*Wars*, V.xviii), or having received the order from Witigis, the cavalry on the Gothic right wing charged. The opposition fled back to the safety of the infantry line, expecting to use the cover of the infantry to regroup before returning to the battle. To no avail; the majority of the infantry wavered and broke, running for the safety of the city. The panic spread to the rest of the army and the entire Byzantine cavalry force routed, pursued for a short distance by the Goths.

The rout would have been a disaster if it had not been for the actions of a section of the infantry that stood their ground. The men around Principius and Tarmatus fought bravely, slowing the Gothic pursuit and allowing the Byzantines to reach the comparative safety of the moat. Eventually, Principius

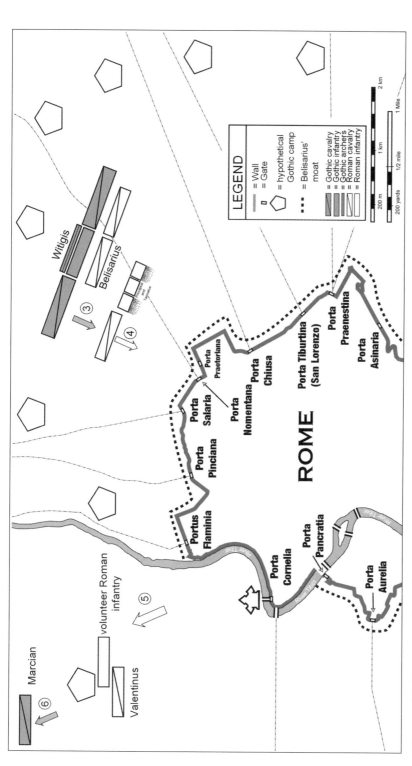

Diagram 17: The second phase of the Battle of Rome. (3): Seeing the Byzantines tiring, the Gothic right charges. (4): The Byzantine cavalry retires on the infantry, most of whom rout. (5): The Roman volunteers charge and begin to sack the Gothic camp. (6): Marcian and his troops retire and watch events from nearby hills.

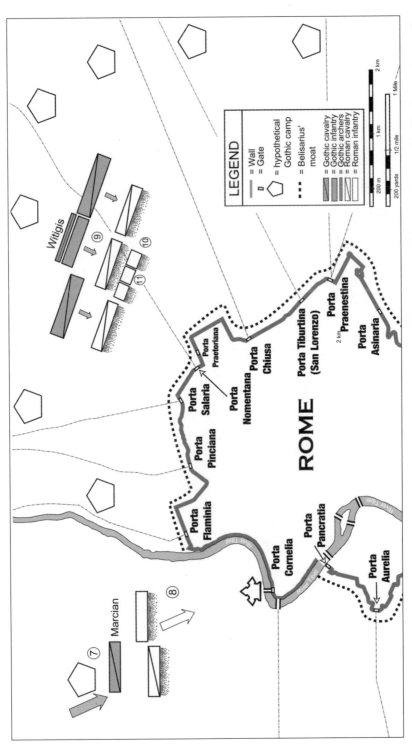

Diagram 18: The final phase of the Battle of Rome. (7): Seeing the Byzantine cavalry and the volunteers rout. (8): The Byzantine cavalry orders a charge. (9): The Gothic line charges. (10): The Byzantine cavalry and most of the infantry routs. (11): The infantry under Principius and Tarmatus holds and allows the rest to retire to the walls.

was overwhelmed and killed, along with forty-two of the Isaurians, whilst Tarmatus continued to fight until he was rescued by his brother Ennes and a detachment of reformed cavalry. Sadly, he was to die of his wounds two days later.

The fleeing Byzantines, covered by this gallant rearguard, reached the city, only to be denied entry by the citizens, who were massed on the wall to watch the battle. Frustrated, they gathered between the walls and the moat. The situation could have resulted in disaster, but the Goths, seeing a large number of people upon the walls, decided not to close with the Byzantines, instead returning victorious to their camps. The battle east of the river was over.

To the west of the river, the Moors and Byzantine cavalry led by Valentinus had again advanced to within missile range of the Goths before settling down to deliver a steady flow of missiles against the enemy. The Goths remained as they had deployed, slightly to the front of their camp, fearing that the Byzantines were trying to lure them into a trap. From a distance the volunteers looked like regular troops, and the Goths believed that the Byzantine cavalry was trying to force them to charge to allow the infantry to manoeuvre between themselves and their camp.

At about midday the Roman volunteers suddenly charged the Goths. Panicked by the unexpected attack, the Goths fled to the cover of the nearby hills, failing even to defend their camp. The attack was to be the undoing of the Byzantines.

The Goths had been frightened by the sheer numbers of the enemy. Yet the Byzantines failed to pursue the fleeing Goths or to destroy the Milvian Bridge, which would have isolated the Goths under Marcian and freed the entire west side of the city from attack. Nor did they cross the bridge themselves to attack the forces of Witigis from the rear. Any of these actions could have changed the outcome of the battle. Instead, the undisciplined forces that had scattered the Goths entered the camp and began to loot it of its valuables.

As the volunteers and the regular troops mingled, Valentinus tried in vain to restore order. Observing the chaos from their vantage point in the hills, Marcian and the Goths regained their courage and charged at the disordered troops on the plain. The Romans and Byzantines were destroyed, many being cut down as they sought the sanctuary of the city walls. The battle had been a disaster, and the Byzantines did not make any further attempt to engage the Goths in open battle.

Belisarius and Witigis as Commanders

Belisarius' role in the defeat is minimised by Procopius. The statement by Procopius that the troops put pressure upon Belisarius to fight may be true, in which case he must still bear a portion of the blame. Yet it may also be false. It is possible that Belisarius himself wanted to fight and was willing to lead the troops into battle. The description of an unwilling Belisarius may simply be a traditional method of averting the blame and placing it firmly with the troops – compare this to Procopius' description of the troops demanding action before their defeat at the Battle of Callinicum (as seen in Chapter 4). It is interesting to note that in both of these battles Belisarius was either 'forced to fight by the troops' and was defeated, or lost the battle and blamed the troops.

It is possible that the defeat was a major miscalculation by Belisarius. Still heavily outnumbered, he may have estimated that the large number of casualties caused by the regular small-scale sallies had reduced morale amongst the Goths, meaning that they would be liable to panic and flee when faced with a much larger force. If so, his guess was hugely mistaken. The troops withstood a barrage of enemy missile fire, for the most part without the ability to strike back. Discipline and morale in the Gothic army remained high. Belisarius' strategy was a failure.

Witigis, on the other hand, gains a lot of credibility from the battle. Although his tactics were uninspired, they were the cause of the victory. Furthermore, his ability to restrain his troops and allow the Byzantines to tire themselves out before delivering a charge that quickly routed the enemy speaks of a Gothic confidence in their commander that in this case was justified. The only incident that stopped the victory from being devastating was the courage of the minority of the infantry under Principius and Tarmatus who fought and covered the retreat to the city. Without them, Byzantine casualties would have been far higher, with unknown consequences for the remainder of the campaign.

Aftermath of the Battle

Recognising the danger of open battle, Belisarius reverted to the earlier hit–and–run tactics that had proved so effective against the Goths. Procopius states that in these Belisarius was 'generally victorious' (*Wars*, VI.I.2). This suggests that on most days the tactics worked, but that occasionally the Byzantine cavalry was caught before they could reach the safety of the city, though possibly without losing too many casualties. This reinforces the idea mentioned earlier that Belisarius relied upon the superior quality of his body-guards and *bucellarii* in these attacks: it is likely that the defeats occurred when a less experienced commander was given control of the sortie and had failed to react in time to the Gothic approach, in much the same way that the Goths had been defeated when they had tried to replicate the ruse and had been surrounded. In the same passage Procopius also indicates that sometimes infantry was sent out alongside the cavalry, possibly with a view to increasing their confidence and experience and so allowing them to become fully integrated with the cavalry as a fighting force.

Procopius gives several examples of such sallies. One of these involved the general Constantinus leading the Huns out onto the Plains of Nero. Late in the afternoon Constantinus realised that the Goths had advanced to close range and were now too close to allow the Huns to retire in safety. Therefore, he led them towards an area where there stood several ruined buildings and a stadium, ordering the Huns to dismount in the narrow lanes between them, where they were safe from mounted assault. His men now began a devastating fire upon the enemy. Finally, when it became evident that the Huns would not soon run out of arrows and their losses continued to mount, the Goths retired in disorder, pursued by the remounted Huns. The Huns then returned to the city.

All of these episodes display that Belisarius, while an an able commander himself, was also ably supported by subordinates who were capable of assessing situations on their own and reaching sound military conclusions.

As the spring equinox arrived, so did the pay for the troops. Euthalius landed at Tarracina with the money, and Belisarius arranged a diversionary attack to allow him access to the city in safety. In the course of these distractions three members of Belisarius' guard were injured by the Goths and their medical attention detailed.

Cutilas, a Thracian, was struck in the head by a javelin, but continued to fight. After the battle, the javelin was removed, but since it was embedded in his skull, the force needed was excessive; he contracted phrenitis, an 'inflammation of the brain', and later died.

Bochas, a Hunnic officer of the guards, was attacked by twelve Goths. One assailant pierced the flesh under his arm and another cut him diagonally across the thigh, both areas which the armour did not cover, As a note to those who study the efficiency of ancient armour, the other ten blows struck his body armour and were turned aside. Unfortunately, the cut across his leg seems to have severed an artery and three days later he also died.

The last of the three, Arzes, was struck by an arrow between his nose and right eye. The physicians were worried about the amount of damage that would be caused by withdrawing the arrow, since the barbs were likely to cause severe injuries when they were pulled backwards. However, one named Theoctistus, feeling the back of Arzes' head, realised that the head of the arrow had gone almost all of the way through. Therefore, he ordered that the shaft of the arrow protruding from Arzes' face be cut off, and then proceeded to cut the back of Arzes' head where the head of the arrow seemed to be resting. Uncovering the head of the arrow, Theoctistus pulled the rest of the arrow through the back of Arzes' head, so removing it without doing any further unnecessary damage. Interestingly, Arzes survived the experience with hardly a scar.

Shortly after the spring equinox, famine and disease began to affect the citizens and troops in Rome. This result illustrates the wisdom and foresight of Witigis in capturing Portus; unable to use the river to transport supplies to the city, the need to transport food by road drastically reduced the daily amount reaching the city. Now, with the outbreak of disease, the Goths ceased to fight as they did not wish to contract the illness themselves.

Instead, Witigis decided to further reduce the level of supplies reaching the city. To the south of the city was a place where two of the great aqueducts approached each other before dividing again to make their separate entries to the city. At this junction the Goths built walls and so created a fortress which they manned with 7,000 warriors in an attempt to cut the supplies coming by road from Ostia, presumably via the Porta Ostiensis. The measure worked, as the situation in the city now became desperate and the citizens demanded that they be allowed to join Belisarius and fight a battle against the Goths. Belisarius refused, claiming that reinforcements were on the way and that shortly he would be able to take offensive action with regular troops.

Accordingly, sometime in September/October 537, Belisarius sent Procopius to Naples to muster all available troops, including any available reinforcements that had arrived, and supplies, ready for transport to Rome via Ostia. There was a rumour that reinforcements had landed and were currently scattered around Campania. Procopius left the city at night by the Porta Ostiensis

Map 14: Events during and after the siege of Rome.

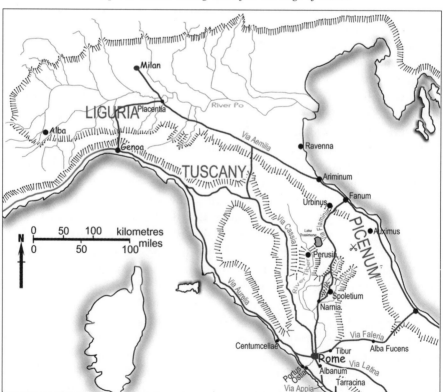

(St Paul's Gate) along with a small bodyguard led by Mundilas to escort him past the newly-created fort guarding the road. As Procopius travelled to Naples, Mundilas and his men returned to Belisarius and informed him that the Goths were not mounting patrols or even moving from their camps at night.

Sensing that Gothic morale was declining, Belisarius sent out cavalry detachments to local strongpoints with orders to restrict Gothic foraging parties. In effect, the Goths were now to be besieged within their own camps, leaving the Byzantines free to gather food and supplies from the neighbourhood without being attacked. Belisarius had previously attempted a similar enterprise earlier, sending Gontharis and a force of Heruls to Albanum. At that time, however, they had been forced to return when attacked by the Goths.

Now, he sent Martinus and Trajan to Tarracina along with 1,000 men. Part of the force was to garrison the city, Martinus and Trajan were to escort Antonina to the relative safety of Naples before setting up strongpoints in Campania to harass the Goths in that region. Similarly, Magnus and Sinthues with 500 men were sent to repair and man the fortress of Tibur, whilst Valerian and the Huns were sent to the Basilica of Saint Paul, which lay 14 *stades* (around 1 ½ miles) south of the city of Rome on the banks of the Tiber, to set up a camp and harass the Goths. Once the base was established, Valerian returned to the city.

The strategy worked; shortly afterwards the Goths began to suffer the effects of famine and disease broke out in their camps, especially that set up to the south between the aqueducts. Unfortunately, the Huns too began to suffer from famine and so left their camp and returned to Rome.

As these events unfolded, Procopius gathered supplies and placed them on board ships ready to sail to Ostia, He also managed to assemble a force of 500 men to reinforce Rome. When he was joined by Antonina, they waited for the orders to return to Rome.

Belisarius regains the initiative

At last, freed from other theatres of war, reinforcements now began to arrive in Italy. The first was a contingent of 300 cavalry led by Zeno, who arrived in Rome using the Via Latina from Samnium. Shortly afterwards, 3,000 Isaurians under Paulus and Conon arrived in Naples, and 800 Thracians under John, nephew of Vitalianus and *magister militum*, along with 1,000 regular cavalry under various commanders, landed at Dryus (see Map 11). These now gathered in Naples before moving to Tarracina, where they joined Martinus and Trajan. The ships with their supplies were ordered to proceed to Ostia, which was still in Byzantine hands.

Fearing the Goths would attack the newly-arrived troops as they moved towards Rome, Belisarius devised a new stratagem as a diversion. Realising that the Flaminian Gate had been blocked, the Goths had built one of their camps close by in order to threaten the walls. At night Belisarius had the wall blocking the gate removed so that he once again had free access to and from the gate. At daybreak, Trajan and Diogenes were sent out of the Pincian Gate with 1,000 cavalry and ordered to attract the full attention of the Goths, if possible forcing them to pursue the Byzantines as they retreated. Trajan and Diogenes were successful, and as the Goths set off in pursuit of the Byzantines, Belisarius led his men out of the Flaminian Gate. Although the new forces failed in their attempt to capture the camp, the majority bypassed the strongpoint and so fell upon the rear of the pursuing Goths. Trajan and Diogenes now rallied their men and charged the Goths from the front. Attacked from both sides, the Gothic forces disintegrated, most being killed and the survivors fleeing to the camps. The Goths were now in no condition to attack the reinforcements as they approached the city.

With their repeated defeats (after the arrival of the wages at the spring equinox, Procopius states that there were sixty nine more skirmishers between the Byzantines and the Goths – *Wars*, VI.ii.37), the onset of famine, disease and the news that an unknown number of Byzantine reinforcements were now approaching the city, the Goths finally lost heart. They sent envoys to Belisarius to arrange for an armistice with a view to negotiating peace.

Declaring that the Byzantines had no right to invade Italy, Witigis offered Sicily to Belisarius in return for an end to the war. When Belisarius asked about those areas of the mainland currently under his control and declared that he did not have the authority to negotiate such a treaty, the Goths agreed to send envoys to Justinian to arrange a peace settlement. The date was now early to mid-December 537. In the meantime, a truce of three months was negotiated to allow the envoys time for their journey. This was good for Belisarius, as it would allow him to billet his troops for the winter and attempt to gather supplies for the coming campaign season.

Constantinus

It was during the time of the truce that Belisarius and Constantinus quarrelled; the second time that Belisarius was to be touched by the hand of scandal during the siege.

The affair was initiated when Constantinus was at Spoletium and, as previously related, confiscated two daggers from a Roman citizen. The citizen was called Presidius and was a Roman living in Ravenna at the outbreak of the war. Rather than face the Goths, he chose to go into exile, carrying with him two daggers with scabbards adorned with gold and precious stones. These represented the remains of his wealth, since he had been unable to take anything else of value with him. He arrived in Spoletium, and, hearing of the daggers, Constantinus sent his guard, Maxentiolus, to take them.

Presidius had travelled on to Rome and, during the course of the siege, had remained quiet about the affair. With the outbreak of peace, he had complained to Belisarius about the theft, which was against Belisarius' instructions concerning the treatment of native Italians. Consequently, Belisarius ordered Constantinus to give the daggers back, but he refused. A stalemate then ensued, most likely because Belisarius left the city and travelled to Campania to collect supplies (Marcellinus Comes. *Additions to the Chronicles*, 538). Upon Belisarius' return, Presidius accosted him in the street and embarrassed him by holding his horse's reigns and explaining the injustice to all within hearing.

Humiliated, Belisarius now called Constantinus and ordered him to relinquish the daggers. When Constantinus again refused, Belisarius summoned his guards. Thinking that he was about to be executed out of hand, Constantinus drew a dagger and attempted to strike Belisarius. He was restrained by Ildiger and Valerian before the guards arrived and he was placed under arrest. According to the *Anekdota*, Procopius claims that Belisarius was willing to release Constantinus once the daggers had been returned, but was persuaded by Antonina to execute the general because she had a grudge concerning remarks Constantinus had made against her (*Anekdota*, 1.22–5 for the cause of animosity; 1.28–30 for the execution). Procopius declared that this was the 'only unholy deed done by Belisarius' (Proc, *Wars*, VI.viii.18), and that it earned him the enmity of Justinian and the Byzantine notables (*Anekdota*, 1.30).

The End of the Siege

As the talks progressed, the reinforcements and supplies arrived at Ostia. Under cover of the non-aggression agreement, Belisarius now transferred all of the supplies to Rome using the river to help in the transportation of the goods. The Goths watched from their vantage point at Portus and the transfer was completed by the winter solstice.

Byzantine command of the sea now began to affect the situation. Unable or unwilling to risk transporting supplies to their garrisons by boat, the Goths were forced to withdraw their troops from Portus and Centumcellae. Due to famine, they were also forced to leave the city of Albanum. Belisarius quickly sent troops to occupy all of the vacated positions. Although the Goths protested that this was in violation of their non-aggression treaty, Belisarius laughed and refused to withdraw his men.

Since he had been reinforced, and confident that he could defend the city, he dispatched some troops further afield in order to put pressure on the Goths. John, nephew of Vitalianus, who had recently arrived with 800 Thracians, along with 400 men from Valerian's command under Valerian's nephew Damianus, and 800 *bucellarii* under Suntas and Adegis, were sent to set up a camp in the vicinity of Alba. John was ordered not to act aggressively or commit any warlike act unless the Goths had broken the armistice first. However, when the Goths did, he was to take control of the district of Picenum, so pushing Byzantine control further to the northeast.

At the same time, Datius, the priest of Milan, along with envoys, arrived and offered to surrender the city and the whole district of Liguria to Belisarius, requesting troops to act as a garrison. In light of the armistice, Belisarius decided to agree but then detained the envoys over winter, thus gaining time and so not being seen as the man who broke the truce.

Unhappy with Belisarius and his deployment of troops around Italy, Witigis decided that the capture of Rome was still possible, given the more relaxed conditions now prevailing. He sent scouts into the Aqua Virgo aqueduct at night to establish whether it could be used for access to the city. The lights of the torches they carried were seen by the guards, and, when it was reported to Belisarius, he ordered an investigation. The Byzantines found extinguished torches in the aqueduct and so posted guards. Consequently, the Goths gave up on the attempt

Instead, Witigis decided upon a frontal assault on the Pincian Gate. Unfortunately for the Goths, Ildiger and his men, who happened to be on duty at the time, saw the Goths forming up for the assault and mounted a pre-emptive attack. Many of the Goths were killed, and the noise of the fighting alerted the rest of the Byzantines to the danger. The Goths withdrew and Witigis considered his options.

He determined that the final attempt on the city would be made against the walls that ran alongside the Tiber. Here, the ancients had relied upon the river to do most of their work and so had erected only a small wall with no towers. Witigis bribed two Byzantines to move along the wall distributing drugged wine to the guards, so allowing the Goths easy access. However, one of the men – probably after taking the money – went to Belisarius and told him of the plot, naming the second man. This individual was arrested and, under torture, revealed the full details of the plan. He was then mutilated, but not killed, mounted on an ass, and sent into the Goths' camp.

At this point, Witigis realised that the siege could not be won. Furthermore, disturbing news now reached him from Ravenna. For with the Goths' breaking of the armistice, Belisarius had sent a message to John in Picenum, ordering him to take control of the area. John with 2,000 cavalry had travelled throughout Picenum, enslaving Gothic women and children, but, following Belisarius' policy, leaving the native Italians unharmed. He was brought to battle by Ulitheus, Uncle of Witigis, but the Byzantines won a resounding victory, killing most of the Goths, including Ulitheus himself.

Procopius records that John was a daring, efficient and experienced officer who used his expertise to help bring the siege of Rome to an end. With nice strategic insight, John had bypassed Auximus and Urbinus, since they both had garrisons and were difficult to assault, and instead had accepted the invitation by the citizens of Ariminum to occupy their city. John recognised that, since the city was close to Ravenna, the Goths were likely to lift the siege of Rome and return to Ravenna to protect their city from the threat of being captured. He was correct: upon hearing the news, Witigis ordered the army to leave Rome and march on Ravenna.

As the Goths withdrew, Belisarius planned one more action against them. Since most of his cavalry was away from the city, Belisarius decided to use his infantry alongside his remaining cavalry. Deciding that if he faced the entire Gothic army he would likely suffer a heavy defeat, he decided to focus the attack on the Gothic troops that had been encamped west of the Tiber. He waited until over half of the Goths had crossed the Milvian Bridge and then assaulted the rear of their retreating columns. The ensuing battle was quick and decisive. Although the Goths resisted manfully at first, they soon broke and fled across the bridge, many being killed or wounded in the crush while more were pushed over the bridge and so drowned in the Tiber. It was now the middle of March 538, and the siege of Rome was over; it had lasted for one year and nine days.

Belisarius and Witigis

The question remains as to why the siege of Rome failed and whether the failure was due to the incompetence of Witigis or the superior generalship of Belisarius.

In one respect Belisarius was extremely fortunate: having recently defeated the Vandals and witnessed their inability to resist his horse archers, he was now facing an army with the same weakness. He had recognised the similarity very early in the campaign and so been confident throughout that he would be victorious (Proc, *Wars*, V.xxvii.28–29). Consequently, during the siege he had used the horse-archers' superior abilities in order to wear down the Goths slowly, constantly defeating them in small-scale encounters and so reducing their morale. However, when he changed his tactics – allegedly under pressure from his own troops, whose morale had been correspondingly increasing – he risked losing control of the battlefield and allowing the Goths the chance to fight the battle on their own terms. The Goths seized their chance and defeated the Byzantines in the only open battle of the siege. Recognising his mistake, Belisarius did not repeat the attempt at facing the Goths in the open, even when pressed by the Romans to do so. It is the sign of a good commander that, if he makes a mistake, he does not repeat it and so suffer unnecessary casualties amongst his men.

Finally, when he realised that the Goths' endurance was waning, Belisarius took positive action and so placed the Goths themselves under the pressures of a siege. By almost continuously retaining the initiative, Belisarius controlled most of the encounters that took place. Apart from the battle, his strategy and tactics utilised the innate superiority of his troops in a specific style of warfare. Overall, he displayed a high level of military competence.

Witigis does not fare as well in the analysis of the siege. Having failed to take the city in the traditional manner, using battering rams, siege towers, and so on, he recognised the importance of the port of Portus in the supply of Rome, and its capture must rate as one of the high points of the Gothic siege. Although the Goths did not entirely surround the city, the large population depended upon vast amounts of goods being transported by ship; the roads did not have the same capacity and so the city faced famine and disease.

Witigis' control of his troops during the Battle of Rome is the other high point of the Gothic siege. Despite losing many casualties without being able to reply, the Goths maintained their discipline and formations until the decisive point of the battle. The timing of the charge caused the Byzantine wing to panic, and the panic spread throughout the army. Without the cover of a small group of infantry, the defeat could have been far worse.

However, in other areas Witigis' strategy does not stand up to inspection. Time and again he failed to take the initiative or respond to the Byzantine hit-and-run tactics with a tactic of his own to nullify the effects of the Byzantine horse archers. Furthermore, he totally failed to grasp the purpose of the tactic and his own attempts to emulate it ended in dismal failure as his troops were incapable of long-distance missile fire.

Finally, the free movement allowed to the Byzantines towards the end of the siege, and the lack of response by the Goths, illustrates that Witigis was a general of average, but limited qualities. He did not maintain the pressure upon the defences that would have allowed the Goths a chance of victory. His lack of forward planning proved to be his downfall.

Chapter 10

The Victory of Belisarius

With the siege over and the Goths defeated, Belisarius now had enough troops to begin the conquest of the rest of Italy. His first act was to accede to the Milanese envoys' demands and send a force of 1,000 men, comprised of Isaurians under Ennes and Thracians under Paulus, to occupy Milan. The whole force was under the command of Mundilas, who had a few of Belisarius' *bucellarii* to act as a personal bodyguard. With the troops went Fidelius, who had been appointed praetorian prefect by Belisarius. He was a native of Milan and was sent to act as personal proof of Roman efficiency and good intentions.

The army travelled by sea from Portus to Genoa, before arriving at Ticinus. Here, the Goths of the region had deposited their wealth for safekeeping, leaving a strong garrison of efficient troops as guards. As the Byzantines approached, the garrison left the city and a pitched battle was fought. The Byzantines were victorious, and in their pursuit came near to capturing the city itself. Shortly afterwards, Fidelius went alone to a church to pray. Upon leaving, his horse stumbled and he fell. This was within sight of the city walls, and a small group of Goths came out and killed Fidelius.

Politically weakened by the loss, the Byzantines moved on and finally entered Milan. They sent small garrisons to the neighbouring cities of Bergomum, Comum and Novaria, plus other strongholds, in order to secure the whole of Liguria for Rome.

When Witigis learned of the defection of Milan, he sent a large army under the command of his nephew Uraias to lay siege to the city. In accordance with their agreement, the Franks sent 10,000 Burgundians to assist Uraias in the siege, although Procopius may have exaggerated the strength of the Burgundian force. No Franks participated, since they were still supposed to be allied with the Byzantines against the Goths.

In Milan, Mundilas prepared to face the Goths. But, as he had left garrisons throughout Liguria, he had only 300 regular troops for the defence, according to Procopius, and so he was forced to rely upon the citizens to help maintain a guard on the walls.

With provision made for the attack on Milan, Witigis followed the roads towards Ariminum, deploying his forces as he went. Gibimer and 1,000 men were to garrison Clusium; Albilas with 1,000 men went to Urviventus; Uligisalus and 400 men to Tudera; Visandus and 4,000 men garrisoned Auximus; and

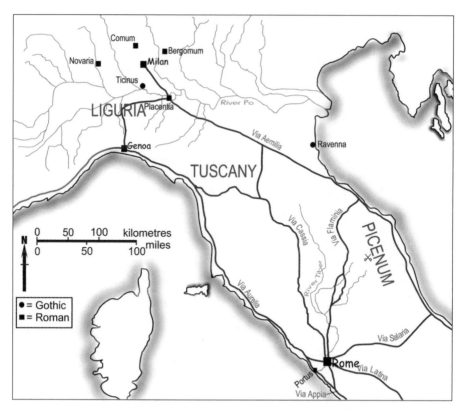

Map 15: Belisarius takes Liguria.

Moras and 2,000 men were to hold Urbinus. Another 400 men were left in Petra (in Picenum), and 500 men each in Caesena and Montferetra. Witigis led the rest to Ariminum to lay siege to the city and so remove the threat to Ravenna.

Correctly surmising that Witigis would attack Ariminum, Belisarius sent 1,000 men under Ildiger and Martinus to the city with fresh orders for John, who currently held it for Rome. Belisarius could be certain that they would arrive before Witigis since the Goths had been forced to use a longer, more circuitous route. The Byzantines still had garrisons in Narnia, Spoletium and Perusia and Witigis wanted to avoid these cities as they would slow his progress towards Ariminum. Ildiger and Martinus used the direct route of the Flaminian Way.

Ildiger and Martinus had orders to proceed via Ancon, which was garrisoned by Conon, take men from that garrison, and then go to Ariminum. Conon was to remain at Ancon. Once at Ariminum, John and his cavalry force was to be replaced by infantry comprising those from the command of Ildiger and Martinus combined with those taken from Ancon. The strategic reasoning

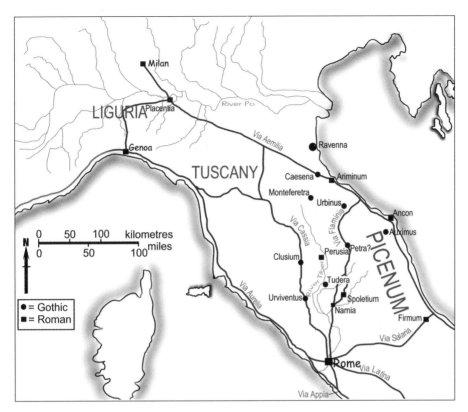

Map 16: Witigis' response.

behind the decision is simple to understand. Belisarius hoped that the presence of only a few troops under an unknown commander would be less of a threat to the Goths, resulting in them not bothering to lay siege to the city, but instead going on to Ravenna and reserving their troops for more vital commitments. On the other hand, if they did decide to lay siege to the city, the cavalry forces under John would be best deployed where their mobility was an advantage. Combined with the cavalry of Ildiger and Martinus, they could pose a real threat to the Goths besieging the city, causing casualties and disrupting supplies.

On the way to Ariminum the road passed through a tunnel cut through where the mountains came down to a river's edge, with the north and south entrances covered by iron gates. This was known as Petra, and Witigis had sent 400 men to act as a garrison at that point. The Byzantines attacked the southern gate and were repulsed, having to resort to scaling the cliffs before the garrison surrendered. Leaving a small force of their own to guard Petra, Ildiger and Martinus continued to Ancon and collected some of the garrison before arriving at Ariminum.

Disregarding Belisarius' orders, John refused to leave. After much argument, Ildiger and Martinus left the infantry from Ancon to supplement the garrison, and returned to Belisarius, accompanied only by the *bucellarii* that Belisarius had sent with John. Damianus and the 400 *foederati* remained with John. Justinian had attempted to nullify just this kind of intrigue and infighting by appointing Belisarius as sole commander for the campaign. In Africa this had worked, due to the speed of the campaign and there being no need to dispatch reinforcements. In Italy, the need for large numbers of additional troops – who needed high-ranking commanders – resulted in a situation where friction began to arise.

The Siege of Ariminum

Shortly after Ildiger and Martinus had left to join Belisarius, Witigis arrived at Ariminum and placed the city under siege. He quickly built a siege tower, but this time it was designed to be pushed by men stationed inside the tower: there was to be no repeat of the failure outside Rome when the oxen had been killed. When the tower was ready, Witigis had it manoeuvred near to the wall, ready for use the following morning. Placing guards around the tower, the Goths retired for the night.

Although the inhabitants of the city panicked, John remained calm. That night he led a force of Isaurians outside the city walls, but, instead of attacking the tower, they quietly deepened the existing trench in front of the wall, throwing the spoil to the wall side of the trench to create an inner earthwork. Late in the night the Goths became aware of activity and quickly mounted an attack, but John withdrew into the city, believing the trench to be deep enough for his purposes.

He was soon proved to be correct. Witigis was extremely dissatisfied with the guards, so had some of them executed. He then began the assault. Observing that the ditch was now deeper in front of the tower, he ordered his men to throw faggots into the trench before pushing the tower forwards. As the tower advanced its weight crushed the faggots and it sank a little into the trench. The advance now ground to a halt, since the tower came against the newly formed earthwork, made from the spoil of the previous night, and could not progress any further.

As the tower was now vulnerable, Witigis decided to withdraw, taking the tower with him. John did not want this, so led a sortie out of the city. After fierce fighting, the Goths succeeded in withdrawing with the tower, but lost so many men that Witigis decided to simply starve out the defenders, who were already low on supplies.

Now that he needed far fewer troops for a siege than for an assault, Witigis dispatched an army under Vacimus to Auximus to join with the garrison there and make an attempt upon Conon in Ancon. As the Goths approached Ancon,

Conon led his troops out and formed a line of battle. Upon seeing the numbers arrayed against them, the Byzantines fled back to the city, where the defenders had already closed the gates. Many men, including Conon, only gained access by climbing ropes let down from the walls.

Unfortunately, the Goths already had siege equipment prepared and immediately attempted to take the city by storm. Using scaling ladders they managed to gain a foothold on the battlements but Ultimuth, a Thracian of Belisarius' guards, and Gouboulgoudou, a Hun of Valerian's guards, drove the attackers off the walls, both being severely wounded in the feat.

Meanwhile, Belisarius left a few men to garrison Rome and sent some to Tudera and Clusium to make camps ready for laying siege to these cities. Upon the Byzantines' approach, however, the Gothic garrisons of both cities surrendered and were sent to Sicily and Naples. Belisarius now detached men to act as garrisons for the two cities.

Hearing of the arrival of Narses the eunuch in Picenum, Belisarius travelled to join forces with him, leaving Rome in mid June 538. Narses was accompanied by 5,000 men with their commanders, including Justinus, the *magister militum*

Map 17: Belisarius makes new plans.

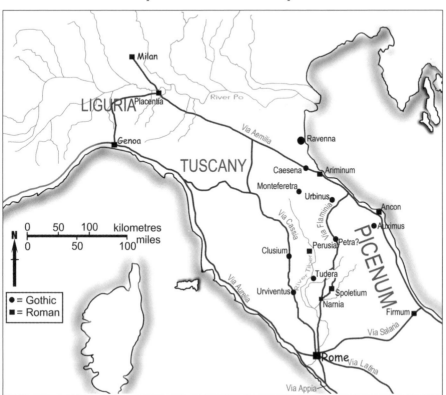

per Illyricum, and Narses, brother of Aratius, who together had beaten Belisarius in battle in the east (see above and Chapter 8). They were accompanied by 2,000 Heruls led by Visandus, Aluith and Phanitheus.

The two generals met near Firmum and held a conference to decide upon strategy. There appeared to be two options that Belisarius could take. One was to assault and take Auximus before attempting to relieve the siege of Ariminum. This would take time and Ariminum could fall before it could be relieved. The other course was to bypass Auximus. This could allow him to arrive at Ariminum in time to lift the siege, but would be at risk of attack from the rear by forces moving out from Auximus.

The talks split the officers into two distinct groups, centred around Narses the eunuch and Belisarius. One stated that they needed to relieve Ariminum, since John had some excellent troops there and he was a brave and energetic commander. This view was supported by Narses, more so as John was a personal friend of his. The other maintained that John was there by his own choice and because he had refused to obey Belisarius' commands. This was supported by those who had followed Belisarius throughout the campaign, and especially those who had served in Africa.

The episode illustrates the division inherent within the Byzantine military framework. Narses the eunuch was a personal friend of John, and was backed by those who had come with him, especially Narses and Aratius the Armenians, since they were fellow countrymen of Narses the eunuch. Those loyal to Belisarius wished John to be punished for his disobedience. Whilst the argument was being waged, a letter arrived from John stating that his supplies would only last seven days before he would be forced to surrender. This was the spur Belisarius needed to make his decision. John and Ariminum would be saved from the Goths.

Belisarius' strategy was to make the Goths believe that they were being faced with a force that greatly outnumbered their own. Accordingly, he divided his forces into four. Aratius and 1,000 men were to make a camp near to Auximus in an attempt to pin the Gothic garrison within the city. They were not to fight except in self-defence. A large force under the command of Ildiger, with Herodian, Uliaris and Narses brother of Aratius were to go by sea to Ariminum, but were not to land near the city unless other Byzantine forces were close by. Another large force under Martinus was to march along the coast road, lighting campfires equivalent to those of a far larger force to deceive the Goths into thinking that the force was bigger then it was in reality. Belisarius himself, along with Narses, would lead the remainder inland via Urvisalia and so come upon Ariminum from a different direction. Procopius (*Wars*, VI.xvii.12) gives the reason for these deployments: the Goths still outnumbered the Byzantines and so Belisarius was unwilling to fight a conventional battle. Therefore, if the Goths saw three Byzantine armies of unknown size – one of which was making itself appear bigger than in reality – approaching from different directions, they would hopefully panic and raise the siege without a fight.

This strategy received a major boost when Belisarius was only one day's travel from Ariminum. His army unexpectedly met a force of Goths and killed the majority of them, the remainder hiding nearby until nightfall. These then returned to Ariminum under cover of darkness and claimed that Belisarius was approaching with a large host. As a result, the Goths made preparations to fight Belisarius as he approached the north of the city. Yet that same night the many camp fires lit by Martinus were observed about 60 *stades* (approximately 7.5 miles) to the east along the coast. The Goths were now filled with fear, which was heightened at daybreak when the Byzantine fleet came into view with Ildiger's troops on board. The Goths did not wait, but gathered most of their belongings and retreated to Ravenna. The siege was raised without a fight and John emerged from the city looking pale and emaciated.

The whole strategy displays Belisarius' abilities as a commander. He was able to foresee the enemy's response and so make maximum use of the forces available. It was an excellent piece of generalship and won the day without a single casualty.

Internal divisions

Unfortunately, the division in the Byzantine army between Belisarius and Narses was now deepened by the actions of John. Upon the relief of the town, the first person to the city was Ildiger, and when Belisarius implied that John owed a debt to Belisarius' son-in-law, John replied that his gratitude was to Narses the eunuch, suggesting that Belisarius had only come to his aid after being persuaded to act.

John's response deserves examination. Although the statement has been interpreted by Procopius as an insult to Belisarius, there may have been more to the reply. In the early Roman Empire, citizens of Rome were bound to one another by the client/patron system. No doubt by the time of Justinian the system had changed, and probably drastically, but the idea of owing a personal debt still remained. It is possible that John was not being insulting as such, but was attempting to avoid an obligation to someone with whom he was at odds politically. In Chapter 2 the complex system in which the bureaucracy and the military operated was outlined. It is likely that if John had accepted Belisarius' comment without demur he would have been obligated to repay Ildiger at some later date in a manner which he would not like. Furthermore, Ildiger was a relative of Belisarius, a man who John had just disobeyed.

By his remaining in Ariminum after Belisarius had specifically ordered him to leave the city, John had laid himself open to attack. It is clear that John, and Narses the eunuch, did not share Belisarius' opinions concerning the strategy

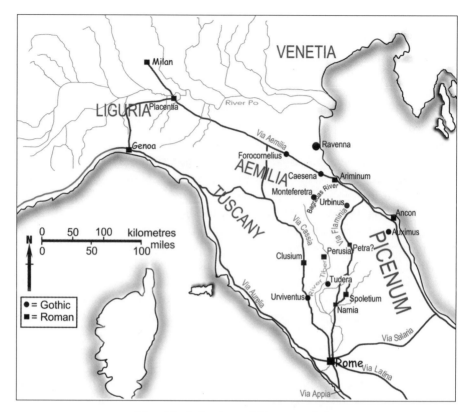

Map 18: Belisarius and Narses in Italy.

to be used to defeat the Goths. Maybe John was unconvinced about Belisarius' military ability as, although he had conquered the Vandals easily, he had not done too well in Persia. The alleged dismissal of the Gothic threat by both John and Narses is likely to have led to the conclusion that Belisarius was of only limited talent. Consequently, John may have wanted Narses, both his friend and certainly a gifted general, to be appointed to the command in Italy. Whatever the cause of the friction, it soon bore fruit for the Goths. Belisarius and John were now intensely unsure of each other. The conflict within the army now increased to a greater level. Narses' aides now began to turn the eunuch against Belisarius, declaring that a man who was a close confidant of the emperor should not be taking orders from a mere general. Realising that things were getting out of hand, Belisarius called a meeting.

At this meeting, Belisarius pointed out that the Byzantine position was now slightly precarious, since they were surrounded by the Gothic garrisons in Ravenna, Auximus, and other cities round to Urviventus. Accordingly, he proposed to send troops to Milan to raise the siege of Mundilas' forces whilst he and the rest of the army advanced to attempt the siege of Auximus. This would allow the Byzantines more room and extricate them from their current vulnerable position. He also warned Narses that he and his supporters were underestimating the strength of the Goths due to the ease with which they had relieved Ariminum. John and Narses may have believed that the Goths were unable to defend themselves and that Belisarius' incompetence was delaying the conquest.

Narses agreed with most of the plan, but argued that Narses and his 'allies', including Aratius, would go to the region of Aemilia, which the Goths were attempting to secure. As well as saving the region, this would simultaneously pin down enemy forces in Ravenna, allowing Belisarius and his troops an almost free hand to do as they wished. He suggested that an attempt on Auximus would fail without such a diversion, as the troops in Ravenna could easily move south and attack the Byzantines in the rear. Being outnumbered and surrounded would be disastrous for the Byzantines.

After some thought, Belisarius, who was worried about splitting his forces too much and leaving them vulnerable, decided that the final decision was his to make. He therefore showed his letter of appointment to Narses, stating that Narses was his subordinate and, as stated in the letter, all should follow Belisarius 'in the best interests of the state' (Proc, *Wars*, VI.xviii.12–29). Showing that he was well versed in Byzantine politics, Narses focused on the last sentence and declared that Belisarius was not acting in the best interests of the state and in that case the letter could be disregarded. The complexities of Byzantine politics had come home to roost.

Yet when Belisarius did act, he did not follow the plan outlined above, deciding instead to spend winter in Rome. However, before the end of the campaigning season he had the chance to further restrict the Goths' control of Italy. As a consequence, on the way back to Rome, he sent Peranius and a strong force to besiege Urviventus, himself leading the rest of the army to lay siege to Urbinus. Narses, John and their adherents followed Belisarius but set up their camp on the opposite side of the city. The envoys that Belisarius sent failed to convince the garrison that they should surrender, so Belisarius began to prepare siege engines with which to assault the city. John, who had on a previous occasion decided not to attempt to attack the city, declared that the city could not be taken. Narses agreed with him, and, although Belisarius begged him to stay, their forces abandoned the siege and returned to Ariminum.

Belisarius' luck now came to his aid again. As he was preparing to assault the city, the spring inside the city upon which the garrison relied for water inexplicably failed. As the assault troops moved towards the city, the Goths appeared on the walls and surrendered to Belisarius. It was now mid December 538 and Belisarius continued on his journey to Rome.

Astonished and dejected by Belisarius' success in a venture he had declared impossible, Narses sent John to take Caesena whilst he remained in Ariminum. The assault failed with heavy casualties, but, undaunted, John moved fast and took Forocornelius (modern Imola) by surprise. Alarmed, the Goths in the area retreated and so John secured Aemilia for Narses.

Meanwhile, hearing from Peranius that the Goths in Urviventus were short of supplies, Belisarius detoured to the town and waited for the inevitable. Shortly after his arrival, the Gothic garrison surrendered.

The loss of Milan

Belisarius could finally return to Rome and set up his winter headquarters in the city, but he had one more action to take before the end of the year. In late December, he sent Martinus and Uliaris to lift the siege of Milan. However, daunted by the crossing of the River Po (possibly in flood due to the seasonal rains) and unsure of the strength of the forces of Uraias, they did not dare to cross the river. Learning that friends were nearby, Mundilas smuggled a message out of Milan, saying that the city was in dire straits. Unsure of what to do, and hearing that John and Justinus were close by in Aemilia, Martinus sent to Belisarius asking for them to join him as reinforcements. Belisarius now ordered John and Justinus to join Martinus. They refused, stating that Narses was their commander. Belisarius now sent a message to Narses, asking him to order John and Justinus to go and aid Martinus raise the siege of Milan. Narses did as Belisarius had asked, and John travelled to the coast to collect ships to transport the army across the Po. On the way, he fell ill and stopped.

With the delay of the relief force, and with famine beginning to take hold, Uraias sent envoys asking for the surrender of the city and pledging the safety of the troops inside. The citizens, however, would have no such pledges as they had betrayed the Goths. Despite Mundilas' protests, the troops agreed to surrender and were escorted to safety outside the walls. The date was February or March 539. The city was now sacked, the men being killed and the women and treasures given to the Burgundians as thanks for their assistance. A further result of the surrender of Milan was that all of the cites in Liguria with a Byzantine garrison, including Bergomum, Comum and Novaria, quickly surrendered to the Goths to avoid the same fate.

With the imminent arrival of spring, Belisarius was preparing for the new campaign season when news arrived of the loss of Milan. Stung by the inactivity of Uliaris, for at least Martinus had requested aid in the attempt to relieve the city, Belisarius refused to speak to him again. Finally, he sent a letter to the emperor outlining the situation and explaining the course of events.

As a final blow to the pretensions of the invaders, when spring arrived it became apparent that their activities in Italy had caused the disruption of the normal agricultural routines and many crops now failed. In the ensuing famine thousands died and Procopius even gives examples of Italians turning to cannibalism in order to survive (*Wars*, VI.xx. 26–7).

Narses recalled

After receiving Belisarius' letter, Justinian did not apportion blame or take any action against individuals. Instead, he simply recalled Narses and again gave Belisarius overall command, this time ensuring that there would be no repeat of Narses' reinterpretation of the text.

Unfortunately, the Heruls that had arrived with Narses refused to stay with Belisarius in Italy. Making their own way out of Italy, they met Uraias and a Gothic force and sold all of their Gothic captives back to the Goths, simultaneously taking an oath not to fight the Goths again. However, meeting Vitalius in the lands of the Veneti, they were overcome with shame and so left Visandus and his troops in the region whilst the remainder returned to Constantinople.

Possibly at the same time as the arrival of the letter recalling Narses, or only shortly thereafter, the Gothic envoys that had been sent to Constantinople in December 537, towards the end of the siege of Rome, were sent back by Justinian. Belisarius retained them in his camp, demanding the release of Peter and Athanasius, the envoys who had been held captive since 536. The Goths agreed to the exchange and the Byzantine envoys were finally released. Belisarius sent them to Constantinople, where Justinian treated them with great honour.

Belisarius lays his plans

Now that he again had sole control of the army, Belisarius laid his plans for the new year's campaign. He decided to take Auximus and Fisula in order to clear the roads to Ravenna from Gothic garrisons. In this way he would ensure that when he did arrive at the Gothic capital he need not fear an attack from the rear. Accordingly, he sent Cyprian and Justinus with their own men, plus a force of Isaurian infantry and a further 500 infantry from the unit commanded by Demetrius, to begin the siege of Fisula. In order to protect them from an attack by Uraias in Milan, he commanded Martinus and John to lead their forces to the Po and so block any attempt by Uraias to raise the siege. If they were unable to stop him, they were to pursue Uraias and continuously harass the rear of his army. Cyprian and Justinus advanced to Fisula and laid siege to the city, whilst Martinus and John advanced to the Po and took Dorthon (Tortona), an unwalled city, to act as their base. Belisarius himself now moved to attack Auximus.

Learning that Belisarius would soon be attacking Ravenna, Witigis despaired and cast around for sources of help. First, he sent envoys to Vaces, ruler of the Lombards, but they were informed that the Lombards were, in fact, already

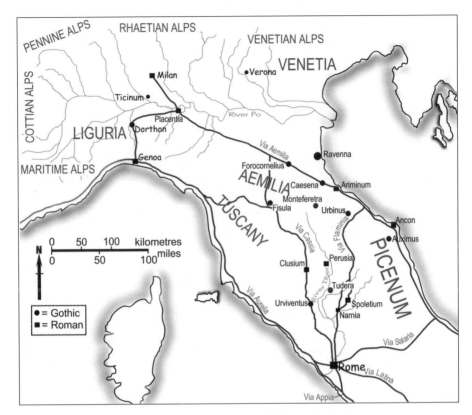

Map 19: The closing stages of the war in Italy.

allied to Justinian. Whilst in conference with his councillors, the Goths realised that the Byzantines had only been able to fight in Africa and Italy due to the peace treaty with Persia. They decided to send envoys to Khusrow, but also chose not to send Goths as their intentions would be plain and may delay talks. Therefore, they bribed two Ligurian priests to pose as a bishop and his retainer and in that guise act as envoys in order to persuade Khusrow to declare war on Justinian.

Meanwhile, Belisarius with the bulk of the army, numbering some 11,000 men, advanced and laid siege to Auximus. The date was either April or May 539. The city was strongly fortified and well sited on the top of a hill. As it controlled the approaches to Ravenna from the south, Witigis had left a strong garrison of proven troops to hold the city and thus act as an advance guard to protect Ravenna itself. Upon their arrival, Belisarius sent his troops to make a circle of camps around the city. Seeing that the Byzantines had become widely spread during the process of building their camps, the Goths sallied from the city and attacked the troops around Belisarius late in the afternoon. Defeated, they retreated to the city and prepared to resist the Byzantine assault.

On the previous day a group of Goths had been sent out of the city to organise provisions. Unaware of the Byzantine approach, these now returned and were caught outside the city. Some managed to sneak into the city, but the rest were destroyed by the Byzantine troops. Belisarius now assessed the defences of the city and decided that it was impossible to take it by assault. Therefore, he decided to put the city under a close siege and so starve the defenders into submission.

As the Byzantines settled down to the siege, they observed that there was an area of lush grass growing near the walls and that the Goths were in the habit of leaving the city to harvest the grass as food for their horses. Consequently, every day there was a small battle between the Byzantines and Goths as the Goths attempted to gather the forage for their mounts and the Byzantines attempted to stop them. Eventually, the Goths decided to ambush the Byzantines. Noting that the hillside around the grass was cut by ravines, they hid men in the depressions and then sent out their foragers as usual. When the Byzantines attacked and were fully engaged, the troops in the ravines leapt out and took the Byzantines by surprise, driving them off with heavy losses and so allowing the forage party to finish their work in peace.

The Goths repeated this tactic several times: although nearby Byzantine troops could see the ambush, their cries were drowned out by the noise that the Goths made during the fighting. Procopius now suggested to Belisarius that the trumpets of the cavalry could be used to sound the attack, and the trumpets of the infantry the retreat. The two trumpets made very different sounds, since those of the cavalry were made of leather and thin wood whilst those of the infantry were made of brass. On the next occasion that the Goths gathered grass, they were attacked by the Byzantines as usual but when they sprang their ambush, the infantry trumpets were blown and the Byzantines retired in safety.

With the siege now laid ever closer, the Goths in the city began to suffer from famine. As supplies ran low they sent an emissary to Witigis to ask for aid. Witigis agreed to send troops, but then remained in Ravenna. Procopius (*Wars*,VI.xxiv.14) notes that this was due to there being a shortage of supplies everywhere due to the widespread crop failures in Italy; Witigis would have had none to spare for the defenders, and if he had moved with his entire army they would likely also have run out of food as they approached the city.

As the siege of Auximus progressed, Cyprian and Justinus laid siege to Fisula, although, due to the topography, this could not be a close siege. Consequently, the Goths mounted many sorties against the Byzantines, but, being defeated, were gradually restricted to the city and the siege here, too, began to take effect. Eventually, these men also sent a message to Witigis asking for help. Since the city was not far from Milan, Witigis sent an order to Uraias commanding him to raise the siege. Uraias moved his army out of Milan and advanced to Dorthon, where he made camp opposite Martinus and John.

However, he did not attack them, believing that his defeat would mean that the Gothic cause in Italy would be lost. Since they were effectively pinning Uraias in place, the Byzantines were also happy to remain in their camp.

The Franks invade Italy

At this vital juncture the Franks, who were in theory allied to both the Byzantines and the Goths, decided to abandon their treaty with both and make an attempt to take at least part of Italy for themselves. Theudibert, king of the Franks, reasoned that, with both the Goths and the Byzantines tired by their long war, conquest of at least part of the peninsula was now feasible.

Leading a force of 100,000 men, according to Procopius, the Franks crossed the Alps into that part of Italy north of the Po. The Franks differed from the Goths and the Byzantines in that, again according to Procopius, they only had a small mounted bodyguard that protected the king. The remainder of the army was composed entirely of foot warriors armed with sword, shield and a throwing axe – the famed *francisca*. Although possibly a little simplistic, since at least some of the infantry would have carried long-range missile weapons such as bows, the description illustrates the main strength of the Frankish army.

The Franks marched through the north of Italy, welcomed by the Goths who believed that they had come as allies. Only when they had secured the bridge across the Po at Ticinum did the Franks show their true colours, attacking the neighbouring Goths, taking much spoil and many captives, before launching an attack on Uraias' camp. The Goths quickly broke and fled past the Byzantine camp. Assuming that Belisarius had arrived unannounced and attacked Uraias, Martinus and John led their troops out of their camp and rode to his assistance. Upon reaching the Gothic camp they were attacked by the Franks and also quickly fled, retiring to the relative safety of Tuscany.

However, Theudibert now halted his large army in an area where the Goths and Byzantines had been camped for quite a while. Supplies were low and, due to their poor diet, the Frankish troops began to suffer from diarrhoea and dysentery. With a large part of the army ill, the Franks were forced to remain stationary, which added to the numbers suffering from disease.

Hearing of the Frankish attack, Belisarius became increasingly worried about the troops besieging Fisula, since they were now vulnerable should the Franks march in their direction. In order to buy time, he sent an envoy to Theudibert, warning him of the consequences should he maintain his aggressive behaviour and remain in Italy. Worried by the possibility of a counterattack, and even more so since possibly up to a third of his army had died of disease, Theudibert decided not to remain in Italy. Instead, he led the remainder of his forces back home over the Alps. Once he had gone, Martinus and John moved their forces back to Dorthon so that they could give an advanced warning to the troops besieging Fisula should the Franks return, as well as guarding them from the Goths in Milan.

Affairs in the empire

It was only due to the relative peace on his other fronts that Justinian had been able to free troops to attempt the conquest of Africa and Italy. The peace was to be shattered by two events. The nearest of these to Italy, and so the one that could be expected to affect the progress of that war, was the Hunnic invasion of the Balkans. With most of the troops from the area already involved in the Gothic war (at the time of the Hunnic invasion Vitalius was advancing with a large body of troops from Dalmatia towards the north of Italy) the Huns advanced as far as the walls of Constantinople before returning to their homeland with a large number of captives and a vast amount of booty. A second wave invaded Greece, bypassing Thermopylae – which was stoutly defended – and ravaged the whole of Greece except for the Peleponnese.

Affairs in the east also began to affect the situation in Italy. Khusrow had been viewing the conquests of Belisarius with alarm, and he had asked his ally Al-Mundhir of the Lakhmids to give him a pretext for declaring war. Accordingly, Al-Mundhir accused Arethas, the Ghassanid ally of the Byzantines, of violating his territory. He then invaded the Ghassanid kingdom, declaring that he was not in breach of the treaty, since he had not been named in it. However, Procopius claims that traditionally the various 'Saracens' allied to Rome and Persia were automatically included in treaties made between those two empires.

Both the Ghassanids and the Lakhmids claimed suzerainty over an area known as Strata, south of Palmyra, and this is where Al-Mundhir attacked. Justinian sent Strategius, the administrator of the royal treasuries, as an envoy, who advised Justinian that he should relinquish claims to the area and so not provide Khusrow with a pretext for war.

However, Khusrow now claimed that the envoys to Al-Mundhir had been sent in an attempt to detach Al-Mundhir from his alliance to the Persians. He also claimed that Justinian had sent a letter to the Huns asking them to invade Persia. Although Justinian denied the claims, it now appeared to be only a matter of time before war was declared.

At this point the two 'Roman' envoys from Italy reached Khusrow. Whether he would have declared war upon hearing their pleas is unknown, since events in Armenia tipped the balance. An individual called Symeon had betrayed the city of Pharangium to the Byzantines during the Persian war, and had been given several villages in Armenia as a reward. Unfortunately, the previous owners did not appreciate the gift and had killed Symeon before fleeing to Persia. Justinian now gave the villages to Amazaspes, Symeon's nephew, but he was denounced by a man named Acacius for both abusing the native

Armenians and for planning to betray Theodosiopolis and other fortresses to the Persians. Following the accusation, Acacius killed Amazaspes and took his place. He then treated the natives badly and they killed him before fleeing to Pharangium. In frustration, Justinian ordered Sittas to invade Armenia. After trying to negotiate a peace, Sittas entered Armenia but was killed in a skirmish. Justinian sent Buzes as a replacement, who also attempted to negotiate, asking for representatives to meet him. Only a single noble named John, who knew Buzes, agreed, taking a few men to the meeting place. On seeing that they were almost surrounded by the Byzantines, his followers fled, but this John stayed and was killed by Buzes. In response, the Armenian nobles now sent envoys to Khusrow to solicit his help.

With the Hunnic invasion and the threat of war in the east, Justinian sent emissaries to Khusrow, admitting writing letters to the Huns, but stating that they were not attempting to provoke the Huns to invade Persia. They also noted the aggressive acts of Al-Mundhir, but it was to no avail. Believing that his moment had come, Khusrow cancelled the treaty and prepared for war. The Persians were always a far greater threat than the Goths, so Justinian decided to end the war in Italy and recall Belisarius to take charge of the war in the east. He determined to send Domnicus and Maximinus as envoys to the Goths with the message that the Goths could have peace if they agreed that Witigis would retain half of the Gothic treasure plus Italy north of the Po, whilst the emperor would gain the other half of the treasure and all of Italy south of the Po.

The Fall of Auximus and Fisula

The Gothic garrison of Auximus did not know of the Frankish invasion and could not understand why Witigis had not sent help. As they were restricted to the city, they decided to bribe one of the Byzantine troops to carry a message to Witigis in Ravenna. Burcentius, a man in the command of Narses, accepted the bribe and took the message to Witigis. Witigis sent a reply outlining the attack of the Franks and stating that he would arrive shortly with the army, once the Franks had definitely retreated from Italy.

Burcentius returned and gave the message to the Goths, replying to his companions' queries as to his whereabouts that he had been ill in a nearby sanctuary. Shortly thereafter, the Goths became frustrated and sent Burcentius to Ravenna again, this time with a message saying that they would be forced to surrender in five days unless help arrived. Again Burcentius returned with an excuse for his absence and passed a message to the Goths saying that help would soon be arriving.

Belisarius was baffled by the defenders' refusal to surrender and decided to find out why they were being so stubborn. He set Valerian the task of catching a Goth for questioning. A Goth was duly caught as he tried to gather grass from the usual source. When questioned he told the whole story of the messages, including the bribe to Burcentius. Belisarius arrested Burcentius, but then gave him to his comrades, telling them that the punishment was in their hands. His army colleagues decided to burn him alive as a warning to others.

Becoming impatient, Belisarius attempted to cut the supply of water to the city. The main source of water was a spring that arose on the side of the hill, just outside the city walls. From there, the spring ran in to a cistern from which most of the water for the city was drawn. Ordering his troops to draw up their battle lines as if to attack the city, Belisarius then sent five Isaurians with tools to break the cistern. Advancing under a cover of shields provided by their fellow troops, the men advanced to the cistern, which was covered from sight of the walls by a vault over the top, and jumped into the water. The Goths, believing that the attackers were going to attempt to weaken the walls, at first made no response, waiting for the wall of shields to advance to a closer range. Then, when they realised the purpose of the attack, they showered the area with missiles. At this, the shield carriers fled back down the hill, but the Isaurians, covered by the vault, began to attack the walls of the cistern.

In desperation, the defenders mounted a sortie in an attempt to stop the work. As they appeared, Belisarius ordered his troops to attack and a battle took place on the side of the hill. Many Byzantines fell, since the Goths had the advantage of the higher ground, until seven Armenians from the command of Narses and Aratius – possibly eager to wipe out the shame of Burcentius accepting Gothic bribes – routed a section of the defenders. The Byzantines advanced through the gap and the defenders retired to the walls. The attackers also withdrew. Unfortunately, the cistern was undamaged, partly because of the superior building methods used in ancient times making the task extremely difficult, and partly because the Isaurians had retreated along with the troops after the skirmish.

Although a failure, the attack had made it clear how important the water supply in the cistern was to the defenders, so Belisarius ordered animal carcasses and lime thrown in to the water to make it unfit to drink. The Goths now had to rely on a small well within the city which did not fulfil their needs, but still they held out.

As the siege of Auximus progressed, the Gothic garrison of Fisula finally surrendered to Cyprian and Justinus. Leaving a garrison in the city, Cyprian and Justinus moved to Auximus and joined Belisarius for the siege there. Belisarius paraded the leaders of the garrison from Fisula outside the walls of Auximus. As a consequence, the garrison began to negotiate for their surrender. Originally, they demanded to be freed and allowed to retire to Ravenna, taking all of their belongings. Yet Belisarius was uncertain what course to take. His next move would be to advance on Ravenna, so it would be a mistake to allow the garrison, who had already proved themselves resourceful and brave, to join Witigis and fight him again. On the other hand, speed was needed, in case the Franks should decide to cross the Alps again and join with the Goths. Belisarius needed to secure Auximus to prevent the Goths attacking him from the rear. Finally, the Byzantine troops, having received the news of the Gothic terms for surrender, were unhappy since they would not receive any rewards for their bravery. Eventually, a compromise was reached in which the Goths kept half of their property, the other half being distributed as booty to the troops, and the Gothic garrison was to join forces with Belisarius, being distributed amongst the Byzantine army. It was now October or November 539 and the siege had lasted for seven months.

The Siege of Ravenna

In haste, as it was now late in the campaign season, either late 539 or early 540, Belisarius advanced towards Ravenna. He dispatched the general Magnus with a large force to go to the farther side of the city and patrol the south banks of the River Po to ensure that no supplies reached the city. Furthermore, Vitalius had meanwhile advanced from Dalmatia and was now in a position to patrol north of the river. It was as Vitalius approached the river that Belisarius' luck helped him again. Vitalius discovered boats loaded with grain that were destined for Ravenna. They had been unable to navigate to the city due to the river falling to a very low level, the cause of which is unknown. Shortly after, the river rose again and the grain was sent to Belisarius for distribution to the troops.

The Goths in Ravenna began to suffer from the perils of starvation, as their supplies had been captured and the Byzantines had control of the sea, so cutting of the supplies usually transported by ship. Seeing that the Gothic position was becoming desperate, King Theudibert of the Franks sent messengers to Witigis, offering his military support in return for a share in the kingship of Italy. Hearing of the offer, Belisarius sent Theodosius, the head of his household, to Witigis to remind him of the Franks' recent invasion and reinforce the belief that they could not be trusted. After deliberating on the matter, Witigis decided to open negotiations with Belisarius with a view to surrender. Whilst Witigis' was considering his options, Belisarius used the pause in the conflict to send Vitalius to Venetia to secure as many towns as he could in that region.

Procopius reports that it was about this time that the grain stores in Ravenna caught fire and were burnt down, all of the grain in them being lost. Although the cause of the fire is unknown, Procopius suggests that the most likely causes are either that Belisarius bribed a citizen of the town to start the fires, or that they were ordered by Matasuintha, the wife of Witigis, who was unhappy because he had forced her to marry him to cement his position on the throne.

Hearing of the siege of Ravenna, and convinced that their cause was now lost, the Goths garrisoning the passes through the Cottian Alps decided that the time had come to surrender. When the news reached him, Belisarius sent Thomas and a force of troops to accept the surrender and secure the passes. When Thomas arrived, Sisigis, the Gothic commander in the region, surrendered himself and ordered all of the garrisons in the region to surrender at the same time. However, Uraias, who had gathered a force of 4,000 men in Liguria after his defeat by Theudibert, was moving towards Ravenna in order to help fight in the siege. When news of the surrender reached him, his troops demanded action, since most of them had families in the Alps who were now in the hands of the Byzantines. As a consequence, Uraias changed direction and immediately laid siege to Thomas and Sisigis.

When word of Thomas' plight reached Martinus and John, who following their defeat had returned to Dorthon, they moved north to help him, taking many Goths captive on the way. By chance, these included many of the wives and children of the troops under Uraias, who immediately deserted and surrendered to the Byzantines. As his force melted away, Uraias retired with his remaining force to Liguria and remained there quietly until later in the year. There was now no source of help for the Goths trapped in Ravenna.

The End of the Belisarian War

It was now that Justinian's envoys arrived at Ravenna and conveyed the emperor's offer to the Goths. The Goths would have agreed to the treaty, but Belisarius, as the general on the spot, refused to ratify it. The army commanders were unhappy with his decision, so Belisarius had a conference during the course of which they agreed to sign a declaration stating that, when the emperor's offer had arrived, there was no real chance of the Byzantines completing the conquest of Italy. Belisarius was very close to a total victory and did not want to leave them with the opportunity to later declare that he could easily have completed the conquest, but lacked either the will or the ability to do so. The officers agreed, and Belisarius was happy since they would not be able to lay charges against him.

Yet even at this late stage the situation changed drastically. The Gothic nobles, who had become disillusioned with Witigis, feared that their surrender would result in their being transported to the east and not allowed to return. In secret, they sent a messenger to Belisarius and offered him the title Emperor of the West. When Witigis heard of the plan, he gave it his whole-hearted support.

Belisarius did not want the position, but believed that he could manipulate the situation to his advantage. He agreed to the deal in principle, and then dismissed the messenger and called a meeting of his officers. He asked them if the capture of the whole of Italy and the surrender of the Goths would be a good thing for the emperor. When they agreed, he set the wheels in motion for the Gothic surrender.

When the Gothic envoys arrived, they made vague statements about surrender, but in secret asked for pledges from Belisarius concerning both their safety and his acceptance of the kingship. Belisarius gave all of the pledges they required except for the ones about the kingship, stating that these should be made later in the presence of Witigis and the Gothic nobles. As the envoys could not believe that he would refuse the kingship, they agreed to his terms and returned to the town.

For his part, Belisarius did not trust those commanders who had previously followed Narses to accept his plan, and believed that they may make a mistake, either on purpose or by accident, that would ruin the plot. As a consequence, he ordered Bessas, John, Narses the Armenian and Aratius his brother to take their troops and disperse amongst Italy's towns, both in order to maintain control as well as to ease the burden of supply on the city of Ravenna.

With everything ready, he ordered a fleet full of grain to land their cargoes at Classis, the suburb of Ravenna which included the port, and, with the remainder of the army, Belisarius entered the city in triumph, watched by the Goths. The Goths had told their women that the Byzantines were 'giants' and that their army was 'vast'. When the women saw normal-sized men enter the city, and in such small numbers, they turned on their menfolk and berated them for their cowardice. The date was sometime in May 540: the Gothic War, which had begun in 535, had lasted longer than either Belisarius or Justinian had hoped.

The War Unfinished

Belisarius now put everything in order in Ravenna. Witigis was kept under guard, but treated in a dignified manner, and Belisarius urged the Goths from districts south of the Po to return home in peace. As the Byzantines had garrisons in all of the major towns, such a move did not threaten the security of Italy, since it was unlikely that the Goths would be able to rebel without a central base to store supplies of food and weapons. On the other hand, as a result of this measure the Byzantines now outnumbered the Goths in Ravenna itself. Belisarius also took control of the Gothic treasury and prepared it for transport to Justinian.

When they heard of the fall of Ravenna, those towns still held by the Goths in Italy made haste to surrender, their leaders travelling to Ravenna for meetings with Belisarius. The only exception was Ildibadus of Verona. He agreed to surrender, but, due to circumstances, was never to reach Ravenna. For when they saw Belisarius preparing the treasury for the trip to Justinian, the Goths realised that he was not going to accept their offer of the kingship. Therefore, they sent envoys to Uraias at Ticinum and offered him the throne instead. He refused, both because the Byzantines would treat him lightly as a relative of the defeated Witigis, and also because he would not win favour by usurping his uncle's throne. He suggested that they offer the throne to Ildibadus, who was energetic, an excellent leader, and, as a nephew of King Theudis in Spain, could expect support from the Visigoths in the ensuing war.

So Ildibadus was summoned to Ticinum to be made the king of the Goths. Although he accepted the throne, he advised the Goths to again offer the throne to Belisarius. When Belisarius refused, stating that he would always be loyal to Justinian, they returned to Ticinum and Ildibadus was recognised as king. Shortly afterwards, at around midsummer 540, Belisarius boarded ship and sailed to Constantinople, ready to go east to deal with the Persians.

Antonina and Theodosius

Whilst in Sicily, Belisarius was approached by a slave called Macedonia and informed of the continued affair of Antonina and Theodosius. Belisarius ordered the death of Theodosius, who fled to Ephesus for safety. However, Antonina managed to convince Belisarius of her innocence, later having Macedonia and her accomplices killed. She also persuaded him to forgive Theodosius and invite him to return. However, Theodosius was worried by the presence of her son Photius and refused. Finally, Antonina pressured Photius into returning to Constantinople and Theodosius rejoined her in Italy.

As the war drew to a close, Antonina and Theodosius, who were continuing their affair, moved with Belisarius into Ravenna. As well as having an affair with his adoptive parent, Theodosius began to gain a reputation for greed. In the wake of the victory in Africa, he made his fortune by dubious means whilst in Carthage. In Ravenna, he continued in a like manner. Fortunately, the stay in the city was to be a short one; when Belisarius was recalled to Constantinople, Antonina and Theodosius returned with him.

The conquest of Italy assessed

The conquest of Africa took less than a year. The conquest of Italy took approximately five years. Yet it is obvious that Justinian expected the war to be over quickly, just like the Vandalic War. This can be seen by the small number of troops allocated and the slow arrival of requested reinforcements. It is possible that the similarities between the events in Africa and the events in Italy prior to the respective invasions had led Justinian to believe that the conquest of Italy would be easy.

The rapid capture of Sicily and the capitulation of Ebrimuth would have been seen as symptomatic of the empty threat of the Goths, hinting that the conquest would be similar to that of Africa. The emperor's hopes were to be unfulfilled. It would appear that he had underestimated the stubbornness of the Goths, especially in their northern homeland.

In one respect the situation in the north of the peninsula proved to be completely different to that in the south, or even in Africa. The lack of defensible towns in the south resulted in a collapse as spectacular as that in Africa. In the north, many towns had built and maintained walls as a response to the crises brought about by barbarian invasions from as early as the second and third centuries. These required time and troops to reduce, both of which were in short supply for much of the campaign. When the reinforcements arrived, Belisarius was able to take the cities one by one, but he still needed a large amount of luck.

Belisarius as a general

If the invasion of Africa gives an indication of Belisarius' abilities in the field, the 'conquest' of Italy demonstrates his abilities at siege warfare. His conduct in siege operations, both defensive and offensive, shows an imagination and a variety of strategies which is almost completely the opposite of Witigis.

Witigis relied mainly on attempting to starve the opposition into surrender, with infrequent assaults being mounted to test the quality of the defence. In some instances, such as in the occupation of Portus with the simultaneous recognition that Ostia was not suitable for supplying Rome, Witigis did display quality strategic abilities. Yet by allowing the roles to be reversed, with Belisarius trapping his forces within their camps at the siege of Rome, and his almost total inactivity in the later stages of the war, Witigis surrendered the initiative without a fight. He seems to have relied upon capturing Belisarius at Rome, and, when this failed to materialise, he did not devise a viable alternative and so lost the war.

Belisarius, on the other hand, was constantly attempting to take the initiative during the siege of Rome, and managed to achieve it so effectively that Witigis ended being besieged within his own camps. Furthermore, when the war entered its later stages Belisarius attempted to relieve the cities under siege by the Goths and focused upon clearing the approach to Ravenna. The fact that he managed to complete his strategy is a sign of the high quality of his generalship in the war, but we should not exaggerate his achievement: Witigis did not provide him with a high level of opposition, and it is possible that many of Belisarius' subordinates could have equalled the general's exploits.

Apart from maintaining the initiative, Belisarius won the war with his realisation that the Goths, like the Vandals, had no answer to his mounted archers, and with his grasp of logistics. Throughout the siege of Rome, and when faced with Goths in the open, he relied upon the abilities of his horse archers to weaken and demoralise the Goths. He succeeded so effectively that the Goths became terrified of their abilities and refused to leave their camps. Furthermore, Witigis later refused to meet him in the open, despite having won the Battle of Rome and shown that in the correct circumstances the Byzantines were extremely vulnerable..

In many ways it was Belisarius' grasp of logistics that helped him to win the war. He managed to keep Rome supplied during the siege, and understood that, by remaining in their camps, the Goths were leaving themselves as vulnerable as if they were actually the besieged, rather then the besiegers. It is quite possible that many of his actions can be interpreted as ways of reducing his own supply problems, as well as putting pressure upon the Goths.

In the war, he made only three mistakes that proved to be costly. The first was in accepting battle outside Rome. Procopius does his best to lay the blame upon the regular troops, claiming that they pressured Belisarius to fight when he did not want to. Yet later, when the Romans demanded that he fight a second pitched battle, he had the strength of will to refuse. Furthermore, the excuse had already been used at Callinicum in the east, where Belisarius again was allegedly pressed by the troops to accept battle against his better judgement. It is probably safer simply to accept that he made a mistake. The Goths had suffered heavy losses, caused by his policy of using small groups of horse archers in hit-and-run tactics. It is easy to understand that he believed that Gothic morale was extremely low and that under pressure they would break; after all, a similar thing had happened at Tricamerum in Africa. He made a mistake and lost the battle. Fortunately, the heroics of Principius and Tarmatus, along with a section of the infantry, allowed the Byzantines to retreat with fewer casualties than they may otherwise have suffered.

His second mistake was to accept the invitation to garrison Milan. The city was too far away from the rest of his forces, and so was vulnerable to attack. Furthermore, it was on the far side of a major river, the Po, and was not easy to either reinforce or relieve when besieged. That said, it is easy to show that the occupation of Milan was a mistake in hindsight: in reality, his detaining the envoys over winter can be interpreted as his being unwilling to make the commitment, and it is probable that he only agreed because of the political implications. Along with Milan he gained control of the area of Liguria, one of the most fertile in Italy. If it was a mistake, it was an understandable mistake.

His third, and perhaps his greatest mistake, was that he rushed the end of the war. It was becoming likely that the envoys sent by Justinian would make arrangements to end the war before Belisarius had completed his military conquest. For whatever reason, whether the pursuit of glory, the desire to simply finish the task, or for some other motive, Belisarius was not prepared to allow the Goths to escape without acknowledging their total defeat. The result was to be disastrous for Rome.

Due to the need for speed, Belisarius failed to comprehend the Gothic fears for their safety and the depth of their desire to remain in Italy: after all, although seen in Constantinople as 'Germans' and foreigners imposing their will on the Italian natives, they had been born in Italy and considered them-selves to be 'of Italy'. If Belisarius had taken more time in the negotiations, he may have listened to and understood their fears and taken steps to allay them After all, the majority of Goths had returned to their homes south of the Po, apparently with no intention of restarting the war. With only a little extra patience the war could have been finished before he left.

He did not take the time, and rushed through the peace negotiations. Convinced that Belisarius was going to accept the kingship, and so ensure that they would not be deported to the east, the Goths accepted their defeat. When Belisarius refused to accept the throne, the situation again became unclear, and the Gothic nobles were uncertain as to their future. With his dismissal of their request to become king, Belisarius alienated the Gothic nobles, as his actions may have been perceived as demeaning the kingship. In these circumstances were planted the seeds for the continuance of the war after Belisarius had been recalled.

There is only one note of caution that remains concerning Belisarius' abilities as a general. He does not appear to have been confident in his use of infantry, instead relying almost wholly on the cavalry. It would be easy to dismiss this by noting that the infantry were obviously of poor quality and had fled from the field at the Battle of Rome with potentially disastrous results.

Yet this is not the whole story. A portion of the infantry, led by Principius and Tarmatus, fought bravely against the Goths. It is clear that, if they had been properly trained by Belisarius and led by officers who did not run away at the first opportunity, they could have formed a valuable asset to the Byzantines, both in attacking enemy fortifications and by acting as a rallying point for the cavalry. By neglecting these troops, Belisarius diminished the fighting strength of his army by disqualifying a section of his troops from taking an effective part in battle.

Despite these reservations, overall the Italian campaign reinforced his reputation and highlighted his military abilities in a way that they had never been shown before, either in Africa or in the east. Now that he was returning to the Persian front, his abilities would be tested against armies that had already shown that he could be beaten. It remained to be seen if his experiences in the west had given him the knowledge and maturity to master the armies of the east.

Chapter 11

The Return to the East

The Reforms of Khusrow

The so-called 'Eternal Peace' that was agreed between Rome and Persia following the defeat of Belisarius at Callinicum is commonly attributed to the desire of Justinian to free troops for the upcoming war against the Vandals. Although there is a large amount of truth in this conclusion, Khusrow also appears to have wanted a peace treaty. However, he understood that Justinian was in a rush and so ensured that he gained the best possible terms.

The reason for the desire for peace was that Khusrow was about to set in motion a system of reforms. In Chapter 4 it was shown that the Persian army was effectively a feudal force consisting of lords who were granted land in return for military service. They in turn conscripted men into the army who thus owed their loyalty to the nobles. Khusrow had determined to change this for a professional force with no loyalty to the nobles, only to the king.

To complete these reforms, Khusrow would have to curtail the power of the nobles. To do this, he enrolled the lesser nobility, the *dekhans*, into the *savaran*. This diminished the influence of the upper nobility and allowed his further reforms to pass, since the nobles no longer had the power to stop them. This created a much larger manpower base from which to recruit the *savaran* heavy cavalry. As a by-product, it correspondingly reduced the number of troops available to serve as light cavalry, especially as horse archers. To overcome the shortage, Khusrow began an active recruitment campaign amongst the tribes bordering the empire, aimed especially at recruiting horse archers.

Possibly due to the *dekhans* being unable to afford the expensive equipment needed to serve in the *savaran*, Khusrow instituted a salary for the army and equipped the troops from state arsenals. In effect, Khusrow created a professional fighting force owing loyalty to the king, so further weakening the power and influence of the nobles.

As was shown in the previous disussion, the command of the Persian army was usually left to the *eran-spahbad*, who was traditionally a member of one of the seven most influential families. The post was now abolished. Instead, command devolved upon four *spahbads*, each of whom was given control of a specific region within the empire.

The *spahbad* of the north was responsible for the provinces of Media, Kurdistan, Azerbaijan and Arran, and also the passes over the Caucasus,

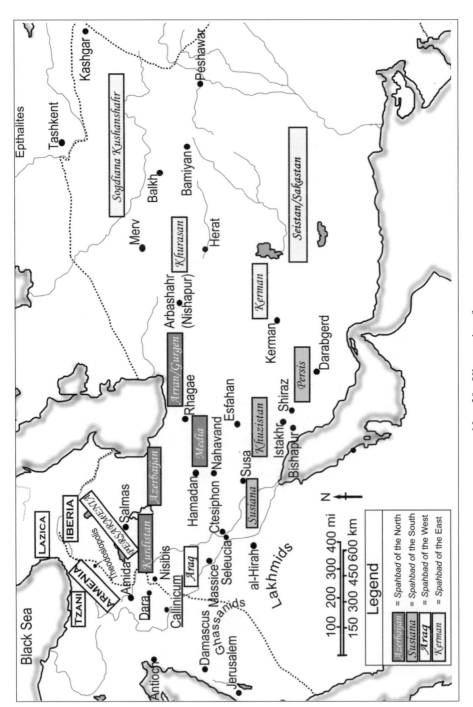

Map 20: Khusrow's reforms.

including the Derbend Pass that had been a bone of contention between the Persians and the Byzantines in the past. The *spahbad* of the east was responsible for the provinces of Khurasan, Seistan and Kerman. The *spahbad* of the south was responsible for the provinces of Persis, Susiana and Khuzistan, including the long coast on the Persian Gulf. Finally, the *spahbad* of the west was responsible for the most important area of all: Mesopotamia (known to the Persians as Araq, 'the Lowland' – modern 'Iraq'). Each *spahbad* was responsible for the recruitment and levying of troops within his designated area, and in theory with ensuring that each of them was armed and equipped in the correct manner.

It was only when these reforms had been completed that Khusrow began to look at the situation regarding the Byzantines in the west.

The Second Persian War
It was obvious that Khusrow was going to invade (the political events leading up to the war have already been covered in Chapter 9). In anticipation of the threat, Justinian divided the eastern command: Belisarius was to be given control of the western portion of the command, Buzes control of the eastern portion, up to the frontier with Persia. Until the arrival of Belisarius, Buzes was given command of the whole.

The First Year: 540
In the spring of 540, Khusrow invaded the Empire. Moving along the west bank of the Euphrates, he bypassed the fortress of Circesium, which was situated on the opposite side, in the angle formed by the junction of the Euphrates and the River Aborras, before arriving at the city of Zenobia. The city refused to surrender, so Khusrow bypassed this city as well and travelled onwards before setting up his camp opposite the city of Sura. Khusrow decided to take the city by storm and in the ensuing attack Arsaces, the commander of the defenders, was killed. As a result, the defenders lost heart and the local bishop was sent to negotiate a surrender. Khusrow decided to appear to be considering the proposal but ordered his troops to follow the bishop as he returned to the fortress and, as he entered, to rush forwards and prevent any closure of the gate. The plan worked, the gate was forced and the city carried by storm. The embassy from Justinian was still accompanying the king as he attacked. They were now released and travelled to Justinian to inform him of the defeat.

Moving forwards, Khusrow sold the captives he had taken to Candidus, the bishop of Sergiopolis, receiving 2 *centenaria* (a *centenaria* was 100 pounds of gold, possibly equal to 100,000 *sesterces* – a vast sum of money) for the 12,000 captives. Furthermore, if Candidus did not pay the money by a set date he would then be liable to pay double the amount.

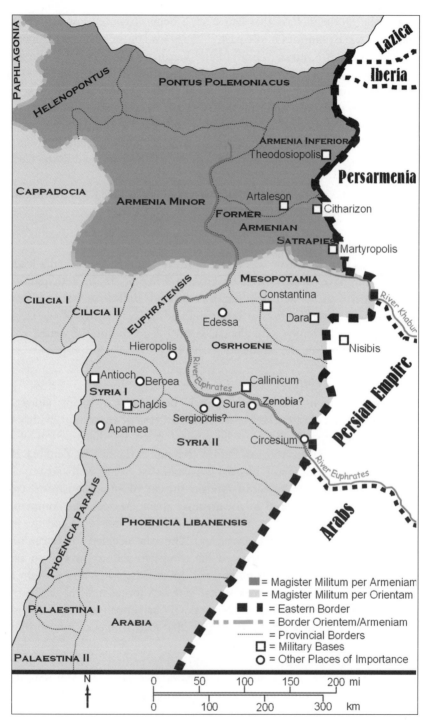

Map 21: The events of 540.

Buzes was in the city of Hieropolis when he learned of the loss of Sura and was told the size of the Persian forces. Therefore, possibly having heard of Belisarius' strategy in the siege of Rome, he proposed to leave part of the army in the city and take the rest out to the hills around it in order to harass the enemy when they arrived. Selecting the best troops, he left the city, but no-one was sure of where he went.

With the citizens of Hieropolis waiting for the expected attack, Justinian also learned of the Persian invasion. Believing that Antioch was Khusrow's target, he sent his nephew Germanus to the city along with 300 men to augment the garrison. Fearing that Khusrow would attack the city simply because the Emperor's nephew was present, Germanus refused to stay in the city and, taking a few men, travelled to Cilicia. In desperation, the citizens decided to offer tribute to Khusrow in the hope that he would then retire to Persia. They sent Megas, the bishop of Beroea, to secure terms, and he arrived in time to see Khusrow launch an attack on Hieropolis. When the citizens of Hieropolis paid Khusrow 2,000 pounds of silver to stop the attack, Megas was forced to offer 2 *centenaria* of gold for the much larger city of Antioch.

Megas returned to Antioch, followed by Khusrow and the Persian army. Khusrow now stopped at the city of Beroea, entered the city and demanded 4,000 pounds of silver from the citizens to leave. When they only offered him 2,000 pounds, claiming that they could not raise any more money, he set fire to the city and launched an attack upon the citadel, where the inhabitants were sheltering.

In the meantime, Justinian had sent two ambassadors to negotiate with Khusrow and they arrived at Antioch shortly before Megas returned with Khusrow's demand. They flatly refused to allow the citizens to pay Khusrow not to attack and Megas was forced to return to Khusrow empty-handed.

Once back with the king, Megas was able to act as a mediator between Khusrow and the Beroeans, of whom he was bishop. The citizens were allowed to leave the city whilst the majority of the garrison joined the Persian army, claiming that they had not been paid for a long time and so renouncing any loyalty to the empire.

With his line of advance secured, Khusrow finally marched towards Antioch. Many of the inhabitants fled upon his approach but the two *duces* of Phoenice Libanensis, Theoctistus and Molatzes, arrived with 6,000 men to help defend the city.

When he arrived, Khusrow immediately demanded 10 *centenaria* of gold, with the suggestion that he might be willing to accept less. The ambassadors in Antioch went to see Khusrow and began negotiations, but the envoy that Khusrow sent to the city was insulted and shot at outside the city walls. Enraged, Khusrow ordered an all-out assault on the following day. The city was taken by storm, sacked and looted. Khusrow retired towards Persia with a vast quantity of captives and booty.

When Justinian's ambassadors now asked for peace terms, Khusrow demanded 50 *centenaria* immediately, followed by 5 *centenaria* per annum to maintain the peace. The envoys agreed to the terms and sent news of the agreement to Justinian. However, on his return journey to Persia, Khusrow broke the contract, arriving at the cities of Apamea, Chalcis and Edessa and demanding large sums of money to leave them unharmed. After paying their ransoms, the citizens of Edessa also offered to buy the freedom of the captives from Antioch, but Buzes forbade the exchange. It was the citizens of the city of Constantina who paid the ransom demanded by Khusrow for the citizens of Antioch.

Whilst Khusrow had been raiding the empire, the peace agreement in Italy had been reached, bringing to an end the first bout of the Gothic War. The troops and commanders thus freed from service in the west now began to arrive in the east. Martinus was sent to Dara, which in the event of continued conflict was an obvious target as it was the headquarters of the *magister militum per Orientem*. He reached his destination shortly before Khusrow and the Persian army arrived and laid siege to the fortress. Martinus and his troops put up a stout resistance to Khusrow, who gave up and finally returned to Persian soil.

Hearing of the demands for ransom and of the Persian attack at Dara, Justinian cancelled the agreement and did not pay any money to Khusrow. As summer was at an end and the campaigning season had now finished, both sides remained quiet and waited for the following year to resume operations.

The Second Year: 541

The Byzantines now made their dispositions for the second year of the war. Valerian was sent to take command of the forces in Armenia and, once winter was fading, Belisarius travelled in haste to the east, anticipating a second invasion by Khusrow. On this occasion Antonina did not accompany her husband, instead remaining in Constantinople in the service of the empress.

The Byzantines had miscalculated; Khusrow was not planning an invasion of Mesopotamia. After the conclusion of the earlier war, the Byzantines had stationed troops in Lazica, quartering them in the traditional manner on the natives of the area. The Byzantine general, Peter, treated the Lazicans badly. Furthermore, the commander at Petra on the Black Sea coast, John Tzibus, described by Procopius (*Wars*, II.xv.9) as 'a man of obscure and ignoble descent', formed a monopoly on imports in the area and began selling the goods at a very high price. As a result, the Lazicans decided to switch allegiances and invited Khusrow to take the country. Spreading the rumour that he was going to the north to fight a Hunnic invasion, Khusrow gathered his troops and moved into Lazica. According to the *Anekdota*, Khusrow also arranged for an

Map 22: The events of 541.

army of Huns to invade Armenia and occupy the Byzantine forces in the area (*Anekdota*, 2.29–31).

When Belisarius arrived in Mesopotamia to assume command, one of his first actions was to send spies into enemy territory to find out what the Persians were planning. He also began to organise his forces. Finding that the troops were terrified of the Persians, badly organised and poorly armed, he distributed equipment and began to train them.

When his spies returned and informed him that the Persians were away fighting the Huns, Belisarius decided that he could invade Persia in relative safety. Joined by Arethas, the leader of the Ghassanids, he called a council of his officers and asked for advice. Most declared a willingness to invade Persia, but the two *duces* of Phoenice Libanensis, Theoctistus and Rhecithancus (who had replaced Molatzes), warned that Phoenicia and Syria would be open to attack by the Lakhmids, so wanted to stay and protect their province. Belisarius pointed out that it was the season of the vernal equinox and that the Lakhmids would be dedicating the next two months to their god and so be unable to attack. (Arethas, although a fellow Arab of the Lakhmids, was a Monophysite Christian, probably along with the majority of his people, and did not, therefore, follow the Lakhmid religious observances.) Belisarius promised that the troops he took with him would be released before the passage of sixty days and allowed to return to their province to defend it from the 'Saracens'. With these reassurances, the generals agreed to his plans. Belisarius decided to attack the city of Nisibis, reasoning that he could not go further than this without taking the city as he would be leaving a strong force to his rear. He now made preparations to attack.

Whilst Belisarius was debating the invasion, Khusrow arrived in the city of Colchis in Lazica and was met by King Goubazes, who made obeisance for his kingdom. Learning that Petra, on the Black Sea coast, was being held in force by the Byzantines under John Tzibus, he dispatched an army under Aniabades to take the city. Warned of the Persian approach, John armed his men and ordered them to remain behind the walls, out of sight and silent. Upon seeing an apparently-empty fortress, Aniabades sent a message to Khusrow informing him of the situation. Khusrow ordered the entire army to advance to the city and ordered an assault, with a ram to break the gate, while he watched from a nearby hill.

Anticipating an easy victory, Khusrow was to be shocked by what happened next: as he watched, the previously-unseen Byzantine defenders made a sudden sally and routed the Persians, many of whom were killed, especially those stationed around the ram. Furious at the unexpected defeat, Khusrow ordered either Aniabades or the officer in charge of the ram to be impaled for their incompetence, though Procopius is unsure about which commander was killed (*Wars*, II.xvii.11).

The Persian king then ordered an all-out assault and, luckily for Khusrow, John was killed by a chance arrow as night fell. On the following day, a projecting tower was undermined and fell, which, together with the loss of John, caused the defenders to lose hope. They sued for surrender, agreeing to join the Persian army. The garrison of Beroea had similarly defected the year before and it is possible that the armies in the east had still not yet been paid.

In the south, Belisarius had advanced on the city and fortress of Nisibis, but, much to the dismay of his officers, he ordered them to camp whilst still some distance from the city. When they protested, he informed them that he was setting the camp at such a distance in the belief that the Persians would emerge and fight. If they did, he wanted to allow plenty of room for a pursuit that would kill or capture a large number of them. In this, he was almost certainly drawing upon his experience during the siege of Rome. For the majority of the siege, Belisarius' own troops had remained near to the city so that any defeat was lessened by their ability to seek sanctuary within the walls very quickly. In contrast, during the Battle of Rome Witigis had deployed the Goths as far as possible from the walls to enable them to pursue the enemy for the greatest distance and so cause the greatest number of casualties.

Belisarius further pointed out to his subordinates that, in the case of a Byzantine attack, Nisibis was the obvious focus point and so he had sent spies here who had informed him that the city was garrisoned by a very large force under Nobades, possibly the *spahbad* of the west. The man was obviously a capable general and the camp was being set as a lure to tempt him to leave the safety of the city. Upon hearing his reasoning, all of the commanders agreed to his commands except for Peter, who, taking John with him, led their men to within ten *stades* of the city. As in Italy, the indiscipline of junior officers would lead to heavy losses for their troops.

The following morning, Belisarius sent word to his men to prepare for battle. He also said that the Persians would attack at around midday, since they knew that the Byzantines were accustomed to eating at that time and so would judge them to be vulnerable. He sent the same messages to Peter and John in their advanced camp. Ignoring the warning, at midday the troops under Peter and John broke ranks for food. Simultaneously, Nobades launched an attack against them. Peter immediately sent messages to Belisarius asking for help, before watching as his men were routed and his standard captured, fifty men being killed.

Peter's messengers were unnecessary. Belisarius had seen the dust being raised near to the enemy city and immediately set the troops in motion. The Goths brought east by Belisarius were the first into the action, followed shortly after by the rest of the Byzantine army. The Persians were routed, yet due to their remaining near to the city walls, they lost only 150 men as they quickly reached safety. They refused to leave their refuge again.

Recognising that the city was too strong to take by storm, Belisarius led the army a day's march further into Persia until he reached the fortress of Sisauranon. In doing this, he had clearly decided that, despite his earlier reservations about leaving a strong force to his rear, the defeat they had suffered would make Nobades wary of leaving Nisibis.

Sisauranon was held by 800 Persians under Bleschames, and the first assault on the walls was repulsed with heavy loss. Therefore, Belisarius decided to send Arethas and a small group of Byzantine troops across the Tigris and further into Persian territory, to gather plunder and information. If the fortress fell, he proposed to lead the rest of the army across the river. Consequently, the Lakhmid forces, accompanied by 1,200 *bucellarii* under John the Glutton and Trajan, crossed the Tigris and began to plunder a rich and untouched area of Persia.

In the meantime, Belisarius captured some Persian deserters who declared that the fortress was short of provisions and about to fall. He then sent an individual named George, who had a reputation for persuasion, to talk to the defenders. After receiving pledges for their safety, the garrison surrendered. The inhabitants, who were mainly Byzantines captured during Persian raids, were set free and the garrison sent to Justinian: they would later be deployed in Italy.

The forces that had been sent ahead had by now taken a large amount of booty. Afraid that when they returned the Byzantines would take all of the spoil for themselves, Arethas ordered some of his men to ride out of the camp, and then ride back declaring that a large force of Persians was approaching. They followed their orders and in the ensuing panic Arethas counselled that John and Trajan should take their share of the plunder and return directly to Byzantine territory, as in this way they would manage to retain their share of the spoil. He would go directly to his own kingdom. In this way, they should be able to avoid the Persians. John and Trajan agreed, and, without informing Belisarius, departed for home.

Troubled by the lack of news, and due to many of his troops catching a fever – with up to one third being ill – Belisarius needed to decide quickly upon his next move. When Theoctistus and Rhecithancus declared that the sixty days were now almost gone and that they needed to return home to garrison their cities, Belisarius convened a council. At the council all agreed that they should return to Byzantine territory. Sending the ill ahead and using the rest as a rearguard, Belisarius safely led his troops out of Persia. Fortunately for Arethas, he never met Belisarius again. Upon his return, Belisarius was reunited with Antonina, a reunion that was to have dramatic consequences, as we will see in due course.

As he was campaigning in Lazica, Khusrow learned of Belisarius' invasion. He also learnt that the Huns that had invaded Armenia had been defeated by Valerian, the Byzantine commander in the area (Proc, *Anekdota*, 2.30). Leaving a garrison in Petra, Khusrow returned to Persia. It was now late in the year and any reprisals against the Byzantines would have to wait for the following spring.

Antonina and Belisarius

The reunion of Belisarius and Antonina was, according to Procopius' account in the *Anekdota*, a bitter one. As was seen earlier, Antonina and Theodosius had continued their affair in Constantinople. Before Belisarius had departed for the war, Theodosius began to feel guilty and became uncomfortable with Antonina's ever-more-outrageous displays of affection. Theodosius again fled to Ephesus, where he became a monk. Antonina managed to persuade Belisarius to request his return, but to no avail. However, when Belisarius left for the war, accompanied by Photius, Theodosius returned and the affair resumed.

At the same time, Antonina took part in ensnaring John the Cappadocian at the request of Theodora. Antonina befriended John's daughter Euphemia and, completely winning her friendship, persuaded her that both herself and Belisarius would join in an attempt to overthrow Justinian. Euphemia told John, who joined the plot, only to have Antonina betray him to Theodora. Narses the eunuch and Marcellus, the captain of the palace guards, arrested him and his property was confiscated, although a small portion was later returned to him by Justinian (Proc, 1.xxv.13–36). Having increased her value in the eyes of the empress, Antonina travelled to the east to join Belisarius.

Her reunion would not be as she expected. Photius had learned that Theodosius was staying with his mother and had reported the matter to Belisarius. Belisarius ordered him to travel to Ephesus and kill Theodosius, secure in the knowledge that when Antonina travelled to the east Theodosius would return there. The account given in *Wars* now differs somewhat from that given in *Anekdota*. In *Wars*, Belisarius was troubled by the lack of news from his advanced army and by the fact that many of his troops had caught a fever, and so had convened a council at which it was agreed that the army should return to Byzantine territory (Proc, II.xix.29–46). In *Anekdota*, Belisarius was influenced by the news of Antonina's impending arrival and so hastened the withdrawal of the troops from Sisauranon. He was consequently accused by the Byzantines of putting his personal affairs before the needs of the state, having always stayed within a short distance of the frontier in order to be ready to return upon Antonina's arrival. Procopius even goes on to say that Belisarius could have taken the Persian capital of Ctesiphon and released the Byzantine citizens held there as slaves, since the Persian army was in Lazica, and there was little in the way of defences to stop him (*Anekdota*, 2.18–26).

Although it is possible that Belisarius could have advanced further than he did, given that he was unaware of the exact position of the main Persian army and lacked the time to lay siege to fortresses such as Sisauranon, the suggestion that he should have taken Ctesiphon is a little absurd. Even if he had taken the capital, his return journey with the ex-slaves would have been slow and easy for the Persians to attack. Belisarius was always careful of his men's lives and it is extremely unlikely that he would ever have countenanced such an invasion without detailed information on the Persian deployments. This part of the story should be seen as an attempt to ridicule the man who Procopius once thought capable of achieving much more, and is evidence of Procopius' slow change of attitude towards Belisarius: he was no longer the conquering hero of Africa

Upon her arrival, Antonina was placed under arrest and treated poorly, but Procopius states that Belisarius did not kill her due to the affection that he felt for her (*Anekdota*, 3.2–3). This may be true, but it is just as likely that, hearing of her service to the empress, he also believed that he would be punished if anything happened to his wife.

At this point the couple were recalled to Constantinople by the empress, as she had heard of events in the east. Photius also arrived in Constantinople, having captured Theodosius, taken all of the money he had with him, and sent him under guard to Cilicia, where Belisarius' *bucellarii* had been sent to spend the winter.

In consideration of her service against John the Cappadocian, Theodora now forced Antonina and Belisarius to be reconciled, at the same time arresting those who had travelled to Ephesus to arrest Theodosius. These men were tortured, including Photius, to reveal Theodosius' whereabouts. Finally, she discovered where he was and had him brought to the palace. Shortly afterwards he was revealed to Antonina and their affair would in all likelihood have continued, had he not shortly afterwards contracted dysentery and died.

Photius, after several attempts, escaped from prison and travelled to Jerusalem, where he spent the rest of his life as a monk. Procopius attacks Belisarius for his refusal to help Photius during his time of imprisonment and after, yet, as it was the empress that was holding him, it is unclear what Belisarius could have done in the matter (Anekdota, 3.29–31).

The series of events had lasted throughout the winter, reaching their conclusion as the campaigning season for 542 approached.

The Third Year: 542

In the spring of 542, Khusrow again led an invasion into Byzantine territory. Following the same route as he had in 540, keeping the Euphrates on his right hand side, he marched until he reached Sergiopolis. The priest of Sergiopolis, Candidus, had earlier promised to pay a ransom for the release of the captives taken during the sack of Susa. He had never paid. Whether under pressure from the citizens who were hoping to avoid an attack, or hoping to avert any punishment by facing the king in person, Candidus went to see Khusrow and pleaded for clemency. Khusrow had him tortured and then demanded double the original amount, as had been agreed earlier. Candidus authorised a payment by giving Khusrow treasures from the sanctuary in the city. Khusrow sent men to the city and took the treasures: it was not enough.

Khusrow now decided to capture the city by ostensibly sending men back to the sanctuary for more but giving them orders to capture the gate and allow the army to enter. However, a Christian in the army of Al-Mundhir by the name of Ambrus crept near to the fortifications and warned the citizens of the plan. When Khusrow's men approached the city they were refused entry. Khusrow immediately laid siege to the city. Some 6,000 men were committed to an assault, but they were repulsed after heavy fighting. Yet the citizens now fell into despair and would have surrendered if Ambrus had not informed them that the Persians' water supply was running low and that they only had enough left to last for two days. Taking heart, the defenders held out until, as predicted, the Persian army lifted the siege two days later and moved in search of water. Candidus was never released from captivity.

Khusrow, possibly after taking advice from his officers and spies, now led the army through the province of Euphratensis (Commagene), heading towards Syria and especially Jerusalem. He had learned that the territory was poorly defended, as it did not expect an invasion, and rich, as it had not been pillaged for a long time.

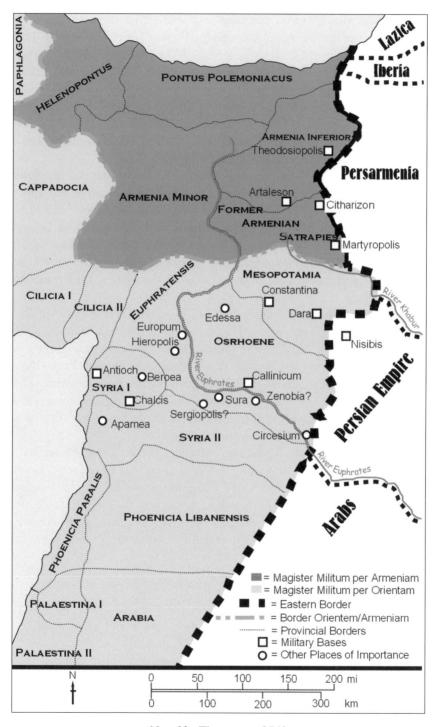

Map 23: The events of 542.

Learning of the invasion, Justinian had sent Belisarius back to the east. Belisarius arrived in Euphratensis at roughly the same time as Khusrow. Justus, Justinian's nephew, and Buzes, along with other commanders, had retreated to Hieropolis upon learning of the Persian invasion. They now sent letters to Belisarius requesting that he join them. Belisarius declined the invitation, instead going to Europum and establishing his headquarters there. He quickly gathered an army before recalling Justus, Buzes and the others to him. Leaving Justus with a few men to act as a garrison, the rest of the commanders and troops marched to Europum and joined Belisarius.

When he learned of Belisarius whereabouts, Khusrow dropped his plans to invade and sent Abandanes to Belisarius to acquire information and also put forward a complaint that Justinian had not sent the ambassadors that Khusrow expected. Belisarius' scouts reported the approach of Abandanes, so Belisarius selected 6,000 men of fine build and stature and led them on a hunt far from the camp. He also ordered his guardsman, Diogenes, and Adiolus son of Acacius to take 1,000 cavalry across the river and so block the route of the Persian army back into Persia.

As Abandanes approached, Belisarius had a pavilion erected and then set the 'huntsmen' on either side, first the Thracians and Illyrians, then the Goths, Heruls and finally the Vandals and Moors. As on the previous day, they were all equipped for hunting not for war. When Abandanes entered the pavilion he immediately complained about the lack of ambassadors from Justinian. These, he said, could have sorted out the difficulties and helped prevent a war. He was dismissed by Belisarius, being informed that ambassadors would not be sent whilst the Persians were on Byzantine territory.

Returning to Khusrow, Abandanes informed the king that Belisarius was a great general, and commanded troops such as he had never seen. He then added that if Khusrow beat and killed Belisarius, he would only have defeated a servant of Justinian; if Belisarius beat Khusrow, the defeat would bring disgrace upon the Persians and damage the whole kingdom. Furthermore, as they were in Byzantine territory, a defeated Byzantine army could retire to its strongpoints and reform; a Persian defeat would see them being pursued in a hostile land with a long distance to travel before they could find sanctuary. Finally, he reported that the Byzantines had a force on the far side of the river. Unfortunately, there were only two routes the Persians could use to return to Persia. They had already travelled upon one route and used up all of the provisions it could supply. The Byzantine cavalry that had crossed the river was blocking the Persian retreat in the other direction. That route also could not be used.

Taken these matters into consideration, Khusrow decided that his only means of escape was to fight a battle and force a river crossing. Yet Belisarius did not want to fight a battle, he simply wanted the Persians out of Byzantine territory. The Persians were allowed to reach the river, where they quickly erected a bridge and crossed over. Once across, Khusrow sent messages saying that he had kept his part of the agreement and now wanted ambassadors to be sent. Belisarius crossed the river after him and kept pressure on Khusrow, who continued his journey out of Byzantine territory. He asked the king to maintain wisdom and treat the Byzantines he encountered on his return journey as friends. Khusrow agreed, providing that a hostage was provided for Byzantine good conduct and the sending of ambassadors.

With his task completed, Belisarius travelled to Edessa and sent a noble of the city to be Khusrow's hostage. However, on his return journey, no longer pressured by the Byzantine army and with no hostage to force the Byzantines to keep to the agreement, Khusrow attacked and sacked Callinicum. As he was there the hostage arrived and, satisfied with the year's events, Khusrow finally left Byzantine territory.

Procopius now claims that all of the troops, who had been scared and outnumbered, as well as the citizens of the east, praised Belisarius for repelling an invasion without fighting a battle. Belisarius was now summoned to Constantinople to be sent back to Italy, where in his absence the situation had become desperate (Proc, *Wars*, II.xxi.1–34). Such is the story given by Procopius in order to win renown for his patron Belisarius. It does not, however, contain all of the information needed to form a true picture of events.

The Plague and Justinian

In 541 disease had broken out in Egypt. Procopius gives us a clear description of the illness, which allows us to clearly identify it. It was bubonic plague. The description in Procopius almost precisely matches the descriptions of the disease from the Middle Ages – including the use of the term *boubon* (*Wars*, II.xxii.17). It rapidly spread and was already in the vicinity when Khusrow invaded Euphratensis and Belisarius arrived at Europum. Their urgency to avoid the disease is adequate explanation for the desire of both Belisarius and Khusrow to end the campaign quickly and leave the area.

Yet Belisarius' ploy of showing strong and fit troops to Abandanes needs explanation. It is likely that Belisarius was demonstrating clearly to Khusrow that not only were his troops fit and free from disease, they were also unworried about catching the disease, instead preparing for a hunt. In effect, this display of strength and bravado increased the pressure on Khusrow. He now realised that he was faced by an army unaffected by the disease and so capable of strong resistance, not weakened by the ravages of plague and so easily defeated or outmanoeuvred. Furthermore, the display of nonchalance contrasted sharply with Khusrow's desire to leave the area as quickly as possible.

Although Belisarius had given the initiative to Khusrow, he was secure in the knowledge that Khusrow did not want to fight a battle, as the ensuing delays would increase his chances of contracting the plague. Belisarius probably surmised that Khusrow's next move would almost certainly be to retreat to Persia. He was correct in his assumption.

Yet his overconfidence nearly proved his undoing. Once the Persians were retreating, Belisarius moved north to Edessa, so relieving the Persians of the threat of attack. It would have done little to maintain the majesty and terror of the Persian ruler if, in a major campaign, his only success was the capture of Candidus and the gaining of a previously-agreed ransom. The sack of Callinicum would have enabled Khusrow to claim a victory, since even though threatened by disease and a Byzantine army under one of its greatest generals, he had still accomplished a major feat.

Due to this, Procopius alleges that Belisarius had to face accusations of cowardice for allowing Khusrow to retire unmolested after his attack at Callinicum (*Anekdota*, 3. 30–1). Although in some ways understandable, such claims were never to receive a general airing or to be brought in front of a court: it would appear that the majority of people recognised the gravity of the situation and applauded Belisarius for his decision not to risk battle with a possibly infected army.

As Belisarius retired to his headquarters, events in Constantinople changed the whole complexion of both his campaign and his career. In 542 the plague had reached Constantinople. According to Procopius the first recorded outbreak was at Pelusium in Egypt (*Wars*, II.xxii.6). From there it had travelled throughout the whole of Egypt, including Alexandria, and along the coast northwards towards Palestine. Possibly being transmitted by the fleas of the black rat, as in the Middle Ages, the disease was carried by ship around the eastern Mediterranean; Procopius noted that it 'always took its start from the coast' (*Wars*, II.xxii.9). The first outbreak occurred in Constantinople in the middle of spring, when Belisarius and Procopius were still in residence before their departure to the east to face Khusrow (*Wars*, xxii.10).

Procopius states that the disease lasted for four months in Constantinople, at first making little impact on the number of recorded deaths. Yet, before long it was claiming 5,000 deaths per day and, at its height, 10,000 per day (*Wars*, xxiii.1–4). Overall, the disease is estimated to have taken 300,000 lives in the capital alone (Norwich, *Byzantium*, p.233). Yet by itself the virulence of the disease in Constantinople is unlikely to have affected Belisarius' career. Circumstances were to change. At some point during the summer (no dates are given by Procopius) Justinian caught the plague.

Belisarius' fall from favour

Obviously there was a time lapse between Justinian contracting the disease and the news reaching the commanders in the east. By the time the news arrived, the whole of the Middle East was suffering from the plague, so the commanders of the armies naturally assumed that, given their experience of the disease, Justinian would die and may already have done so. At a meeting it was agreed that the army commanders would not endorse any replacement chosen to be emperor in their absence from Constantinople.

The decision was to have grave consequences. Theodora's only source of power was her marriage to Justinian. If Justinian died, she would have to quickly search for an imperial replacement, presumably marrying the man in the process of making him emperor. This was the only way in which she would be able to maintain her hold on power if Justinian died. When news reached her of the meeting in the east she interpreted it as a personal attack, since it would be unlikely that the generals would approve of her choice of emperor. The individual would be ousted and her grip on power lost. The throne would then pass to one of the generals, most likely Belisarius, since he had the most popularity with the people.

With her fate resting upon the health of Justinian, she watched and waited for Justinian's recovery. Fortunately for her, he survived. As soon as his survival was assured, Theodora struck. The two generals who were thought to have instigated the fateful meeting – namely Buzes and Belisarius – were recalled to Constantinople. Belisarius was never to return to the eastern frontier. Unaware of events in the capital, the generals arrived in Constantinople.

Taken by surprise, Buzes was thrown into the dungeons, charged with treason (*Anekdota*, 4.6–12). He was to remain there for twenty-eight months, until Theodora relented and he was released. However, by some chance Belisarius had not attended the meeting in person. Without that evidence, it was difficult to lay the same charges against him. However, he was charged instead with reserving for himself money taken in the Vandal and Gothic campaigns that should have been delivered to the emperor. He was stripped of the rank of *magister militum per Orientem*, with the title being bestowed upon Martinus. The empress also confiscated all of his wealth and forbade his friends and associates from communicating with him. Finally, his *comitatus* was disbanded, with the officers and palace eunuchs casting lots for the individual units (Proc, *Anekdota*, 4.13–16).

Belisarius as commander in the East

In the east, Belisarius only served in two out of the three years of campaigning before his final recall to Constantinople. In both of these Procopius raised doubts about his competence. The question remains as to whether these claims were merely malicious or whether they had a basis in fact.

In his first year on campaign, the second year of the war, Belisarius only advanced a short distance into Persian territory. Procopius ascribed this to his desire to confront Antonina concerning her affair with Theodosius (*Anekdota*, 2.19–20). However a close reading of the text reveals that Procopius thought that this had only reinforced his resolve to retire ('This information, however, led him much more quickly to the decision' – *Anekdota*, 2. 20). The analysis shows that, whatever he thought of Belisarius' private life, Procopius – even in the vindictive *Anekdota* – grudgingly concedes that Belisarius had acted properly in deciding to withdraw.

The factors that affected this decision readily support the hypothesis. Firstly, Khusrow was reported as being engaged against the Huns, yet, with an army that could be composed entirely of cavalry, it was possible that he could arrive unexpectedly and so take the Byzantines by surprise, possibly with disastrous consequences. Secondly, although Belisarius' strategy had effectively pinned Nobades in Nisibis, the city still had a large garrison. The arrival of Khusrow with a large force of Persians would free the garrison and so enlarge the forces under Khusrow's immediate command. In such circumstances, discretion was required, not an ill-informed advance deep into Persian territory. When Procopius claims in the *Anekdota* that Belisarius could easily have taken the Persian capital of Ctesiphon, he did so in hindsight, knowing that the Persians could not have interfered with the action (*Anekdota*, 2. 25).

In Belisarius' final year of campaigning, both Belisarius and Khusrow were constrained in their actions by fear of the plague. Although Belisarius could have forced a battle, it could easily have been lost due to the large numbers of the invading army. Furthermore, even if he had won, remaining in the area could have led to his troops contracting the disease, which would have decimated his forces and so left the east vulnerable to attack. As it was, with disease possibly already present in the Persian army, a withdrawal was the wisest move, since it protected his own troops whilst likely leaving the Persians decimated by the disease and consequently vulnerable. Belisarius would not have known that the plague was destined to devastate both empires, leaving them both weaker than they had been originally.

Therefore, although it is possible to castigate Belisarius over his lack of aggression, an analysis of the possible reasons for his decisions allows us to understand the motives behind his decisions. It is possible that a decision to make a decisive strike at the Persians in either of the two campaigns could have resulted in Khusrow suffering a major defeat, yet on balance Belisarius made the only decision that was open to him. Throughout his campaigns he rarely threw away the lives of his men without strong strategic or tactical reasons. In the east, he decided that the risks outweighed the potential gains and the casualties he would suffer. The continuing care Belisarius took with the lives of his men no doubt contributed to his lasting popularity with the troops.

Finally, although it is possible to claim that Belisarius made a grave mistake in gaining the animosity of Theodora by refusing to accept her nomination for the throne in the event of Justinian's death, his actions are understandable. As a close friend of Justinian and as a powerful figure in Constantinople, Belisarius could not have stood by and allowed a rival to become the ruler of the empire. It is unlikely that any new emperor would allow the continued existence of such a powerful competitor as Belisarius. Consequently, Belisarius was in a no-win situation as he would be seen as either the supporter of an extinct line or a threat to the existing one. Yet in one respect his decision making was to be very fortunate. He refused – or was unable – to take part in the meeting that decided not to accept any candidate proposed by Theodora. It is possible that Belisarius assumed that, if he took no active part, he would be more readily acceptable as a candidate for emperor from among the military leaders. Almost by accident, the decision not to attend instead saved his own life.

Chapter 12

Italy again

Italy after Belisarius

In 540 Justinian had sent Alexander to reorganise the new territory upon the imperial model for taxation. The choice would prove to be a mistake. He was nicknamed 'Snips' after a set of curved cutters that he used to trim the edge off coins whilst still allowing them to appear round. In this way he was able to build up a store of the metal and so increase his personal wealth. Upon his arrival in Ravenna Alexander announced an investigation into the taxes paid by the Italians to the Goths since they had arrived in Italy with Theoderic nearly a century before. He found that the natives had underpaid the Goths and declared that the underpayment was now due to the emperor. He also stopped the corn ration that was given to the poor at St Peter's in Rome. Obviously, these actions immediately began to alienate the Italians to the imperial cause (Proc, *Wars*, VII.i.31–33).

Alexander also launched an inquiry into the financial condition of the troops, charging many of them with fraud and of costing the state money, putting many of them on trial and then fining them large sums of money. Whilst some of the money was forwarded to Constantinople, much was retained by Alexander. Finally, he reduced the expenditure on the army. Although his actions increased the cash in the empire's coffers, as well as enlarging his personal wealth, they began to undermine the loyalty of the troops, many of whom became increasingly unwilling to fight. His actions would later be highlighted by Gothic rulers as the negative aspects of imperial rule.

Alexander's actions were to some extent mirrored by the actions of the Byzantine commanders Justinian had left in Italy. Ignoring Belisarius' earlier guidelines, they began to treat the natives badly, taking what they wanted whenever they desired from whoever owned it. The troops followed their example, possibly being spurred on by the knowledge that Alexander's decisions were depriving them of what they believed were their rewards for their victory.

All of this is in contrast to the state of affairs under Belisarius, whose self-restraint had resulted in him being trusted by the natives, and who did not allow his troops to take goods from the natives without payment. The imperial conquest began to turn sour.

Ildibadus

Upon hearing that Belisarius had left Italy, Ildibadus had taken control of the remnants of the Goths. He slowly gathered his forces together, being joined by several Byzantine deserters, unhappy with the conditions under Belisarius' successors. Beginning with approximately 1,000 troops at Ticinum, slowly the Ligurian and Venetian towns and cities changed allegiance and pledged their support.

Map 24: Italy during Belisarius' absence.

The Byzantine general Vitalius now advanced into Venetia with a force of Byzantine troops accompanied by Heruls. Meeting Ildibadus at Tarbesium (Treviso), Ildibadus defeated Vitalius in battle and forced him to retire. Despite this promising beginning, things quickly went awry for Ildibadus. First, he quarrelled with Uraias, the man who had suggested he be crowned king. According to Procopius, Uraias' wife entered the baths in which Ildibadus' wife was present. Uraias' wife completely ignored the queen, who complained to Ildibadus. Shortly after, Ildibadus had Uraias put to death. The incident caused dissension in the Gothic ranks, as many disagreed with the execution.

However, nothing was done before Ildibadus made his second, fatal, mistake. He organised the marriage of a man and woman in his court. One of his guards, Velas, was in love with the woman and took exception to the arrangement. Taking advantage of his privileged position, he assassinated Ildibadus at a banquet. At this juncture the tribe of the Rogi, a subdivision of the Goths who had fiercely maintained their independence, declared their leader Eraric as king.

Eraric

Hearing of the death of Ildibadus and fearing that he would be next, Totila, Ildibadus' nephew, sent messengers to Constantianus. Totila was in control of Tarbesium, and he agreed to surrender the town in exchange for sanctuary. Constantianus agreed and a date was set for the exchange. Before the transaction could be completed, the Goths lost patience with Eraric. They offered the kingship to Totila, who informed them of his deal with Constantianus and of the date that it would be fulfilled. He said that if Eraric was killed before that date, he would accept their offer instead.

Throughout this period, when the Goths had been in disarray and vulnerable, none of the Byzantine generals in Italy other than Vitalius had united their forces and taken any aggressive action. Possibly due to this inactivity, Eraric despatched envoys to Justinian to ask for the same peace treaty that had been offered earlier: namely, that the Goths would be allowed to retain all of Italy north of the Po whilst the empire controlled all of Italy to the south of the river. Procopius also claims that Eraric's envoys in secret offered to surrender the whole of Italy in return for a large sum of money, and this may be one of the reasons for the Goths' antagonism towards their new king. Whatever the cause, the negotiations came to nothing as Eraric was killed by his own troops and Totila was declared king.

Totila and the War for Italy

When news of the death of Eraric reached Justinian, he realized that during this period in which the Goths were paralysed by internal dissensions his generals in Italy had done nothing. He now sent a letter reprimanding them for their inactivity and demanding action. Accordingly, John the nephew of Vitalianus, along with Bessas and Vitalius all now travelled to Ravenna, meeting Constantianus and Alexander 'Snips', who were already there. Leaving garrisons in the other cities, they marshalled their forces before marching against Verona, planning to capture the city before moving on to Ticinum where Totila had his headquarters. Constantianus and Alexander led 12,000 men under eleven commanders (Proc, *Wars*, VII.iii.2–5) towards Verona, setting their camp about 60 *stades* from the city where the plains stretched all the way to Mantua.

From this point onwards their actions showed the limitations of military campaigns run by committee. When Marcian, a citizen of the Veneti who was an imperialist at heart, offered to bribe a friend of his who was a guard at Verona, the Byzantine generals accepted. However, they decided that one of them needed to lead an advance party that would rush the gate and hold it until the main force arrived. None of them wanted to actually take part in such a risky venture. Eventually, Artabazes agreed to undertake the task. Artabazes was the Persian general who had surrendered the fortress of Sisauranon to Belisarius in his eastern campaign the previous year (541). He had been deployed to Italy by Justinian to reinforce the forces fighting the Goths.

With only 100 men Artabazes took control of the gate, attacking the Gothic troops in the vicinity and killing the guards on the nearby walls. The entire Gothic garrison, fearing that this was a major Byzantine assault that had already secured a gate and a section of the walls, fled to a nearby hill over-looking the city. Unfortunately, the main body of the Byzantines was still 40 *stades* (about 5 miles) away. Procopius states that they had stopped whilst the generals argued over the plunder that would be taken when the city fell (*Wars*, VII.iii.15–16). Seeing from their vantage point that there were only a few Byzantines in the city, the Goths returned and attacked Artabazes and his men, driving them from the gate and on to the city walls, where defence was easier. The Byzantine generals finally resumed the advance only to find the gate closed against them.

As the army approached, the men on the walls called for them to come to their aid, but instead the army retired to a safe distance and watched while they fought on. Realising that help was now impossible, the men on the walls jumped off in an attempt to escape death. Many were killed by the fall, but others – including Artabazes – fell upon soft ground and survived.

Artabazes was furious with the generals for both failing to advance quickly enough to support his attack upon the town, and also for failing to take any action to help when they saw that he and his men were in difficulty. As the attack had failed, the army left Verona and moved across the Po towards Faventia (Faenza).

Totila received news of the events at Verona and realised that the Byzantines were badly commanded, being led either by a committee or by a single commander with a divided command, rather than a gifted individual. He immediately decided to take advantage of the situation. He summoned the Goths from Verona to join him in Ticinum, leaving behind only a garrison to maintain their command of the city. Upon their arrival, he marched against the Byzantines with his whole force of some 5,000 men.

As the Goths advanced towards them, the Byzantines held a debate to decide what they should do. Artabazes advised that although they outnumbered the enemy, and despite the fact they had been defeated by Belisarius, they should not underestimate the Goths. He suggested that they should wait until the Goths began to cross the River Po, wait until half were across, and then launch an attack whilst the Goths were divided. As the debate continued the Byzantines remained stationary.

Unobserved by the Byzantines, Totila arrived at the Po. He dispatched 300 troops with orders to travel down river for 20 *stades* in order to cross and come up behind the Byzantine camp. In this way, they could attack the Byzantine rear at the height of the forthcoming battle.

Crossing the river unopposed, Totila marched towards the Byzantine camp, and at his approach the Byzantines formed their battle lines. Before the battle began, a Goth called Valaris rode between the armies and laid down a challenge to individual combat. Artabazes accepted the challenge and killed the Goth, but not before being mortally wounded himself, dying three days after the battle. The battle itself now began and raged fiercely until the 300 Goths sent down the river by Totila arrived and, as planned, attacked the Byzantine rear. Taken by surprise, the Byzantines panicked and fled.

A short time later, Totila sent an army under Vledas, Roderic and Uliaris to lay siege to Florentia (Florence). Not expecting to be attacked, the Byzantines in the city had not gathered provisions for a siege, so immediately sent a message to Ravenna asking for help. An army was sent under Bessas, Cyprian and John the nephew of Vitalianus. Upon their approach the Goths withdrew to the valley of Mucellis (Mugello) and the Byzantines, learning that they were still in the vicinity, decided to force a battle.

Leaving a small garrison in Florentia, the Byzantines advanced towards the Goths. The Byzantine commanders decided to send a small, picked force of men under one of their number in advance of the main body. In this way, it was hoped, the Goths would be surprised and, when they were fully engaged, the Byzantine main body would arrive and the battle would end. The commanders decided to draw lots to decide who would lead the advance party, and John the nephew of Vitalianus won the dubious prize of going ahead of the main force. Unfortunately, the other commanders now refused to follow the plan and give him their best troops. He was forced to go ahead leading only his own contingent of men.

The Goths saw John and his men approaching and retreated to the top of a nearby hill. John led his men in an assault upon the position, but, outnumbered and downhill, they were forced back and then routed. As they ran, a rumour spread that John had been killed. When they reached the main body of troops, the rumour of John's death spread and the entire army now fled, each of the commanders leading their troops to different towns and cities, as circumstances dictated. Once in position, they settled down and prepared to be besieged. They no longer had any thought of leaving their sanctuaries, or of uniting and fighting the Goths in open battle. John himself made his way to Rome.

Most writers have followed Procopius in his castigation of the Byzantine commanders in Italy. Their refusal to cooperate and join together in order to defeat Totila resulted in a prolongation of the war. If they had acted in concert at an early stage, they may have been able to defeat Totila before he was able to build up his forces. These historians, along with Procopius, neglect to mention one salient factor: in 542 the plague arrived in Italy and the commanders were staying in place in order to avoid catching it.

Either dismissing the threat of the disease or deciding that the risk was worth the possible gains, Totila decided to maintain an active stance. He now showed the political and personal abilities that were to make him the Byzantines' most formidable foe; he showed respect to all of the prisoners he had taken, treating them all courteously and with kindness. When the treatment was contrasted with the behaviour of Alexander 'Snips', who was acting on behalf of the Emperor, the captives found it easy to change sides and pledge their allegiance to Totila.

So ended the campaign season of 542. There was plague in Constantinople and Justinian was only slowly beginning his journey to a full recovery; Belisarius was in disgrace for relieving the emperor of spoils taken in the Vandal and Gothic Wars. The Goths were resurgent in Italy, having beaten the armies that had ventured to face them in open battle, with the Byzantine forces now penned into their cities and waiting to be attacked.

The campaign of 543

At the start of the new campaign season, Totila quickly retook Caesena and Petra, but was resisted when he attempted to gain control of the towns in Tuscany. Therefore, he bypassed Rome – the scene of Witigis' defeat – and entered Campania and Samnium. Taking Beneventum, he razed the city walls to the ground. It appears that he believed the Byzantines to be superior in siegecraft – both in the taking and the holding of towns – so wanted to deny them the opportunity to fight in sieges. He was, however, confident in his ability to defeat them in open battle. With no walls, the towns of Italy could not harbour the Byzantines and they would be forced to fight on his terms.

Totila's political wisdom also began to bear fruit. Naples was garrisoned by Conon with 1,000 Byzantine and Isaurian troops. Setting up his camp nearby, Totila sent a force which retook Cumae and other strongholds near to the city. In this way he captured many of the wives and families of Italian senators who had been living in the region, believing themselves to be safe from attack. Totila now freed the captives, so winning a reputation for wisdom and humanity. Whether this was done in imitation of Belisarius, or was a result of his natural disposition is not known. What is known, is that he now began to acquire esteem amongst the Italians for his honesty and honour.

Totila waited outside Naples, but, realising that no troops were going to be sent out against him, he dispatched small contingents throughout Apulia and Calabria. With the towns having no walls and so putting up little resistance, he soon controlled both of these territories and was able to collect their taxes for his own uses.

The loss of this revenue, coupled with the strict budgetary measures of Alexander 'Snips', soon resulted in the soldiers' pay being in arrears. The troops became increasingly unwilling to leave the cities and risk their lives for the emperor. Furthermore, the Italian landlords from Apulia and Calabria also lost their incomes, since they had moved to the towns to protect themselves and so could do nothing to stop Totila claiming their rents. As a result, the Italians became increasingly restless.

Justinian's response

Since the Battle of Mucellis, the Byzantine commanders had refused to leave the towns to which they had fled. Constantianus was in Ravenna, John nephew of Vitalianus in Rome, Bessas in Spoletium, Justinus in Florentia, and Cyprian in Perusia. The other, lesser commanders were in whichever town they had sought refuge with their troops. Realising that these commanders were unable to make decisions together, Justinian appointed Maximinus as *praetorian prefect* and gave him supreme authority in Italy. Unfortunately, according to Procopius, he was 'inexperienced, timid, and prone to delay' (*Wars*, VII.vi.12). Sent from Constantinople with a fleet and army (consisting of Thracians under Herodian and Armenians under Phazas the Iberian, plus a few Huns) Maximinus reached Epirus in Greece and halted.

After a long delay, Maximinus sent Demetrius, who had previously served under Belisarius, to Sicily. Learning that Conon in Naples was hard pressed to resist the Goths, Demetrius decided to act, although he had only a few men with him. Accordingly, he gathered a large fleet and stocked it with grain for the city. Assuming, correctly as it turned out, that the Goths would believe this to be a large army, he set sail. The Goths were fearful for their safety, but the fleet sailed past and proceeded to Portus, where Demetrius hoped to spend a little time in gathering extra troops from the area. However, the Byzantines in the area had only recently been defeated by the Goths and refused to join him.

During this time, the Neapolitans had become ever more desperate and finally sent another Demetrius, known as the Cephalonian, who was governor of the city, to Rome to ask for help. Frustrated in his attempts to raise an army, Demetrius agreed to help the Neapolitans and sailed for Naples. It was too late. By this time, Totila had learnt of the composition of the Byzantine fleet. As they neared Naples, the Gothic fleet attacked the Byzantines, defeating them and capturing all of their ships and cargoes. The Byzantine Demetrius escaped in a small boat, as did a few others, but most were captured or killed, including Demetrius the Cephalonian. He was taken alive before Totila. During the siege, he had been accustomed to stand upon the walls and hurl insults at the Goths and their king. As a punishment, Totila cut out his tongue and chopped off his hands. He was then allowed to return to the city.

After a very long delay in Epirus, Maximinus, the new commander of the Italian armies, reached Syracuse. Learning of his arrival, messengers from all over Italy arrived to ask him for help. Finally, he sent Herodian, Demetrius – who had returned to Sicily – and Phazes to Naples by sea. As it was now close to winter, the fleet was caught in a storm and blown aground near to the Gothic camp. Most of the troops were killed or captured, including Demetrius. Herodian and Phazes and a few others managed to escape, but it was now clear that there was to be no relieving army for the city of Naples.

Demetrius was paraded before the walls and forced to tell the Neapolitans that they could no longer expect any help from the Byzantine army. After negotiations, the citizens agreed to surrender in 30 days if no army arrived to help them. As a sign of his confidence, Totila extended the deadline to three months, in order to emphasise the hopelessness of their cause. The strategy worked. Shortly after the negotiations, and long before the deadline, the city surrendered.

Totila now worked upon improving his image. He collected food for the city, and himself organised its distribution so as to minimise the number of deaths caused by people eating too much food after reaching the edge of starvation. He also allowed the Byzantine troops to go free, but when they decided to sail to Rome a strong wind kept them in the harbour. Finally, Totila gave them horses and pack animals and they headed for Rome by the land route. When a Neapolitan complained to Totila that his daughter had been raped by one of his men, Totila had the man imprisoned and then executed. In this way he began to gain the loyalty of the native Italians. In direct contrast, the Byzantine troops who were not immediately threatened by the Goths plundered the territories around their cities and so alienated the natives from their cause. Slowly, army discipline began to collapse.

A further repercussion of the capture of Naples was that the Goths now occupied a large port on the western coast of Italy. As a consequence, Totila gathered a fleet in the port with which to control the Tyrrenhian Sea (Proc. VII. xiii. 6).

Totila's next move was to send messengers to the senators of Rome asking them to revert to their original allegiance. John, nephew of Vitalianus, prevented the senators from sending a reply, but Totila sent a second letter stating that the Byzantines would be unharmed if they supported him. Suspecting the Arian bishops in the city of colluding with Totila, the Byzantines evicted them from the city. After sending the letters, Totila dispatched an army to Dryus (Otranto) with orders to ask the city to surrender. If it refused, it was to be laid under siege. With the rest of the army, Totila himself moved to lay siege to Rome.

As their control of Italy slipped away, Constantianus sent a letter to Justinian, signed by all of the other commanders, stating that they were unable to fight the Goths.

Belisarius reappointed to a command

In Constantinople, Belisarius had been living simply as a private citizen, and although allowed access to the palace, he was not allowed into the presence of Justinian and Theodora. According to Procopius, he only retained a few attendants, which was very different from his recent exploits accompanied by thousands of *bucellarii* and a large household. Procopius also alleges that Belisarius was poorly treated by the emperor and empress, who allowed their lackeys to treat him with contempt, and that he lived in fear of assassination – possibly on imperial orders (*Anekdota*, 4.20–22).

It is possible that this treatment had two distinct causes. The first is that the empress wanted to punish Belisarius for his alleged inclusion in the plot to replace her husband on his death. This would have stripped Theodora of her power and rendered her vulnerable to attack from her enemies. It is not hard to see why Theodora would want to punish him for his actions.

The second revolves around Antonina. Procopius claims that Antonina and Belisarius had quarrelled after her services for the empress. It is likely that Theodora wanted to impress upon Belisarius the importance of Antonina in maintaining his position at court. Without her, he would not have the same level of influence in political and military affairs. Furthermore, the reliance went both ways. By having Belisarius, the empire's leading general, tied to her close friend and confidante, Antonina, Theodora ensured that the likelihood of Belisarius leading a successful revolt against Justinian was slim; even if he did and won, Antonina would be in a position to intercede on her behalf with the new emperor.

Shortly afterwards, Theodora agreed to allow the restoration of Belisarius to the imperial grace. Again according to Procopius, Theodora emphasised that Belisarius was being restored to favour due to the intercession of Antonina, to whom the empress owed a favour thanks to her recent service. She also pointed out that Belisarius' attitude to the emperor and empress would be judged by his treatment of Antonina (*Anekdota*, 4. 27–30). The circumstances surrounding his restoration to favour reinforces the idea that the whole episode was contrived in order to reduce Belisarius from his lofty position as conqueror of the west and remind him that he was subordinate to both Justinian and Theodora. It further suggests that it was at least in part engineered to ensure that he remained loyal to Antonina, and was thus kept subordinate to Theodora.

The majority of Belisarius' wealth was restored, except for a portion that was given as a present by Theodora to her husband. To further secure his loyalty to the imperial family, his daughter Joannina was betrothed to Anastasius, one of Theodora's grandsons, although Procopius suggests that this was also a way for Theodora or her descendants to acquire his personal wealth after he had died (*Anekdota*, 5. 20).

Once restored to imperial favour, Belisarius asked to be reinstalled as *magister militum per Orientem*, and to be sent to the east to fight the Persians. His request was declined, possibly at the request of Antonina, who declared that she did not want to go back to the place where she had been insulted in front of everybody (*Anekdota*, 4.38). However, a further reason for the refusal presents itself. There was an urgent need for a commander in Italy and Justinian may have already decided to send Belisarius back to the scene of his earlier triumphs. Instead of being reinstated as *magister militum per Orientem* he was given the lower rank of *comes sacri stabuli* (count of the sacred stables). Whilst still a senior post, the appointment must be seen as evidence that Belisarius had not been fully restored to imperial favour. Moreover, the post of *magister militum per Orientem* was still held by Martinus and it may have been impolitic to have removed him from office after such a short tenure.

The Return to Italy

For his new campaign Belisarius was not given the troops that had recently served under him. They were needed in the east to face the Persians. Furthermore, his *comitatus* had been distributed by lot amongst his fellow generals and he does not appear to have been able to recruit a substantial number of *bucellarii* to form his household. Instead, he travelled throughout Thrace, his home province, offering a bounty to volunteers willing to join him. He was joined in this exercise by Vitalius, *magister militum per Illyricum*, who had recently returned from Italy.

Map 25: Belisarius in Italy.

After collecting around 4,000 men, Belisarius decided to make for Salona and from there, following Vitalius' advice, proposed to take the land route to Ravenna (Proc, *Wars*, VII.xiii. 14). With the Goths controlling the Italian peninsula outside the towns, Belisarius decided not to travel straight to Rome. He did not yet have enough troops to face the Goths in open battle and he was certain to be seen and his presence reported to Totila; there was no chance of taking the Goths by surprise.

Meantime, at Dryus the Byzantines were in such dire straits as their food supplies ran low that they agreed to surrender the city on a specific date should no outside help arrive. Belisarius loaded provisions on to ships and sent Valentinus to save the city. Arriving unannounced, the ships entered the harbour unmolested, and when the Goths besieging the city saw the fleet, they abandoned the siege and retired to join forces with Totila. Valentinus stocked the city with provisions and replaced the sick and malnourished garrison with fresh troops that he had brought from Belisarius. However, the new troops set out to plunder the countryside around the city and, in an accidental encounter with a Gothic force, were routed and forced to retreat to the city, having lost 170 men. Leaving the city with provisions to last them for a full year, Valentinus returned to Belisarius, who was still at Salona.

Once Valentinus had arrived back at Salona, Belisarius sailed to Pola. Totila quickly learned that he had landed and attempted to discover the composition of his army by sending a fake message from the Byzantine commander at Genoa. The messengers had instructions to spy on the Byzantine army, taking note of the numbers and types of troops present. Belisarius was completely fooled by the ploy and Totila now knew the nature of the army he had brought to Italy.

Whilst Totila had been spying upon Belisarius, the citizens of the besieged town of Tibur betrayed the town to the Goths. The garrison escaped but the Goths put the town to the sack, taking a large amount of spoils and captives.

In the meantime, Belisarius moved to Ravenna and attempted to persuade the Byzantines and Goths in the region to accept service with him. The appeal failed: not a single man was willing to reenlist in the army under Belisarius. There was a single major reason for their refusal to reenlist. Although they may have retained their loyalty to and respect for Belisarius, they knew that he would at some time be sent elsewhere again and they would be left with the same generals in Italy that they had previously abandoned. Alongside a reversion to the poor policies of lesser generals, there also remained the possibility of punishment for their desertion by generals other than Belisarius.

Unwilling to remain inactive, although he did not have enough troops to mount significant expeditions, Belisarius sent his bodyguard Thurimuth and some *bucellarii*, along with Vitalius and some Illyrians, into Aemilia. Camping near to Bononia (Bologne), they exerted pressure upon the surrounding area, inducing some fortresses to surrender. Before they could secure their gains, one night the Illyrians decided to return home, claiming that they were owed back-pay. In reality, it is more likely that they were worried about a Hunnic invasion that was currently devastating their homeland.

Totila learned of their departure and sent an army to attack Vitalius. Vitalius and Thurimuth were informed of the Goths' approach and set up a series of devastating ambushes. The Goths were either destroyed or routed and, once the outcome was certain, Thurimuth returned to Ravenna to report to Belisarius. Although the loss of the Illyrians was a serious blow, overall the venture had been a success, so Belisarius now sent Thurimuth, Ricilas, and Sabinianus with 1,000 troops to help the garrison of Auximus, which was under the command of Magnus. The town was still under siege, but the reinforcements managed to enter the town by night completely unobserved.

Once inside, it was decided to send out some scouts to discover the strength and position of the besiegers before mounting a series of sorties. Unfortunately, Ricilas became drunk and personally went out on reconnaissance. He was killed, and although an attack by Thurimuth's men routed the Goths and retrieved the body, it was decided in a conference that there were too few men available to defeat the enemy, but too many to act as a garrison; the extra men would simply use up the supplies faster and so hasten the capitulation of the town. Thurimuth and Sabinianus decided to leave the town by night, but a deserter informed Totila of the plan. He put in place an ambush of 2,000 men, which killed 200 Byzantines and captured the pack animals, servants, weapons and clothes of the troops. The remainder of the Byzantine force, including Thurimuth and Sabinianus, fled to Ariminum.

Still desiring to retain some of the initiative, Belisarius decided to restore one of two fortresses that had previously been dismantled by Witigis. Pisaurus (Pesaro) and Fanus (Fano) had both had their houses destroyed and the walls reduced to half their original height. As Pisaurus was in a region which was good for the pasturing of horses, Belisarius had the entrances measured and gates made in secret. Once complete, he ordered Thurimuth and Sabinianus with a force of men to retake the fortress and rebuild it. Totila heard of the attempt and led an army to assault the fortress. The attack failed and Totila withdrew to his camp near Auximus.

As a final move, Belisarius sent two of his personal guards to Rome with instructions for Bessas to remain within the walls and not attempt any sallies or forays outside. With the refortification of Pisaurus, Belisarius had used all of his available men; he could not do anything now other than wait. Totila had the initiative.

Totila became aware that all Byzantine movements had ceased, so, although winter had arrived, he decided to test the strength of the strongest towns, secure in the knowledge that they would receive no outside help. The first two towns he laid siege to were Firmum (Fermo) and Asculum (Ascoli) in Picenum.

Belisarius did not have spare forces with which to send help to the two towns. In desperation, he sent John the nephew of Vitalianus to Constantinople with instructions to act as swiftly as possible. John carried a message to Justinian begging for a large army and also for money to cover the arrears in pay for the troops, as many were now unwilling to fight. He further requested a supply of fresh horses and other equipment, as much had been lost in the various defeats that had been inflicted on the Byzantines by the Goths. Finally, he requested the return of his *comitatus* plus the recruitment of a large force of Huns and other mercenaries. He was aware that the Goths had yet to discover a counter to the use of massed horse archers, and wanted to take advantage of their inabilities.

John did not fulfil his task. Although when in Constantinople he married the daughter of Germanus, the emperor's nephew, he failed to convince Justinian of the need for speed in dispatching the reinforcements to Belisarius. Despite Procopius' castigation of his failure, it is not surprising. As we saw earlier, the Huns had only recently invaded Illyricum, the war was continuing against Persia, and there was a major rebellion in Africa. As a further –and major – factor, there had recently been a recurrence of the plague in Constantinople. The empire's resources were stretched to the limit.

These arguments would have done nothing to help the citizens of Firmum and Asculum, since both cities surrendered. Totila moved on and now laid siege to Spoletium and Asise. Neither of these cities were to fare any better. Spoletium was held by Herodian, who made an agreement with the Goths that if no help came within thirty days he would surrender the city. Procopius states that Herodian may have surrendered very easily, since he was worried about facing prosecution for his earlier failure to act against the Goths. Given the treatment of Belisarius after his actions in the east, such a worry is under-standable. Naturally, the overstretched Byzantines could not help the city and Herodian surrendered as agreed. Asise was held by Sisifridus, himself a Goth. When he was killed in a sally against the besiegers the heart went out of the city's defenders. They immediately surrendered to the Goths.

In contrast to these two cities, following their surrender a message was sent to Cyprian in Perusia, demanding that he surrender the city and offering a large sum of money as a reward. When Cyprian refused, Totila bribed one of his bodyguards, Ulifus, to kill Cyprian. Yet, when Ulifus succeeded both in killing Cyprian and in escaping, the troops and citizens still held firm and Totila retired from the city. Lifting the siege, Totila marched on Rome.

The Second Siege of Rome

Like his predecessor Witigis, Totila fortified a number of camps around the city with which to control movement both to and from it. When a number of Goths approached the city walls, Artasires and Barbation sallied against them – against Bessas' wishes – and routed them. However, they pursued the Goths into an ambush from which Artasires and Barbation escaped with only a few men, the rest being killed. Following this defeat, no more sorties would be allowed by Bessas. With Totila cutting the land routes and the navy stationed in Naples cutting the sea routes, severe famine quickly set in at Rome.

With Rome confined under siege, Totila sent a contingent of troops to Placentia, the only city in Aemilia in Byzantine hands, to either take the city by storm or to starve it into submission. Upon its arrival, the army's leaders offered terms to the Byzantine defenders, but these were refused and so the Goths began a siege. Again, due to the lack of supplies in much of Italy, the city was quickly reduced to starvation rations since they were already low on supplies.

Belisarius realised that he did not have the troops needed to effect the relief of Rome. Leaving Justinus to command the garrison in Ravenna, Belisarius, accompanied by 'a few men' (Proc, *Wars*, VII.xiii.19), travelled across the Adriatic and through Dalmatia to Epidamnus (Durazzo), from where he sent a message to Justinian requesting that reinforcements be sent to him. By this time Justinian had troops to spare for Italy, so sent a force of Byzantines and barbarians, under the command of John nephew of Vitalianus and Isaac the Armenian, brother of Aratus and Narses, to Epidamnus.

To help alleviate his manpower problems, Justinian sent Narses the Eunuch to the Heruls in order to persuade them to send an army to Italy to help Belisarius. The Heruls agreed and a large force set out led by Philemuth, amongst others. The intention was to winter in Thrace before joining Belisarius in spring. The move was to prove extremely fortunate. Accompanied by John the Glutton, the Heruls moved towards Thrace and, by chance, encountered an army of Sclaveni which had been plundering Byzantine territory. The Heruls defeated the Sclaveni and released all of their captives, who were allowed to return home.

In another attempt to wrest the initiative from the Goths, Belisarius now sent Valentinus and Phocas, his bodyguard, to join Innocentius in Portus with orders to harry the Gothic camps. Upon their arrival, they sent a message to Bessas informing him that they would be launching an attack on the main Gothic camp and requesting that he make a sortie and join the attack.

With 500 men, Valentinus and Phocas rode to the Gothic camp and began to fire arrows into it. They killed a few men, and the uproar the attack caused was heard by the people in Rome. However, Bessas made no attempt to leave the city and the Byzantines withdrew to Portus.

Valentinus and Phocas now sent a second message to Bessas, informing him that they were going to repeat the attack and again requesting that he send forces out of the city to join them. The attack never took place. A deserter informed Totila of the Byzantine plans and he ambushed Valentinus and Phocas as they were en route to the Gothic camp. Valentinus, Phocas and the majority of their men were killed in the ambush.

At this time Pope Vigilius (537–555) was in Sicily. Determined to help the Byzantine citizens, he loaded ships with grain and sent them to Portus. Unfortunately, the Goths controlled the actual harbour. The ships were taken by surprise and all of their provisions taken by the Goths. Shortly afterwards, Vigilius was summoned to Constantinople by Justinian to take part in the 'Three Chapters' controversy.

Totila in the ascendant

As winter began, the Byzantines in Placentia began to suffer from the worst effects of famine – so much so that some of them turned to cannibalism in order to survive. It was not enough. The garrison finally surrendered and the last city in Aemilia fell to Totila.

In the city of Rome the situation was becoming desperate. Pelagius the Deacon (Pope Vigilius was in Constantinople) was sent to Totila to negotiate a set period of truce, after which the city would surrender if no help came. Confident in his victory, Totila refused the offer.

The citizens asked Bessas for food, knowing that he had a large store set by for the troops. Bessas refused, and the troops made money selling their extra food to the citizens at hugely-inflated prices. Things now became so desperate that rich Romans began to run out of money and were reduced to bartering with the troops to exchange their possessions for food. When the troops' food also began to run out, many citizens left the city, either bribing the guards to let them out of the gates or escaping over the walls. The majority died in the attempt.

Belisarius reacts

At the beginning of the new campaign season, Belisarius – who had remained in Epidamnus over winter – was joined by John the nephew of Vitalianus and Isaac the Armenian. John advised that they should sail across the Adriatic before marching across land to Rome. Belisarius disagreed with the idea, instead sending John to southern Italy to secure the region of Calabria before marching on Rome. Belisarius and the rest of the army would sail directly to Rome.

John set sail first, but met a gale and was forced to take refuge in the harbour at Dryus. A force of Goths had been sent to lay siege to the city, but when they saw the fleet arrive they raised the siege and fled north to Brundisium. Assuming that the Byzantines were sailing further south, they sent messengers to Totila to advise him of their assumptions. Totila set his army on alert and ordered his commanders in Calabria to maintain control of the passes across the Apennines. Shortly afterwards, Belisarius set sail, intent on sailing directly to Portus.

The Goths in Calabria managed to overcome their initial fright and slowly began to relax, so they were completely oblivious when John ferried his troops across to that region. Recognising that Rome was likely to be the target for Belisarius' campaign, Totila remained on his guard and took measures to prevent any help arriving in the city. About 90 *stades* south of the city, the River Tiber became narrow. At this point Totila placed long timbers across the river and constructed a tower on either side to obstruct passage up the river. Leaving garrisons in the towers, Totila withdrew to his camp. Not long afterwards, Belisarius landed at Portus.

John the nephew of Vitalianus

After his landing in Calabria, John captured two Goths. He executed one of the Goths, and, unsurprisingly, the second Goth cooperated. He showed the Byzantines where the Goths at Brundisium pastured their horses. The Byzantine infantry immediately mounted the horses and the whole force attacked the Gothic camp. The majority of the Goths were killed, the remainder fled to Totila's camp near Rome. Having secured the area, John acted with restraint in an attempt to secure the locals' loyalty.

With his reputation growing, John advanced to Canusium, which he took. Tullianus, the leader of the Brutii and Lucani, agreed to hand over Bruttium and Lucanium if, this time, the Byzantines behaved in a proper manner. John agreed to the terms, a deal was struck and Tullianus accompanied the army on their travels.

Hearing of the loss of Bruttium and Lucania, Totila dispatched a force of 300 Goths to shadow John, but not to engage in combat. Wary of falling into a trap, John stopped his attempts to rejoin Belisarius as ordered, instead retiring to Bruttium. Totila had sent Rhecimundus with a force of Goths, plus Byzantine and Moorish deserters, to guard Rhegium and the Bruttian coast. The army was taken unawares by John, who destroyed the majority of the force – since they were deserters from the Byzantine army – and captured Rhecimundus and some of the Goths. Despite the victory, John still refused to combine forces with Belisarius near Rome, even though Belisarius pointed out repeatedly that he was only being blocked by 300 Goths based at Capua. Instead, John retreated to Cervarium in Apulia and remained there.

Belisarius attempts to supply Rome

Frustrated by John's refusal to act, Belisarius determined to force supplies through to Rome. He sent men posing as deserters to spy on the Gothic camps and the towers on the river. Upon their return he lashed two wide skiffs together to form a stable base. He then had a tower that was taller than those of the Goths built upon the skiffs. Once completed, he had a small boat fastened to the top of the tower and filled it with pitch, sulphur, resin and other flammable materials. At the same time, he took 200 fast boats and had wooden walls built on them with loopholes cut for his archers. The boats were then filled with grain and other supplies ready to sail to the city.

He left Isaac the Armenian in charge at Portus with strict instructions not to leave the city under any circumstances. He also left Antonina in the care of Isaac. Furthermore, he left troops to guard the approaches to Portus so that Isaac could not be the victim of a surprise attack. Finally, he sent a message to Bessas announcing his imminent arrival and ordered Bessas to mount an attack on the Goths on the following day in order to distract them from his own forces. The order was, as usual, to be ignored; according to Procopius, Bessas was by now the only individual with grain left in the city and was making a fortune selling it to the senators for vast sums of money. He did not want the relief force to arrive and cut off his source of income or the relief of the city to see the start of his own prosecution (Proc, *Wars*, VII.xix.14).

Once all these measures were in place, Belisarius embarked on one of the 200 fast boats and the relief force set out, accompanied by an infantry force that marched along the right (east) bank of the river. It was now that he was surprised to find that, a little downstream from the barrier of long timbers, the Goths had secured an iron chain across the river. Fortunately, upon his approach the Goths defending the chain fled and he was able to quickly dismantle the obstacle.

As he advanced upon the bridge, the Goths – warned of his arrival by the men who had been guarding the chain – were rushing out of their camps and running to help in the defence of the structure. On the east side of the river the road from Portus came near to the bridge and here Belisarius brought the skiffs close to the Gothic tower. He ordered the small boat on the top of his own tower to be set on fire, and it was then thrown on to the Goths' lower tower. Immediately, the Gothic tower caught fire and was quickly destroyed by the flames, the Goths also losing the 200 men that were stationed inside it. In disarray, the Goths withdrew and Belisarius began the task of destroying the bridge.

Events beyond Belisarius' control now forced his hand. In Portus, Isaac heard of the capture of the chain and decided that he wanted to take part in the momentous events taking place. Accordingly, he took 100 men and mounted an attack on a nearby Gothic camp, where Totila had left a certain Ruderic in charge. Ruderic was injured in the fighting and the Goths withdrew. With no thought to their safety, the Byzantines began to plunder the camp. The Goths reformed and realised that there were only a few Byzantines in the camp, wandering about in total disorder, so they launched a counterattack. Many Byzantines were killed and the rest were driven off, but Isaac himself was captured.

Unaware of these events, Belisarius recieved word that Isaac had been captured. As Isaac had been ordered to stay in Portus, the only logical explanation was that the Goths had assaulted the city and taken it. The only hope was to attack them while they were still in a state of disarray in the newly-captured city. Abandoning his attempt to supply Rome, Belisarius ordered an immediate withdrawal and rushed back to Portus. Only when he reached the city did he realise his mistake: the city was safe and the attempt to resupply Rome had failed. Procopius states that he was so distressed by the whole situation that he fell ill, nearly succumbing to the fever (*Wars*, xix.33–4). Two days later, Ruderic, the Gothic leader, died of his wounds. When he died, Totila had Isaac executed.

Although it is possible to view the return to Portus as a mistake, such a judgement is unfair to Belisarius, given the information he had. It is obvious that Belisarius realised the importance of Portus as the only safe base for his army. When he gave Isaac instructions not to leave the city under any circumstances, he was ensuring that Portus could not be lost. When he heard reports of Isaac's capture, he naturally assumed that the port was lost and returned to attempt its recapture. Only when he returned did he recognise that his decision had lost the chance to slip supplies into Rome. Although an understnadable mistake, the decision was to lose Rome to the Goths.

The Loss of Rome

In Rome, Bessas was now focusing entirely on making money, paying no heed to his military responsibilities.. As a result, the soldiers were neglecting their duties and only a skeleton force was manning the walls. The remaining citizens were wasting away due to the famine caused by the siege.

It was at this point that four Isaurians used ropes to let themselves down from the wall at night and approached Totila with a proposal. They manned the Asinarian Gate at night and offered to let Totila into the city, since he would be able to enter unobserved due to the negligence of the army commanders. Totila agreed to their proposal and promised them large sums of money if the plan succeeded. Two Goths accompanied them on their return to Rome and reported to Totila that their reports had been true: there was no force on the walls to stop the Goths if they attacked at night.

Totila was suspicious and, when he failed to act, the Isaurians returned and repeated the offer. Two different Goths were sent with the Isaurians and again the report showed that the plan would work. Not only did Totila still hesitate to act, a reconnaissance force from Rome captured ten Goths not far from the city. Under questioning, they told the whole story of the Isaurians' offer, since it was well known to all of the Goths. Bessas and Conon dismissed the story and failed to act and so stop the Isaurians.

For a third time the Isaurians made the same offer to Totila, and again he sent a number of Goths with them when they returned to Rome, and again the report was that the plan would succeed. This time, Totila decided to act. On the following night, he ordered the army to gather in silence and approached the Asinarian Gate (see Map 13). Four Goths armed with axes climbed the ropes used by the Isaurians and entered the city. With the axes they smashed the bars holding the gates closed, opened the gates, and finally the Goths entered the city.

In the darkness, Totila kept his men under tight control, fearing that the Byzantines might regroup and ambush his forces if they were scattered around the city. As word spread that the Goths were in the city, the Byzantine troops fell into confusion, some taking refuge in sanctuaries, others following their unit commanders out of whichever gate in the walls was nearest. Bessas himself escaped along with some of the Roman nobles, whilst others took sanctuary in the Church of St Peter.

Throughout the night Totila was repeatedly informed that Bessas had fled the city, but still he maintained a tight control of his troops. However, when day came he was approached by Pelagius the Deacon who pleaded with him to spare the lives of the citizens. Totila acceded to the request, with the result that less than 100 people were killed in the capture of the city. He further ordered his troops not to molest any of the citizens, but allowed them freedom to plunder the city of its wealth and himself laid hands on the treasure that Bessas had accumulated but not been able to take with him when he fled. According to Procopius, Totila 'won great renown' amongst the Italians due to his moderate treatment of the captured city, which fell on 17 December 546 (*Wars*, VII.xx.31).

After the capture of the city, Totila assembled the senators and berated them for their betrayal of the Goths. He relieved them of their offices and gave the posts to the four Isaurians who had betrayed the city to him, along with Herodian, the man who had surrendered the city of Spoletium. In the hopes of securing peace, he sent Pelagius the Deacon and Theodorus, a Roman orator, to Justinian with the offer of a Gothic alliance. The attempt failed as Justinian sent them back with the reply that Belisarius was the commander in Italy and that he was empowered to make such decisions.

It took time for the envoys to travel to and from Constantinople. Meanwhile, in Lucania John gave Tullianus command of a unit of 300 Antae (a tribe living to the north of the Danube), who were excellent troops in rough ground. Tullianus supplemented them with a force of peasants and used the combined army to hold the passes into Lucania against the Goths. When Totila learned of this development, he gathered his own force of Italian peasants and sent them, with a small force of Goths, to force the passes. When the two sides met there was a battle, which the Byzantines won mainly thanks to the superior skills of the Antae at fighting in rough terrain. The Gothic forces were forced to withdraw after suffering heavy losses.

When he heard of the defeat, Totila determined to raze Rome to the ground and then march with the entire army against John and Tullianus. He had torn down about a third of the city walls and was considering burning many of the important buildings in the city when a message arrived from Belisarius. Belisarius had learnt of his decision and the message implored him not to set fire to the city: Rome was full of noteworthy buildings that were a memorial to the building ability of the ancients that had constructed them. Furthermore, if Totila was victorious, he would be destroying his own property and, if he lost, such an act would negate any chance of mercy being shown towards him. It would also damage his reputation in Italy for clemency and toleration. After much consideration, Totila let the buildings remain. Leaving Rome entirely deserted, he stationed the main force of the Goths in a camp 120 *stades* west of the city in order to pin Belisarius in Portus, then led the remainder of his forces against John and Tullianus.

Hearing that Totila was advancing against him, John fled to Dryus with his troops. Totila sent messengers ahead telling the peasants gathered with Tullianus that, if they returned to their fields, the farms would be confiscated from their landlords and given to them instead. Naturally, the peasants left and Tullianus fled. The Antae retreated and joined John at Dryus. The Goths entered Lucania but dispersed and wandered around the countryside in small groups. Seeing this, John sent out a large force of Byzantines that ambushed and killed many of the Goths. Therefore, Totila ordered his troops to gather at Garganon (Gargano) and remained there inactive.

With Totila in Lucania, a Roman citizen by the name of Martinianus approached Belisarius and offered to feign desertion to Totila and then work for the Byzantines. Belisarius agreed to the offer, and Martinianus 'deserted', having his wife and one of his two children returned to him by Totila as a reward. His second child was retained by the Goths as a hostage. Martinianus was sent to Spoletium, where he persuaded fifteen Byzantine deserters to help him betray the city to the Byzantines. He next sent messages to the Byzantine garrison at Perusia asking for troops to help him. After the death of Cyprian, a Hun named Odalgan had assumed command at Perusia, and he himself led a force to Spoletium. The fifteen deserters killed the garrison commander and opened the gates to the Byzantines. Most of the Gothic garrison was killed, the rest captured and taken to Belisarius in Portus.

Belisarius decided to go to Rome and reconnoitre the area, with a view to retaking the city. A deserter informed Totila of his plans and the Goths organised an ambush. Belisarius marched towards Rome with 1,000 men and was ambushed en route by the Gothic forces. Surprisingly, the Goths were defeated in the skirmish but, although victorious, Belisarius decided to immediately return to Portus rather than continue towards Rome. He obviously realised that the Goths were relatively well-informed about his movements and decided not to expose himself to further danger unnecessarily.

In the south, the citizens of Tarentum invited John to take control of the city. Accordingly, he left a garrison at Dryus and led a few men towards Tarentum.

The city had no walls to defend, so John organised the fortification of the isthmus covering the harbour. He collected the Tarentines and other Italians living in the area behind the newly-constructed walls then, leaving a garrison, he returned to Dryus. With these developments, the Calabrians began to consider rebelling from Gothic rule.

Meanwhile, Totila left the captive Roman senators under guard in Campania, left a garrison in the city of Acherontis, and led the remainder of his forces towards Ravenna.

At Portus, Belisarius resolved to retake Rome. Leaving a few men in Portus as a garrison, Belisarius marched with the rest. Totila had destroyed about one-third of the circuit walls and all of the gates to the city. Belisarius did not have the time needed to effect proper repairs to the walls, and did not have the large number of skilled workmen needed to replace the gates rapidly. Therefore, he ordered his men to pile the rubble left by the Goths into the holes in the walls, taking care to make the outer face of the walls appear as smooth as possible. In this way, he would have hoped to divert the attention of any Gothic attack away from these weak points. He also set in motion work on manufacturing new gates to replace those destroyed by the Goths. As his position was still insecure, he set stakes around the ditch he had constructed during the first siege of the city, so protecting his men from attack while they worked, and in twenty-five days the walls of the city had been repaired to the best of his ability given the limited time available.

During this period many of the Roman citizens returned to the city, partly because of the relative safety the rebuilt walls afforded, but mainly due to Belisarius having brought a large amount of supplies with him by river. The area had yet to recover agriculturally from the previous battles and sieges, and there was a distinct shortage of food around Rome.

Totila, who was advancing north towards Ravenna, was informed of Belisarius' retaking of Rome and arrived in front of the city before Belisarius was able to install new gates in the walls. Camping overnight on the banks of the Tiber, the Goths launched a furious attack upon the empty gateways at sunrise. Belisarius had stationed his best men in the gateways and ordered the rest to man the walls and give supporting fire as the Goths attacked. The fighting was fierce, but as the entrances to the gateways were narrow the Goths were unable to make their superior numbers count. Furthermore, they lost many men due to the heavy volume of missiles being fired from the walls. With both sides exhausted, the fighting stopped at sunset and the Goths withdrew to their camp. Whilst the Goths rested overnight, the Byzantines kept guard and took the time to spread large numbers of caltrops around the gateways to help them in their defence.

On the second day the Goths again launched an assault, but the Byzantines gained the upper hand and a number of troops launched a sortie against the

Goths. The Goths withdrew for a considerable distance and the Byzantine forces leading the pursuit were in danger of being surrounded. Fortunately, Belisarius observed the danger in time and ordered a large force to rescue them from their perilous situation. After the second day of battle, the Goths had lost many men killed and wounded and the Byzantines were exhausted, so both sides rested for many days.

Once rested, the Goths prepared another assault, but this time Belisarius led the army out to meet them. In the ensuing battle Totila's standard bearer was killed and his standard fell to the ground. After a fierce fight, the Goths retained the standard but were routed with heavy loss. Retiring to their camp, dissension now arose amongst the nobles. Many of them complained that when he had chance Totila had neither razed the walls of Rome to the ground, nor left a garrison in the city. Due to Totila's mistakes, the Goths were now faced with the need to lay siege to the city all over again. Totila decided that another siege of Rome would be unprofitable, so the Goths destroyed most of the bridges across the Tiber to restrict Byzantine movements and, lifting the siege, moved to Tibur. Here they rebuilt the fortress that they had previously dismantled and settled in for the winter. In Rome, Belisarius had the time needed to remake the city gates. Once completed, he sent the keys to Justinian and also settled down for the winter.

Yet the Goths were stirred to activity by events in Perusia. The Goths besieging the city became aware that the defenders were low on rations, so sent to Totila to bring the army north in order to take the city. Despite resistance, the Gothic nobles were persuaded to make the attempt and the army moved to Perusia.

Whilst Belisarius had been retaking Rome, John nephew of Vitalianus had begun the siege of Acherontis. Learning that Totila was busy assaulting the walls of Rome, John chose a picked force of cavalry and force-marched to Campania in an attempt to rescue the Roman Senators being held there by the Goths. Aware that John might make such an attempt, Totila had sent a force of cavalry to Campania to stop him. The majority had made camp at Minturnae and had rested there to care for their horses. Some 400 men were sent on to Capua and the adjoining towns to act as scouts and locate the Byzantine forces.

Undetected, the Byzantine forces reached Capua at the same time as the 400 Goths and a fierce battle began. John won a decisive victory and the surviving Goths retired to Minturnae. However, once they reached Minturnae the combined Gothic forces retired to rejoin Totila, who by this time had moved to attack Perusia. In order to retain their reputation, the Goths informed Totila that a large Byzantine force was now at large in Campania.

John found seventy Byzantine deserters in the Gothic camp who elected to rejoin the Byzantine army, but he only released a few Roman senators, since the majority had escaped to Portus during the Gothic sack of the city. He did find many of the wives of the senators and these were released. The result was that many senators who would otherwise have been constrained in their actions due to the threat to their wives were now free to choose their own destinies.

There was another consequence to John's actions. Totila now believed that he had lost face to John and decided that John needed to be punished in order for Totila to regain his standing. Leaving a small force at Perusia to maintain the siege, Totila headed towards Lucania. John had set up camp with 1,000 men and posted scouts along the roads in order to guard against just such an attack. Totila was expecting this, so he marched off-road through the nearby mountains, which were considered to be impassable. John's scouts realised that there was a Gothic army in the region, but were unable to pin down its location. Therefore, they returned to John's camp, arriving after night had fallen. By a coincidence, Totila arrived there at the same time.

Totila now made a major mistake. Although he had the larger force, he decided to attack at night. Furthermore, he did not use the element of surprise to his best advantage by surrounding the camp. Instead he launched an immediate attack with predictable results. In panic, the Byzantine troops fled away from the attacking Goths. However, since Totila had only attacked on a narrow front, the majority of the Byzantine troops escaped. In this they were helped both by the lack of opposition around the perimeter of the camp and by the covering darkness. Only about 100 Byzantines were killed by the Gothic assault. John, together with Arufus the leader of the Heruls, escaped to Dryus and the Goths plundered the Byzantine camp before returning to Perusia.

Finally having troops spare, Justinian at last felt able to respond to Belisarius' repeated requests and send reinforcements to Italy. Firstly, Pacurius and Sergius with a few men arrived in Italy and joined forces with Belisarius. These men were followed by two more groups, one of 300 Heruls led by Verus and the other of 800 Armenians led by Varazes. Verus landed at Dryus but refused to join with John the nephew of Vitalianus, instead advancing to the neighbourhood of Brundisium and making camp. Totila marched to meet him, but the Goths were seen by the Heruls, who hid in some nearby woods. Surrounded by the Goths, the Heruls lost 200 of their men before the fleet carrying the Armenians approached the coast. Totila, assuming that the fleet was carrying a large force of reinforcements, retired, and Verus and the Heruls joined the Armenians and sailed to Tarentum. There they were joined by John and his troops.

The final reinforcements were under the command of Valerian, *magister militum per Armeniam*. Justinian recalled him from the east and ordered him, along with his *comitatus* of over 1,000 men, to go to Italy. Valerian arrived at the Adriatic coast, but, as it was near to the winter solstice, he decided to remain there for winter to help ease the problems of supply in Italy. Valerian sent 300 men to join John and inform him of the decision.

In the meantime, Justinian sent a message to Belisarius informing him of the imminent arrival of reinforcements and ordering him to unite with them in Calabria and then take the war to the Goths. Belisarius received the emperor's orders and, leaving Conon in charge of the Byzantine garrison, took 700 cavalry and 200 infantry and sailed to Sicily before going on to Tarentum. However, a storm arose and he was forced to halt at Croton, which had no walls and no supplies. He decided to remain in place with the infantry, sending the cavalry under Phazas the Iberian and Barbation, one of his guards, to guard the passes into the area, since there were only two of them and they were narrow and easy to defend. In this manner he hoped not only to guard against attack but also by dispersing the troops to help ease the difficulty of supply.

The two passes over the mountains were the Petra Sanguinis (Rock of Blood) and the one known as Lavula to the locals. The only other entrances to the area were at the two ends of the mountains, but one was covered by the garrison at Rusciane, the naval base of Thurii, whilst the other was controlled by a fortress – possibly Rossano – which had earlier been garrisoned by John.

The cavalry sent by Belisarius towards the fortress encountered by chance a force sent by Totila to take the fortress. Although they were outnumbered, the Byzantines immediately attacked the Goths, killing over 200 of them and forcing the rest to flee. The survivors returned to Totila and reported the presence of Byzantine forces in the area. Due to the ease of their victory, the Byzantine cavalry became complacent and failed to maintain a proper guard on the pass, wandering the area in small groups.

Totila investigated and, when he had learned of the Byzantine deployment, selected 3,000 cavalry to attack the Byzantines. When they struck, Phazas happened to be camped nearby and he and his men fought back bravely. Although they were all killed, their resistance allowed many Byzantine troops to escape.

The troops that had been destroyed were classed by the Byzantines as an 'unusually efficient fighting force' (Proc, *Wars*, VII.xxviii.16–7), so when Barbation reached Belisarius with the news of the defeat, as well as giving his opinion that the Goths would soon be arriving, Belisarius ordered all of the men to board ship and immediately sailed to Messana in Sicily. In the meantime. Totila learned that the fortress at Rusciane was low on supplies, so he advanced and laid siege to the place. It was here that he spent the next winter (548).

In the New Year, Justinian sent 2,000 men by sea to Italy and ordered Valerian to cross the Adriatic and join Belisarius. Valerian set sail and landed at Dryus, where he found Belisarius, along with Antonina. At this point Belisarius sent Antonina on a mission to Constantinople to intervene with the Empress Theodora to gain the troops and provisions he needed to prosecute an aggressive war against the Goths. He also sent orders to John to join him at Dryus.

Two events now helped to shape the nature of the war. At Rusciane, the garrison, commanded by Chalazar the Hun and Gudilas the Thracian (one of John's guardsmen) comprised 300 Illyrian cavalry and 100 infantry that had been sent by Belisarius. These men opened negotiations with Totila and agreed that if by midsummer no help had arrived, they would surrender to him.

Simultaneously, the garrison in Rome killed their commander, Conon, and then sent priests as envoys to Justinian. They accused Conon of trafficking in grain and other goods at their expense, demanded pardons for his death and requested the arrears of pay that they were owed. They stated that if their demands were unfulfilled, they would hand the city to Totila. Justinian immediately granted their requests and the city was retained in Byzantine hands.

When John arrived at Dryus, Belisarius, Valerian and the other commanders joined him aboard ship and their combined forces sailed to relieve Rusciane. The troops in the fortress saw the ships approaching and determined not to surrender to Totila, even though the date for their surrender had arrived. Unfortunately, a storm blew up and scattered the ships before they could land. Gathering again at Croton, the fleet made a second attempt to relieve the garrison. On this occasion, the Goths saw the fleet and determined to resist them as they landed. Mounting their horses they rode down to the beach and formed up opposite the fleet. In the face of such determined opposition the army refused to land, instead returning to Croton.

Once back in Croton, the commanders held a conference in which it was decided that Belisarius should proceed to Rome and that John and Valerian would march overland to Picenum, relieving any strongholds in the region that were still under siege by the Goths. It was hoped that this move would force Totila to raise the siege of Rusciane and force him to follow the troops as they moved north. As planned, John began the march to Picenum with 1,000 men. However, being worried about journeying over land, Valerian and his troops sailed to Ancon (Proc, *Wars*, VII.xxx.17).

The plan did not work. Totila selected 2,000 men and sent them to Picenum, remaining with the other 1,000 to finish the siege of Rusciane. Recognising that their position was hopeless, the garrison again entered negotiations. Totila agreed to free the garrison as long as Chalazar was handed to him, as Chalazar was the one who had encouraged resistance when the Byzantine fleet had been sighted. The garrison agreed and Chalazar was executed by Totila. The other terms of the agreement were the ones that can now be seen as standard for Totila: the remainder of the garrison could either keep their arms and equipment and join his forces as equals of the Goths, or they could leave their belongings behind and go where they wished. Only eighty of the 400-strong garrison opted to make the long march to join Belisarius. The rest joined the Goths. Totila further ordered the confiscation of all of the property of the local Italians. They were, however, allowed to go free and unharmed wherever they desired.

After Belisarius had reached Rome, word finally came from his wife in Constantinople. When she had reached the capital, she had found that the plan to solicit the aid of the empress was a failure, since she had died on 28 June 548. Instead, Justinian had agreed to recall Belisarius to the capital, so ending his exploits in Italy.

Belisarius recalled

Procopius' gives three reasons as the cause of Belisarius' recall from Italy. The first of these is that Antonina, upon finding that the empress was dead and her mission impossible, instead urged Justinian to recall Belisarius (*Wars*, VII.xxx.25). The second is that Belisarius himself asked to be recalled from his hopeless war in Italy (*Anekdota*, 5.16–7). The third is that Justinian needed to recall Belisarius due to the renewed threat of war with Persia, and the possible need to send him to command operations in the east (*Wars*, III.30.25; 36.4).

It is highly likely that Antonina requested his recall from Italy. With the empress dead, her only source of influence, wealth and power rested with Belisarius. Furthermore, due to her political intrigues as the right hand of Theodora, Antonina would have made many enemies. If Belisarius was killed in Italy and his protection removed, Antonina would be unlikely to survive. She needed him to return safely as quickly as possible.

It is also possible that Belisarius himself requested a recall via Antonina. The situation in his second campaign in Italy was very different to that of his first. Without either the troops or the finances necessary to fight a successful war, it is likely that Belisarius would want to extricate himself and so avoid a long conflict that he could never win; maybe he believed that Justinian would never fully support the war with men and materiel.

It may be that Justinian wanted to recall him for a campaign against Persia, yet of the three explanations this is the most unlikely. After his return from Italy, Belisarius was only once more sent to fight an enemy of Rome, and it was not Persia, as we shall see. That he was not used as a general apart from one instance suggests that he was not recalled for his military abilities.

There might, in fact, be yet another reason for Belisarius' recall. Justinian had recently lost Theodora, the wife that had helped to formulate policy both abroad and at home. Without her assistance, which had been a constant since his coronation in 527, it is likely that Justinian had a gaping hole in his decision-making apparatus. Belisarius was required by Justinian to help in the role of advisor. Whatever other attributes can be given to Belisarius, his honesty and straightforward approach was likely to be indispensable to Justinian at a difficult time of readjustment.

Before leaving for Constantinople, Belisarius made two final dispositions to try to keep Italy in Byzantine hands. In Rome he left a garrison of 3,000 men under Diogenes, and Rhegium was garrisoned by Thurimuth and Himerius.

Belisarius as general in Italy

Procopius, being the major source for the events, is usually followed when he lays the blame for the lack of success with Justinian. However, Procopius' account – and therefore any conclusion based upon it – is heavily biased. At no point, for example, does Procopius acknowledge that there were limits to the empire's reserves of manpower and that these were overstretched due to the Persian War, the revolts in Africa, and the continued invasions of the Balkans by the Huns, Slavs and others. Furthermore, at no point in his *History of the Wars* is the catastrophic effect of the plague upon reserves of manpower noted. In fact, as has been noted by Teall (1965), between 542 and 546 all Byzantine military projects ground to a virtual halt as the full effects of the epidemic made themselves felt. When Belisarius was in Italy, Justinian simply did not have the necessary men spare to send to Belisarius.

To compensate for the lack of manpower, it is likely that Justinian was relying to a great degree upon the aura that surrounded Belisarius. He had now acquired a great reputation as a general and was recognised as a man of his word. Unfortunately, it was also recognised that Belisarius would not always be the man in charge and the replacement sent by the emperor was likely to have no such high ideals and be prone to ignore the natives and indulge in corrupt practices. Belisarius could make any promises that he liked; the natives now knew they would only be kept as long as he was present in person.

One further point needs to be borne in mind when assessing Justinian's response to Belisarius' pleas for troops: the quick conquest of the south of Sicily and the surrender of the Goths during Belisarius' first campaign are likely to have caused Justinian to seriously underestimate the capacity of the Goths to resist. When Belisarius was first recalled from Italy, the war had been all but over, and there would have been no reason to suspect that the Goths would be able to make such a startling recovery and regain control of the majority of Italy in such a short time.

Unsurprisingly, upon his redeployment to Italy there was no mass Italian uprising in favour of Belisarius, nor did any of the deserted troops accede to his requests to return to their former service. The integrity and respect felt for the general was no longer a shield against the mistrust of the emperor and his other appointees. Belisarius was now in a position where he could not win except by overwhelming military strength, and, as we have seen, during his five years in Italy the necessary troops were never to be available.

Although his actions during his second period in Italy showed that he was still attempting to take the initiative and force Totila on to the back foot, at very few points did he manage this due to the lack of resources. Maybe the best that can be said about this period is that, thanks to his efforts, the Goths failed to completely evict the Byzantines from Italy during a period when their position in the peninsula was extremely weak and vulnerable.

Yet this raises a further point about the war in Italy. Both the Goths and the Romans suffered from the same handicap: namely, the difficulty of maintaining both the numerous garrisons and a field army of sufficient force to give a good chance of victory in the field. Battle was to be avoided.

This must surely be connected to the lack of commitment shown by many native Italians to either the Goths or the empire. A large number of Italians were – understandably – reluctant to commit themselves to either side when they were unsure of who would be victorious; choose the wrong ally and there would in all likelihood be serious repercussions when you were defeated. Yet, by their lack of commitment, the Italians ensured that neither side would be in a secure enough position to attempt to defeat the opposition. As long as Belisarius was prying for weak points and attempting to subvert the Italians to the imperial cause, they would waver and the fight would hang in the balance. Once he had been recalled, the generals that were left failed to make any move to gain the alliance of the Italians and, realising that the imperial cause was, as a consequence, in decline, many Italians decided to join with the Goths. In part, this helps to explain both the lack of large scale operations in Belisarius' second stay in Italy, as well as the rapid collapse of imperial power when he left.

It is noteworthy that, after Belisarius' recall, Totila ordered the resumption of the games at Rome and then launched an attack on Sicily. The first was a direct challenge to Justinian, since only the emperor could give permission for games to be held. The second was a sign that Gothic power, which a few years before had been on the verge of total defeat, had been spectacularly resurrected by Totila. To submit to these indignities was unthinkable. However, by this late date the effects of the plague were starting to recede and the empire was slowly recovering its strength. Available troops were freed for service in Italy and a large number of *foederati* and allies was collected and sent under Narses to finally defeat the Goths.

Chapter 13

Twilight

Whilst Belisarius was travelling back to Constantinople, a conspiracy had been formed to murder Justinian. The conspirators were Artabanes, Arsaces and Chanarangas. Artabanes, an Armenian, had been created *magister militum per Africam* in 546 for his loyalty, and had fallen in love with the emperor's niece, Praeiecta. She had gone to Justinian and asked for permission to marry Artabanes. The couple were given permission to marry and Artabanes was recalled to the capital. There, he was applauded by the people and honoured by Justinian, who made him *magister militum praesentalis* and *comes foederatum*, as well as giving him an honorary consulship. His happiness was not to last. Learning of his elevation, his existing wife arrived from the east before the marriage could take place. The Empress Theodora supported his wife's claims, and although after Theodora's death he renounced his wife, by that time it was too late: Praeiecta was married to another. Unhappy with the course of events, Artabanus was receptive to the approaches of Arsaces and Chanarangas and joined the plot against Justinian.

The conspirators decided to move after Belisarius had returned, since it was likely that he would be acclaimed emperor upon the death of Justinian and his unquestioned loyalty would likely mean the death of the conspirators. Therefore, he also was to be killed.

The plot was exposed to several court officials, including Marcellus, yet they withheld the information from Justinian, since as yet there was little firm evidence. However, when Belisarius approached the city the plot was revealed. Under torture, all of the details were unmasked, yet Artabanes was only held under arrest in the palace and had his titles removed. Later, he would be restored to favour when there was a shortage of competent generals to fight in all of the theatres of war opened by Justinian.

Belisarius returns to Constantinople

After his return to Constantinople, Belisarius settled down with Antonina. According to Procopius, he was accorded first place in dignity, although out-ranked by others (*Wars*, VIII.xxi.2–3). This may be true, though it may also be an exaggeration by Procopius in order to elevate Belisarius' stature in the eyes of the populace. Whatever the reality of his standing with the people, Belisarius does appear to have been honoured by Justinian. Throughout his lifetime of service he had remained loyal to the emperor, despite some extremely difficult circumstances, and Justinian may have realised that Belisarius deserved rewards. Consequently, he was reinstalled as *magister militum per Orientem*, and may also have been made either *comes protectorem* or *comes domesticorum* (Proc, *Wars*, VIII.xxi.1). It is unclear from Procopius which of these posts was held, although by this time both were honorific titles with little real power and no military responsibility.

Earlier, Joannina, the daughter of Belisarius and Antonina, had been betrothed to Anastasius, the grandson of Theodora. Now that Theodora was dead, Antonina declared the engagement cancelled, much to the dismay of the young couple, who appear to have become genuinely attached to each other. According to the *Anekdota*, due to the cancellation of the engagement Belisarius was now the victim of gossip suggesting that he was dominated by Antonina (*Anekdota*, 5.24–7). In spite – or possibly because – of all his achievements, Belisarius was now a figure for jealousy and rancour.

The end of the war in Italy

In Italy, without Belisarius in command the situation quickly deteriorated. Although he had achieved little, the threat of his presence may have helped curb the aggressive tendencies of Totila. Once Belisarius had gone, Totila was to take the initiative in dramatic fashion.

As Belisarius withdrew in 548 the Franks occupied Venetia, and in the following year the unpaid garrison of Rome lost patience with the emperor and betrayed the city to Totila. Neither of these may have happened had Belisarius still been in Italy, since his reputation as a warrior may have deterred the Franks and his reputation for fair play may have led the garrison in Rome to hope for eventual payment by the government.

However, in response to the new challenges Totila acted fast. Possibly in an attempt to elevate his standing with the native Italians, he decided to revive the staging of the games in the Circus Maximus. Furthermore, with the threat of Byzantine aggressive action removed, Totila sent his fleet to ravage Sicily, leaving garrisons in some of the strong points. Furthermore, he was able to secure the capture of Sardinia and Corsica, neither of which had been garrisoned by the Byzantines (Proc, *Wars*, VIII.xxiv.31–33).

The whole series of events was a distinct shock to the Byzantines. Justinian appears to have been astonished by the extent of the Goths' recovery – at this point only the cities of Ravenna, Ancon, Dryus and Croton in Italy were still in Byzantine hands. Furthermore, by the staging of the games, and especially by the raid on Sicily and the taking of Sardinia and Corsica, Totila had sent a clear message of strength, defiance and scorn to the emperor. In response, Justinian decided to send Germanus with a large force to complete the conquest. To further this aim, Germanus married Witigis' widow, Matasuintha. In the meantime, Artabanes was given command of an army and sent to regain mastery of Sicily, a task which he quickly completed (Proc, *Wars*, VIII.xxiv.1–3).

Following his appointment, Germanus set about raising troops in the Balkans, but before he could depart for Italy he was distracted by a Slav invasion across the Danube directed at Thessalonica. Deterred – possibly by Germanus' reputation – the Slavs turned west and entered Dalmatia. Germanus was now free to invade Italy. Unfortunately, the unexpected happened: Germanus died suddenly of an illness.

After a delay, Justinian finally ordered Narses the eunuch to take command. The reasons for the choice are unclear, but Narses had one ability that would make him the ideal choice: he had the strength of character necessary to dominate the generals still present in Italy and force them to follow his orders.

Narses spent most of 551 in Thrace and Illyria recruiting, training and organising his troops. It is thought that his army may have comprised as many as 35,000 men (see, for example, Norwich, *Byzantium*, p. 251), although Treadgold, (*Byzantium and its Army*, 1995, p. 61) gives the more reasonable number of 20,000 men for the total army. Included in the army was a core of Byzantine troops, supplemented by men collected from Thrace and Illyricum. They were joined by the remnant of Germanus' forces, led by John nephew of Vitalianus. Following a recent treaty agreement, the Lombards sent 2,500 heavily-armed cavalry, accompanied by 3,000 fighting men as servants. There were also 3,000 Heruls, 400 Gepids, a large number of Huns, and Cabades nephew of Khusrow with many Persian deserters (Proc, *Wars*, VIII.xxvi.10–13). Following the apparent recovery of the Goths, Justinian was determined to finish the war once and for all.

In 552 Narses ordered his army to gather at Salona. He did not take the sea route to Italy due to the presence of a large Gothic fleet in the southern Adriatic. Instead, in the summer of 552, after a delay caused by another invasion across the Danube (this time by a large number of Huns), he entered Italy by land from the north. Totila gathered his troops and moved to face the invasion. It was to prove a mistake: at the Battle of Taginae, he was defeated and killed. Undeterred, the Goths decided to crown Teias as their new king. Whilst the Goths were making their choice, Narses began the siege of Cumae where Totila had deposited the majority of his treasury (Proc, *Wars*, VIII.xxxiv.19, 21).

In the following year, 553, Teias gathered the remainder of the Gothic army together and marched towards Narses. Again, the decision to fight an open battle was to be fatal. At the Battle of Mons Lactarius, Teias was defeated and killed by Narses. That same year a Frankish army under Lothar and Butilin invaded Italy and defeated the Byzantines' Herulian allies, whilst the Byzantines took the city of Lucca and Aligern surrendered Cumae to Narses.

In 554, the vanguard of Lothar's army was defeated, and shortly afterwards Lothar died. Upon his death, his army quickly disintegrated and returned home. Meanwhile, Butilin was heavily defeated by Narses at the Battle of Casilinum.

In 555 the last major Gothic force surrendered at Campsa. Yet some of the cities remained loyal to the Goths and the last one to surrender, Verona, only did so in 561.

The Three Chapters

It is not known what Belisarius' reaction was to the appointment of Germanus, and later Narses, to the command in Italy. Since Belisarius had only recently been recalled and had achieved little in his five years of command in Italy, it is unsurprising that he was not chosen to lead the army of invasion in 550 or 551/552. It may also be possible that Justinian remained jealous and that he did not want Belisarius to win more renown by completing the conquest. Alternatively, as suggested previously, we must bear in mind the possibility that Justinian was in need of people he could trust around him to give him sensible, unbiased advice now that Theodora was dead. Given his past record, Belisarius was an ideal man to fill such a position. Justinian could not afford to lose his most loyal and trustworthy advisor.

When Belisarius returned to Constantinople the religious debate of the 'Three Chapters' was in full swing. At this time there were major divisions between the Orthodox Church, which dominated the west and the majority of the east, and the Monophysites, who were mainly to be found in Egypt, Syria and Palestine. The Orthodox Church followed the decision of the Fourth Ecumenical Council of Chalcedon (451) which maintained that Christ was one man possessed of two natures, while the Monophysites maintained that Christ had only one nature, the divine.

In an attempt to diffuse the situation, Justinian had – under pressure from Theodora – issued 'The Three Chapters', an edict condemning the writings of Theodore of Mopsuestia, Theodoret of Cyrrhus and Ibas of Edessa. The edict declared that these writers were too supportive of Nestorian beliefs. Nestorianism, first preached by Nestorius (appointed bishop of Constantinople in 427) declared that Christ had two distinct persons, one divine and one human. This belief was now only held by a small and dwindling minority and it would appear that Justinian may have been attempting to unite the Orthodox and the Monophysites against a common 'enemy'.

The attempt failed. The Monophysites, who had been hoping for real concessions were unappeased and the Orthodox bishops of the east only accepted the ruling under pressure. However, in the west the teachings of Theodore, Theodoret and Ibas had been approved by the Council of Chalcedon, supported by the Orthodox church. Accordingly, western bishops believed that the move had been an attempt to favour the Monophysites and the papal legate in Constantinople pronounced the ban of the Church upon the patriarch of Constantinople as a response to the edict.

Summoned to Constantinople from Sicily, Pope Vigilius found himself opposing the emperor and, fearing for his safety, he took sanctuary in the Church of Saints Peter and Paul. Appointed as one of the *'memorati iudices'*, Belisarius was sent to Vigilius and, along with his colleagues, succeeded in persuading the Pope to leave the sanctuary and continue to participate in the debate. Although Belisarius was no longer used in a military role, the fact that Justinian was willing to use him in such a delicate mission, plus the fact that Vigilius was willing to listen to the delegation, make it obvious that he remained in favour and was seen as a man of influence.

Despite returning to the palace, Vigilius realised that he was under close supervision and in a position equivalent to close arrest. Accordingly, he fled to the Church of St Euphemia in Chalcedon. This was more than just a clever escape: by placing himself in the same church where the Council of Chalcedon had deliberated in 451, Vigilius was making a very clear statement of his intentions.

Sent to see the Pope for a second time, Belisarius and his associates could not on this occasion persuade Vigilius to return to Constantinople. Instead, Vigilius sent a letter known as the *Encyclica* to the emperor, putting his own views and proposing negotiations, whilst simultaneously excommunicating the patriarch of Constantinople and two eastern bishops.

The matter dragged on, through the deliberations of the Fifth Ecumenical Council held at Constantinople, until the defeat of Totila and the removal of the Goths as a threat in Italy. Realising that he now had no need to keep the Italian bishops on his side, the emperor struck. He sent a letter to the council asking them to condemn/excommunicate Vigilius and pass the emperor's edict. The council agreed and Vigilius was banished to an island in the Sea of Marmara, while Theodore and Theoderet were anathematised. Strangely, it was decided that the offending letter attributed to Ibas was not written by him, and so he was not anathematised.

It is interesting to note, however, that in the intervening period when the Pope decided to reply in a negative manner to the conclusions of the Council, he summoned Belisarius along with three other secular individuals and three bishops, and requested that they carry his judgement to Justinian. Although they refused to carry his message, it is significant that Belisarius was still placed highly enough in the esteem of the emperor and of the Pope that he was considered vital to communication between the two at a very difficult time. His political good sense and support seems to have been highly valued by both.

Spain

Whilst Narses was defeating Totila at the Battle of Taginae, Justinian had already made plans to intervene in Spain. Earlier, in 534, Belisarius had sent a force along the north coast of Africa to evict the Visigoths from their stronghold at Septem (modern Ceuta). Although in 547 King Theudis made an attempt at recovery, his force had been heavily defeated.

Yet the situation began to deteriorate for the Visigoths. As in both Vandal Africa and Gothic Italy, the Visigothic rulers of Spain had internal difficulties with their subjects which finally erupted in 550/551. In a situation equivalent to that of Gelimer with Tripolitania and Sardinia, the new King Agila was faced with two simultaneous rebellions. In this case, it was the 'Romans' of Cordova and his kinsman Athanagild that rebelled.

Realising that he was faced with yet another opportunity at conquest, Justinian ordered Narses to detach Liberius along with approximately 2,000 men from his army and send them to Spain. They landed in 552 and so began the reconquest of large parts of the south of Spain. After three years of campaigning the Byzantines captured Cartagena, helped by the disunity of the Visigoths who were divided in their support between Agila and Athanagild.

Realising that they were faced with a similar peril to the Goths and Vandals, the Visigoths took matters into their own hands. In 555 Agila was murdered by his own troops and Athanagild became sole king. Nevertheless, due to their temporary weakness, the Visigoths were forced to negotiate with the Byzantines, who were allowed to keep most of the territory under their control, including the Balearic Islands.

Persia

Meanwhile, the war with Persia dragged on. In 547 Justinian sent 8,000 men to support Goubazes, ruler of Lazica, who had transferred his allegiance back to the Byzantines. Although the Byzantine attack on Petra was interrupted by Mehr-Mehroe arriving with 30,000 Persian troops, such a large force could not be adequately supplied so was later forced to withdraw, after reinforcing the garrison in Petra.

In 549 there were battles in Lazica, but these were inconclusive until Byzantine reinforcements arrived to tip the balance. Dagisthaeus dismounted many of his cavalry to form an infantry phalanx that stopped the *savaran*, the Persian general being killed and his army defeated.

In 551 the Byzantines determined to finally take Petra. Despite a stubborn defence, the city fell at last. Although Mehr-Mehroe arrived with an army containing elephants and laid siege to Archaeopolis, these were defeated with heavy losses (Proc, *Wars*, VIII.xiv.1–44).

In a reversal of fortune, in 554 Mehr-Mehroe counter-attacked again and this time captured the city of Telephis, held for the Byzantines by Martinus.

(Agathias. II. 19.5 – 21.11). Escaping from the city, Martinus attempted to capture Ottogaris in 555 but was heavily defeated.

Finally, in 556, Martinus beat a Persian army said to be 60,000 strong in the final battle in Lazica. The war gradually petered out, but peace was not signed until 560/561, when a fifty-year peace was declared upon the payment of 30,000 gold *solidi* by the Byzantines.

The Last Battle

We have little information concerning Belisarius' activities between the controversy of the 'Three Chapters' and the late 550s. It is likely that he remained in Constantinople to act as a councillor to the emperor and was given duties commensurate with his standing as a successful and highly-regarded international figure. It is almost certain that he was in the capital when a new outbreak of plague occurred in 558. It is also probable that he may have given up hope of being given a military appointment or of achieving military glory, yet there was to be one final chance.

It has been noted that possibly the weakest frontier and the one most often crossed by armies intent on plunder was the Danube. Throughout Belisarius' campaigns one of the most recurrent themes is that of potential reinforcements being needed to expel either Slavs or Huns after they had crossed the Danube and attacked the Balkans. In 550 Germanus had been stopped from invading Italy by an irruption of Slavs, and in 552 Narses was similarly impeded by an invasion of Huns.

In 559 there was yet another invasion across the Danube. An army of Kutrigur Huns led by Zabergan crossed the frozen Danube in March and invaded Byzantine territory. Passing through the provinces of Scythia and Moesia, they invaded Thrace before the army split, with one part heading towards Greece and the other, led by Zabergan, heading for the Chersonese (Agathias, V.11.5–7).

According to Agathias, Zabergan had determined to cross into Asia Minor, an area completely unplundered and extremely wealthy in comparison to the often-ravaged Balkans: consequently, he led 7,000 troops to attempt the crossing (Agathias, V.12.4–5). After taking a large number of prisoners and a vast quantity of booty, the Huns passed the Long Walls and approached Constantinople (Agathias. V.13.1–5).

At this point Agathias denounces Justinian for his disregard for military affairs. Agathias claims that the army, which had once numbered 645,000 men had been allowed to decline until only 150,000 men remained (V.13.7); he had also allowed the quality of the troops in the capital to decline, due to his neglect and abuse and his failure to pay their wages. Furthermore, they were no longer concentrated in the city ready to be deployed but were scattered around Thrace, intent upon their own business (V.14.2–5). As a final concern, the

Scholari (Guards) were now of poor quality, due to their being composed of friends of the emperor or of men who had paid large sums to enrol in the unit. Therefore, when the capital was under threat, the men comprising the 'elite force' surrounding the emperor were not actually soldiers at all (Agathias, V.15.1–6).

Advancing steadily, the Huns reached the village of Melantias on the River Athyras, only a short distance from the capital itself. Understandably, there was panic in the city. With all of his generals engaged abroad and unable to return at such short notice, Justinian had only one course of action open to him. He appointed Belisarius to take command against the Huns.

However, it seems likely that there were no combat-ready troops left in Constantinople to meet the crisis. We are told by Agathias that Belisarius only had '300 heavily-armed veterans from Italy' (V.16.2). These were probably the last remnants of his *comitatus*, left over from his earlier days of military activity, retained as his personal bodyguards; even in peace he would have needed a certain number of attendants in accordance with his dignity and status.

Map 26: The Balkans and Melantias.

Strangely, these men are described as being armed with 'shields and javelins' by Agathias, where they might have been expected to be armed with bows (Agathias.V.19. 4). Although it is possible that they did indeed have bows that are simply not mentioned by Agathias, there is a possible explanation for their armament. It is not unreasonable to assume that these men were a dedicated group of Goths, Vandals or other Germanic tribe armed in their native fashion and dedicated to the service of Belisarius. Alongside these he was followed by a large number of unarmed civilians from the capital and peasants who had lost their farms during the Hunnic advance.

Camping at the village of Chettus, near to the Huns at Melantias, Belisarius had the peasants and civilians dig a large trench around his camp before lighting a large number of campfires to exaggerate the size of his force and sending out spies to keep an eye on Hunnic movements (Agathias,V.15.2 – 16.4–5). At first the Huns were subdued by the threat, but once they learned of the true composition of Belisarius' forces they prepared to attack. Zabergan with 2,000 Huns detached himself from the main force and advanced towards Chettus (Agathias, V.19.3). In the meantime, Belisarius was having trouble with the raw levies. They had become overconfident and were totally unprepared for a real battle. As a result, Belisarius made a speech that sobered the men, leaving them more cautious but still confident in eventual victory (Agathias, V.17.1–11).

Learning from his scouts of Zabergan's approach, Belisarius deployed his forces. Judging that the Huns' approach would lead them through a nearby wooded glen, he split his 300 veterans into three groups of 100. Two of these divisions were sent into the woods on either side of the glen, and ordered to wait for a signal from Belisarius before emerging to attack the Huns in the flank and rear. In this way, Belisarius hoped to constrict the enemy within a very tight space, so negating the advantage of their superior numbers. Belisarius remained in the centre with the remaining 100 veterans, and he deployed the untrained men behind him, with orders to shout and make a lot of noise (Agathias.V.19.4–5).

When the enemy saw Belisarius' small force they advanced to meet him in the glen. Belisarius led the charge with his men, with the main force of peasants and citizens holding their ground and causing as much noise as they could. He also gave the signal for the troops in the woods to charge into the flanks and rear of the Huns. Agathias relates that the noise and the confusion caused by the swirls of dust created by the peasants was out of all proportion to the size of the battle. The Huns now did exactly what Belisarius had anticipated; they drew together 'so tightly that they could not defend themselves, since there was no room to use their bows and arrows or to manoeuvre with their horses'. Stunned by the noise and dust, the Huns were finally broken by Belisarius' frontal assault and, as the peasants and citizens advanced, they fled in disorder.

Even now, Belisarius retained control; the pursuit was orderly and did not allow the Huns to regroup and counterattack, since the Byzantines retained their order and so did not present a target vulnerable to such a move. The nature of the attack and their defeat so terrified the Huns that they did not even use the 'Parthian-shot' tactic for which they were famous, instead fleeing without any attempt at resistance (Agathias, V.19.7 – 20.1).

Retreating to Melantias, Zabergan immediately broke camp and the Huns withdrew. At the same time, the Huns that had advanced to the Chersonese had started their assaults. However, Germanus the son of Dorotheus defeated their attempts to take the city, even destroying an attempt by the Huns to attack the city from the sea by using small skiffs against their hastily-made armada of reed boats (Agathias. V.22.3–8).

Both groups of defeated Huns now came together under Zabergan, and learned that the assault on Greece had also failed. Yet Zabergan refused to leave Byzantine territory without something to show for his efforts, so he ransomed the captives they had previously taken before returning to their homes north of the Danube.

According to Agathias, the episode served to highlight the difference between Justinian and Belisarius: the population of Constantinople lauded Belisarius for saving them in their hour of need and defeating the Huns when heavily outnumbered (V.20.5); they castigated Justinian for his seemingly cowardly action in ransoming the captives and so 'buying' peace (V.24.1). Yet Agathias saw further than this, and relates that Justinian now stopped the tribute to a separate group of Huns, led by Sandilch, claiming that the money that was due to them had instead been paid to Zabergan and his horde; if they wanted the money, they needed to get it for themselves. As a consequence, the Huns of Zabergan and Sandilch spent a long time in a war against each other, so leaving the empire free from attack and so weakening the two groups that by Agathias' time they had fallen under the control of other barbarians and no longer existed as separate entities (V.25. 6).

Belisarius as general

This last battle shows that Belisarius had lost none of his ability to motivate and control his men and ensure that they followed his plans for engagement. Furthermore, the manner of the ambush and the reasoning behind the decision to use it illustrate that he had lost none of his strategic or tactical ability after such a long time taking part in only civilian affairs. As a final observation, his deployment of the large number of civilians and the manner in which they contributed to the battle with only a little risk to their lives show that he had retained his desire to keep casualties amongst his own forces to a minimum. The battle was a model for those who are outnumbered and outclassed by the enemy.

The last acts

Sadly, Belisarius victory was later used against him. Men of rank remained jealous of his abilities and his influence with the emperor and so began a rumour that he was aiming at the throne; as a result, he was not given any recognition for his deeds against the Huns (Agathias, V.20.5–6).

Furthermore, when another group of Huns invaded the Balkans in 562, Belisarius was overlooked for command against them (as noted by Norwich, *Byzantium*, 1989, p.261). It is possible that, in this instance, a younger general could be trusted to lead the fight against the Huns: after all, Belisarius was by now aged around 60. Instead of military glory, Belisarius was embroiled in conspiracy. In November of that year a plot against the emperor was uncovered and two of Belisarius' staff implicated. Under torture, one of the men named his master as conspirator. Belisarius was formally accused in December 562, when Justinian removed his dignities and privileges and began an inquiry. Under house arrest, Belisarius accepted the situation without protest and waited for the judgement of the emperor.

After a full investigation, Belisarius was found not guilty of plotting to kill Justinian and was restored to favour with all of his previous titles in July 563. The later story that Justinian had Belisarius blinded and forced him to sit in the Lausus Palace with a begging bowl is a complete fabrication.

In Italy, Narses was forced to defend the country from two rebellions. The first was in 563, led by Amingus the Frank and Widin the Goth. The rebellion was defeated and both men were killed. The second was in 565, led by Sindual the Herul. Again, the rebellion was defeated and Sindual was captured and hanged. These would be the last consequences of Belisarius' invasions of which he would have been aware. He died in March 565 aged around 60 years. Antonina survived him, but it is not known when she died. Only eight months later, in November 565, the Emperor Justinian also died. It was the end of an era.

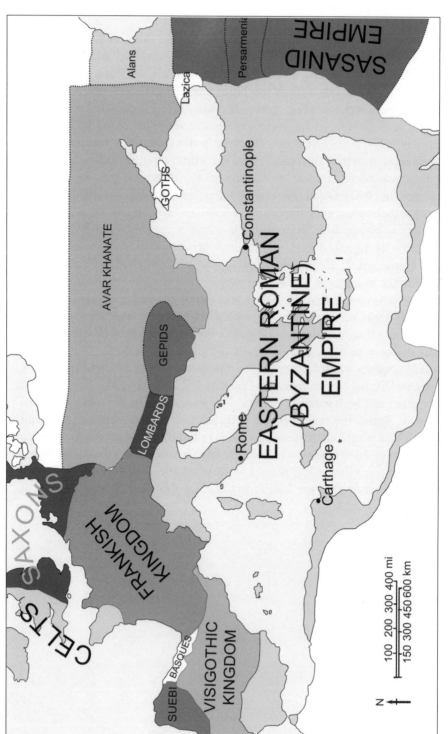

Map 27: The Empire on the death of Justinian.

Chapter 14

Conclusion

Epilogue

The Byzantine re-conquests were not destined to last. In Spain, a revival of Visigothic power gradually reduced the Byzantine possessions until, in the year 631, they were eliminated from the peninsula.

In Italy, events were much more complicated. In 568, only three years after the death of Belisarius, the Lombards invaded Italy, disrupting the province, annexing the north of Italy and establishing the duchies of Benevento and Spoleto in the centre and south. Although control of the remainder remained in Byzantine hands, the long, tortuous border with the Lombards remained a constant threat and siphoned away much needed revenue and manpower. This unsatisfactory arrangement would last until the eleventh century, when the Byzantines were finally expelled from Italy.

The almost-constant warfare on these two fronts would be a drain on the empire when facing its two greatest crises of the seventh century. The first of these was the Persian invasion led by Khusrow II, which, in a series of campaigns over 10 years (607–616), conquered Syria, Armenia, Lazica and Iberia, before culminating in 616 with the capture of Egypt. The Emperor Heraclius was only able to overcome the danger by first forming an alliance with the Khazars (recently established in the Caucasus) and then invading Persia. After the capture of his capital by Heraclius, Khusrow II was deposed by his nobles and a peace agreed that ceded all of the conquered territories back to the Byzantines.

The second crisis came shortly after the Persian War. This was the eruption of Islam. Without warning, a major new military force was unleashed on the world. Within a very short space of time the armies of the Prophet conquered Syria, Egypt, Mesopotamia and Tripolitania from the Byzantines. The Byzantines were lucky: at the Battle of al-Qâdisiyyah in 636 the Sasanids suffered a major defeat at the hands of the Arabic forces. Sasanid Persia came to an end shortly afterwards. As the Byzantines grimly held on in Asia Minor, the Muslims seized the province of Africa in 696, and swept along the North African coast before overrunning Visigothic Spain by 711.

Due to these upheavals, secure control of the western provinces retaken during the reign of Justinian varied considerably. Complete control of Italy lasted for only three years – although partial control of Italy remained for a

244 Belisarius: The Last Roman General

further 300 years; whilst in Africa the empire continued to reign for a little less than 150 years.

The ultimate loss of the provinces of Spain, Africa and Italy could make all of Justinian's campaigns seem futile, and it is possible to claim that the manpower used would have been better withheld in reserve and saved against the upcoming Sasanid and Islamic assaults. Yet it should be remembered that Justinian had no warning of the coming crises and that some of the results of the reconquest were both beneficial and long lasting. The province of Africa, along with Sicily and the Balearic Islands, seems to have slowly recovered and been an asset to the empire, contributing taxes and (possibly) manpower whilst being an integral part of the empire's trading network.

This gives a clue as to what may have been possible had Justinian's conquests lasted. A fully integrated Italy – including Rome, the major focal point of the earlier imperial trading network – is likely to have seen a slow re-emergence of a more varied trade under imperial sponsorship. It is also possible that Italy itself would have recovered financially and agriculturally from the wars and become a valued member of the provincial system. The consequence of the Lombard invasion was that recovery and integration would not happen. The long border with the Lombards prevented northern Italy from ever being truly stable. This made it impossible to promote either the levels of trade needed by the empire or the agricultural recovery needed to fulfil the potential Italy could have had under sole Byzantine rule. Therefore, Justinian's conquests might have worked rather than being a drain on imperial resources and could, in the long term, have contributed to the strength and durability of the Empire. We know now that it was not to be, but to suggest that the attempt was futile and a waste because of events Justinian could not have foreseen is inappropriate.

Justinian's policy

We might now consider how much of Justinian's western reconquests were a premeditated attempt to restore the 'Glory of Rome' and how much was opportunism in the face of events.

In Chapter 6 the causes of the invasion of Africa and the intense diplomatic exchanges needed to give the offensive a chance of success were analysed in detail. The main conclusion that can be drawn from the analysis is that there is little evidence for a long-term plan for imperial recovery. It would appear more likely that the invasion was only considered after the coup of Gelimer, the imprisonment of Hilderic and Gelimer's refusal to send him to Constantinople. It may be that Gelimer's refusal to submit to Justinian's demands, even when threatened with war, forced Justinian's hand: a failure to act would have undermined his authority, both at home and abroad. As a consequence, it is possible to see the war against the Vandals as a political act made in response to immediate events rather than the calculated act of an emperor determined on a Byzantine revival.

In Africa, the Vandals had become politically fragmented and open to attack. Their realm had fallen after a war of only nine months' duration. During the course of the Vandalic War a similar series of events occurred in Italy, with Gothic political disunion mirroring the earlier situation in Vandal Africa. To a religious individual like Justinian, such a repetition may have appeared like a sign from God. It would seem likely to Justinian that this was a God-given opportunity and that an invasion of Italy would result in a rapid victory as had occurred in Africa.

Indeed, up until the capture of Rome Justinian's belief would have seemed well-founded. The whole of the south of Italy fell, with only Naples offering any resistance and with a mass surrender of the defenders in the region. When Belisarius retook Rome, Justinian would have been extremely satisfied with the course of his reign: large areas in the west retaken at minimal loss. The fact that the war would drag on for over twenty years would not have been obvious at the time.

Furthermore, events in Spain reflected the events in Africa and Italy. As the war in Italy came to a close, the ruling nobility in Visigothic Spain divided behind two candidates for the throne. As was to be expected, Justinian moved quickly, ordering troops to be sent to take advantage of the situation. In the case of Spain, however, the Visigoths appear to have recognised their danger – after all, the events in Africa and Italy would be well known – and quickly reunited under one leader. The reconquest ground to a halt and a united Visigothic kingdom slowly forced the empire to retreat. In all of these cases, without the internal political divisions in the ruling elite the Byzantines would have been extremely hard pressed to achieve their goals.

It is commonly assumed that Justinian came to the throne with a master plan to regain the west. Recognising Byzantine weakness, he first negotiated a peace with the Sasanids before launching his western expeditions. This supposition suggests that Justinian had complete understanding of Byzantine political and military strengths and weaknesses. Yet the fact that he continued and widened the campaigns of expansion, even when war again broke out in the east, suggests that the claim is false. Such an enlargement of the original conflict would be unacceptable if Justinian accepted that he could not fight wars on more than two fronts. As a consequence, it can be suggested that there was no 'grand plan' to annex the lost western provinces.

The 'reconquest' was a series of unconnected wars, each following on from the previous conflict in a series of natural progressions. In all of these Justinian was hoping for a quick end to the war, as had happened in Africa. This explains his willingness to expand in the west whilst still fighting in the east: the western wars would – hopefully – quickly be brought to a satisfactory conclusion, releasing the troops needed to fight the Sasanids.

Belisarius

For the present purpose, the main question concerning the 'reconquest' is the role and ability of its major player, Belisarius. He has always received an excellent report from historians, who have based their opinion on the early sections of Procopius and especially the battles of Dara, Ad Decimum and Tricamerum. On the whole, the earlier losses in the east and the battle of Rome have been ignored or marginalised in order to promote Belisarius' abilities as a general. In order to determine whether Belisarius deserves his reputation as one of the finest generals of the Byzantine period, we will analyse his career chronologically to gain a clear idea of his abilities.

In his early battles in the east Belisarius was on the winning side once, at the Battle of Dara. The battle was a resounding success and appears to have been the result of Belisarius having a clear strategy in place, and of his predicting the Persian moves and having the tactical flexibility necessary to overcome them. The battle should be classed as one of the outstanding single military victories in warfare. Yet the winning of individual battles, however brilliantly, is not necessarily the most important attribute of a general; it is winning the whole conflict that counts. Belisarius did not achieve this goal.

The first battle in the east is unnamed by our sources, yet it is clear that Belisarius and Sittas were soundly defeated. The Battle of Tanurin which followed was the first described in which Belisarius played a leading part. In this battle the Byzantines were on the offensive and the Sasanids had the time to prepare defensive positions, luring the Byzantines into attacking across pre-dug trenches.

In the third battle, at Mindouos, Belisarius was again defeated but again we are not given any details of the engagment. However, the fact that he was now promoted suggests that, for whatever reason, the defeat was not seen to be as a result of his abilities. The most likely reason is that Belisarius was a junior partner in the early battles, and that the main blame for defeat rested with his superiors and not him. Conversely, in the only battles where he was sole commander he won an outstanding victory at Dara, whilst he was cleared of blame for the defeat at Callinicum by the enquiry that followed. As a consequence, the defeat at Callinicum was relegated to the background whilst the victory at Dara was promoted as an outstanding military action – possibly for internal and external political reasons.

In one way, however, these defeats do seem to have affected Belisarius. From this point onwards he remained essentially a cautious commander, looking after the well-being of his men and taking care with their lives. Although this may also have been necessary as a result of his being given very few troops to work with, it appears that the defeats in the east, which were on the whole offensive battles, permanently affected his conduct: he would prefer to fight defensive battles. The fact that he lost several major battles where he was on the offensive – such as Tanurin, Callinicum, and Rome – but was extremely effective defensively – such as at the siege of Rome – supports the conclusion.

The campaign in the east was won by a mixture of diplomacy and the threat of war, coupled with the fact that both parties wanted peace – Justinian to deal with the Vandals and Khusrow to begin his overhaul of the Sasanid administrative and military organisation. Although a second victory after Dara could have ended the war sooner, Belisarius' defeat at Callinicum ensured that the war would grind on for longer than was absolutely necessary.

In Africa, Belisarius appears to have had little control over the two battles in which the Byzantines were victorious. At the Battle of Ad Decimum, even Procopius allows that he did not want to fight and was actually attempting to evaluate the strength of the Vandals when he was caught in an encounter battle. Although luck certainly played a large part in the battle, the calmness he displayed in the face of the unexpected and the speed of his decisions resulted in a substantial victory, achieved by what must be described as superior generalship.

The Battle of Tricamerum was a different affair. A close reading of Procopius suggests that Belisarius had little influence on the deployment of the troops, with John the Armenian deploying the troops before the battle. There are two possible ways of interpreting the events which followed: either John remained in control of the battle, since Belisarius had arrived late and did not have all of the necessary information to hand, or Belisarius arrived and took control. As was suggested in Chapter 6, the likelihood is that John deployed, either with a plan for the upcoming battle in mind or in a standard array due to being taken by surprise. In this scenario, John remained in overall control of the elite troops in the centre whilst Belisarius took command of the rest of the army.

However, whichever of these cases is the truth has little bearing on an assessment of Belisarius as a commander. If he took full control of the army, he should be credited with gaining an outstanding victory. The overall plan for the battle and the timing of the attacks in the centre, along with that of the general assault which caused a complete Vandal collapse, shows a commander in top form. If, on the other hand, he allowed John to remain in control and only commanded either one or both wings, he again deserves a lot of credit. Although the credit for the overall plan should go to John, Belisarius deserves praise on two counts. One is for his common sense in recognising that John had a better picture of the situation and for allowing him to retain command. This shows that Belisarius knew his limitations and trusted in the ability of his senior officers. The second follows from the fact that John now became embroiled in the conflict in the centre and may have been unable to give commands in the heat of battle. Belisarius is probably the commander whose judgement and timing allowed the all-out attack across the front to succeed in routing the Vandals. Whichever option is chosen, Belisarius gains a lot of credit for his actions in the battle.

If Belisarius gains credit from his conduct in Africa, his strategy in Italy up to the Battle of Rome deserves a higher level of commendation. The continued policy of controlling his troops and protecting the natives paid dividends, with the whole of the south surrendering without resistance. Furthermore, when Ebrimuth, the Gothic commander in the south, submitted – whether from a desire to retire in comfort in the east, or from a dislike of Theodahad, or from the assumption that Belisarius was certain to win – he was treated with courtesy, and this in all likelihood enticed the others to yield.

Yet it is after the successful capture of Naples that Belisarius earned the approval of the Italian populace as a whole. The refusal of the citizens to surrender meant that, by the accepted rules of war, once the city was captured the victors had the right to take anyone or anything they desired. Belisarius' order to return all of the captives to the city was a gesture that would result in the surrender of both Rome and Milan, since they now knew that they could expect fair and generous treatment from Belisarius. After assuming control of Rome, Belisarius' deportment and confidence, combined with his tactical and strategic insights, ensured that the city would be safe from Gothic attack. This is the sign of a general at the top of his game.

Shortly afterwards, however, he was to suffer his only defeat in Italy at the Battle of Rome. Although Procopius lays the blame with the troops, since they forced Belisarius to fight against his will, the truth of the claim is open to question. The excuse had already been used at the Battle of Callinicum, where Belisarius had also lost. It is possible that at Callinicum the claim was vindicated, since Belisarius was cleared by the inquest into the defeat. At Rome, the declaration that Belisarius had again reluctantly agreed to fight at the insistence of his men is more open to question. At Callinicum Belisarius was still a relatively unknown general who may indeed have succumbed to pressure: by the time of the Battle of Rome Belisarius had established a reputation as a general and, since he had compelled his men to return the captives at Naples, it is clear that he had control of the troops. He should have been able to refuse any request by the troops that they fight a battle. It is more likely that Belisarius, a master of the ruse and defensive strategy, became over confident and fought the battle on his own initiative. After the defeat, and facing censure, the blame was laid on the troops – calling to mind the Battle of Callinicum – and the excuse accepted. Yet even if the excuse is accepted at face value, it does not show Belisarius in a favourable light. Although Procopius claims that Belisarius recognised the dangers of battle, the general who could so dominate his men that they would return captives does not deserve credit if he then yields to their demands to fight. Whatever the cause of Belisarius leaving the city to fight, he gains no credit for losing the battle.

Although not a major defeat, mainly thanks to the actions of Principius, Tarmatus and their troops, the Battle of Rome taught Belisarius a valuable lesson: the Gothic troops, despite numerous defeats in small-scale engagements, remained effective in the field of battle. He would not underestimate their valour again. For the remainder of his time in Italy he relied upon the use of deception, artifice and siege in his attempt to defeat the Goths. The fact that in this he almost entirely succeeded is the sign of a great general.

After his recall and return to the east he continued to rely upon strategy and hoax in order to defeat the Sasanids. In this he succeeded on the whole, forcing the Sasanids to retire from strong positions and slowly attempting to regain the initiative from Khusrow. Yet his refusal to fight a major battle may be due to a different cause: it is possible – though not provable – that the defeat at Rome affected his confidence and resulted in a desire to avoid risking all in a single engagement. On the whole, however, his conduct in the east should be seen as a continuation of his use of deception, artifice and siege in order to win the war – or at least prevent the Sasanids from gaining the upper hand. On the whole, he succeeded in his aims.

Upon his return to Italy, he continued to avoid battle, although at this late stage whether he wanted to fight or not was not an issue: he was never to be given the resources needed to face the Goths in an open battle. Yet his continuous movement and his reputation appears to have to some degree restricted the offensive desires of Totila, who only unleashed his full military abilities after Belisarius' final recall, quickly reducing the Byzantine control to only a few towns and re-establishing a presence in Sicily, Sardinia and Corsica.

The final battle against the Huns allows us to establish a firm opinion of Belisarius' residual abilities at an older age. His bold decision to split his troops, despite being outnumbered, allowed him to attack the Huns from three different directions, resulting in a collapse in their morale and eventual defeat. Even with hindsight it is hard to imagine how else he might have won the battle against such odds. Belisarius' ability to foresee the Huns' response demonstrates that he retained his military flair into old age.

There is one further aspect of Belisarius' performance as a general that is usually overlooked: his personality. As was seen in Chapter 3, Zacharias described Belisarius as a man not open to bribery, who was kind to the natives, and who did not allow the army to injure them. He maintained this practice throughout his military life and it gained him a formidable reputation for honesty and decency – which is in contrast to the reputation of the majority of the Byzantine generals and bureaucrats mentioned in Procopius. The result was that the inhabitants of Africa and then Italy chose loyalty to the empire over loyalty to the Vandals and Goths. The net result was that he needed to leave fewer men to act as garrisons and so maintained a larger army in the field than would otherwise have been possible: an important factor since he had a limited amount of manpower to work with. His integrity would encourage others to treat him fairly and would entice his opponents to surrender in the knowledge that they would be treated with respect and allowed to retain their dignity. It is interesting to note that when Gelimer was part of Belisarius' triumph in Constantinople, Belisarius performed obeisance to the emperor at the same time as Gelimer. Although the reasons for this simultaneous *proskineisis* will never be fully known, it is possible that at least part of this was in order to minimise the humiliation felt by Gelimer at having to surrender.

Belisarius was obviously a man of strong character and outstanding moral bearing, especially when he is compared to his compatriots. The only time when he failed to maintain high moral integrity was when the Goths offered him the kingship of Italy. His desire to return to Constantinople having secured total victory resulted in him misleading the Goths into thinking that he was going to accept their proposal. In an ironic twist, it is likely that the manner of his refusal resulted in the Goths prolonging the war and Belisarius later having to spend several wasted years in Italy attempting to fight a war that he could not win.

As an overall judgement of Belisarius, therefore, it is possible to reach a simple conclusion. This was a man who was far above average in his military ability and very far above others in his moral integrity. His grasp of strategic considerations was unmatched and his reactions to events almost faultless. The fact that he lost battles due to either bad planning or by being pressured into fighting by his own men when at a disadvantage means that he cannot be placed on a par with outstanding military leaders such as Julius Caesar or Alexander the Great, but his abilities place him not far below their level. Although at times – such as in the Battle of Ad Decimum and at the siege of Naples – he can be said to have been lucky, this should not make us underestimate his abilities, since luck has always been a major factor in warfare. As Napoleon once said after listening to references for a candidate for promotion, 'I do not doubt that he is a good general, but is he lucky?'

Appendix I

Chronology

235	Death of Severus Alexander: beginning of 'Third Century Crisis'.
260	Valerian defeated and captured by Persians: Antioch sacked.
306–327	Reign of Constantine I (the Great).
357	Battle of Strasbourg (Argentoratum): Julian defeats Alamanni.
376	Valens allows Goths to enter Roman territory.
378	Gothic rebellion: Valens defeated and killed at Battle of Adrianople.
382	Theodosius signs treaty with Goths, who are given land in the Balkans.
395	Hunnic raids across Caucasus Mountains.
406	Rebellion of Constantine III in Britain: Vandals, Alans and Sueves cross frozen Rhine into Gaul.
409	Vandals etc cross into Spain.
410	Rome sacked by Alaric.
418	Visigoths settled in Aquitaine.
451	Attila invades Gaul: defeated by Aetius at Battle of Catalaunian Plains.
453	Death of Attila.
454	Battle of the Nedao, collapse of Hunnic Empire. Murder of Aetius by Valentinian II.
455	Assassination of Valentinian III: Sack of Rome by the Vandals.
461	Majorian attempts to reconquer Africa from the Vandals, attempt fails.
466	Euric, king of Visigoths, leads conquest of Southern Gaul and Spain.
468	Anthemius with eastern support attempts conquest of Vandal Africa, fails.
472	Orestes becomes *magister militum* in the west. Emperor Julius Nepos forced to withdraw to Illyricum. Orestes has own son declared Emperor as Romulus Augustulus.
474	Rule of Vandals in Africa recognised by Byzantine (Eastern Roman) Emperor Zeno.
475	Rule of Visigoths in Southern Gaul and Spain recognised by Emperor Julius Nepos in Illyricum.
476	Odovacer establishes himself as *magister militum* in the west. Deposes Romulus Augustulus and establishes his own rule in Italy. Traditional date for the end of the Western Roman Empire.
488	Theoderic, king of the Goths in the Balkans, ordered by the Byzantine Emperor Zeno to 'recover' Italy.

493	Theoderic's siege of Odovacer in Ravenna lifted by truce: Theoderic kills Odovacer.
c.500	Birth of Procopius.
502	War begins with the Persians, after Kavadh has subjugated Armenia with the aid of the Eastern or Hepthalite Huns. The Bulgars defeat a Roman army.
503	The Persians take Theodosiopolis and Amida.
505	The *magister officiorum* Celer invades Persia and reaches Ctesiphon. An invasion by the Western Huns across the Caucasus brings an armistice.
506	Anastasius signs a seven-year truce with the Persians.
507	Byzantine fleet raids Italy.
508	Clovis, king of the Franks, captures the Visigothic capital Toulouse and establishes his own capital at Paris. He is made a consul by Anastasius.
517	The Slavs raid as far as Thermopylae. Defeated by Germanus.
518	Death of Anastasius. Justin elected emperor.
525	Byzantine war with Persia. The Persians move against Iberia, which is conquered despite a small army sent by Justin.
526	Death of Theodoric the Great, king of the Ostrogoths. His 8–10-year old grandson Athalaric becomes king. His mother Amalasuintha assumes guardianship. The generals Sittas and Belisarius invade Persarmenia.
527	Justin becomes ill: his nephew Justinian is elevated to co-emperor. Belisarius promoted to *Dux Mesopotamiae* (June/July): Procopius appointed his secretary. Death of Justin: Justinian sole emperor (August).
528	Justinian sends John son of Rufinus to conquer the Crimea with a combined land and naval expedition. Byzantines defeated by Persians in Lazica. Sittas appointed as first *magister militum per Armeniam*. Belisarius takes part in first recorded battle: a defeat. Al-Mundhir raids Syria. Bulgars raid Thrace.
529	Justinian suppresses a Samaritan revolt. Belisarius appointed *magister militum per Orientem* (April). Mundus made *magister militum per Illyricum*: his presence deters attacks until his death in 536.
530	At the Battle of Dara Belisarius defeats the Sasanid Persians.
531	Hilderic is deposed by his cousin Gelimer. Belisarius is defeated by the Sasanid Persians at the Battle of Callinicum. Inquest into the defeat; Belisarius is recalled and replaced by Mundus as *magister militum per Orientem*. Dorotheus, the *magister militum per Armeniam*, defeats Persians near Martyropolis. Death of Khavadh. His son Khusrow Anushirvan ('the Immortal Soul') becomes king. Sabir Huns mount extensive raid across the Caucasus. The Franks move east of the Rhine and conquer Thuringia.
532	The Nika Revolt in Constantinople. Belisarius and Mundus allegedly kill 30,000 people in the Hippodrome. Revolt ends.

533   'Endless Peace' signed between Byzantines and Persians. Sardinia rebels from Vandal rule; Tzazon sent by Gelimer to restore Vandal control. Tripolitania rebels from Vandal rule. Belisarius sent to Africa to conquer the Vandal kingdom. The Battle of Ad Decimum (13 Sept): Belisarius defeats Gelimer. Gelimer is joined by his brother Tzazon after his reconquest of Sardinia. He then confronts the Byzantines for a second time, but is defeated at the Battle of Tricamerum (Dec). Tzazon is killed but Gelimer escapes. Belisarius sends troops to take control of the Balearic Isles and Straits of Gibraltar.

534   Gelimer flees to the mountains but surrenders to Belisarius at last at Mount Papua. Many Vandal troops are recruited for the Roman army. Belisarius recalled to Constantinople. Rebellion of the Moors in Africa. The Romans fortify Ceuta at the Straits of Gibraltar. The Ostrogothic king Athalaric dies of alcohol abuse. His mother Amalasuintha marries her cousin Theodahad, who succeeds Athalaric. The Franks invade Burgundy and kill the Burgundian king, Godomar. They divide large parts of Burgundy amongst themselves. Byzantines and Goths clash in Dalmatia.

535   Amalasuintha, queen of the Ostrogoths, is murdered by Theodahad, who allegedly smothers her in her bath. Justinian uses the pretext to invade Italy. His armies under Belisarius occupy Sicily and under Mundus occupy Illyricum. To secure Frankish help, Witigis cedes Provence to the Franks.

536   Stotzas rebels in Africa: Belisarius returns and defeats rebels outside Carthage. Belisarius returns to Sicily prior to war in Italy. Germanus sent to Africa, defeats Stotzas at Scala Veteres. Belisarius lands in Italy, marches north and conquers Naples. He continues north and enters Rome (9 Dec). Theodahad tries to negotiate, but the Ostrogoths depose him and elect Witigis in his place as 'King of the Goths and Italians'. Witigis marries Matasuintha (granddaughter of Theoderic) and recalls the Gothic forces from southern Gaul (which is then occupied by the Franks).

537   The Ostrogoths under Witigis begin the siege of Rome (late Feb/early March). Battle of Rome and defeat of Belisarius (spring).

538   After a year, the Goths raise the siege of Rome (March). Belisarius takes control of Ariminum, which the Goths place under siege, and Milan. Arrival of reinforcements under Narses.

539   The siege of Ariminum is relieved and the Byzantine siege of Auximus begins. Witigis gains aid from the Franks, who send 10,000 Burgundians to support him. The Goths and Burgundians retake Milan. The women and children are given as slaves to the Burgundians for their help. The Goths retreat under pressure from Belisarius. Belisarius besieges Witigis in Ravenna. The Goths propose a peace treaty in which they keep the territory north of the River Po, with the rest of Italy going to the Empire. Under their king, Theudibert, the Franks invade Italy, but are forced to retreat when disease breaks out in their army. Justinian limits all production of weapons to state-owned *fabricae*.

540   Goths offer Belisarius kingship of Goths and Italy. After the food supply is destroyed by fire, Ravenna falls (May). Belisarius captures Witigis, together with the Ostrogothic treasure. The Ostrogoths elect Ildibadus as their new king. Belisarius leaves Italy. Witigis is paraded in Belisarius' triumph before being given a pension and settling in the east. Witigis' Gothic troops that are captured are enlisted into the Roman army. Ildibadus defeats the Byzantines at Tarbesium. Bulgars ravage Thrace and Macedonia. Khusrow declares war and invades Byzantine territory. He captures many cities including Antioch, which is destroyed.

541   Ildibadus is assassinated and Eraric is made king. Eraric is in turn assassinated and Totila becomes King. Totila builds a fleet and begins the attempt at Gothic recovery. Belisarius is sent to the east. Khusrow campaigns in the east and captures Petra, the Byzantine-held fortress in Lazica. Belisarius attacks Nisibis, before capturing the fortress of Sisauranon. Plague in the eastern provinces.

542   Roman assault on Verona fails. Totila successful at Faventia, then attacks Florentia. Byzantines defeated in the Battle of the Mugello. Totila occupies most of southern Italy. Khusrow again invades the East. Belisarius leads an army to face the Persians and manages to persuade them to retire – possibly out of fear of the plague. Plague reaches Constantinople and possibly reaches Italy. Justinian catches the plague: Belisarius arrested concerning accusations of planning to replace the (assumed-to-be-dead) Justinian: loses post of *magister militum per Orientem*.

543   Gothic naval victory. Totila occupies Naples and marches on Rome. Moorish rebellion in Africa.

544   Belisarius returned to imperial favour: made *comes sacri stabuli* and sent back to Italy with only a few reinforcements. Goths lay siege to Auximus. Kutrigur Huns and Bulgars ravage Balkans. Moorish insurrection (ends 548).

545   War in Italy between Totila and Belisarius. Totila attacks Rome. Byzantines relieve Auximus. A five-year truce is signed between Khusrow and Justinian. Stotzas killed in Africa at Sicca Venerea. Guntharis' rebellion in Africa; he is killed by Artabanes.

546   Totila conquers Rome (17 Dec). Belisarius retreats from the city, which is sacked by the Ostrogoths for forty days. Justinian leaves Pannonia to the Lombards.

547   The Goths leave Rome, after which the city is again occupied by Belisarius. Totila wins battle in Campania. The Byzantines retake Ceuta from the Visigoths.

548   Totila blockades Roscianum and defeats Belisarius' *comitatus* in battle. Death of Theodora wife of Justinian (June 28). Belisarius is recalled to Constantinople. The Visigothic king Theudis is assassinated by Theudegisel. Death of the Frankish king, Theudibert.

549   Byzantine-Persian War in the east. Totila lays siege to Rome. Sclaveni invade Balkans. The Visigothic king Theudegisel is assassinated and succeeded by Agila.

550   Justinian orders Germanus to Italy, after marriage to Witigis' widow Matasuintha. En route, Germanus defeats a Slav invasion of the Balkans, but then dies of illness. The unpaid garrison of Rome surrender. Totila invades Sicily, Artabanes retakes Sicily. Bessas lays siege to Petra in Lazica.

551   Narses appointed as commander in Italy. Totila's fleet raids Greece. Ancona blockaded by the Goths: Byzantines win naval battle off Senigallia and siege raised. Goths capture Sardinia and defeat a Byzantine expedition sent to retake the island. First embassy of the Avars reaches Constantinople.

552   Narses invades Italy: at the Battle of Taginae Totila is defeated and killed. Teias made King of the Goths. Narses besieges Cumae. Byzantine army under Liberius lands in Spain to support the Visigoth rebel Athanagild. Beginning of reconquest of south of Spain for the Empire.

553   Teias defeated and killed by Narses at the Battle of Mons Lactarius. A combined Franco-Alamannic army (under Lothar and Butilin) invades Italy and defeats Narses' Herul allies. Byzantines take Lucca. Cumae surrenders to Byzantines.

554   Lothar defeated and dies: Narses beats Butilin at Casilinum.

555   Surrender of Gothic force at Campsa. Byzantines capture Cartagena in Spain.

556   Jews and Samaritans riot.

558   Recurrence of plague in Byzantine Empire.

559   Huns invade Balkans: Belisarius defeats Hunnic force at Melantas.

561   Byzantine-Persian peace treaty. Byzantine conquest of Italy complete.

562   Kutrigurs invade Balkans.

563   Narses defeats rebellion of Amingus the Frank and Widin the Goth in North Italy. Moorish revolt in Africa.

565   Sindual the Herul rebels in Italy: hanged by Narses. Death of Belisarius (March). Death of Justinian (November).

568   Lombards invade Italy.

Appendix II

Select Personalities

To list all of the people involved in Belisarius' wars would take an entire book in itself. This list only includes those whose stories are deemed worthy of inclusion, and also the majority of those called John, in order to help clear any confusion by the repetition of the name.

al-Mundhir   King of the Lakhmids and ally of the Persians.

Amalasuintha   'Queen' of the Ostrogoths, daughter of Theoderic the Great. Guardian and regent for her son Athalaric, who succeeded Theoderic. She then attempted to maintain control by allying herself with her cousin Theodahad, the next in line to the throne, but he ignored their agreement and had her imprisoned and killed.

Ammatus   Brother of Gelimer, king of the Vandals. On Gelimer's orders he killed Hilderic, whose throne Gelimer had usurped. Killed at the Battle of Ad Decimum.

Antonina   Wife of Belisarius. Said by Procopius to be of very low birth, at the time of her marriage to Belisarius she already had a son, Photius, and a daughter (who married Ildiger). Antonina and Belisarius had only one daughter, Joannina. She outlived Belisarius though the date of her death is unknown.

Aratius   An Armenian, brother of Narses and Isaac, with Narses defeated Belisarius in an unnamed battle in the east before defecting to the Byzantines and serving alongside Belisarius.

Arethas   King of the Ghassanids and ally of the Byzantines, Arethas fought alongside Belisarius in the east before deceiving Belisarius in 541. They never met again.

Artabanes   An Armenian who served Khusrow before deserting to the Romans. Due to his ability and previous rank, rose quickly within the Byzantine hierarchy. Annoyed with Justinian over his inability to marry Praeiecta, Justinian's niece, he joined a conspiracy against Justinian. Although the plot was uncovered, Artabanes was later appointed in command of troops in Sicily and under Narses the Eunuch.

Artabazes	An Armenian who surrendered Sisauranon to Belisarius before being sent to serve in Italy. Led the (failed) attempt on Verona and was later fatally wounded fighting in single combat prior to the Battle of Faventia.
Athalaric	Grandson of Theoderic the Great, succeeded his grandfather in 526 aged c.8. Seemingly ignored by his mother Amalasuintha (acting as regent), he was the centre of an opposition to her policies. Despite his extreme youth, he took part in epic drinking bouts and died of alcohol abuse in 534, aged c.16.
Belisarius	Born c.500; died 565.
Bessas	Served alongside Belisarius in Italy, after being sent into northern Italy, he delayed his return to join Belisarius in Rome and was nearly caught by the Goths at Narnia. Served in the defence of Rome at the Praenestine Gate. Was defeated in battle by the Goths after Belisarius' recall and thereafter stayed in Rome. He repeatedly failed to sally when outside attempts to raise the siege of Rome were made. He allegedly made money selling food at high prices during the siege, but was forced to leave this behind when the city fell to Totila.
Buzes	Fought in the Battle of Dara but missed Callinicum due to illness. After 540 shared command in the east with Belisarius until in 542 he and Belisarius were accused of attempting to replace Justinian (who had caught the plague) without reference to Theodora. Remained in prison for two years and four months. Later served as *magister utriusque militum* in the east.
Constantinianus	Sent by Justinian to defend Salona in Illyricum, took control of Dalmatia and Illyricum and defended it against Gothic attack. His presence forced the Goths to fight a war on at least two fronts.
Constantinus	General serving under Belisarius in Italy, showed himself a capable commander and was in charge of the Porta Flaminia during the siege. He was unable to control his troops during the Battle of Rome and the ensuing Gothic counter-attack resulted in his defeat. Alleged to have stolen two daggers from a native Italian, contrary to Belisarius' policy; he refused to surrender them and, in fear of his life, attempted to stab Belisarius. He was arrested and executed, a deed that Procopius claims was the only stain on Belisarius' reputation.
Cyprian	Served under Belisarius in Italy. Left behind in Italy after Belisarius' recall, he was presumably one of the commanders who failed to act as Gothic power revived. In 545 he refused to surrender Perugia to Totila and was murdered by one of his own guards, who had been bribed by Totila.

Dorotheus   The *magister militum per Armeniam*. Twice defeated the Persians in 530, and again in 531, before driving a Sabir Hun attack back through the Caucasus. In 533 was sent under Belisarius to attack the Vandals. His death in Sicily caused mourning throughout the army.

Ebrimuth   Commander of the Gothic forces in South Italy. Surrendered to Belisarius on his arrival.

Eraric   Made king of the Goths in 541, he was assassinated after a rule of five months.

Gelimer   King of the Vandals; usurped the throne from Hilderic after defeating the Moors and gaining an alliance with them. Facing the Byzantine assault under Belisarius, he was defeated at Ad Decimum, then rallied the surviving Goths only to lose again at Tricamerum. Was taken captive to Constantinople and made obeisance to Justinian before retiring to estates in Galatia.

Germanus   Nephew or cousin of Justinian, he was a capable general who was given irregular commands within the empire, for example to deal with the African mutiny. Following the Gothic recovery after the final departure of Belisarius, he married Witigis' widow Matasuintha before making preparations for the invasion. He died of an illness before the attack could begin.

Godas   A (Gothic) slave of King Gelimer who was put in command of Sardinia. Revolted and appealed to Justinian for aid. Killed by Tzazon before the aid could arrive.

Herodian   Served under Belisarius in Italy. After serving loyally through-out the campaign, he surrendered Spolitium to Totila in 545 – allegedly in fear of reprisals from Belisarius.

Hilderic   King of the Vandals, deposed by Gelimer and killed by Ammatus.

Ildibadus   Made king of the Goths in 540 after the defeat and capture of Witigis, he offered the crown to Belisarius. After a promising start, he fell out with Uraias, who he then murdered. He was then killed in turn by one of his own bodyguards.

Ildiger   Son-in-law of Antonina, wife of Belisarius, travelled to Africa with Belisarius but stayed behind when Belisarius was recalled. Took part in the Battle of Scala Veterae before joining Belisarius in Italy, where, during the siege of Rome, he defeated a Gothic assault on the Porta Pinciana. Accompanied Belisarius on his recall to Constantinople.

Isaac   Brother of Narses and Aratius. When they renounced Persia and joined Justinian, he negotiated the surrender of Bolum – a fortress he was commanding – to the Byzantines. He joined Belisarius for his second campaign in Italy. Left to guard Portus, he abandoned his post and attacked a nearby Gothic camp. In the ensuing fight he was captured and later executed by Totila.

John the Armenian	An Armenian, he was sent ahead of the main force to scout prior to the battle of Ad Decimum. Later, he was dispatched with the cavalry and appears to have been in control of the deployment and possibly of the strategy used during the Battle of Tricamerum. Ordered to pursue Gelimer, he was on the verge of capturing the Vandal king when he died after being accidentally shot by one of his own men.
John the Cappadocian	Promoted by Justinian, he earned the hatred of the citizens of Constantinople, who demanded his removal during the Nika Riots. Reinstated, he continued in power until his enemy Theodora manufactured a plot against Justinian in which he was implicated. Forced into exile, he was recalled by Justinian after the death of Theodora, although not given the same power as previously.
John the Glutton	One of the officers of Belisarius' bodyguard, he served under Belisarius in Italy and went with him to the east. In 541 he was sent with Arethas and Trajan on a probe into Persia. Tricked by Arethas, he returned to Byzantine territory with much booty without orders from Belisarius. In 542 he was one of the men who accused Belisarius of complicity in the refusal to accept a candidate for emperor chosen in Constantinople (ie by Theodora) as Justinian had contracted the plague. He later took part in Narses' expedition against the Goths.
John nephew of Vitalianus	A close friend of Narses the eunuch, he was sent to reinforce Belisarius in Italy in 537. Used extensively by Belisarius during and after the siege of Rome, he was sent to garrison Ariminum but later refused to leave despite orders from Belisarius after the arrival in Italy of Narses. The army was forced to relieve the siege and John thanked Narses, rather than Belisarius or Ildiger (who was first to the city). After Belisarius had been recalled, John remained in Italy and was criticised for mounting only passive resistance to Totila. The rift between Belisarius and John was never healed and he later refused to follow Belisarius' orders in Belisarius' second campaign in Italy. Later, he accompanied Narses on his successful expedition against the Goths.
Justin	Byzantine Emperor (518–527).
Justinian	Byzantine Emperor (527–565).
Kavadh	Sasanid Persian King (531–579).
Khusrow	Nicknamed Anushirvan (The Immortal Soul), Sasanid Persian King (531–579).
Marcellus	High-ranking officer who first served with Belisarius in Africa, fighting at the Battles of Ad Decimum and Tricamerum. He was killed along with Cyril by Stotzas, during the African mutiny.

Martinus[1]   One of the commanders of *foederati* that served in Africa, he took part in the campaign alongside Belisarius. After victory he remained in Africa during the mutiny before being recalled and sent to Italy with reinforcements for Belisarius, where he took part in the Battle of Rome. He then took an active part in the conquest of Italy, in the later stages being paired with John nephew of Vitalian – possibly in an attempt to control John, who was never comfortable following Belisarius' orders. Thanks to his loyalty and military ability, after Belisarius was stripped of his rank in 542, Martinus was made *magister militum per Orientem*, fighting Khusrow in the east. He had varying fortunes but his final victory (allegedly over a 60,000-strong Persian army) helped secure the Peace Treaty of 560/561.

Matasuintha   Daughter of Amalasuintha and granddaughter of Theoderic the Great, after seizing the Gothic crown in 536, Witigis married her in an attempt to fully legitimise his rule. After his defeat, she was married to Germanus prior to his attempt to conquer Italy, but became a widow upon his premature death.

Mundus   Mundus was related to the Gepid noble families. In 529, after service with the Goths under Theoderic the Great, he offered to serve Justinian and was appointed *magister militum per Illyricum*. He showed himself a capable general and his presence deterred barbarian attacks across the frontier. During the Nika Riots he was by chance in Constantinople and, along with Belisarius, took part in the slaughter in the Hippodrome which ended the rebellion. In 535 he invaded Dalmatia – then held by the Goths – defeated them and took Salona. In the following year, a Gothic force invaded Dalmatia and, in a battle near Salona, Mundus' son Mauricius was killed. Infuriated by the loss of his son, Mundus defeated the Goths but was himself killed. His death resulted in renewed barbarian attacks across the Danube.

Narses the Eunuch   An Armenian, he rose high in power during the reigns of Justin and Justinian. Sent to Italy with reinforcements for Belisarius, he was convinced by others that he was better suited to command. Frictions with Belisarius led to Narses' recall. He was later appointed to lead the final assault upon Gothic Italy, following Belisarius' recall to Constantinople.

Narses   An Armenian, brother of Aratius and Isaac. With Aratius defeated Belisarius in an unnamed battle in the east before defecting to the Byzantines and serving alongside Belisarius.

Photius
Son of Antonina and stepson of Belisarius, he gave his loyalty to Belisarius rather than his mother. Accompanying Belisarius and Antonina in the invasion of Italy, he was aware of the affair between Antonina and Theodosius. Having reported the affair to Belisarius, he arrested Theodosius and confiscated his money. However Theodora had Photius arrested and tortured to reveal Theodosius' whereabouts. Photius escaped from Constantinople and lived the rest of his life as a monk in Jerusalem.

Pitzas
A Goth, given control of western Samnium – possibly by Witigis. Prior to Belisarius' invasion, he surrendered to Belisarius and was given a few troops with which to maintain control of the region for the empire.

Principius
A *bucellarius* of Belisarius. Along with Tarmatus he requested permission to lead the infantry at the Battle of Rome, as Belisarius had decided not to allow them to enter the battle. Following the rout of the cavalry, the majority of the infantry also fled but a core of infantry around Principius and Tarmatus held firm and by their sacrifice enabled the cavalry to escape. Principius and Tarmatus both died.

Procopius
A native of Caesarea in Palestine, he died circa 565. Procopius was Belisarius' *assessor* (legal advisor) and private secretary. He wrote an account of the wars, much of which he witnessed first hand.

Pudentius
A citizen of Tripoli in Africa, he organised a rebellion against Vandal rule prior to Belisarius' invasion of Africa.

Solomon
Belisarius' *domesticus*, he fought at Ad Decimum and Tricamerum before being given the majority of Belisarius' *comitatus* and left in Africa to crush the Moorish uprising. In his first battle against the Moors he dismounted his cavalry in order to attack the enemy, who had surrounded themselves with camels to frighten the Byzantine horses. In the second, he managed to manoeuvre troops around the rear of the Moors' camp and so caused panic – according to Procopius, the Moors lost 50,000 casualties. Unable to prevent the troops from mutiny, he was nevertheless held in such awe that the mutinous troops could not bring themselves to assassinate him. After Belisarius' had returned and dispersed the rebels, Solomon retained control until the arrival of Germanus, who finally crushed the mutiny.

Sittas
Roman general, in 528 appointed first *magister militum per Armeniam*, led the first campaigns in which Belisarius was given high command. Defeated, he continued to serve in the east until killed in battle in 539.

Stotzas

One of Martinus' *comitatus*, he was elected leader of the African mutiny following Belisarius' recall from the province. Laid siege to Carthage but at news of Belisarius' arrival he broke camp and fled.

Tarmatus

A *bucellarius* of Belisarius, along with Principius he requested permission to lead the infantry at the Battle of Rome, as Belisarius had decided not to allow them to enter the battle. Following the rout of the cavalry, the majority of the infantry also fled but a core of infantry around Principius and Tarmatus held firm and by their sacrifice enabled the cavalry to escape. Principius and Tarmatus both died.

Theodahad

Nephew of Theoderic the Great, after the death of Athalaric in 534 Amalasuintha, in an attempt to maintain control, asked him to be the next king but to allow her to maintain her power. Agreeing to her conditions, he was crowned king but he ignored their agreement and had her imprisoned and killed. His actions now determined Justinian on invading Italy. Following Belisarius' successes early in the campaign, and the capture of Naples, the Goths turned against Theodahad, elected Witigis, and Theodahad was killed.

Theoderic the Great

King of the Goths and Italians (493–526).

Theodorus the Cappadocian

General and astute politician, he was elected leader of the African mutineers in Carthage but managed to persuade Solomon, Martinus and Procopius that he had had no choice in the matter and arranged for their escape to Sicily. He refused to surrender the city to Stotzas prior to Belisarius' return. Along with Ildiger, he was left in command of Carthage when Belisarius returned to Sicily.

Theodosius

Adopted son of Belisarius and Antonina. Alleged to have been having an affair with his (adoptive) mother throughout the African campaign, in Sicily he was betrayed to Belisarius, who ordered his death. Theodosius fled to Ephesus before Antonina convinced Belisarius of his innocence and he was told to return. However, he refused until Photius (Antonina's son) was no longer in the vicinity. Worried by Antonina's outrageous displays of affection, he again fled to Ephesus. When Belisarius left for the east, Theodosius returned but Photius informed Belisarius, who ordered Photius to kill him. He was only arrested, and later Theodora tortured Photius to learn of his whereabouts. Returned to Antonina, shortly afterwards contracted dysentery and died.

Tzazon Brother of Gelimer, he was sent to Sardinia when news of Godas' rebellion reached Gelimer. Retaking the island, he missed the Battle of Ad Decimum but returned in time for the Battle of Tricamerum, where he was killed.

Uraias Nephew of Witigis, served faithfully until Witigis was captured by Belisarius. Offered the crown, he refused and instead recommended Ildibadus, who was subsequently crowned. However, shortly after he fell out with Ildibadus and the king had him killed.

Vigilius Pope (551–555) Allegedly appointed by the order of Theodora, he came into increasing conflict with Justinian over the debate of the 'Three Chapters', at the end of which he was banished to an island in the Sea of Marmara.

Vitalius *Magister militum per Illyricum*; first served in the Balkans before joining Belisarius in Italy. Later in the campaign he was paired with John nephew of Vitalianus, possibly in an attempt to control John and restrict his tendency to ignore Belisarius' orders. After Belisarius' recall, he was the only general credited by Procopius with taking an active role against the Goths. During Belisarius' second campaign in Italy, an attempt by the Goths to attack him resulted in them suffering extremely high casualties as, in combination with Thurimuth, he trapped the pursuing troops in a series of devastating ambushes.

Witigis King of the Goths (536–540).

Select Bibliography

Although there has been a lot written about Justinian and his reign, there has been surprisingly little about Belisarius himself. Below is a list of books and articles that are relevant to the life of Belisarius. The majority have their own bibliographies for anyone wishing to delve further into the period.

Primary Sources (by translator)

Bosworth, C E, *The History of al-Tabari: Vol. 5; The Sasanids, the Byzantines, the Lakhmids and the Yemen* (Albany, 1999).

Dennis, G T, *Maurice's Strategikon* (Philadelphia, 1984).

Dennis, G T, *Three Byzantine Military Treatises*, (Washington DC, 1985).

Dewing, H B, *Procopius: History of the Wars*, in 5 volumes (London, 2001).

Dewing, H B, *Procopius: Secret History (Anekdota)* (London, 2004).

Frendo, J D, *Agathias: The Histories* (Berlin,1975).

Jeffreys, E, Jeffreys, M., and Scott, R, *The Chronicle of John Malalas: a Translation* (Melbourne, 1986).

Milner, N P, *Vegetius: Epitome of Military Science* (Liverpool, 1996).

Mommsen, T, *Marcellinus Comes: Additions to the Chronicle* (1894), available online at http://www.thelatinlibrary.com/marcellinus1.html.

Thomson, R W, *The Armenian History Attributed to Sebeos*, in 2 volumes (Liverpool, 1999).

Secondary Sources

Bishop, M C and Coulston, J C N, *Roman Military equipment from the Punic Wars to the Fall of Rome* (Exeter, 2006).

Boardman, J, Griffin, J, and Murray, O, *The Oxford History of the Roman World* (Oxford, 2001).

Boss, R, *Juastinian's Wars: Belisarius, Narses and the Reconquest of the West* (Stockport, 1993).

Burns, T S, *Barbarians within the Gates of Rome*, (Bloomington, 1994).

Bury, J B, 'History of the Later Roman Empire' (1958), available online at http://penelope.uchicago.edu/Thayer/E/Roman/Texts/secondary/BURLAT/home.html

Cameron, Averil, *Procopius and the Sixth Century* (California, 1985).

Cameron, Averil, *The Later Roman Empire* (London, 1993).

Coulston, J C, 'Later Roman Armour 3rd-6th Centuries', in *Journal of Roman Military Equipment Studies*, 1 (1990), pp. 139–160.

Farrokh, K, *Shadows in the Desert: Ancient Persia at War* (Oxford, 2007).

Farrokh, K, *Sassanian Elite Cavalry: 224–642* (Oxford, 2005).

Fossier, R, (ed), *The Cambridge Illustrated History of the Middle Ages: 350–950* (London, 1989).

Gibbon, E, *History of the Decline and Fall of the Roman Empire*, in 4 volumes (Liverpool, 1861).

Goldsworthy, Adrian, *In the Name of Rome* (London, 2003).

Greatrex, G, *Rome and Persia at War 502–532* (Francis Cairns, 1998).

Heather, Peter, *The Fall of the Roman Empire* (London, 2005).

James, Simon, *Excavations at Dura-Europos 1928–1937: Final Report VII; the Arms and Armour, and other Military Equipment* (London, 2004).

Jones, A H M, *The Later Roman Empire: 284–602* (Oxford, 1986).

Kennedy, David, 'The East', in John Wacher, (ed), *The Roman World* (London, 1990), pp. 266–308.

Ladner, Gerhardt B, 'On Roman attitudes towards Barbarians in Late Antiquity', in *Viator*, 7 (1976), pp. 1–26.

Lillington-Martin, C, 'Archaeological and Ancient Literary Evidence for a Battle near Dara Gap, Turkey, AD 530: Topography, Texts and Trenches', in A S Lewin and P Pellegrini (eds), *The Late Roman Army in the Near East from Diocletian to the Arab Conquest* (BAR, 2007).

MacDowall, S, *Late Roman Infantryman: 236–565 AD* (Oxford, 1994).

MacDowall, S, *Late Roman Cavalryman: 236–565 AD* (Oxford, 1995).

MacDowall, S, *Germanic Warrior: AD 236–568* (Oxford, 1996).

Mahon, Lord, *The Life of Belisarius: the Last Great General of Rome* (London, 1829; reprinted with a new foreword by J Coulston, Yardley, 2006).

Martindale, J R, *The Prosopography of the Later Roman Empire*, volume IIIa (Cambridge, 1992).

Moorhead, J, *Theoderic in Italy* (Oxford, 1997).

Nicolle, D, *Romano-Byzantine Armies: 4th–9th Centuries* (Oxford, 1992).

Norwich, J J, *Byzantium: the Early Centuries* (Bungay, 1998).

Parker, A J, 'Trade within the Empire and Beyond the Frontiers', in John Wacher, (ed), *The Roman World* (London, 1990), pp. 635–57.

Randers-Pehrson, J D, *Barbarians and Romans* (London, 1983).

Rawlinson, George, *The Seven Great Monarchies of the Ancient Eastern World: Vol. 3 Parthia New Persia* (New York, 1876).

Southern, P and Dixon, K R, *The Late Roman Army* (Cambridge, 2000).

Stephenson, I P, *Romano-Byzantine Military Equipment* (Stroud, 2006).

Teall, John L, 'Barbarians in Justinian's Armies', in *Speculum*, 40 (1965), pp. 294–322.

Thompson, E A, *Romans and Barbarians: the Decline of the Western Empire* (Wisconsin, 1982).

Tomlin, R S O, 'The Army of the Late Empire', in Wacher, John (ed), *The Roman World* (London, 1990), pp. 107–120.

Treadgold, W, *Byzantium and its Army: 284–1081* (Stanford, 1995).

Ure, P N, *Justinian and his Age* (Harmondsworth, 1951).

Wacher, John (ed), *The Roman World* (London, 1990).

Whitby, M, *Rome at War: AD 293–696* (Oxford, 2002).

Wolfram, H, *History of the Goths* (Berkeley, 1990).

Index